D0331267

THE
GRIT
BENEATH
THE
GLITTER

Tales from **THE REAL LAS VEGAS**

EDITED BY **HAL K. ROTHMAN** AND **MIKE DAVIS**

UNIVERSITY OF CALIFORNIA PRESS BERKELEY LOS ANGELES LONDON

University of California Press
Berkeley and Los Angeles, California

University of California Press, Ltd.
London, England

© 2002 by The Regents of the
University of California

Library of Congress Cataloging-in-Publication Data

The grit beneath the glitter : tales from the real Las
Vegas / edited by Hal K. Rothman and Mike Davis.
    p. cm.
Includes bibliographical references and index.
   ISBN 0-520-20529-4 (cloth : alk. paper)—
ISBN 0-520-22538-4 (paper : alk. paper)
   1. Las Vegas (Nev.)—History—20th century.
2. Las Vegas (Nev.)—Social conditions—20th
century. 3. Las Vegas (Nev.)—Economic
conditions—20th century. I. Rothman, Hal, 1958–
II. Davis, Mike, 1946–
F849.L35 G75 2001
979.3'135034—dc21

                         2001005925

Manufactured in the United States of America
11 10 09 08 07 06 05 04 03 02
10 9 8 7 6 5 4 3 2 1

The paper used in this publication is both acid-free
and totally chlorine-free (TCF). It meets the
minimum requirements of ANSI/NISO Z39.48–1992
(R 1997) (*Permanence of Paper*). ∞

Contents

HAL ROTHMAN AND MIKE DAVIS

Introduction
The Many Faces of Las Vegas

THE NEON OASIS

No city in American history has ever changed its clothes as frequently or as rapidly as Las Vegas. No place has grown so fast in so many ways without allegiance to any of the forms of identity its past fostered. Nowhere has each incarnation of existence been more fleeting, more transitory, less based in anything but the human imagination. Reinvention has been the essence of the place, but what can you expect from a town with no compelling natural reason to be where it is? Malleability is the watchword of Las Vegas, a supple response to the changing cultural, intellectual, economic, and social trends of the nation and the world.

In the beginning, there were the first people of the Mojave Desert, the Paiute, and the miraculous, life-saving springs that the Spanish called Las Vegas, "the meadows." In the mid nineteenth century, Manifest Destiny made this natural oasis a pivot of competition between Brigham Young's Nation of Deseret and Gold Rush California. At the beginning of the next century, the Union Pacific Railroad built a town to repair trains en route between Salt Lake City and Los Angeles. When the railroad closed its shop to punish the city for its support of the national railroad strike of 1922, Las Vegas was left to die in the desert, to sink back into the sands from which it had sprung.

California's thirst for water and the federal dollars it brought saved the hamlet from withering into another Nevada ghost town. In the late

1

1920s, Boulder Dam construction stimulated a new boom, and gamblers and bookmakers expelled from Tijuana and Los Angeles in the late 1930s planted the seeds of the modern casino resort. World War II brought defense industries, a huge airbase, myriad GI paychecks, and a new highway to LA, a lifeline to the outside world. The Cold War added the Nuclear Test Site and the mushroom cloud that was once the city's eerie official emblem.

Cowboys and mobsters, bankers and corrupt trade unionists watered this postwar garden and harvested its sweet, and sometimes bitter, fruit during the so-called golden age of the 1950s and 1960s. The reclusive Howard Hughes, never seen by the Nevada public, transformed Las Vegas again in the 1960s, which ended with a series of dramatic buy-outs and consolidations. Hotel chains, headed by Hilton, followed, preparing the way for the corporate revolution that took shape during the 1980s.

As family or mob-owned casinos were transformed into giant gaming corporations and merged with hotel chains and entertainment monop-olies, the pace of change dramatically accelerated. Two generations of resort development were compressed into a single decade. Typical Strip locations metamorphosed from overgrown motels into gambling theme parks with Disneyland-like rides, upscale shopping, and world-class spectacles and illusions. People even began to bring their kids.

The 1997 opening of Showcase on the Strip signaled yet another new dawn for the fastest-growing metropolis in North America. Topped by an enormous Coca-Cola bottle out of a Warhol reverie, the Showcase is an entertainment superplex, with United Artists theaters, SKG Game-works, the All-Star Café, and Surge Rock, a faux climbing rock named after Coke's latest sibling. The brainchild of two young entrepreneurs, Barry Fieldman and Robert Unger, Showcase is a perfect melding of entertainment and shopping, a new concept already oft repeated, tar-geted like a cruise missile at the under-thirty market. With the most potent symbol of global capitalism, the Coca-Cola bottle, now crowning the Strip, Las Vegas can claim its rightful place among the great growth engines of the postmodern economy.

Since 1998, the Strip can also boast of offering the public not only Mike Tyson and Wayne Newton but Picasso and Renoir. The upscale counterweight to the youthful populism of Showcase is Mirage Resorts' newly opened Bellagio, where $285 million of impressionist and modern art graces the property, making it a strange hybrid of the old-fashioned slot palace and the Louvre. Steve Wynn, then Mirage's chairman and impresario deluxe, sold his personal stock to pay for the art for his project. The 3,000-room Bellagio, built around a nine-acre manmade lake, is one of the new billion-dollar resorts that have followed in the wake of the MGM Grand (1993) and New York New York (1997). But just as the dreadnought was inevitably followed by the superdread-nought in the naval arms races of the early twentieth century, the current generation of supercasinos will soon be matched by hyper-resorts like the $2.5 billion, 3,000-room Venetian—complete with canals and gon-doliers—that opened in 1999. The price of poker has risen in Las Vegas; the ante is now so high that only the largest sources of world capital can play in the big-time building bonanza that the town has become. No longer an overgrown gambling palace, a carpet joint in gambling parlance, Las Vegas has become one of the premier resort cities in the world. Even Mecca can't boast as many visitors each year, and while both cities promote forms of prayer, their aims are very different.

The transition from the Mafia to Coca-Cola and Picasso is, of course, a modern corporate fairy tale. The old Las Vegas was the epitome of socially sanctioned deviance, a vast liberty port for the Eisenhower-era middle classes, a place where people could cast off their sins as they did in the deserts of the Bible. In an age when Americans reveled in their industrial might and anticommunist righteousness, the mob oasis in the desert was a pleasure most parents did not tell their kids about. It was the place where the money in the cookie jar went—a secret shared by Mom and Dad (or by Dad and his buddies). The antipode of nine-to-five existence, it was emphatically not a place to build churches, offices, and factories.

This was true as late as the 1980s, when CitiCorp located a service center in Las Vegas. The Manhattan financial giant was so certain that its credit clients would hesitate to mail payments to a Las Vegas address ("So that's what the bank is doing with our money!") that it invented a fictitious town, "The Lakes, Nevada," to receive payments and reassure customers.

With the opening of Showcase and the Bellagio, the transition to a Strip offering something to everyone, from millionaire highrollers to small children, is complete. Las Vegas has merged its shady past (since *The Godfather,* a subject of romantic nostalgia) into a mainstream pres-ent, "a gaming and entertainment theme-park for the world," according to one account. The second most popular tourist destination on the planet, the new Las Vegas can stimulate, titillate, and be safe, clean, and fun all at the same time. Las Vegas has followed the path from gambling to gaming to tourism to entertainment with a success that causes other places to salivate and slavishly imitate the once-shunned Sin City.

Wall Street and the international financial markets have applauded the remake. Since 1990, the annual visitor turnover has increased from 21 million to more than 30 million, and blue-chip financial markets now routinely fill the role once played by the mob-controlled Teamsters' Pension Fund. At the same time, jealous and fiscally starved cities around the nation now see Las Vegas's alchemy of sunshine, gambling, and entertainment as a magic recipe for economic revitalization. Las Vegas has developed a peculiar cachet: it is the success story—the ugly duckling who becomes a swan—that others covet and try to emulate. In a richly ironic reversal of fortunes, as Hal Rothman demonstrates in "Colony, Capital, and *Casino*" and Bill Thompson affirms in "Nevada Goes Global," the pariah has become the paradigm; the colony, the colonizer. The progression to corporate sources of capital for development has made the town a driving force in America's transition to a service economy.

The gaming leviathan can, of course, continue to grow at breakneck speed only if it can colonize the future as well as the present. A new generation of tourists have begun to follow their own celebrities and pop idols to the hipper parts of the post-polyester Strip. About a mile east of the Strip, the Hard Rock Hotel, where the entrance sports Stevie Ray Vaughan's adage "If the house is rockin', don't bother knockin', c'mon in," opened up this niche. Planet Hollywood, which yet may become the flagship of the new order, wanted a hotel to give Generation X-ers a chance to rub shoulders with owners Bruce Willis, Demi Moore, and Arnold Schwarzenegger, while dancing to Third Eye Blind, Matchbox 20, and the Cherry Poppin' Daddies. Most industry pundits agree that the future of Las Vegas will ultimately depend on its ability to integrate gaming with virtual reality and other interactive entertainment technologies.

Las Vegas, in other words, has become a vast laboratory, where giant corporations, themselves changing amalgams of capital from different sectors, are experimenting with every possible combination of entertainment, gaming, mass media, and leisure. Architecturally, the Las Vegas Strip has become a Möbius Strip where casinos merge into malls into amusement parks into sports venues into residential subdivisions into casinos again. Its fundamental malleability, so essential to its transformation from the peripheral to the paradigmatic, has become an envied trait. As Steve Wynn, the CEO of Mirage Industries, told *Time* magazine: "Las Vegas represents all the things people in every city in America like. Here they can get it in one gulp." In a big-gulp culture, Las Vegas has become latest in American dream capitals.

THE FACTORY TOWN

Popular culture often visualizes cities from a single, monotonous viewpoint: the Hollywood Hills in the case of Los Angeles, or the Upper East Side in the case of Manhattan. Las Vegas, of course, is always the Strip at night, five miles long and eight blocks wide, with only darkness and desert at the margin. The residential city—the life world of the miracle workers who create the spectacle—is invisible. This perfectly suits the reigning rhetoric that constitutes the literary and cinematic Las Vegas.

The bulk of outsider reportage on the city falls into two general genres: the male gambling adventure and the middle-American freak show. The first, immortalized by Hunter Thompson's drug-overdosed bestseller of the 1970s, *Fear and Loathing in Las Vegas*, is a gonzo odyssey through temptation, peril, addiction, and a terminal hangover, in which women feature only as bimbo props. Las Vegas in this mode is the ultimate white-guy place—a timeless refuge from feminism, where women are still just commodities and loving every minute of it. As Francisco Menendez argues, movies made in and about Las Vegas—from Lewis Milestone's *Ocean's Eleven* (1960), which brought us the Rat Pack, to the postmodern alcoholic fantasy of John O'Brien and Mike Figgis's *Leaving Las Vegas* (1995)—replay this same overarching theme, set to cater to the social emotions of the moment.

The other preoccupation of Vegas writing is with the bizarre extremism of the average Middle Americans who blunder their way, like herds of dazed, overfed cattle, through the fleshpots of the Strip. Mom and Dad from Sioux Falls—she's in her new wig, he smokes a cigar—have never been stranger, or more normal: "casino zombies" in the words of one writer. Las Vegas has become the favorite setting for hip anthropologists to mock the distended appetites of the majority; in the process, they tell us more about their own faux elitism than they do about the people they are observing.

But Vegas is another world when you enter the gaming palaces from an employees' entrance in a back parking lot. (And we can safely bet that no *Rolling Stone* correspondent or postmodernist philosopher has ever done this.) Or when you leave the Strip to explore the everyday American neighborhoods—rich, poor, and in-between—that now make up a desert metropolis of 1.2 million people. In the daylight, the neon phantasmagoria of the city dissolves into hardworking lives of ordinary dignity and extraordinary aspiration. Here are the alternative narratives and biographies that give the lie to the overtorqued prose that refuses to see the grit beneath the glitter.

Autobiographical essays here by Brian Frehner, Shannon McMackin, and Bill Thompson reframe Las Vegas as home. They invert the typical literary-tourist view of the city: the phantasmagoric landscape becomes a resounding ordinariness, against which remarkable lives are etched in even greater contrast. Las Vegas has become a template for postindustrial, entertainment-driven urbanism at a level and a rate far beyond that of other communities; simultaneously it has become the economic life raft for several postwar generations of workers displaced from their traditional jobs and homes by technological change and globalization. Nowhere else in the United States can an unskilled worker earn middle-class wages and have them mean so much; nowhere else can blue-collar work catapult the next generation into skilled professions with the consistency it does in Las Vegas. The city is many Americans' last-ditch stand, F. Scott Fitzgerald's elusive "second act," the place where, for a variety of reasons, they go to perform an increasingly elusive trick: reaching the brass ring of the American Dream.

In the first generation came the refugees from declining copper camps like Butte and dying factory towns like Lowell, as well as a surprising migration of working-class Mormons from rural Nevada and Utah. They were followed in later decades by waitresses from New Jersey truck stops, unemployed miners from southern Arizona and Sonora, factory workers from East Oakland, deindustrialized steel workers from Youngstown, African-American farm tenants from Mississippi, and most recently, vast numbers of "reverse Okies," the grandchildren of an earlier generation of refugees who fled a California Dream gone sour during the 1991–95 recession that downsized southern California's defense industry.

Las Vegas also functioned as a magnet for everyone who worked in illegal gaming around the country. After the opening of the Flamingo in 1946–47, virtually every hotel and casino manager on the Strip was "connected." Whole coteries, from mob bosses to hat-check girls, arrived from Chicago, Minneapolis, Youngstown, northern Kentucky, and other major illegal gambling centers. They monopolized the best jobs and created a close-knit town with its own codes and moralities. The "hoods," as the daughter of one referred to her father and his associates, were as thrilled by the glamour of Las Vegas, as were the tourists they needed to complete their fantasy community. Las Vegas was heaven, the place where the living they made was legal. They filled the best jobs, hiring other outsiders even for positions as dealers, and created a town that turned on various markers of self-identification that only other members of the club recognized.

In the halcyon early mob era, even maids and busboys were on a first-name basis with pit bosses and casino managers. Old workers recall the familylike intimacy of the immediate postwar generation of casinos. Although some of the darker aspects of that world still remain, Harvard MBAs, not mob family consiglieres, now call the shots. The scale has radically changed.

Twelve giant, industrialized resorts each employ 6,000 to 8,000 workers. While most cities' economies have been restructured into smaller units of production, contemporary Las Vegas has tended toward gigantism and comprehensive integration reminiscent of the Henry Ford era. Dominated by a handful of companies that employ almost 25 percent of the local workforce and wield enormous power in local life, today's Las Vegas recapitulates Detroit or Pittsburgh of the 1960s. At the base of Las Vegas's postindustrial job pyramid is the labor of women. The two largest job categories in southern Nevada's economy are servers/waitresses (15,000) and room cleaners/maids (10,000). In addition to carrying tons of food and drink, as well as walking hundreds of miles, in any normal work year, a waitress must maintain the "hospitality attitude"—smiles and reassurance—that keeps the public at the slots and gaming tables. For decades, Las Vegas waitresses, and their sisters in other casino occupations, including showgirls, have fought to eliminate sexual harassment as a management-tolerated part of their job description. But as Amie Williams shows, the prosperity that unskilled workers enjoy in Las Vegas comes at a price.

Maids' work demonstrates that postindustrial labor can be every bit as grueling and dangerous as work in a steel mill or shipyard. According to the Department of Labor, housekeeping is the fourth most hazardous occupation in the economy, with a phenomenal rate of back injury and high levels of exposure to toxic chemicals. Formerly, black immigrants from the South provided the core of the housekeeping labor pool; now Latinas from Mexico and Central America are the fastest-growing element in it.

There is extraordinary historical significance in the fact that the current president of the powerful Las Vegas Culinary Workers Union is an

African-American maid, Hattie Canty, who came to Las Vegas from the rural South and raised ten children while working thirty years first at nonunion and then later at unionized hotels. The Culinary Workers, who were nearly destroyed during the original corporate phase in the 1970s, successfully reconstituted their position during the 1980s and emerged in the 1990s as a significant political and social force, as well as the primary advocates of social justice in Nevada. Only the Nevada Resort Association exerts its will in politics as comprehensively as the Culinary Union.

In the late 1980s and early 1990s, when the economic and political influence of trade unions collapsed, the Culinary Workers began to rebuild and extend their power within the burgeoning casino economy. It took a decade of strikes, demonstrations, and mass arrests, but Las Vegas is now "the last Detroit," the most dynamic union town in the country. With 50,000 resort employees under contract and ever-increasing influence on local and state politics, the Culinary Workers have become the core of a broad union-community coalition fighting to defend high wages and equal employment opportunity. Courtney Alexander explains how this culture of solidarity at the workplace has reshaped Las Vegas.

The essence of the Las Vegas Dream, in other words, is not the mythic windfall at the blackjack table, but rather the dignity of life that high wages and a union contract make possible. It is a simple fact that here—and in very few other places in the United States—a waitress or a maid can afford to own her home, send her kids to dance classes or Little League, and look forward to quality medical care and a comfortable retirement. The big unionized resorts on the Strip, now including Mandalay Resort Group, MGM Mirage, Park Place, and the Frontier—after the union triumphed in the longest labor strike in American history—are surprising islands of middle-class prosperity in the otherwise low-wage national service economy.

Despite its once tawdry image, Las Vegas was the place where the twentieth century ended. As New York once defined the commercial economy of America and Chicago used its big shoulders to become the city that epitomized industrialization, Las Vegas has become a vision of the future. It offers the most highly developed version of low-skilled service economy in the nation and possibly the world. Its labor is largely unskilled, but the distribution of its employment follows a highly desirable inverted pyramid. Thousands upon thousands of solid-paying jobs offer a place for the unskilled to succeed, an opportunity to sacrifice yourself to the future, to find a way to propel your kids up the socio-economic ladder as did generations of immigrant and blue-collar parents. Unlike Silicon Valley, which creates few low-skilled jobs in comparison to better-paying skilled ones, Las Vegas puts the excised, the economically disenfranchised, and the left-behind back to work in jobs with an economic future. For many tossed on the scrapheap of economic history, the very words "Las Vegas" signify prosperity and an oddly postmodern combination of hope, money, glitz, and action. It has become a repository for the aspirations of the many, displaced from industrial work, seeking reinvention, and embracing a changing American culture as a salve for their woes. In Las Vegas, people seem to believe, the prosperity spawned by tourism and gaming can make them whole, financially and spiritually. Las Vegas now melds fun, work, and wealth, showing a path toward the brightest vistas of the postindustrial world. It is the first city of the twenty-first century.

In this sense, Las Vegas is unique: it uses the mechanisms of an industrial culture of which it was never part to recreate the lost prosperity of the postwar era, the great economic aberration that stretched from 1945 until 1974. Daily, Las Vegas becomes more like the rest of the nation—in where the money comes from, in who makes the decisions, and in the demography, education levels, and other sociocultural traits of the community—but it retains a certain inviolability. Las Vegas has a template for the future that many seek to imitate, but for most, from Atlantic City to the Native American casinos across the land—the results are not the same. Dropping the Las Vegas template on other communities doesn't produce the same results—regional identity, history, and sociocultural structure muddy the picture. Is Las Vegas a paradigm or an oddity, unique or a model?

THE CITY OF THE FUTURE: THE NEW AMERICAN NIGHTMARE?

Las Vegas also has its burgeoning economic and environmental contradictions. Building the first "arid metropolis"—the only major North American city not adjacent to some significant natural source of water (Los Angeles has its river, as does Phoenix)—has required radical innovations in the nature and form of urbanization. Simply put, the rules that have governed urban growth elsewhere in the nation do not apply in Las Vegas. The current boom has defied all naysayers, yet there is a perceptible unease in upper circles. Las Vegas is like a huge jumbo jet in which neither the pilot nor the crew, much less the passengers, have any idea of where it is ultimately headed or how high and far it can fly.

This translates into something entirely new; discerning, addressing, and solving the problems of a postindustrial, postmodern city requires more than the mechanisms chosen by other, more traditional places. The result is a kind of confusion. The traditions of Nevada and the needs of Las Vegas's future stand in stark contrast to each other. While the developers, builders, and real estate people who benefit from growth reap the rewards, larger numbers of Las Vegans, new and old, sit in traffic jams and breathe dust particulate from the torn-up desert. In the most severe and evident dimension of this phenomenon, Las Vegas is engaged in an ongoing conflict with the Environmental Protection Agency. The city cannot conform to national air pollution standards; as long as construction in the desert continues, dust particulate matter will keep the city from compliance.

A growing number of blue-collar Las Vegans, both longtime residents of minority communities and new immigrants of all backgrounds, scrape for a living on the low-rent fringes of the Strip. Newcomers and some locals—those least successful at finding suitable jobs in the past—compete for employment at the edges of the entertainment industry. In many cases, newcomers, possessing skills more suited to the current market, displace already marginalized locals. Southern Nevada advertises ambitious plans for economic diversification, but for the foreseeable future incoming labor will compete with residents in a struggle for a toehold on the economic ladder. For every five newcomers who arrive in Las Vegas, three natives and neonatives leave. For some, the hope of prosperity in the Las Vegas economy is the biggest roulette wheel of all.

The most poignant symbol of this Darwinian economy has been the increasingly visible poverty and homelessness in the shadow of the hyperbolic Stratosphere in an area once called "the Naked City," after the showgirls who once sunbathed there in the buff in the afternoons. Here the forces of economic marginalization and urban redevelopment have united in a sinister compact to displace some of the Strip's poorest residents. There, as Amie Williams chronicles, life is truly a struggle, especially for the young.

Although African Americans in Las Vegas today hold many distinguished political and union posts, they still face obstacles that mirror those elsewhere in the country. The black middle class has fled its old neighborhood, Westside, for opportunities in the multiracial white "burbs," leaving the inner city to fend for itself. This accentuates the gap between the well-off and upwardly mobile and the less skilled, creating two African-American Las Vegases, one visibly prosperous and another increasingly alienated and despondent. For those who arrive with skills and resources, Las Vegas is not the panacea it once was, a place with better opportunities than those offered by the places they came from. Worse, the multiple-shift life of Las Vegas affects families, as does the transience of the community. In Las Vegas, the community structure so essential elsewhere is more fluid and less stable; even institutions such as churches are oddly weaker here, less the glue that holds the community together than groups struggling for the support of the community. African-American newcomers find the core black community of Westside less attractive than the larger city; those who can afford to do so move to the suburbs, leaving a distraught inner city. The tensions that flared up there in the three weekends of "Rodney King" riots in Westside in 1992, which Mike Davis chronicles, had less to do with events in Los Angeles than with Clark County's own dismal heritage of discrimination, its typically high rate of joblessness among black youth, and the excruciating relations between the community and Metro Police. Although middle-class African Americans, including newcomers from California, are finding a place in Las Vegas's booming suburbs, working-class residents of Westside worry about the erosion of their marginal foothold in the gaming industry as many of the larger casinos turn to Latino immigrants as a new supply of cheap labor.

Children with Spanish surnames, meanwhile, are an emergent majority in Las Vegas public schools. Latinos, who made up 13 percent of the school population in 1991–92, had increased to 23 percent, almost 45,000 students, in 1997–98. In 1999–2000, fully one-third of students in grades K-5 had Spanish surnames. The Latino immigration over the past decade is one of the major currents reshaping Las Vegas life, yet Latinos have virtually no political representation in local government. Like black Las Vegans, they complain of overcrowded schools, poor social services, bottom-end casino jobs, and police brutality. The situation of Latinos in the largely nonunion building industry illustrates the larger problem of the low-wage trap. The incredible construction boom of the past decade has ballooned the labor force to nearly 60,000 (a significant number with Spanish surnames), but wages remain depressed. A crew of four "Mexicans" (as Latinos of every nationality are called by their employers) will frequently split $500 for two and a half days of grueling work sheet-rocking a new house in a trendy suburb.

These working conditions offer little hope of eventual prosperity, of stability, of ownership of a home like the ones these workers build. They are left out of the "Last Detroit," this last bastion of remarkable prosperity for the unskilled made possible by unionization, the artificially low cost of living, and the elixir of life in Las Vegas, the tip. Outside of the realm of well-compensated labor, many Latinos receive poor pay and only the most basic benefits, leaving them transient.

Postindustrial Las Vegas is also Darwinian in surprising ways. As in the great industrial cities of the nineteenth century, growth proceeds with insufficient attention to its consequences. The result has been a lack of adequate services, recreational facilities, public space, and other amenities that residents of major cities take for granted. As Eugene Moehring, the most distinguished historian of Las Vegas, observes, the state's tax structure has failed to keep pace with its growth. As a result, virtually every public institution, from libraries and parks to schools and welfare, is grossly underfunded in relation to present demand. Despite its huge gaming turnover, Nevada remains one of the most fiscally regressive states in the union, depending upon sales taxes to generate a disproportionate share of revenue, to which, in turn, investments in infrastructure essential to the resort industry have first claim. As a result, schools and playing fields are overcrowded, while huge, publicly subsidized construction projects pour billions into private coffers. The impetus for much of this development increasingly comes from private developers. Las Vegas may become the first city where public space is privately funded.

Unfortunately, as Robert Parker reveals in his study of social inequality in southern Nevada, there is little relief in sight. From the standpoint of the overburdened public sector, the boom is no longer self-financing. Each new resident now costs more than the tax revenue he or she generates for local government. The obvious remedy in a place with a libertarian ideology and oriented to a regressive tax schedule is to make the gaming industry shoulder a larger share of the costs, but this is like shouting at a mountain. The needs of Las Vegas and Clark County are overshadowed by the ever-increasing political clout of the industry.

The competition for scarce public resources will only grow fiercer in the foreseeable future. In addition to the astonishingly fast-paced growth of its suburbs, Clark County must deal with the special needs of the most rapidly increasing demographic stratum: the 22 percent of the population who identify themselves as "retired." Literally walled off from the rest of the community in their retirement havens in Summerlin and Green Valley, retirees have become a potent voting bloc, which among other things has opposed issuing bonds to relieve school overcrowding. Their potent opposition in 1994 to a major school bond issue awoke the grafted middle class, a one-issue-at-a-time constituency focused on schools and traffic, and nearly split the town along generational lines. A second bond issue, which passed with more than 60 percent of the vote, and which senior coalitions avidly supported, helped close the rift between these grandparents and other people's grandchildren, but deep suspicions remain.

Growth has also brought other problems. As the dreams of some of the many who see Las Vegas as salvation are dashed, crime has become more commonplace. In the mob era, as Debbie Reynolds once remarked, the only people who got killed were the ones who deserved it, but today's Las Vegas has crime like any other city—with one major exception. The Strip and resort corridors are among the most effectively policed urban areas in the world. Crime is typically committed by locals on locals. In "Inside Jean," Constance Devereaux looks at one consequence of dashed dreams: the doubling of Nevada's prison population over the past fifteen years. Thirty miles southwest of Las Vegas, the town of Jean consists almost entirely of two giant casinos in imitation riverboat style, a "welcome center" for tourists, and a grim-looking state prison basking in the reflected neon glow.

Las Vegas has also begun to recapitulate the seven deadly sins of Los Angeles, which is not terribly surprising considering that one-third of its new residents hail from there. Las Vegas's water problems, as Jon Christensen chronicles, are reminiscent of those of southern California at the turn of the twentieth century. Looming large is the issue of where the water to sustain continued growth will come from. If Las Vegas can corral its own Owens Valley, the parallels between it and its southern California counterpart will be even more pronounced.

Some of Las Vegas's problems resemble those of great cities of the past; others are specific to the postindustrial, postmodern landscape. All require the application of social, political, economic, environmental, and cultural capital for their solution. The resolution of these problems will determine whether Las Vegas fulfills its promise as a prototype for the urban twenty-first century.

A PLACE OF ITS OWN

Las Vegas has long been a carpetbagger's dream, a place where self-proclaimed hip intellectuals and grandstanding writers can project their own neuroses, their fears and needs. But the city these outside observers see is a reflection of themselves. It is not the locals' town, not where Las Vegans live. To these writers, Las Vegas is little more than a canvas on which to paint their fantasies. Their renditions sound forced and stale to locals. No wonder that when asked by a group of visiting journalists what the biggest problem Las Vegas faced was, Hal Rothman responded: "People who come from other places who don't know shit about the town and want to write about it!"

He should be forgiven the hostility. Carpetbaggers—outsiders—have always transposed their mythology onto Las Vegas, and the town has always been mutable. It has been what they needed it to be—colony, pariah city, place to cast off sins, den of iniquity, locus of opportunity— but never what it was to the people of the place. The journalists' trick of the quick visit is foolish in Las Vegas: writers from *Time* to the *National Geographic,* from the *New Republic* to *George,* have failed to see more than the very tip of the complexity of the place. Outsiders have often mistaken malleability for gullibility or lack of sophistication, for guile or venality. They have seen the spectacle, but never ventured far beneath; they miss the mask that locals put on to offer outsiders what they want, regarding it instead through their "noir naïf" sensibilities, as Norman Klein puts it. They see evil because they're predisposed to see evil, not because it's necessarily there. They don't know how to see anything else. Las Vegans are quite practiced at giving people what they want without divulging the soul of their place. Unlike other tourist towns, Las Vegas has no illusions about itself; it is what it is and despite the mask of glamour and glitz, it offers no illusions. In Las Vegas, it is always about money, and in late capitalist postmodern America, there's nothing unusual about that except the frankness in acknowledging it.

This is a locals' collection. Most of the authors live and work in Las Vegas, were raised here, chose here, or found an opportunity here. None live on the Strip; a few may gamble or otherwise take advantage of the amenities of life in the neon city, but most live lives that are quite ordinary, little different in texture from the ones they might live in San Francisco or Seattle, New York or Atlanta. They live in what has been the fastest-growing city in the nation for the past decade, amid its traffic and dust, with its limits and possibilities. That alone makes this collection unique. No one has ever before stopped to ask the people of Las Vegas what they think of their place.

PART I **IMAGE AND REALITY**

NORMAN M. KLEIN

Scripting Las Vegas
Noir Naïfs, Junking Up, and the New Strip

Just beyond New York New York, the visitor to Las Vegas enters a zone of unknowing. The sidewalk gets as gritty and nondescript as the industrial edge of Puebla, Mexico. These gritty patches are important clues. In Puebla, factories and body shops encircle the baroque city center, grim reminders of a colonial tradition still in force. Wealth is shipped away, leaving zones of unknowing next to the glamorous eighteenth-century Zócalo and belle époque department stores. Vegas is also part of a colonial tradition, the American West, where mining companies and now gaming corporations ship profits out of state, leaving rough patches just beyond the glamour.

Indeed, the grander the illusion, the more dysfunction it hides. Otherwise, why try so hard? As part of my eccentric research into mass culture, I have been walking through (and clicking or sitting through) every special effects environment I can find, from action "ride" movies, to video games, to the Ringstrasse in Vienna and the Zócalo in Puebla. In each of these, I have spotted zones of unknowing like the rubble along the Las Vegas Strip. The grit in these lost patches is easier to "read" than the finished product only meters away. The seam indicates where the process is uneven. Despite all the enchantment, this economy is continually in drift. On the surface, back at New York New York, there is order—the themed space, the sparkling gimmicks. But beneath that order is a neurotic struggle to industrialize desire. After all, what is a gambler's "impulse"? It is a fractionalized turn of the head—so brief, but so essential that it can be maddening to locate, more a game of chance than gambling itself. With a slot machine, at least the house knows the odds. But to guess which casino will receive the impulse—that problem is subtle enough to be unsettling.

Of course, these seams do not remain for long. Often, the second time I visit a zone of unknowing, perhaps six months later, it has been cleaned up. If not, then I assume that the management must be in trouble. I suspect that the zone between New York New York and Caesars Palace will be shiny soon enough. But for a few months, it will be a useful reminder that while the Strip has "lively pedestrian and sidewalk life," it still has vast contradictions to overcome. From the earliest history of the Strip, when it was merely the road out of town, casino planning ignored sidewalks. For decades, cabs brought guests from one casino to another to keep the spell going.

At the same time, city control of the streets was unwelcome. Recently, Hal Rothman tried to bring a TV crew for a segment on Treasure Island. He set up at the sidewalk overlooking the casino, then was told that he had to leave; it was private property. Finally, he was shuttled to the "public" sidewalk below, a narrow strip of concrete utterly out of sight of Treasure Island.

It is inaccurate to call this policy "pedestrian friendly." Do the casinos really want people drifting down streets through a collage of flyers about escort clubs and hotel strippers? They would prefer gamblers to walk along scripted, glassed-in corridors where you can feel the cybernetic hum of slot machines. In time, a monorail will keep pedestrians on track to gamble. More overhead pedways will be added, because no one lingers on those; you rush across, away from the traffic below. Pedways might as well be rope bridges over a canyon. Indeed, when the pedestrian plan is finished, Vegas will be less a walkable city than a kind of iron lung you can walk through—keep spending or the oxygen may stop.

So, for a few months perhaps, some desert rubble reminds us that Las Vegas was a railroad crosswalk not that long ago, in fact, as late as 1930. The hotels between the rubble momentarily appear a bit more uncertain, as if the dry heat might reclaim them. That uncertainty will be noticed by casino planners, probably already has been. So we should avoid talking about the eye candy for a few pages. Simply concentrate on the contradictions within the designed space of the Strip.

These zones of unknowing certainly reveal a contradiction endemic to the casino business. But we must put aside the excitement about "architainment." That titillation plays into the illusion. Still, the new hotels are vital clues. Let us review the basics of architainment: first of all, eye candy on the façades has replaced neon. There is more narrative architecture on the Strip, an allegorical nod to pedestrian cities. The architectural historian Alan Hess calls it "a radioactive Manhattan." Very systematically, the earlier logolike iconography of the Stardust, the Dunes, and the Aladdin has been imploded. Today, their 1960s neon modernism is practically gone, along with the seedy lounge acts, icy showgirls, and gangsters behind the scenes. To counter the expansion of gaming across the United States over the past twenty years, corporate Las Vegas is now marketed as a resort destination. And like themed retail outlets everywhere, Las Vegas resorts have to look both international and baronial, linking tourism, retail sales, and cinema on a scale never possible before. The new casino-hotels also elaborate on older designs for casinos, especially the trope I call the "unfinishable object." For example, in 1993, I visited Luxor soon after it opened, and my son took a photo of me in front of the Sphinx. When I leaned back, part of the wall fell off in my hand. It was as light as meringue. Beneath the stucco shell and the chicken wire—of the "first pyramid built in 2,600 years"— the wall was made of styrofoam. Later that week, I was told that Luxor had a shelf life of perhaps twenty years, and that it would have to change drastically before it actually began to age. When I returned to see the wall in 1998, it was gone, of course, replaced by more eye candy.

Never quite finishing a casino leaves patches like these zones of unknowing, but why is this financially advantageous? In Reno, I interviewed an architect working on the Eldorado, a simulation of the mining industry—panning slot machines. The eye candy there is gargantuan, with huge mining machines in the center and even an oversized replica of Bernini's Triton Fountain in a corner. By contrast, near the restaurants at the Eldorado, I found a curious dichotomy, even for casino architecture. A very expensive Victorian cherrywood saloon/tearoom was positioned directly alongside one of the most primitive murals I have ever seen. The architect told me that this is a common practice, called "junking up," leaving patches suggesting that the casino is not quite finished. The management wants guests to assume that the odds are not finished either.

Management studies the Eldorado in blocks of twenty to thirty feet to see how the flow of traffic generates profits. In other words, the unfinishable object serves several purposes at once. It inspires gambling, and also the need to return months later to see what has been added. But most of all, it is the only way to fine-tune profits inside a casino.

The "new" Strip dates from 1993, when Luxor, Treasure Island, and the refurbished MGM Grand followed the new Caesars Forum, "the most expensive shopping mall per square foot in the world." Leases inside these new hotels are vastly higher than in the older Las Vegas. Guest rates have soared, to hundreds of dollars a night, testing how high they can go. To promote this five-star image, the hotel is split off more from the casino, particularly at the Bellagio (unless you are in the Mirage/Bellagio slot club; hotels must have wiggle room somewhere in the price, so as not to lose their lower-end clientele entirely).

Catering to the lower end, in zones of unknowing, there are still nests of squat, late 1950s trailer park tourist blockhouses, embarrassing reminders of the indispensable discount Las Vegas. Vegas is continually double marketing—from trailer parks (overnight gamblers visiting by Greyhound from just across the border) to high rollers, now at the Monte Carlo, soon to be shifted over to Bellagio. This contradiction never seems to go away; it just gets recalibrated. Or it gets aestheticized inside a hotel like New York New York. From a nondescript side door, we wind our way into a simulation of the Lower East Side, immigrant America's ur-space, now featuring Il Fornaio pasta. That's essentially all the ethnicity we need. On the left, the fake stalls along Brooklyn's mythical Delancy Street are gaming tables.

Despite what seems obvious, we must not allow ourselves to turn into "noir naïfs" while researching casinos. Doing so obscures more than it reveals. I tend to be a terrible noir naïf when I visit Vegas. For example, as a classic case of naive research, I decided to "look" wrong at the San Remo to see if I could force a clue about how surveillance operated (to pass the time while a friend went to the bathroom). It seemed easy enough to stand out there. That weekend was dominated by hordes of Japanese and Puerto Rican tourists. I tried to stare oddly at the craps table. The lady pit boss, who looked as if she had just overhauled a truck, eyed me strangely. I kept "standing out," thinking she would cue the security people. Later, I was told that she was simply trying to guess when I would get to the tables. She didn't think I was counting anything; she could see through me instantly. My fantasies outran my good sense. That can happen so easily. I often warn students: Evil never wears a black hat. It comps you a room, offers you a $6.95 buffet. It is homespun, very ergonomic, easy listening, user friendly. It is in the business of never showing its dark side, of giving you a good nine cents on every dime. But in Vegas, do I know how to take my own advice?

Indeed, a long-range strategy is required. No amount of simply staring will accomplish much. Critics need to get shrewder to decipher the policies behind the eye candy. That does not mean practicing "noir naïveté"; it means finding more precise critical tools. Some of these tools may date back centuries; others will be very recent. They help propel us beyond the self-evident, beyond news updates that Las Vegas has grown more pedestrian friendly. I doubt that any sapient biped within a hundred miles of the Strip has failed to notice that. Even the booster literature offers "walking tours" of the Strip. We need to find layers beneath the boosterism—paradoxical codes built into the design itself. Let me review a few tools that fit the evidence left by architectural and economic planning—a somewhat anecdotal introductory list that, it may be hoped, will spark much more. As my first tool, I always begin with the same phrase (in lectures, other essays): the casino is a scripted space with illusionistic effects, where the audience is a central character and the narrative is about power. In the case of casinos, power suggests the house's edge and a ubiquitous franchise entertainment economy—the electronic baroque of the gaming industry. The audience makes up stories while held in the cybernetic embrace of gambling. This embrace resembles the thrill of video games or theme park rides, but it is more intense, more existential, more about money and fate. At the heart of the electronic baroque, however, is the designed script itself.

HAPPY IMPRISONMENT: THE LABYRINTH EFFECT

A visitor writes about getting lost in the Caesars Palace casino every time he goes. But it is fun getting lost, "a challenge." Also, you always find your way out eventually. "Wish me luck for the next Xtreme Adventure at Caesars I attempt to take."

This is what I call Happy Imprisonment, or a labyrinth effect. You have infinite choice, but seemingly no way out. Happy imprisonment is a rare pleasure in casinos, and in narrative architecture generally—in mega malls, even in video games, and on the Internet. Casino spaces are scripted particularly as ergonomic labyrinths. Entrances and exits remain askew. Lighting and ceiling heights vary from one specialty aisle to another. The atmosphere is immersive—englobing; domes or parabolic ceilings feed into arcaded channels or glass-barreled vaults. Finding your way back from the bathroom can be difficult. Cacophony is avoided, as well as aural specificity. The entire place hums blissfully. You cannot hear where "it" was. You never leave, but always arrive. It is easy listening, user friendly imprisonment.

SLOTS: THE METROPOLITAN SUBURB IN MINIATURE

Lately, I have been learning a bit about slot machines, how they fit into the script at casinos. Slot machines earn upwards of 70 percent of all gaming profits. They cost about $10,000, last up to ten years, and are generally recalibrated every two or three years. They are the golden goose, particularly now that they are computerized. Apparently, the chips inside calculate within thousandths (or, I am told, even millionths) of a second. Thus, the wheels (reels) turning around are merely for show. Players generally do not trust a screen that looks too much like a computer. The odds seem worse. Slots that look too much like a video game seem too controlled. However, the new slots will be fiercely digital inside, including a vast feedback, statistical control package for casino owners that takes away the need for as many paid human hands to count and miscount. Also, the software will not significantly boost the price of a slot machine. And, finally, with 20,000 more rooms on track to open by 2002, and market shares dividing even more, the owners will need more edge. The power of software companies will grow; people speak of "killer software in an era of slower growth." The script in the machines will include more reward action games like those on CD-ROMs today, a trend pioneered by Odyssey slots in the early 1990s. These include "game within a game" bonus features, carefully hidden (a labyrinth reward, what I call "sim" cheating); and "pick-a-game" (multigame) choices—up to twelve choices, from keno to poker to various slot games—all on a single machine, like a remote control programmer for gamblers. And, finally, the backgrounds behind the slot reels will become far more elaborate. Odyssey specializes in cyberstaging for backgrounds: Arabian riches; bonus vacation maps; bananarama animated monkey hosts; Fort Knox as an adventure game; the Three Wishes magic lantern under a glittery sky reminiscent of Disney's Pinocchio; the Riddle of the Sphinx, lit like an Indiana Jones mystery; Phantom Belle (a live-action southern belle deals, then smirks and hides her cards just above her cleavage); Buccaneer Gold (an atmospheric pirate deck modeled on the woodsy imagery of Myst); a glowing yellow palm reading for Lady of Fortune; a magic wand coming to life in Top Hat.

Slot machines are clearly the future for gaming. At casinos like the MGM Grand, they dominate; they resemble kinetoscopes that remind us of the golden 1930s at MGM, beneath the massive movie screen. By contrast, at the Monte Carlo, slots are much more hidden; there, the gaming tables dominate, framed by rectangular molding on the ceiling, recalling Monaco and the high rollers that the Monte Carlo has tried to lure. Of course, here, too, myths precede facts: high rollers generally have their own private spaces, with restricted entrances, not on casino floors. Tables on the main floor at the Monte Carlo merely suggest James Bond in a tuxedo at baccarat.

At New York New York, gaming tables suggest an imaginary prole-tariat, craps on the Lower East Side in 1915, with the velvet tables submerged under canopies. Apparently, however, the appeal of craps is diminishing. As of 1950, perhaps, or 1955, when the Strip really took off, craps was very much perceived as a sidewalk sport. The war added to its romance: many GIs identified craps with months stuck on a ship; the Sergeant Bilko or Damon Runyon mystique came to mind. Craps suggested the nineteenth-century mining-town West as well; that was essential to the Vegas Vic promotional campaign of the late 1940s into the 1950s. Today, very few men remember playing craps in a submarine or at the motor pool. Increasingly, the anonymity of the slot machine is more soothing for men and women alike: the bodiless cybernetic dealer; poker as private, not communal.

In short, while Vegas may be more "pedestrian friendly," the slot machine yet again raises the question of where is everyone walking to— not through neighborhoods, not inside a world of mixed use. They make their way through narratized retail shopping as tourists; this is utterly different from the patterns of the industrial city or the baroque city that are being idealized. I won't say worse, only different. I leave moral judg-ments for others. Of course, my urban nostalgia probably shows through anyway. But my taste for thin-crust pizza and chewy bagels is irrelevant. Instead, let me repeat the key issue: the new Vegas Strip en-hances the interior narrative, not the communal process. That is not particularly evil, simply a new version of what Baudelaire meant by mixing your solitude in crowds of people. It is less like walking through New York in 1930, more like gambling on a movie set. It is part of what I call "the metropolitan suburb," where streets are privatized and urban interiors operate like cable TV with a food court.

We make too much of the myth that thousands of people watching the volcano at the Mirage constitute an urban experience. Why in that sentence do we leave the term "urban" undefined? Certainly, we do not mean urban in the sense of Parisians in a Daumier lithograph watching the *saltimbanques* perform. Do we really imagine any return at all of the warm evening we see in Whistler's famous painting of the fireworks in Venice? That world is utterly gone, has no roots in Vegas, no matter how glamorous the condensed New York, Bellagio, Paris, Monaco, and Venice become. The city circa 1900 involved much more bricolage, more traces of mixed use. It was a world that dressed differently for every meal, from the workers at dawn to the carriage trade at lunch, to the café crowds later on. In Vegas, we only find bricolage by mistake, where the script misses a street, in zones of unknowing, or in the mix of classes on foot.

The slot machine is a symbol of the globalized electronic economy. It stands for cybernetic controls across many markets at once. New computerized digital tracking services perform like a cyborg for the house: tracking players, slots, tables, revenue sources, demographics, doing the taxes, providing "up to the minute WIN reporting," player photos, electronic signature identification, messages for players on screens in their hotel rooms. For the trackers on the casino floor, there are portable hand-held tracking devices; for their bosses, multiple casino access. This is indeed a software chimera, the tail of a serpent attached to the head of a lion. It combines business graphics with the Internet, cinematic memory, remote control systems, and banking—franchise capitalism at your fingertips. Increasingly, digital slots will operate without coins in cashless casinos, like ATM gambling machines that simply debit your Master Card. Even many Native American casinos, from Cherokee, North Carolina, to Deadwood, South Dakota, are wired for such digital tracking services.

IMMERSION

We wait for the sea battle at Buccaneer Island in front of Treasure Island, for the pirates to sink the British frigate one more time. The entire site has been designed around a scenario, like a nineteenth-century panorama of the Battle of Waterloo. A Portuguese island in the Caribbean is taken over by the Spanish, then falls to pirates. "That way," explains the designer Charles White, "we could rationalize a lot of Middle-Eastern attitude and Moroccan influence." And this (looking at the bottom line) would please Arab high rollers; beyond each hidden script, there is a bottom line, with yet another script, the image of Moslem gaming in Vegas. These back story movie scripts help designers fill in atmospheric details. Pieces of imaginary shipwrecks turn into pirate lairs. The stern of a pirate wreck clings to a hillside.

Bellagio has a similar cinematic back story, about a fictional Italian immigrant, the son of chefs who settled in Las Vegas earlier in the century. It gradually builds a fantasy version of his place of birth; he even starts collecting impressionist art. The Hotel Bellagio is imagined as eighty years old; it simulates the prehistory of a Las Vegas that never was. This scenario requires panoramas on a lavish scale—including $300 million in trophy art—and expensive wood paneling, as if one had been given a special pass to a private club. It needs "immersive" effects, not unlike the lighting and spectacle from Disney Imagineering or Industrial Light and Magic. "Immersion" is a term commonly used in the digital industry to refer to any ambient design that is audience-centered; it places the guest inside the themed fantasy (which may include dressing up the streets as well, which are then monitored often by casino companies).

To be immersed in the lights and props of a Las Vegas casino feels more like film production and less like the movie premiere. In the original Flamingo Hotel (1946), Bugsy Siegel recreated the spirit of a Hollywood nightclub. Today at the MGM Grand, at Caesars Palace, and particularly at all of Steve Wynn's hotels, the guest is transported directly into movie set design. Through devices in scale and overhead gimmickry, the foreground tends to expand outward, to absorb the guest like a friendly dragon.

Visually, this expanded foreground is a rather complicated shift in the way scripted spaces operate, away from the dioramic (viewer set outside the frame) and increasingly toward the panoramic (wraparound effect). To englobe the space, ceilings may be interrupted like film cuts by parabolic shapes: curved hanging objects; animatronic trickery; shadow boxes of pirate treasure; overhanging faux shrubbery.

At the same time, there is casino business as usual. Gaming tables, slot machines, sports gaming, and the hotel and food area have to be designed for maximum profit, yet match the overall theme. There is an ongoing debate as to how theme and gambling should be merged or isolated for proletarian and upscale clients respectively. For example, does the main room need to feature the blackjack tables or diminish them?

The movie set and the profit motive must be married in some way. As I mentioned earlier, there are quick edits every twenty feet or so. Mini-sets sharpen each area to maximize profits. (By mini-sets, I mean the fixed-point breaks in the decor indoors, as well as in the eye candy outdoors.) To enhance these mini-sets, the design often relies on fixed-point perspectives, moments to stop: flashes of trompe l'oeil (copies in unusual materials); video walls; display cases near the ceiling. Fixed-point illusion is a Renaissance visual pleasure, very antique magic; it provides boundaries where needed, yet makes the guest feel like an insider, "in the know." For an instant, trompe l'oeil movie tricks seem to reveal secrets; this might be the influence of Universal Tours, but more the spirit of George Lucas and Steven Spielberg.

Of course, casino architects also draw on baroque and Renaissance trompe l'oeil. For example, Jon Jerde's designs for Bellagio, even for the Fremont Experience, refer to sixteenth-century Italian illusionistic architecture. But the overall strategy is consistent across the architainment on the Strip. The imagery must be abbreviated, foreshortened in some way, but look extremely three-dimensional, deep focus. Often, the effects are modeled on Disney Imagineering, particularly the Pirates of the Caribbean (designed by Marc Davis in 1964), the point of origin for theme park immersive spaces in Orlando as well. To sum up: immersion relies on compositing, but in a sculptural architectural way—blue-screen and digital trickery, one layer upon the other, but also trompe l'oeil sculpture reminiscent of eighteenth-century German baroque churches.

CONDENSED CITIES

Through immersive devices, replicas of cities can be shrunk to the scale of a hundred acres or less. Bally's Paris is less than twenty acres; it's across the street from Lake Como, down the block from Venice, near Rome and New York. Obviously, these are "condensed" spaces, but not simply because the Chrysler Building is foreshortened against the Empire State Building. They are condensed in Freudian terms: mutual narratives that distract by overlapping the same space, like the topology of a dream. These overlays can leave zones of unknowing of a different sort than rubble on streets: sutures in the architainment, within the mini-sets themselves. Does the guest sense which buildings are "missing" in New York New York? Not really. More likely, the guest feels point of view, like the chiaroscuro in cinema—a dark accent that adds contour and suggests a controlled world for your visual pleasure.

Indeed, movie sets are for our civilization the quintessential condensed spaces, a recorded memory cut short because the camera must keep moving. The film *Titanic* is essentially all the streets of a city that movies generally show, a theatricalized backdrop three streets long, and short streets at that. Logically enough, a *Titanic* hotel has been discussed for a site just off the Vegas Strip.

Consider the broader implications of a condensed city: tourism converts neighborhoods into a blackness off screen, not seen, only the cinematic long shot where the murderer slinks away into the night; it condenses space into camera time. A world becomes a tour by automobile—this is particularly essential for the pedestrian Strip. Vegas monumentalizes that time/space paradox of driving, even when you walk through it.

Also, consider the cybernetic controls implied by condensed cities. Architainment selects what of the whole we see and chooses instantaneously—no time for resistance—like a search engine delivering on the Web or a movie camera panning a city before the action starts. And yet beneath the false skyline of New York New York, for example, like the antlers of a great moose, there is a single head—the casino, or the hotel, one building that supports the rest. The visitor probably finds the interior soothing, a world under control. The sum of all of these (indoors/outdoors) becomes a computer-like menu—abbreviated, accessible, and air-conditioned wherever possible. You make your choice, a happy prisoner.

What do condensed cities reveal about franchise capitalism in the electronic baroque era? They mix elements from practically all the businesses that share in this baroque—tourism, cinema, and the fixed perspectives provided by the automobile. New York New York is a composite of how it might feel inside a car on the Staten Island Ferry as the skyline pulls in; or perhaps on a Sunday drive in Manhattan. We walk through what the view through a windshield would show us (of course, it is nearly impossible to say for certain what the guest "actually" sees in his or her mind's eye). The Strip has been a road out of town to the airport for generations. That was its originary moment. All human settlements, no matter how genteel they get, refer back to such points of origin.

What do condensed cities say about the context of urban life today? They monumentalize the death of cities as we have known them, much the way Disneyland's Main Street in 1955 reminded guests that small towns were dying. It is homage to what is gone. Oddly poignant, it can be charming, very hip and politically correct, like the jungle shop for extinct animals inside the MGM Grand, with its animatronic replacements for animals that will soon be irreplaceable. The city becomes a petting zoo, a backdrop for photographs; or a botanical gardens for a landscape of rare plants. It is a cheerful funeral, if possible out of scale, foreshortened to add grandeur. The Eiffel Tower is so close to the street, it seems to bump you off the curb, as does the Empire State/Chrysler Building. The vertigo of the skyscraper is enhanced, even if the buildings are half-scale.

Wherever possible, the condensed space in Vegas is not miniaturized. Somehow, through forced perspective, it still has to suggest scale. Vegas cities are part of an epic resort, not a Japanese contemplative garden (although Japanese theme parks certainly rival those in the United States). The Eiffel Tower looms directly against the street, as does the Statue of Liberty. The nine-acre Lake Como, like the pirate village along Treasure Island, is foreshortened to look even bigger. The Coke bottle that dominates the Coca Cola sim-museum hugs the street as well (drink soda pop condensed from around the world). I am reminded of the theatrical machines that relied on foreshortening in seventeenth-century Europe, of the vast tradition of forced perspective and optical tricks that peaked in the baroque era.

Steve Wynn, the archduke of Vegas baroque, has called the architect Jon Jerde (Treasure Island, the Fremont Experience, Bellagio) a "Bernini for our time." Jerde himself likes to compare himself to Borromini, a rival Bernini distrusted. Both Wynn and Jerde are profoundly aware of the late feudal nature of this world of megamalls and hypertrophic casinos. Instead of the industrial nation-state represented by Manhattan in 1920, we have retail, franchise capitalism, where entertainment and investment merge in real estate, urban planning, global ad campaigns, global licensing. It very much resembles the mercantilism of the seventeenth century, whether that of the Counter-Reformation in Italy or central Europe, or of Colbert on behalf of Louis XIV.

Condensed cities are baronial palaces with stylized moats and drawbridges: the public approaches only with permission. There is a profound sense in all the Vegas promotion I see that these condensed cities are the palace jewels. They are Versailles for the multitude, but let us never imagine that palaces are democratic sites. I do not care deeply whether the old cities return, much as I love them. I am more concerned that we may lose our urban political heritage. As a culture, we are being asked to dispose of our first and second amendment rights for a good cup of latte and a chance to walk past architainment. To repeat, for emphasis—these are ducal domains, cities for public ritual, but not for "democratic ways," to use Louis Sullivan's expression.

These ergonomically restricted spaces, like being trapped in traffic but with a great CD sound system, will grow more comfortably restricted as the decades wear on. Ours is a much more class-driven culture. Steadily, institutions like genteel casinos are emerging to give us rituals to celebrate the new restrictions.

Do not be fooled by the mix of classes and races who walk along the Strip. Crowds are not by definition a symbol of democracy. Crowds of that sort used to honor the birthday of the baron as well. We must not confuse happy imprisonment with political freedom, remote controls with democratic controls. To shop and gamble freely is now the bulwark of the republic. It is also not the bubonic plague—no noir over-simplifications. What results is not the worst of all possible worlds, surely, but neither is it simply a new fashion. Architainment is a ducal fantasy on behalf of cinematic tourism. And cinematic tourism symbolizes the revival of a feudal economy, sponsored by franchise licensing and digitalized gambling. No one will die of it, but no one will be liberated by it either. Monuments are not crimes. They merely announce who is in charge of our public memory.

Las Vegas of the Mind
Shooting Movies in and about Nevada

Snow covers a Chicago sidewalk. At the curb stands the "All-American Gas Station," a front for organized crime. Several sedans, circa 1975, drive past as a large Lincoln cuts through the fresh snow at the station's entrance and parks next to one of the gas pumps. The Lincoln's door opens and out comes a huge man with salt-and-pepper hair wearing a winter coat. He looks around to check if he is being watched and enters the gas station, carrying a heavy briefcase.

The man is Frank Marino, part of Nicky Santoro's "crew." Money skimmed from the Tangiers casino in Las Vegas is in his briefcase. The Tangiers has secret ties to a midwestern crime syndicate, and a payoff in dollars about to be delivered to the aging Remo Gaggi, head of the Chicago mob.

"Cut," says a sharp voice.

"Cut, and back to one," orders another voice.

The sharp voice belongs to the New York filmmaker Martin Scorsese, who now paces beside the Academy Award–winning cinematographer Robert Richardson. Next to them, a 65mm film camera focuses on the wintry scene. Through the camera's lens, the skyline of hotels and casinos reveals that the gas station is really located at the edge of downtown Las Vegas, not Chicago.[1]

On the street, the dated "picture cars" return to their first positions. The Scorsese veteran Frank Vincent, who plays the role of Frank Marino, backs the Lincoln out through the snow-covered entrance. Two film crew members sporting backpacks with hoses hurry to restore the mantle of white by spraying it with a foamy substance that, on-screen, will look like fresh snow.

For this shot, a large-format film camera is being used so that a matte of the Chicago skyline can be added to the scene months from now in postproduction. This process shot will last no longer than four seconds of screen time, but shooting it here will save the crew the trouble of leaving its home base, Las Vegas—where most of the film takes place. The movie is *Casino,* a $50 million Universal Pictures production.

By Christmas 1995, audiences all over the country had seen *Casino,* the story of organized crime's decline in Las Vegas in the late 1970s and early 1980s, written by Nicolas Pileggi and Martin Scorsese. By the end of 1995, Las Vegas had also been featured prominently in Joe Eszterhas and Paul Verhoeven's *Showgirls* and John O'Brien and Mike Figgis's *Leaving Las Vegas.*

Not everyone would see these films at the theater, but the advertising machine and the media blitz behind Hollywood films today made it nearly impossible not to know of them. Television spots, print ads, and cable specials make the public aware of films' plots and show images from their climactic moments. The public has second, third, and fourth opportunities to catch films on pay-per-view, cable, or at the local video store. Images used to promote films not only rekindle memories of what the film was about but reaffirm popular notions about Las Vegas and Nevada.

Not only are more films shot on location in Nevada each year, but the Silver State is specified more and more as a locale in film scenarios. A movie set in Nevada has come to have specific meaning in the mythology of film storytelling. Early in film history, footage shot in the state was used in adventure serials, westerns, and prehistoric sagas, but in the past few decades, film narratives have integrated Nevada itself into their plots, thus constructing a pop-culture conception of the state. This impression is filled with images, icons, and new stories that reflect our need to include Nevada in our shifting pop culture mythology.

Today, Las Vegas is rendered in narrative film as a moral testing ground, a special world in which a movie character's fidelity, integrity, and family are challenged by power, gambling, sex, and greed in a variable landscape of neon, desert, or science-gone-wrong. To appreciate how Las Vegas is currently depicted in film, one must first look at the state's early filmmaking history, the creation of the State Motion Picture Division, and the reinvention of Las Vegas's own image. These provide the proper context from which to appreciate the changing cultural conception of Nevada, and how film stories set in the Silver State have evolved over the years.

At the turn of the century, Nevada was nearing the end of a two-decade depression framed by the decline of the Comstock Lode and the Tonopah mineral discoveries in 1900. At this time, boxing was a controversial sport. Participants and promoters risked felony convictions in other states. However, because of its poor fiscal situation, Nevada welcomed prize fighting—its first attempt to attract tourism.[2]

The first event recorded on film in Nevada was a boxing match between James J. Corbett and Bob Fitzsimmons in 1897. That year, Nevada lawmakers answered Governor Reinhold Sadler's request for additional revenue measures by passing a bill that licensed prizefights. The fight aroused national outrage because Nevada law had legalized boxing. It was the beginning of a negative image the rest of the country would construct about Nevada, an image fed by later legislation emphasizing "easy divorce" and gambling, and another that would influence Nevada's portrayal in motion pictures.[3]

The Corbett–Fitzsimmons fight occurred six years after Thomas Alva Edison and William K. L. Dickson patented the Kinetoscope, the original movie machine, in 1891. The next recorded entry in the state's filmography was another boxing match in Reno on July 4, 1910. Thirteen years after Corbett–Fitzsimmons, Nevada scandalized the nation once again—this time by mixing races in the ring. The former heavyweight champion Jim Jeffries was brought out of retirement to fight the first black heavyweight title holder, Jack Johnson. The hostile crowds were reported to be "downright dangerous," not only because Jack Johnson was black, but because he was living openly at his training camp with his white wife.[4]

The result of the match was that Johnson pummeled the aging Jeffries and took him out in the 15th round of a scheduled 45-round fight. Johnson's impressive performance apparently appeased the crowd. The box-office record of 15,670 tickets sold would not be surpassed until years later. The preservation of this spectacle on film allowed Americans across the nation to witness the event. Interested spectators no longer had to use their imaginations to connect pictures to written reports; instead, they had a chance to "experience" the fight with their own eyes. That side of Nevada became "real" through the medium of film.[5]

The first attempt to shoot a narrative film in Nevada dramatized the event that pulled the state out of its twenty-year depression. In 1913,

Yale Feature Films shot a four-reeler entitled *The Tonopah Stampede for Gold*. In his manuscript "Cinema in the Silver State," the Nevada film researcher Gary Du Val suggests that, since only prerelease items are available on this film, and since there is no record of a screening, the film may never have been released. What makes this movie about men trying to stake their claims during the Nevada gold rush notable is that it featured, as themselves, acting governor Tasker L. Oddie and Jim Butler, the man who discovered the Mizpah and Butler mines.[6]

Back in the teens, it was not surprising to see untrained actors starring in silent films. Such was the case with Helen Holmes, the daughter of a railroad executive, who was lucky enough to meet Mack Sennett's Keystone Comedies star Mabel Norman, who promised her: "I can get you work in the movies if you have enough money to get some good clothes." Holmes joined the ranks of those brave film serial heroines in peril. In 1915, she came to Nevada to shoot episodes of *The Hazards of Helen*— the longest-running serial of all time.[7]

There were 119 episodes of *The Hazards of Helen*, of which episodes #20 through #23 were shot in Nevada. In this case, the state was a generic backdrop rather than a specific locale. Each installment revolved around a train, a villain, and Helen—who always proved resourceful in even the most dangerous situations. The company worked quickly, shooting an episode a week, and chartering a train that would transport them every morning to the vicinity of Bard and Sloan, where the surroundings were deemed "sufficiently wild and romantic to suit."[8]

Helen Holmes returned to Nevada the next year with her director, co-star, and fiancé, John P. MacGowan, to shoot another episode: *The Girl and The Game*. The company hired some locals, and this time a portion of the episode featured Reno. One scene, staged atop the Majestic theater, included a pan of most of the existing town.[9]

Northern Nevada was featured several times in early silent movies. In 1919, Robert Z. Leonard shot *The Scarlet Shadow* and *What Am I Bid?* in the Lake Tahoe area. Both melodramas starred his then wife, the silent film star Mae Murray. In 1921, Nevada residents Captain H. M. Joss and the producer John Carrico made the western *Black Steve of the Sierras,* billed as the first "All-Nevada picture creation." Even then, Nevadans were determined to show the film industry that the state had all the resources necessary to make movies.[10]

In 1922, Paramount Pictures shot *The Covered Wagon* (1923), later to be labeled the first epic western, and one of several big-budget silent pictures that featured Nevada's desert. Its director, James Cruze, man-

From *The Hazards of Helen* (1915).

aged a cast of 3,000, including 1,000 Native Americans brought in from Wyoming and New Mexico. Two years later, John Ford shot his own large-scale western in Nevada, *The Iron Horse* (1924), which tells the story of young lovers who endure the obstacles of the coupling of the Union Pacific and the Central Pacific railroads. It was shot at Dodge Siding and Pyramid Lake, Nevada, and became Ford's first success.[11]

Nevada's untamed landscape continued to attract film productions. In 1926, Samuel Goldwyn sent the director Henry King to Nevada to scout for the perfect desert location in which to stage a "super-colossal" picture. *The Winning of Barbara Worth,* starring Ronald Coleman and Vilma Banky, was Gary Cooper's debut picture, a melodramatic romance set against a vast desert irrigation scheme. The production company established the town of Barbara Worth, Nevada, in the Black Rock Desert as a publicity stunt. After a tight eight-week shooting schedule, the company of three thousand people left, turning the site into an instant ghost town.[12]

In southern Nevada, Hal Roach wrote and produced *Black Cyclone* (1925), a love story where horses play the major parts and humans are the supporting characters. He set up a unit on the Home Ranch in the Moapa Valley. The Valley of Fire also served as a location for several films, among them the 1939 caveman saga *One Million b.c.,* co-directed by Hal Roach and Hal Roach, Jr., which featured Lon Chaney, Jr.,

From *One Million B.C.* (1940).

Victor Mature, and Carol Landis and included some uncredited directing by D. W. Griffith.[13]

During the 1920s and 1930s, Nevada was used mostly as a backdrop
of arid landscapes. The major exceptions were pictures that were shot
in and about Reno, a city that developed a distinct reputation with the
American public. In 1920, the silent-screen star Mary Pickford traveled
to Reno and waited for six months to get a divorce so she could marry
Douglas Fairbanks. The high visibility of her stay paved the road for
fashionable celebrity divorces, and Reno would eventually become
known as the "divorce capital of the world."[14]

Legalized prostitution and rumors that it had become a major center
for laundering stolen cash helped cement Reno's image as "sin city." It
represented what the country continued to see as Nevada's immorality.
Movies set in Reno promised a sultry melodrama to audiences outside
the state.[15]

The relegalization of gambling in Nevada in 1931 further perpetuated
and cemented the state's bad name. While Nevada offered legal prostitution, divorce, and gambling, Hollywood self-censored the material it
put on the screen. Back in 1915, the U.S. Supreme Court had found that

motion pictures were not to be granted the free speech protection guaranteed to newspapers and other media. This decision, along with several Hollywood scandals in the early 1920s, prompted film producers to create a self-regulatory organization called the Motion Picture Producers and Distributors of America in an attempt to forestall external regulation.[16]

In 1930, a document was drafted known as the Production Code, which "attempted to explain the general moral principles by which producers should be guided as well as to spell out specific directives regarding the depiction of crimes against the law, sex, dances, religion, vulgarity, 'repellent' subjects, and other potentially objectionable material." With religious groups threatening to boycott offending movies, filmmakers respected the code. It remained in effect until the 1950s.[17]

Films made in or about Nevada in the 1930s, 1940s, and early 1950s must therefore be seen in the context of the Production Code. Pictures with "Vegas" in the title began to proliferate in the 1940s when the Hoover Dam's construction caused sudden growth in Las Vegas. Some films were shot on location, while others used stock footage of casino exteriors and were shot back in California. One of these was *Las Vegas Nights* (1941), a musical remembered, not because of its plot, but because it introduced Frank Sinatra to the silver screen.

The "sin city" mantle began to pass from Reno to Las Vegas during this period. In 1952, Howard Hughes produced *The Las Vegas Story*, starring Jane Russell and Victor Mature, a *Casablanca*-like tale of a woman finding her old love in a land of greed and being forced to decide whether or not to stay with her husband. The twist is that, unlike Paul Henreid's character in *Casablanca,* the husband is not a leader of the anti-Nazi underground but an embezzler—and perhaps a murderer.[18]

The Las Vegas Story was filmed on location at the Flamingo, and Hughes, who ran RKO at the time, was quoted as saying that the location "represented all that is glamorous and exciting about Las Vegas." The movie also starred Hughes's protégée, Jane Russell, whose shapely figure had caused censorship problems during the release of Hughes's earlier western *The Outlaw* (1943). Despite these enticing elements, and a much-publicized ad campaign, the public stayed away and critics savaged the picture.[19]

However, *The Las Vegas Story* is best remembered for the controversy during its production. The film's screenwriter, Paul Jarrico, had refused to testify for the House Un-American Activities Committee on the grounds of self-incrimination. This led to Jarrico's immediate dismissal by Hughes. The Writers Guild arbitrated and RKO decided that Jarrico's name should remain on the credits, despite two additional writers having been brought onto the project. Hughes overrode the arbitration and spoke out against "communist influence in Hollywood" and "red sympathizers and dupes" in the film industry.[20]

The concerns of the Cold War affected Nevada in other ways. By 1952, most nuclear testing occurred less than a hundred miles away from Las Vegas at the Nevada Test Site. This spawned several grade-B science fiction films that used Nevada as a radioactive backdrop, among them *The Atomic Kid* (1954), *The Amazing Colossal Man* (1957), and *The Beast of Yucca Flat* (1960).

While Hollywood was engaged with Senator Joseph McCarthy's witch hunts in the early 1950s, movies lost their edge. The pervasive fear that the House Un-American Activities Committee had engendered made studios produce movies that would placate the Production Code office. Hollywood also lost audience share to the new medium of television. In 1948, when Howard Hughes had gained control of RKO, about 360 million people went to the movies every week. By 1952, weekly attendance at the movies had dropped dramatically to 200 million.[21]

In response, filmmakers tried to woo audiences back into theaters. One approach was to make films that could, once more, boast shooting in actual locales. As sound and camera equipment became more portable, film units could once again venture outside the studio gates. Hollywood film producers were, however, met with a cumbersome permit process and a web of additional fees when they tried to shoot on location in California.

Since Joss and Carrico's *Black Steve of the Sierras* (1921), there has been an active interest in trying to lure filmmaking to Nevada. In fact, filmmakers had used the state as a generic location as many times as they had scripted Nevada as a specific locale. The University of Nevada, Reno, and the scenic vistas around Lake Tahoe served as picturesque backdrops, just as the Nevada desert had served adventure serials, westerns, and *One Million B.C.* In the early 1960s, the film industry remained in a slump, but Nevada made a comeback as a specific location with pictures set in Las Vegas. Frank Sinatra and his "Rat Pack" played World War II veterans attempting to rob five Vegas resorts on New Year's Eve in *Ocean's Eleven* (1960). *Viva Las Vegas* (1964) would be remembered as the ultimate Elvis picture, fusing elements of the King's

From *Viva Las Vegas* (1964).

past movies with the glitzy background of Las Vegas. Both Sinatra and Elvis would become inextricably linked with the town that described itself to the outside as the entertainment capital of the world. Las Vegas was moving beyond its image as "sin city" and was beginning to establish its mythical stature on screen.

In the 1960s, however, Robert Sklar observes in his book *Movie-Made America*, "the children of the post-war baby boom—the infants who kept their parents home from the movies in the late 1940's—began to come of age. They themselves had grown up in the television era and had logged tens of thousands of hours before the small screen. Oriented to the visual media as no previous generation had been, they experienced a steady diet of entertainment equivalent to the 'B' movies of the 1930's."[22]

The baby boomers were ready to be recruited into the ranks of film fans. Hollywood countered this challenge by reaching back to its genre traditions to please this new audience. By the mid 1960s, those who worried about the movies' ability to corrupt were outnumbered by those curious enough to attend. Hollywood discovered that controversy would sell as many, if not more, tickets. The Production Code had become outdated and was replaced by a ratings system.

Culturally, films rose once more as they had in the 1930s, this time playing to an audience that had been trained by television. Hollywood began to shift its focus toward the successively younger generations that were buying movie tickets. By end of the 1960s, Hollywood was courting a new generation who would be mentored by, come of age with, and sometimes allow their lives to be defined by movies.[23]

The common experience of television, and now film, created a popular culture that allowed audiences to share collective notions of stories, characters, and locales. Vegas was displayed prominently in the James Bond series when Sean Connery made his return in *Diamonds Are Forever* (1971). In this picture, the Las Vegas Valley is replete with casinos, mobsters, nuclear warheads, and Willard Whyte—a movie version of Howard Hughes, played by the singer and sausage magnate Jimmy Dean. Recalling Hughes's mysterious hermitlike existence in his top floor suite at the Desert Inn, Whyte is sequestered in his own hotel, the Whyte House. It was Howard Hughes himself who approved the script and gave the producers full access to the city. Las Vegas was no longer just a backdrop; its history was used and repackaged, however ridiculously, by this box office success.

The fictional geography of Las Vegas began with *Ocean's Eleven*'s detailed description of the five Las Vegas casinos targeted for the heist: the Sahara, the Sands, the Flamingo, the Riviera, and the Desert Inn. It continued in a sanitized tour with Elvis and Ann-Margret in *Viva Las Vegas*, which takes place during the Las Vegas Grand Prix and not only features Strip hotels but uses Hoover Dam and the campus of Nevada Southern University (now the University of Nevada, Las Vegas). *Diamonds Are Forever* completes the tour, featuring the International (now the Las Vegas Hilton) as the Whyte House as well as other Las Vegas landmarks. Las Vegas locations became an integral part of the fabric of each of these movies. No longer just backdrops, the locations, real or fictionalized, are required in order for these stories to take place.

While Las Vegas was redrawn by these pictures, Nevada's links with organized crime were about to be presented to a worldwide audience in a believable context. *The Godfather* won the 1972 Oscar for Best Picture. Two years later, its sequel won another Oscar for Best Picture. These were the first Academy Award–winning films to portray Nevada in an openly disreputable light. *The Godfather,* based on the novel by Mario Puzo, tells the story of the fictional Corleone family and their organized crime empire. Fredo, the black sheep of the Corleone family, is sent to Vegas to work at the fictional Tropigala hotel-casino, run by the flamboyant Moe Greene. Later, Michael Corleone, played by Al Pacino, finds out that his brother Fredo has been shamed publicly, leading to Greene's gangland-style execution at the end of the film.[24]

The Godfather II goes further by placing the Corleone family retreat at Lake Tahoe, Nevada, and including several scenes featuring a local senator, played by G. D. Spradlin, who is intent on extorting money from the Corleone family if they persist on developing new casino interests in Nevada. Michael, the new Godfather, deals with the senator's threats by framing the politician for the murder of a young prostitute at a local whorehouse run by Fredo. By this time, Michael has assumed a guise of respectability, but he is not beyond using force to protect the interests of his "family."[25]

Earlier generic portrayals of mobsters and hoodlums are transformed in these films into a nexus of organized crime, casinos, and the Nevada state government. The critical and popular success of *The Godfather* and its sequel impressed on audiences worldwide the picture of a Nevada run by the mob and corrupt state officials.

These two films played to these real and popular conceptions of Nevada's ties to organized crime, and where the veracity of events ended and the fiction began became irrelevant. Unlike *Ocean's Eleven, Viva Las Vegas,* and *Diamonds Are Forever,* which respectively integrate Las Vegas into the caper picture, the musical, and the action movie, *The Godfather* pictures play along the lines of a historical epic. The caliber of the script, the direction, the design, the cinematography, and the acting, combined with the award-winning recognition of both films by the critics and the film community, elevated these films in stature, turning popular perception into accepted fact.

The fantastical image of Las Vegas and the "real" rendering of Nevada were two images that conflicted in years to come. Either Nevada was a benign oasis filled with neon promising luck, glamour, and adventure, or it was a sleazy place populated by criminals, gamblers, and prostitutes, with little hope and plenty of broken dreams. In the next twenty-five years, both images prevailed. At first, the negative image was a cause of great concern to the state, and, specifically, to the resort community.

During the 1970s, Nevada remained determined to entice filmmakers in a concerted effort to diversify its financial base. The state's goal was to try to make movie and television production the third industry behind gaming and tourism. Although the growth of movie production in Nevada is intertwined with the flowering of Las Vegas as resort community, that history was not without its own growing pains. Efforts to attract movie production to the state on a regular basis remained unsuccessful, and interested locals demanded a state agency that would court Hollywood.

For years, other states' film commissions had bent over backward to get movie producers to locate their productions there. They lured film companies by providing what was not available in California: easy access to sites and permits, discount lodging and office facilities, and the attractiveness of a "right to work" state. Yet, in 1978, Nevada remained the only western state without a film commission. This meant that film and television productions were at the mercy of hotels and service providers, and on their own when it came to scouting locations or securing permits.[26]

In his book *Adventures in the Screen Trade,* the screenwriter William Goldman recounts his experiences when he wanted to use the MGM Grand (now Bally's) as a location for shooting a remake of *Grand Hotel* in 1977. Norman Jewison was to direct, and it was to be a big-budget musical. At the time, no film had ever been shot at the MGM Grand and no filmmaker had seen its size or interiors, making it virgin territory.[27]

Deals were made, the picture was a "go" project, but then, as Goldman describes it, "a Metro executive (literally) woke up from a sound sleep and realized that Jewison got final cut on his pictures, and what if he decided to ridicule the Grand?" As Goldman counters: "Neither Jewison nor I ever dreamed of ridiculing the Grand. We wanted to make this wonderful bubble, an entertainment, very pure and very simple, with the best musical talents we could find. An exposé of the dark side of Vegas's underbelly was not what he had in mind. Nor did we want to mock the ladies in curlers or the men in leisure suits. And we weren't after a tract that preached the evils of gambling."[28]

But Jewison had "final cut" in his contract, which meant that the Metro executives could not risk the possible disgrace of their establishment. Final cut is one of the most coveted items in a director's contract, so Jewison was not going to give up his right. The Metro executives gave in with one major exception: Jewison and Goldman could do whatever they wanted with everything outside the hotel, but anything shot inside would be controlled by Metro. This concession meant little to the film-makers, because 99 percent of the story takes place inside the hotel, but the point the executives were making was clear: what the public saw would be controlled.

Both Jewison and Goldman left the project, but four years later they were contacted again by Metro to consider it. This time Goldman hesitantly went to Las Vegas to explore location possibilities. As he was touring one of the gigantic suites, a hotel employee said to him, "[T]his is the one Mr. Ashby used."[29]

In just four years, the people who had denied Goldman and Jewison free access had allowed Hal Ashby to film *Lookin' to Get Out* (1982), the story of two New York losers who escape to Las Vegas. It had yet to be released, but Goldman managed to get hold of the script. The story hinged on the pair impersonating a friend of one of the hotel executives over the phone, thereby fooling the hotel staff and getting everything for free at the MGM Grand.

Lookin' to Get Out had been approved by the MGM executive staff after being refused by Caesars Palace across the street and had used all the locations that *Grand Hotel* had intended to use. Moreover, it exploited the dark image of Vegas that Goldman and Jewison had had no interest in exploring. This included "a scene where one of the male leads waits outside in the corridor so his buddy, inside, can get a blow job from a whore."

The inconsistencies that Goldman discovered at the MGM during the preproduction of *Grand Hotel* were not the only type of roadblock film-makers faced while shooting in Las Vegas in the late 1970s and early 1980s. The TV series *Vegas* followed the exploits of detective Dan Tanna, who operated out of the Desert Inn. The show's producers shot all over town, but found it difficult to operate because service providers charged the production ludicrous prices. Bob Hirsch, formerly director of the Nevada Motion Picture Division, regretfully recalled the series being billed $300 for a bag of ice.

In 1982, Nevada's newly elected governor Richard Bryan made good on his campaign promises to establish the Motion Picture Division of the Commission on Economic Development. This office would entice film, television, and commercial productions to come to Nevada and

From *The Electric Horseman* (1979).

provide them with a formal liaison to monitor abuses either by providers or by the productions themselves.[30]

There has always been a delicate balance between the art and business of making movies. A film is considered successful by a studio if it is accepted at the box office or if it garners the requisite amount of prestige, thus making the write-off more attractive. The problem that studios have with "A" pictures is that their cost is now typically from $20 to $60 million, and there is no guarantee that a film will be either a popular or a critical success. Studio executives therefore hedge their bets by relying on several factors in producing a motion picture: a director's or star's track record, story elements similar to those of past successes, or high production values that may stimulate audience curiosity.[31]

A state's motion picture division faces similar challenges when determining whether a film will benefit the territory. Of course, if a film spends a lot of money in the state, it obviously meets the requirement of bolstering the economy. Yet determining which movies to favor when the production slate is full can be as tricky as deciding whether a movie should be put into production.

A concern to any state motion picture division is that the state might be misrepresented or shown in a negative light. The more immediate reason that box office numbers and critical reception of Nevada-themed films are important to state officials is because films that gain widespread attention present their images of the Silver State to the broadest audiences. In effect, the powerful medium of film could reinforce or combat the desired perception.[32]

In the past, the armed forces and government agencies such as the FBI have refused to cooperate with film companies because of "negative portrayals" of their organizations. Indeed, the Las Vegas resort community had been reluctant to align itself with the portrayal of organized crime in the hotel/gaming industry. In 1984, John Chiero, then president of the Tropicana, spoke out in the press against the NBC-TV movie entitled *The Las Vegas Strip War* because it mentioned organized crime in a story about hotels on the Las Vegas Strip. Surprisingly, the context was not a negative one; in the film, a casino owner down on his luck refuses money from potential investors when he figures out that they may be mobsters.[33]

Nevada representatives yearned for the state to be portrayed as a magical place devoid of crime, addicted gamblers, and immorality, as in the movie *Starman* (1985), the story of an innocent alien in human form who uses his extraterrestrial powers to win at a slot machine so that he can escape in a new car. This vision of Las Vegas was not far from the one Goldman was trying to achieve in *Grand Hotel,* and it was the kind of film that the Film Commission was interested in bringing to Nevada.

In 1987, the TV producer/director Michael Mann was given support to shoot *Crime Story* on location in Las Vegas as long as it showed organized crime as a thing of the past. The show focused on Nevada mobsters circa 1950. Frank Sain, the Las Vegas Convention and Visitors Authority chief, was said to have no public image concerns as long as *Crime Story* never moved its episodes into the 1980s.[34]

In 1988, Barry Levinson's *Rain Man* won several Academy Awards, including Best Picture. Charlie Babbitt, a self-centered young hotshot, played by Tom Cruise, is forced to travel with his grown autistic brother Raymond, played by Dustin Hoffman. When Charlie realizes that Raymond is a whiz at math, he takes him to Caesars Palace in Las Vegas to count cards in blackjack. The characters win big, allowing Charlie to get out of his financial jam.

Again, this was the kind of benign rendering of Nevada on film that the Nevada Motion Picture Division wanted to foster. Finally, here was a critically acclaimed, heartfelt story that stayed away from the seamy side of Nevada. As seen through the eyes of the autistic Raymond in *Rain Man,* Las Vegas is impressive, lavish, and conquerable. This was not a gambling picture per se, but it perpetuated the image of Las Vegas as a magical place.

A screen-writing competition was instituted by the Nevada Motion Picture Division in 1990 to encourage the writing of films about Nevada or that could take advantage of Nevada locations. In 1992, in an effort to ensure that only an accurate, positive image of Nevada was depicted, the Nevada Motion Picture Division attempted to push through a bill in the state legislature requiring approval of the script of any motion picture to be shot in the state. It was voted down for fear it would be seen as censorship and drive away filmmakers.[35]

In 1994, downtown Las Vegas stood in for hell in the mini-series *The Stand,* adapted from a Stephen King novel, in which survivors of a deadly virus make pilgrimages to two messiah-like figures: a mystical old woman in Utah and a forbidding, devil-like character who now rules Las Vegas. The message is clear: Las Vegas symbolizes all that is wrong with humanity.

By 1995, Nevada gave up its self-imposed three-decade limit on assisting productions portraying historical mob involvement in Las Vegas when Martin Scorsese wanted to film *Casino* there. The film is set in the late 1970s and early 1980s and depicts the events that led to Tony Spilotro's death, and Frank Rosenthal's inclusion in the infamous casino "black book." Despite the fact that the film did not flatter Las Vegas, its big budget made it an attractive project for Nevada. Moreover, the Nevada Motion Picture Division knew that *Casino* would help demonstrate to the rest of the filmmaking community that a big-budget production with A-list talent could be shot entirely in-state.

The *Casino* production team remained in Las Vegas for seven months shooting Nicolas Pileggi and Martin Scorsese's 140-page screenplay. Most big-budget films set in Nevada use the state for exterior locations and casino interiors, and then retreat to Los Angeles or New York sound stages to finish the rest of the production. *Casino* was an exception. In it, not only do Las Vegas and its surroundings provide the requisite Las Vegas interior and exterior shots, but Nevada locations stand in for

From *Casino* (1995).

Chicago, Kansas City, Beverly Hills, Palm Springs, a tropical retreat in Costa Rica, and even a cornfield in Indiana.

The film's budget was large, and Scorsese's track record with this kind of material allowed him to dictate the specifics of the production. In fact, shooting on location extended the schedule by several weeks—more income for Nevada, but not good news to studio accountants.

In *Casino*'s case, concern about whether it was an accurate portrayal of real-life events was eclipsed by the money and exposure the project would give the state. However, to audiences who have seen the film, the decline of the Las Vegas mob is no longer an abstraction, but a specific set of images and events that will be inextricably linked to their recollection of Nevada history.

Furthermore, the film's views on gambling, Nevada's premier industry, are as cynical and outspoken as those of "Ace" Rothstein, the film's main character, who tells the audience in voice-over narration: "At the time, Vegas was a place where thirty million suckers flew in every year on their own nickel and left behind a billion dollars."

Ironically, that same year, the Nevada Motion Picture Division would not be able to provide Mike Figgis with hotel locations for his low-budget film *Leaving Las Vegas*. In a 1996 interview, Bob Hirsch made it clear that the main reason was the film's bleak portrayal of its characters, its sometimes brutal plot, and its negative view of Las Vegas. "No hotel wanted to be associated with that kind of script."[36]

Ironically, *Showgirls*, a film that was released unrated because of its sexual content, was shooting in Las Vegas at the same time. The main character is also a hooker, and the film depicts both drug abuse and a corrupt staff at the Stardust hotel.

Figgis went public to protest what he called the censorship of his script. The Nevada Motion Picture Division insisted that no hotel casino wanted to be linked with his material. In the end, Figgis shot in Laughlin and filmed what he needed "guerrilla" style on the Las Vegas Strip. Despite its low budget and low-profile director, *Leaving Las Vegas* received many more nominations and awards than *Casino*, and *Showgirls* is now remembered as one of the worst films ever shot in Nevada.[37]

But Nevada's image on film has managed to evolve. The negative aspects of Nevada have been fused to stories seeking to depict the state as mysterious and alluring. Nevada's mythic place in film narrative evolved slowly. In terms of storytelling on film, it is important to note that screenwriters continue to draw on ancient myths and folktales. The elevation of film into a pop-cultural experience in the late 1960s allows these mythical landscapes to be widely shared. Screen stories continue to evolve by borrowing from old tales to create new myths that mirror the culture's preconceptions.

In film stories, the journey of the protagonist from an ordinary world into a special world to confront his or her fears has endured as the most popular structure for a feature-length narrative. These stories have evolved from the mythical deeds of the more traditional archetypal hero into the darker adventures of an innocent main character in a fairy story.[38]

In this mythology, Nevada is a special world in which "ordinary people" are tested. A 1980s version of this myth was attempted on a large scale by the same director who had been responsible for linking Nevada to organized crime on screen. In September 1980, the director of *The*

Godfather films, Francis Ford Coppola, invited 350 guests to Ruther-
ford Vineyards in California to announce that "something incredibly
great was about to happen." That something was his next film, *One
from the Heart,* a fantasy love story set in Las Vegas, which attempts to
combine and reinvent several classic film genres.

Unfortunately, after *Apocalypse Now,* Coppola had grown weary of
location filmmaking, so the film would not be shot in Nevada. He was
also determined to use new technologies and a process he called the
"electronic storyboard" to shoot the film. This required studio control,
so Coppola's newly purchased and freshly baptized Zoetrope Studios
rebuilt Las Vegas in northern California.[39]

Michael Goodwin and Naomi Wise reconstruct that time in their
book *On the Edge: The Life and Times of Francis Coppola:*

> The real Las Vegas wasn't as good as the Las Vegas of the Mind. He [Cop-
> pola] wanted magical images that would go right past reality to achieve some
> kind of superreality, something like a live-action version of a Disney ani-
> mated film. If he shot in the real Las Vegas, it would be just another rela-
> tionship movie. Dean Tavoularis (the production designer) could build him
> a Las Vegas infinitely shinier, brighter, and more artistic than the one in
> Nevada.[40]

On February 4, 1981, Coppola held a press conference at his studio,
three days into shooting *One from the Heart.* There he recalled how as
a young man he had lost $1,000 in Las Vegas in an attempt to raise
money for a film. He then explained why the movie was set in Vegas.
"It's a perfect place to set a love story. . . . One minute the city says,
'come, come and get me,' and the next, it looks like Burbank and you're
drunk and broke."[41]

But Coppola did not have to travel to Nevada to lose money on *One
from the Heart.* The expensive sets, the new technology, and the mixing
of genres created a movie that was visually incredible, but resulted in a
story that could not live up to its images. The tale of a Las Vegas couple,
Hank and Frannie, who stray from each other one fourth of July, only
to return to each other's embrace the next day, failed to capture the
imaginations of audiences and critics.[42]

Coppola had indeed taken Las Vegas and reinvented it in his own
back lot. Little did he know that Las Vegas was about to begin redefining
itself in a way that would surpass his vision. The magical images, the
superreality, and the live-action version of an animated film would all
come to pass. Vegas would, indeed, become shinier, brighter, and more
aesthetically designed in the years to come.

In the mythology of screen stories, a new myth set in Nevada had been born, but Coppola failed to make it work. The biggest difference between Coppola's lovers in *One from the Heart* and the couples that would be tested in the city of sin in years to come was that Coppola's pair are Las Vegas residents. Las Vegas's seductive and destructive powers, which Coppola seeks to depict, only work for those who come to Vegas from the outside, not for those who live there and work within its system.

The next fifteen years would see the development of the new myth in which a young couple are tested by Las Vegas. In order for this myth to work, at least one of them has to travel voluntarily to the neon city, so that they cannot be dismissed as victims of Nevada, but are understood to be active participants in a bind that they have created for themselves. Once they have survived this testing, their relationship deepens and their lives change. This pattern plays out in *Lost in America, Honeymoon in Vegas, Indecent Proposal, Leaving Las Vegas,* and *Vegas Vacation.*

Albert Brooks's comedy *Lost in America* (1985) helped begin to codify this new screen myth. In this story, yuppie spouses David and Linda Howard, played by Brooks and Julie Haggerty, decide to "drop out" of society and hit the road in their own materialistic version of *Easy Rider.* They cash out their assets, buy a Winnebago, and leave Los Angeles to live their dream life. The first stop on their tour is Las Vegas, where they plan to renew their vows at a wedding chapel before traveling on into the American wilderness.

On arrival at the Desert Inn in Las Vegas, David decides that they can wait to renew their vows until the next morning. Their first experience in Nevada does not bode well. The desk clerk cannot provide them with a bridal suite, and David's continued attempt at bribing him only results in securing a junior bridal suite—a small room with two teeny heart-shaped beds.

That night, David wakes up to discover that Linda has left the room. He finds her in the casino at the roulette table where she has been gambling the entire night. The news is worse than he fears: in the past few hours, she has managed to lose their entire nest egg, making it impossible for them to live out their fantasy.

David asks to talk privately to the casino manager, played by Garry Marshall. Upstairs in an office in the Desert Inn, David attempts to use his talents as an LA advertising executive to persuade the casino manager to return their nest egg to them.

"My wife and I have dropped out of society," David explains.

The casino manager twists his head uncomfortably, failing to understand what David is getting at.

"We really just were gonna roam across the country and find ourselves, uh, just like they did in *Easy Rider*."

"Easy what?"

"*Easy Rider,* the film?"

"Oh, I didn't see that film."

"Great movie. You gotta see it, it's historic."

David and Linda belong to a generation that has been mentored and inspired by films. They are too young to have taken part in the 1960s counterculture but have experienced it by watching the granddaddy of all road movies. Although their plan bears little resemblance to *Easy Rider* in reality, they crave Captain America and Wyatt's quest for freedom—the freedom to "do your own thing."

The casino manager empathizes with David and Linda, and immediately reassures David that his rooms and his meals are now "comped." But David continues, determined to explain to the manager how he and Linda are special, and how the whole situation can be turned to everyone's advantage.

"As the boldest experiment in advertising history, you give us our money back," David pitches.

"I beg your pardon," the casino manager interrupts.

"Give us our money back. Think of the publicity." David explains. "The Hilton Hotel has these billboards all over Los Angeles where the winners of these slot machine jackpots, their faces are all over L.A. and I know that works. I've seen people at corners look up and say, 'maybe I'll go to the Hilton.' Well, you give us our money back. I . . . don't even know, now, cause I'm just coming off the top of my head, but a visual where if we had a billboard and the Desert Inn handed us our nest egg back. This gives the Desert Inn really . . . " David is at a loss for a second, then suddenly he blurts out, " . . . Vegas is not associated with feeling."

"[T]hose people on those signs, they won," the casino manager explains. "You lost." That's exactly the campaign, David counters: after reviewing his and Linda's situation, the Desert Inn gives them their money back. The casino manager explains that if they did that, everyone would want their money back. David explains that he and his wife are different; they made a mistake, and the Desert Inn has the power to correct it.

David continues, "[I]n the campaign, you make a clear distinction between the bold, who would be my wife and I, and then all the other schmucks who come here to see Wayne Newton."

"I like Wayne Newton," the casino manager says.

"I said Wayne Newton?" David asks, realizing he has made a mistake.

"What were you talking about? I heard you say schmucks see Wayne Newton. I like him. That makes me a schmuck?"

And so the scene continues, with the casino manager struggling to explain to David why his proposed "The Desert Inn has heart" ad campaign won't work, and David trying to pitch "Las Vegas, a Christmas place to be." The casino manager tells him that people know what to expect when they come to Vegas: "[P]eople come here, to gamble. They want to go to a hunting lodge, they go to Wisconsin. They want to rest, they go to New Orleans. They want to gamble, they come to Vegas. That's why it's called gambling, Las Vegas, gambling."[43]

Funny as the scene may be in the context of 1985, a decade later, Las Vegas evidently fired that casino manager and hired David to do its publicity. David's incongruous pitch "Las Vegas, a Christmas place to be" is not far from the ad campaigns of the 1990s, oriented to bringing the entire family to Las Vegas.

David and Linda began the archetypal figures that would form the new screen myth: the tale of the young couple arriving in Nevada to be tested in sin city. On screen, Nevada is henceforth no longer reserved for adventurers, burn-outs, and compulsive gamblers; it also lures innocents, who fall prey to the vices it has to offer. The appeal of this story is that the couple manage to overcome the obstacles they face and in their own way discover how important they really are to each other.

Lost in America ends by warning its viewers in its end credits: "To those few that have the courage to drop out and find themselves, may God be with you and take you through Utah, avoiding Nevada completely." However, films have continued to depict Nevada as a magnet to screen innocents. Las Vegas functions as the mysterious forest once did in fairy tales. It is an unknown and frightening environment, but one that the central characters will eventually overcome.

Honeymoon in Vegas (1992), for instance, is a comedy in which a young couple, played by Nicolas Cage and Sarah Jessica Parker, travel to Las Vegas to get married. After arriving in Nevada, their relationship shifts dramatically when he "loses" her in a high-stakes card game at Bally's to a professional gambler, played by James Caan. The film goes to great lengths to connect itself with Elvis's *Viva Las Vegas,* including having Cage jump out of an airplane dressed as an Elvis impersonator.

From *Honeymoon in Vegas* (1992).

The plot of *Indecent Proposal* (1993) uses Las Vegas similarly, but this film, shot at the Las Vegas Hilton, plays as a drama. A young married couple, played by Woody Harrelson and Demi Moore, come to Las Vegas in hopes of winning enough money to pay their mortgage, which they manage to do. Their greed is played upon by Robert Redford, playing a tycoon who offers the couple a million dollars for the opportunity to sleep with Moore.

In both films, the couples realize their love for each other and successfully reunite. Las Vegas acts as a testing ground to see how far seemingly honest characters will bend their morality, and then to what lengths they will go to get it back. In 1994, a *Time* article entitled "Las Vegas, U.S.A.," featured on the cover of the magazine, concluded that Las Vegas had not changed, but that America had.[44]

Even *Leaving Las Vegas* was marketed to fit the new myth. The film tells the tale of a drunken screenwriter (also played by Nicolas Cage, in an Oscar-winning performance) who comes to Nevada to drink himself to death. He encounters a hooker, played by Elisabeth Shue, picks her up, and eventually moves in with her, biding his time until his death. Despite the film's grim material, the emphasis is on the love story that develops between the characters, and Cage's death is his way "of doing his own thing."[45]

The film's marketing also conformed more to the new myth of the couple who come to Vegas to find each other. Discrepancies from this paradigm in the scenario were compensated for by the expectations created by the marketing campaign. In the end, audiences were convinced that they had seen a love story and not the abysmal tale in which the Nevada Motion Picture Division had failed to find merit.

In one hundred years of film history, there have been only a few films shot in Nevada about Nevada residents. The best example is John Huston's *The Misfits* (1961), a psychological drama about contemporary cowboys, the "misfits" of the film's title, who hunt down wild mustangs and sell them to be butchered for dog food. Marilyn Monroe is an emotionally unstable Reno divorcee. Clark Gable plays an aging cowhand who falls in love with her, and Montgomery Clift is a cowhand and rodeo rider. Monroe is deeply upset by the men's determination to capture the horses, and the men are obsessed with who will end up with Monroe.

But audiences have voted with their wallets and show no interest in seeing Nevadans and their personal problems on screen. Nevada does not exist as a real place where real people live and have problems, but only as a mythologized world outside reality, which endures in the imagination and on the film screen. Nevada has not only lived up to its reputation but has been transformed by it, making visitors believe their preconceptions, rather than try to understand what it takes to live in the desert alongside the neon.

Even older conceptions of Las Vegas, such as Hunter S. Thompson's *Fear and Loathing in Las Vegas*,[46] which was brought to the screen in 1998 in a film directed by Terry Gilliam, are dated. The fictionalized Las Vegas journey of Hunter S. Thompson and Oscar Zeta Acosta, as they attempt to cover a national race and crash a police convention while high on every possible drug, no longer rings true. At the end of the millennium, *Fear and Loathing* is a strange historical artifact that lacks the context for us to understand the rantings of the film's main character, Raoul Duke, as he tries to sum up the 1960s and define what Las Vegas means to them.

The fact is that the Las Vegas that Raoul Duke and his sidekick Dr. Gonzo once experienced simply does not exist. The Las Vegas of *Fear and Loathing* is now a romantic notion that no longer draws a crowd. The transformation of Las Vegas has also been a physical one, witnessed on screen.

Since the publication of *Fear and Loathing* in 1971, Las Vegas has been intent on changing the filmic geography laid out decades earlier. Its destruction of the old has even been recorded in several films.

Upon completion of the Treasure Island hotel, Steve Wynn offered film production companies the option of filming his implosion of the Dunes hotel to make way for a new property. When no one took him up on his offer, Wynn produced a TV movie, *Treasure Island: The Adventure Begins* (1994), which centers around a young boy who comes to Las Vegas with his family.

The boy is meant to be a close screen cousin of Steven Spielberg's Elliot in *E.T.* (1982), another young boy distanced from his family and needing to find meaning in his life. The boy in Wynn's film does this by meeting up with a kindly pirate and looking for treasure on the Treasure Island property, as well as at the Dunes. The movie even features Steve Wynn as himself in a few scenes with the boy and his parents. It ends with the boy managing to escape in time before the Dunes implodes.

The destruction of Las Vegas landmarks was recorded in a series of films. The Dunes was used again by *Casino,* in which the Rothstein character laments the corporate takeover of Las Vegas. It signals the end of an era, and is followed by the destruction of the Landmark hotel by aliens in Tim Burton's *Mars Attacks* (1996). In 1997, a 747 carrying a cargo of prisoners crashes into the Sands hotel in the climactic scene of the pathetic action adventure film *Con Air.*

The drug-induced hell experienced by the anti-heroes of *Fear and Loathing* has been replaced by the foibles of the American family unit now faced with just how "Las Vegas" can they become. In *Vegas Vacation* (1996), Clark Griswold walks down the Las Vegas Strip a broken man. As played by Chevy Chase, Griswold has managed to lose his family to Las Vegas: his son Rusty is somewhere on the Strip posing as a high roller named Mr. Pappagiorgio, his daughter Audrey has become an exotic dancer, and his wife Ellen has left him, not for just any other man, but for Wayne Newton himself.

This is the fourth movie of the National Lampoon *Vacation* series. The first installment mercilessly satirizes a road trip that ends at a closed-down WallyWorld (read Disneyland), and Clark's faithfulness is put to the test by the alluring Christie Brinkley. *European Vacation,* the second film, challenges the Griswold family by pitting them against a landscape filled with culture, international espionage, and people who don't speak "American." In *Christmas Vacation,* the third film, Clark tries to force his family and their relatives to enjoy the Yuletide season at whatever the cost, even their happiness.

Like it or not, the Griswolds have become the big-screen representatives of the American family in pop culture. *Vegas Vacation* does not steer away from the formula of Clark trying to force his family to have a good time. At the outset, Clark and Ellen Griswold struggle to agree on the perfect place to celebrate their twentieth anniversary with their family. Clark attempts to convince Ellen that Las Vegas is the ideal place to celebrate with their teenage kids. Like *Lost in America*'s David Howard, Clark wants to take Ellen to Vegas so that they can renew their vows. When Ellen questions his decision to take a family vacation in Las Vegas, Clark shows her a brochure entitled "Las Vegas, a Family Kind of Place."

Indeed, the Las Vegas that the Griswolds encounter has become the Las Vegas that Howard is trying to sell to the Desert Inn manager in *Lost in America.* Las Vegas is no longer just gambling as Garry Marshall insists. *Vegas Vacation* sets out to prove, if not lampoon the fact, that Vegas is everything that the Griswolds might covet.

The Griswolds aren't gamblers; they consider themselves to be "the others" that Howard talks about, despite the fact that Ellen falls under the spell of Wayne Newton. Vegas is no longer the adult gambling joint from which to begin a couple's journey into the American wilderness; it has transformed itself into a 24-hour amusement park that can seduce each and every member of the American family.

However, the new myth remains the same. Las Vegas is a place that transforms its visitors. Even in *Vegas Vacation,* with its agenda to spoof the new Las Vegas and make filmic references to *Indecent Proposal, Rain Man,* and *Showgirls,* the dramatic function of the special world remains the same. Las Vegas is a moral testing ground, in which the Griswolds' fidelity, integrity, and family are challenged by power, gambling, and greed.

At the end of the screenplay, Clark has definitely been tested. Not only has he lost his offspring and wife, he has gambled away all their money. As he walks down the Vegas Strip questioning his worth, he spots the Stratosphere Tower, the world's tallest observation platform. With the intention of jumping, Clark rides the elevator up to the top, passing tourists wearing T-shirts that read "Las Vegas is for Lovers" and "Las Vegas is for Children."[47]

From the top of the Stratosphere, he sees the Vegas lights and thinks about how much better off his family will be without him. Will Clark jump? Probably not. In any case, this is only in the screenplay. This scene was dropped from the film itself and replaced with a milder one that plays out at the newly constructed Fremont Street Experience.[48]

In the end, *Vegas Vacation* is just another fairy tale set in Las Vegas: a place that tests all the characters who pass through it. Like it or not, Las Vegas has become a special world in the mythology of film storytelling. Only part of it exists in Nevada; the rest resides in the mind of the audience.

NOTES

1. This establishing shot would normally be shot by a second unit or by an assistant director, but Scorsese always insists on being present and directing every frame.

2. Robert Laxalt, *Nevada: A Bicentennial History* (New York: Norton, 1977), 89–95.

3. Russell R. Elliott, *History of Nevada* (Lincoln: University of Nebraska Press, 1973), 200.

4. Laxalt, 94. Kristin Thompson and David Bordwell, *Film History: An Introduction* (New York: McGraw-Hill, 1994), 7–14.

5. Laxalt, 94.

6. Gary Du Val, "Cinema in the Silver State" (MS, 1992 [?]), 124; Elliott, 211–12. Laxalt, 73.

7. Eldon K. Everett, "Helen Holmes—The Railroad Girl," *Classic Film Collector*, winter 1973, 37. Ally Acker, *Reel Women* (New York: Continuum, 1991), 253.

8. Du Val, 49.

9. *Las Vegas Age*, January 30, 1915, 1: 6.

10. Du Val, 12, 42, 109, 129.

11. Ibid., 24, 60; Thompson and Bordwell, 165–68.

12. Barbara and Myrick Land, *A Short History of Reno* (Reno: University of Nevada Press, 1995) 63, 64.

13. "We Ought to Be in Pictures: Selling Las Vegas to TV and Movies," producer/reporter Claudia Collins (Las Vegas, NV: KLVX), 1981; *Las Vegas Review Journal*, April 13, 1939, 1: 6; Du Val, 12, 89.

14. Laxalt, 95.

15. Ibid., 89, 96–98.

16. *Movies and Mass Culture*, ed. John Belton (New Brunswick, N.J.: Rutgers University Press, 1996), 135–49.

17. Ibid., 136.

18. David Barnett, "'The Las Vegas Story': Bad Flick, but a Good Fight," *Las Vegas Review Journal,* March 22, 1987, CC 6–7, 14.

19. Ibid., CC 7.

20. Ibid.

21. Ibid; Robert Sklar, *Movie-Made America* (New York: Vintage Books, 1994), 249–68.

22. Sklar, 300.

23. Ibid., 286–304.

24. *The Godfather,* directed by Francis Ford Coppola. With Marlon Brando, Al Pacino, and John Cazale. Paramount Pictures, 1972.

25. *The Godfather II,* directed by Francis Ford Coppola. With Al Pacino and John Cazale. Paramount Pictures, 1974.

26. "We Ought to Be in Pictures" (cited n. 13 above).

27. William Goldman, *Adventures in the Screen Trade* (New York: Warner Books, 1983), 262–73.

28. Ibid., 264.

29. Ibid, 270.

30. Carol Cling, "Bryan Meets the Stars on Movie Set," *Las Vegas Review Journal,* August 4, 1984, B1; "Bryan Meets with Film Execs," *Las Vegas Review Journal,* October 29, 1985, B5.

31. Low-budget pictures operate on a similar, but baser level. The makers of these films guarantee their success by using a well-worn genre, and having a required amount of sex and violence.

32. Candace Kant, "City of Dreams: Las Vegas in the Cinema, 1980–89" (Master's thesis, UNLV special collection, 1989).

33. Scott A. Zamost, "Crime Inference in 'Strip War' Irks Trop Exec," *Las Vegas Sun,* November 27, 1984, B1–2.

34. Caryn Shetterly, "*Crime Story* Returns to LV," *Las Vegas Sun,* June 6, 1987, B1–2.

35. Cy Ryan, "Movie-Script Bill Blast," *Las Vegas Sun,* August 14, 1992, A7; "Film Control a Dumb Idea," *Las Vegas Sun,* August 16, 1992, D2.

36. In 1998 Bob Hirsch left his job as head of the Motion Picture Division and was replaced by the seasoned Charlie Geocaris, former film commissioner from Chicago.

37. Ruth Stein, "Mike Figgis Gambles and Wins: *Leaving Las Vegas* a Critical Success," *San Francisco Chronicle,* November 7, 1995, E1.

38. Christopher Vogler, *The Writer's Journey: Mythic Structure for Storytellers and Screenwriters* (Studio City, Cal.: M. Wiese Productions, 1992), vii–viii, 3–9. Bruno Bettelheim, *The Uses of Enchantment: The Meaning and Importance of Fairy Tales* (New York: Vintage Books, 1989), 22–41.

39. Michael Goodwin and Naomi Wise, *On the Edge: The Life and Times of Francis Coppola* (New York: Morrow, 1990), 290–337.

40. Ibid., 301.

41. Ibid., 306–7.

42. Ibid., 321–37. Peter Cowie, *Coppola* (New York: Scribner, 1990), 145–65.

43. *Lost in America,* directed by Albert Brooks. With Albert Brooks, Julie Haggerty, and Garry Marshall. Warner Bros., 1985.

44. Kurt Andersen, "Las Vegas, U.S.A.," *Time,* January 10, 1994, 42–51.

45. *Leaving Las Vegas,* directed by Mike Figgis. With Nicolas Cage and Elisabeth Shue. Miramax, 1995.

46. Hunter S. Thompson, *Fear and Loathing in Las Vegas: A Savage Journey to the Heart of the American Dream,* illustrated by Ralph Steadman (New York: Random House, 1971). See also Terry Gilliam and Tony Grisoni, *Not the Screenplay to Fear & Loathing in Las Vegas,* with the complete storyboards by Terry Gilliam (New York: Applause, 1997).

47. Elisa Bell, "Vegas Vacation," rewrite by Robert Cohen, Stephen Kessler, and Mike Wilkins, second draft, May 9, 1996. *Vegas Vacation,* directed by Stephen Kessler. With Chevy Chase, Beverly D'Angelo, and Wayne Newton. Warner Bros., 1996.

48. The Fremont Street Experience has covered up what used to be a traditional image of downtown Las Vegas with a gigantic video screen that extends from one side of the street to the other.

Discordant Infrastructure

While the spectacle of the Las Vegas façade overwhelms any visitor's views, the automobile becomes a visual infrastructure. Architecture, social ceremony, travel, conspicuous consumption; all are reflected by the utility and subliminal presence of the automobile. Power lines, fences, gateways, traffic, and even the irony of a commercial lot full of expensive and in-need-of-repair motor boats deconstruct the popular image of Las Vegas. The glitter is an illusion, and visitors ignore the frame of the car window or the truck blocking their view. The ostentatious display of light and power is sufficient. Recently designated a "scenic route," the Strip has become a postmodern main street, the ultimate expression of car culture. Nuptial ceremonies are handled by "drive-ups" and celebrated by crudely drawn hearts on darkened car windows. Bob Stupak's Stratosphere Tower, one of the recent additions to the Las Vegas skyline, is already entangled in power lines. The arch, gateway to wealth and progress, now advertises free parking. Freeways are arteries in constant need of repair. The vast number of vehicles traveling through one intersection at night leave a flow of lights and visual marks of constant motion. Airplanes are either adding contrail grids to the desert sky or lying dormant as museum relics or mothballed fleets. Trees are planted in movable containers. Every structure, sign, and view offers metaphoric testimony to the insecurity that mobility implies. If necessary, even the trees could be moved . . .

Originally designed as a driveway for large casino parking lots, the Strip has become the national archetype of the automobile-oriented street. It was officially designated a Scenic Route on March 21, 1996. Although scenic byways are eligible for additional federal and state funding, nearly one hundred hotel and casino owners contributed $1.9 million for the beautification of a four-mile stretch of the Strip during 1994–95.

"Just Married—What You Looking At" car on the Strip. More than 158,000 people are married in Las Vegas each year, and more than 6,000 people move to the city each month.

The Stratosphere Tower, view from the Department of Energy building, Highland and Presidio. Phase I of the Stratosphere cost $550 million and included 1,500 rooms with another 1,000 planned. As of 2000, there were 125,000 hotel rooms in the city limits.

The Stratosphere Tower, view from the lot of Marine Services, Inc. Las Vegas lies in the Mojave Desert and averages only four inches of rainfall per year. Its groundwater is nearly exhausted, but Las Vegas annually receives 300,000 acre-feet of Colorado River water.

Little White Chapel sign on Las Vegas Boulevard near Park Paseo.

Sunset at Main Street and Bridger Avenue. More than 6.3 million vehicles and 36 million people visit Las Vegas each year (as of 2000).

Deconstructed highway, Las Vegas. In 1990, Clark County approved a $2 billion transportation plan that redesigned the spaghetti bowl. According to the records of the county health district and the regional transportation commission, the number of vehicle miles traveled in the valley was approximately 18.6 million in 1990—double what it had been in 1988—and it continues to rise.

View of intersection along Las Vegas Strip from the Excalibur overpass. The MGM Grand Hotel is the largest hotel on planet Earth, with more than five thousand rooms. Las Vegas has more than 125,000 hotel rooms.

Mothballed commercial airplanes, Las Vegas Boulevard and Dewey Drive, Las Vegas.
McCarran International Airport has been one of the busiest airports in the United States.

Trees in planters, abandoned motel, Las Vegas Boulevard and Dewey Drive.

"Just Married" and Suntrek Adventures vehicles, The Luxor pyramid, Las Vegas.

PART II **NUTS AND BOLTS**

Growth, Services, and the Political Economy of Gambling in Las Vegas, 1970–2000

The growth of Las Vegas has been a constant source of interest to the media and public alike. From the celebrated opening of Bugsy Siegel's fabulous Flamingo in 1946 to the majestic arrivals of Caesars Palace, the MGM Grand, and their spectacular successors, Las Vegas has become an icon of modern popular culture.

Since the early 1970s, the town has continued to boom, largely thanks to gambling (or gaming, as it is called in Nevada). Ten new major hotels arrived in that decade and a half dozen more in the 1980s. While Circus Circus (the hotel section opened in 1971), Harrah's (1974), and the Marina (1974) as well as the Maxim, Imperial Palace, and Barbary Coast (all in the late 1970s) added to the Strip's allure, the Rio, Palace Station, Gold Coast, Arizona Charlie's, Sam's Town, the Santa Fe, and other notable places helped extend the casino frontier onto new streets and into the suburbs. Downtown Las Vegas also flourished in the 1980s with Fitzgeralds skyscraper and Steve Wynn's dramatic transformation of the old Golden Nugget.

The late 1980s and early 1990s witnessed still another round of development, as the twin casino cores on the Strip and downtown continued to grow. The Strip, in particular, expanded at both ends and in the middle. In 1989, Wynn established a new standard of excellence when he opened the Mirage. With its white tigers, bottle-nosed dolphins, exotic atrium, and erupting volcano, the hotel quickly surpassed Hoover Dam as the state's leading tourist attraction. This mega-resort, along with Wynn's intentions of building his pirate-themed Treasure Island in the Mirage's parking lot, forced neighboring Caesars Palace to invest millions and build The Forum Shops, an upscale, "Roman-style" shopping center, in its parking lot. Treasure Island itself opened in 1993. Circus Circus Enterprises further energized the Strip's south end that same year when it completed the pyramid-shaped Luxor Hotel next door to its medieval Excalibur resort, which it had unveiled in 1990. Across the street, the billionaire Kirk Kerkorian raised the stakes for everyone when he launched his MGM Grand Hotel on the site of the former Marina resort. With its four casinos, over 5,000 rooms, and theme park, it instantly became the world's largest hotel.

On New Year's Eve 1996, Circus Circus Enterprises imploded the old Hacienda Hotel, which for years had stood as a lone sentinel greeting highway tourists from southern California. But it had to go. Before it did, the venerable Hacienda found itself engulfed by a wave of urbanization that stretched far to the south, leaving the old resort in the midst of traffic jams spawned by the recent appearance of the Luxor, Excalibur, and MGM Grand. Indeed, the intersection of Las Vegas (Boulevard) and Reno (Avenue), which was little more than sagebrush desert a few years ago, is today a bustling reservoir holding back traffic from the sprawling corner of the Strip and Tropicana, with its elevated pedestrian walkways spanning all four corners. The arrival of the Monte Carlo (1996) and New York New York (1997), along with the rush of tourists, and the postmodern transformation of the south Strip forced the demolition of the Hacienda. In its place, Circus Circus has erected Mandalay Bay, a 43-story "tropical paradise" that opened in 1999.

Of course, this prosperity has not been limited to the south end of the Strip. The middle has been boosted not only by the efforts of Wynn and Caesars Palace, but by Sheldon Adelson, who imploded the renowned Sands Hotel in 1996 to make way for its successor, the Venetian, in 1999. Several years earlier, Wynn had imploded both towers of the former Dunes Hotel to clear the land for his much-anticipated Bellagio, which, at $1.6 billion, rivals the Venetian as the most luxurious resort ever built. All of these events, along with the opening of the Paris Hotel and Casino across from Bellagio, pushed the Las Vegas visitor count well past thirty-three million in 1999. And there is more in the offing. The newly rebuilt Aladdin Hotel officially replaced its dilapidated predecessor in 2000. Major changes are also in store for the Desert Inn. In March 2000, Steve Wynn sold Mirage Resorts to Kirk Kerkorian for more that $6 billion. With his share of the profit, Wynn and his wife

Elaine then purchased the 250-acre Desert Inn Hotel and have begun plans to build a spectacular new resort. The increased tourism generated by these events has also affected the long-dormant north end of the Strip. In 1995, William Bennett, the former CEO of Circus Circus, purchased the Sahara Hotel and adjacent lands as a prelude to his multimillion dollar renovation and expansion of the old resort. When completed, the new Sahara, along with Carl Icahn's recapitalized Stratosphere Tower (at 130 stories, the tallest structure west of the Mississippi) Hotel and Casino should transform the north Strip once again into a busy tourist center.

Farther north, downtown Las Vegas is also undergoing nothing short of a revolution. The Fremont Street Experience, an enclosed electronic canopy that has converted the city's casino core into a semi-enclosed mall, opened in December 1995. Along with this, the impending development of former railroad lands behind the Plaza Hotel, together with the Neonopolis festival mall off Fremont Street, will sweep downtown Las Vegas back into the tourist limelight.[1]

Powered by a vibrant economy for most of the past quarter century, the Las Vegas Valley saw its population skyrocket from 273,000 in 1970 to almost 1.2 million by 1998—an influx that, in some years during the 1980s and 1990s, made it the fastest-growing metropolitan area in the United States. Of course, resort development has not been the sole force behind the city's expansion. Las Vegas's recent appeal to retirees, job seekers, and new businesses is multifaceted. For many people, the tax climate, like the sunny weather, has been a major inducement. Unlike most western states, Nevada has no franchise tax, personal or corporate income tax, or inheritance-estate-gift taxes. Statutes limit Nevada's ad valorem property tax rate to $3.64 per $100 of assessed valuation, and the latter to no more than 35 percent of the land's "full cash value." In fact, a 1995 survey credited Las Vegas with having the second-lowest per capita taxes among America's 100 largest cities.[2]

This has attracted large corporations like Hilton, Hyatt, and even Marriott, as well as small businesses. Low taxes, a strong right-to-work law, and plenty of unskilled, cheap labor (boosted by the large influx of Hispanics since 1970) attracted hundreds of small employers in the 1980s and 1990s. While the Culinary and related unions continue to maintain a formidable presence on the Strip, much of the metropolitan area's labor force remains ununionized. This advantage, along with relatively cheap fuel costs, inexpensive housing, and a convenient location, have helped the Nevada Development Authority lure Citicorp, Ocean

Spray Cranberries, Inc., Ethel M Chocolates, and many other companies to Las Vegas in the past twenty years. In addition, the creation of the Foreign Trade Zone in 1986 strengthened Las Vegas's growing appeal as an international business center. By 1995, over eighty companies operated in the zone.[3]

While the town has long enjoyed the benefits of good weather and low operating costs, it has worked hard to develop other advantages, especially in transportation. During the past quarter century, Las Vegas has emerged as a busy transshipment center. Building upon the foundation laid by the railroad in 1905 and more recently by the opening of its jetport in 1963 and Interstate 15 in the early 1970s, Las Vegas has become a major shipping point for cargoes as well as passengers. The expansion of McCarran International Airport in the 1980s and 1990s brought not only additional terminals and runways for tourists but new facilities for handling mail and freight. In the late 1980s, Las Vegas became the Southwest's major distribution center for mail, a role that led to construction of a giant post office near the airport and special gates for handling the agency's jumbo jets. Then, in April 1993, McCarran officials opened their new International Cargo Center, which more than doubled the air freight passing through the metropolis.[4]

Thanks to the airport, Interstate 15, and other factors,[5] the service sector dominates the local economy, and casino profits are the engine driving the city's growth.[6] Las Vegas's gross gaming revenue rose steadily from $1.6 billion in 1980 to $4 billion in 1990 and $5.4 billion four years later, with no sign of a slowdown. Thanks to Las Vegas's 90,000 hotel rooms (the most of any American city), the number of visitors also increased from 10 million in the early 1980s to 29 million in 1996, a figure second only to Orlando.[7]

The phenomenal success of the resort makers, along with Las Vegas's overall economic expansion, has dramatically extended the urban canvas. Since 1970, the physical development of the metropolitan area has continued to be shaped by historic forces. The city of Las Vegas itself has largely failed to snare most of the new tax base created by the boom. Because of state legislation after World War II that prevented cities from annexing unincorporated townships without their county's approval, Las Vegas has never been able to capture the Strip or any of its mushrooming suburbs south of Sahara Avenue. To the northeast, the vigorous annexation campaigns of North Las Vegas in the 1960s have blocked the central city's growth in that direction. So, Las Vegas's expansion has been limited mainly to the north and west.

Because of its vast tracts of open land and scenic vistas, the west has been the main direction of expansion for the municipality. A new real estate frontier opened in the mid 1980s when the Del Webb and Howard Hughes corporations agreed to build Sun City Summerlin on the vast land holdings of the late billionaire. Since the city of Las Vegas stood between the new community and Lake Mead, the developers decided to join it in order to use its convenient waste water system and other urban services. But Summerlin is far more than a retirement community. Its developers ultimately envision a huge suburb of more than 25,000 housing units, schools, and shopping centers, catering to old and young alike. Already by the mid 1990s, this new wave of building had reached county lands south of the city line. And developers of Summerlin South, whose lands will host a substantial tax base, have decided to follow the Strip's earlier example and not join the city. As a result, the 1995 state legislative session witnessed a bitter confrontation between city and Clark County power brokers over who would collect the sales tax revenues generated in Summerlin South. The county won the latest round in its half-century-long struggle with the city, but Las Vegas, along with Henderson (founded in 1941) and North Las Vegas (1917), were clearly concerned about the ramifications of this decision for their future interests.[8]

Henderson, the second-largest city in the metropolitan area, has also battled with county authorities to realize its ambitions. While the urban sprawl emanating from the Las Vegas casino core finally reached Henderson in the early 1980s with the construction of Green Valley, this valuable new tax base, like Spring Valley (begun in 1982) west of the Strip, was also under county control. Still, Henderson's aggressive construction of sewer mains in the 1960s and 1970s positioned it to grab dozens of new subdivisions to its south, east, and west, thereby thwarting Clark County's designs. Henderson itself has undergone something of a transformation in the past two decades. It began in the early 1980s with the development of Green Valley, the metropolitan area's first master-planned community. Located near Henderson's western border, Green Valley needed urban services and access to the city's sewer system. And so Henderson was able to annex this development, whose planned environment quickly attracted many professionals, university professors, and small business owners. Green Valley's continued growth eventually brought a freeway connection to downtown Las Vegas and Interstate 15, while also awarding the city a substantially expanded tax base.

The momentum created by these events has caught the attention of ambitious developers. In the past decade, southern Nevada's housing boom has encouraged a substantial influx of out-of-state capital to Spring Valley and Summerlin, but especially to Henderson. Perhaps the most ambitious project has been "Lake Las Vegas," a 2,245-acre planned community, touted as "the largest privately funded development under construction in North America." A joint venture of Santa Barbara and Texas investors, the complex involved the damming of Las Vegas Wash (a tributary of the Colorado River) in the east valley hill country before the water reached Lake Mead. The engineering requirements to accomplish this feat were staggering: the developers had to build an earthen dam eighteen stories high, 4,800 feet long, and 716 feet wide to create a 320-acre lake, 145 feet deep, with ten miles of shoreline. On the south side is the luxurious South Shore development. Built on 503 acres, it ultimately will consist of 450 estate and custom homes with an equal number of "golf villas," townhouses, and condominiums that will, according to the company's president, William Foote, make it "the premier address in Southern Nevada." Mediterranean-styled homes will be terraced into the hillsides to ensure "almost every homeowner a superb view." South Shore hosts "Marseilles," an ultra-exclusive enclave of 35 estate home sites ranging from $350,000 to $1.95 million. There will also be other upscale gated communities. All will enjoy views of the lake and mountains, as well as the new Jack Nicklaus–designed championship golf course that winds its way from the highlands down to the lake. The centerpiece of it all will be the lake, together with the hillside streams and waterfalls it will supply.

Thanks to Green Valley, Lake Las Vegas, and dozens of other projects in the southeastern sector of the metropolitan area, Henderson became America's fastest-growing city in 1997. Between 1990 and 1994, its population more than doubled, soaring past the 100,000 mark. Amazingly, Henderson has passed Reno to become Nevada's second-largest city.[9] The housing boom in the metropolitan area has continued virtually unabated since the 1970s. In fall 1995, for example, 108 projects were under way in the valley, the most ever at any one time. Of these, more than 30 were master-planned communities. There certainly has been no lack of demand. And this upward trend in the housing market has only increased; in 1997, an average of 5,857 people moved to the Las Vegas area each month, six times the national average.[10]

Clearly, the past fifteen years have been a bonanza for casino owners, land developers, and the metropolitan area as a whole. But there is trouble in paradise. The spectacular growth of Las Vegas has strained local services, spawned a major infrastructure crisis, and, most significantly, enthroned a powerful elite of casino executives, Steve Wynn and Sheldon Adelson among them, who attempt to shape public policy by actively bankrolling candidates for office. All three of these issues are interrelated, because the interests of the gaming industry often diverge from those of the city, county, and state.

About a decade ago, the distinguished Nevada historian James Hulse wrote a book entitled *Forty Years in the Wilderness,* in which he demonstrated how Nevada's gaming community has historically been hostile to environmental concerns, minority rights, and education.[11] Today, the threat to state programs is again real, because the political economy of gambling is probably the strongest it has ever been. Nevada is no stranger to corporate co-option of its political system. In the nineteenth and early twentieth centuries, mining companies and railroads based in Virginia City, Goldfield, Reno, and San Francisco largely controlled the politicians in Carson City. But there was always a significant constituency of farmers, ranchers, and union miners to act periodically as a counterbalance. With the growth of Populist sentiment in the 1890s, reinforced by a strong national movement to control railroad rates and other abuses, the mine-railroad coalition weakened significantly during the Progressive Era, when the proposals of Theodore Roosevelt and Woodrow Wilson inspired a series of state reforms that tempered laissez-faire in many Nevada industries.

Of course, special interests always have enjoyed some influence at the state capital. But even after the relegalization of gambling in 1931 and the development of Las Vegas in the postwar era, the gamers, while a political force, did not enjoy the same laissez-faire environment as their predecessors. The mob's presence guaranteed that. In the 1950s, Republican Governor Charles Russell's support of the regulatory powers of the Nevada Tax Commission, along with several major court decisions, firmly established the state's supremacy over Las Vegas and Reno casino owners. Even with the casinos' substantial campaign contributions to Russell's Democratic successor, Grant Sawyer, there was no change in policy. Under Sawyer's leadership, the Nevada Gaming Commission and Black Book were created to strengthen regulation of mob and non-mob casinos alike. In the 1950s and 1960s, despite the efforts of Norman Biltz and other influential lobbyists employed by elements of the casino industry in Las Vegas and, to a lesser extent, Reno, the state maintained its dominant position in the relationship. And this continued under the governorships of Paul Laxalt, Mike O'Callaghan, Robert List, and Richard Bryan.

The casinos, with their ability to generate thousands of dollars in campaign contributions, always had the ears of these governors, as well as of most state legislators. Certainly, they were consulted about revenue policies, especially the all-important gaming tax. There is no doubt that they played an influential role in 1981 when Republican Governor Bob List persuaded the state legislature to reduce the property tax and raise the sales tax from 3.5 to 5.75 percent, in an effort to shift the state's revenue base to the latter. Overall, state property taxes dropped by an average of 50 percent in just one year. For Caesars Palace, MGM Grand, Hilton, and other major property owners, this was certainly a beneficial reform, but it forced the state to rely more on the volatile sales tax. As former Governor O'Callaghan recently observed, this tax shift was directly responsible for Las Vegas's infrastructure crisis and the state's lack of funding for many programs in the 1990s.[12] The danger of this policy became immediately evident in 1979, when a national recession combined with competition from Atlantic City and other factors to create a brief tourist recession in Nevada. In an effort to cut expenses, List denied state employees cost-of-living increases and imposed a hiring freeze that affected most positions in the state government. By 1981, however, the recession had ended, tourism rebounded, and state workers won a generous 23.6 percent cost-of-living increase, spread over two years, to offset the sacrifice they had made during the previous two years of high inflation.[13]

Throughout the late 1980s and early 1990s, there was a general expansion of government spending, driven by a renaissance in gold and silver mining, heavy defense spending, and the continued boom in Las Vegas and Reno, as well as growth in Laughlin and other new gaming centers along the state's borders. But national and world events disrupted this round of prosperity. The end of the Cold War in the early 1990s (including the cessation of nuclear testing in 1992) made the Silver State even more dependent upon the casino moguls, just as they were trying to export gaming to other states. President Clinton's closure of military bases, especially in California and Texas, created a brief drop in tourist spending that cut sales tax and gaming revenues. Along with other factors, this forced Governor Bob Miller to impose a series of budget cuts in 1992–93. These resulted in a new series of wage and hiring freezes across the board in state government, along with reduced funding of programs for the mentally ill and others. Once again, state employees willingly sacrificed cost-of-living increases and took on increased workloads to help out the state. At the same time, their payments for dependent health insurance from the state insurance plan, which was also cut, reached $300 a month, forcing many to switch to sharply reduced benefit options or HMOs.

The economic downturn proved only temporary, however, and 1994 and especially 1995 saw Las Vegas rebound with record profits and lead the state out of its crisis. As noted, three major casinos debuted in Las Vegas alone in 1993, and they helped to short-circuit the recession and inspire a new round of resort construction.[14] Moreover, by early 1996, at least seven major hotels were either under construction or in the blueprint stage.

In 1995, gaming profits and tourism hit all-time highs, but—ominously—so did the influence of gamers in Carson City. The increased economic power of the Las Vegas casino industry and the rising tide of fiscal conservatism (which in 1994 awarded Republicans, who were heavily supported by the casinos, control of the state senate and a tie in the assembly) bodes ill for the public sector. These two factors are related, because in the past few years Nevada and especially Las Vegas casino interests have shifted their campaign contributions in the direction of Republican candidates for the state senate and assembly. They also have rewarded pliable Democrats such as Governor Bob Miller.

The recent growth of Las Vegas gaming's power and the Republicans' influence have dramatically strengthened the political economy of gambling. In the 1990s, more than at any other time in the state's modern history, the casino elite exerted a strong influence, if not control, over many lawmakers in Carson City. Nevada's chief executive was another reason for this. Although a professed Democrat, Miller came from a "well-connected" gaming family in Las Vegas, and enjoyed political support from nearly every major casino owner in the state. Not surprisingly, he saw many issues their way.

A clear barometer of that support was evident in 1994 when Steve Wynn openly supported Miller over Las Vegas Mayor Jan Laverty Jones in Nevada's Democratic gubernatorial primary. In the 1990s, Wynn became a political force to be reckoned with. He strongly encouraged voter registration among his thousands of employees, openly communicated his political concerns to them, and contributed heavily to pro-gaming candidates. As the local political consultant Don Williams recently observed, "[W]hen Steve Wynn picks up the telephone, most politicians jump. He doesn't get everything he wants, but he rarely loses."[15]

Governor Miller has been a prime beneficiary of Wynn's largesse. Thirteen of the fifteen top contributors to Miller's 1994 reelection campaign were (mostly Las Vegas–based) casino companies or their top executives. Wynn alone gave $70,000, exploiting a loophole in the state law limiting any corporation's gift to $20,000 by spreading separate donations across four subsidiaries, a move that drew the ire of Common Cause in Nevada. Miller also received thousands of dollars from two major slot and video poker machine manufacturers, Bally's and International Game Technology (IGT). Another major contributor was Barrick Gold, the state's largest gold mining company.[16]

The political economy of gambling is alive and well not only in Nevada's executive mansion but in the state legislature (especially the Republican State Senate), both houses of which are dominated numerically by Las Vegas area politicians. During the 1995 session, the casino industry, led by two Republican state senators, Sue Lowden of Las Vegas and Reno's Bill Raggio, led the fight against any tax increases. Lowden, the wife of the then prominent Las Vegas casino owner Paul Lowden (who, at the time of her election in 1992, owned the Sahara and Hacienda hotels on the Strip, as well as two others), became chair of the Senate Taxation Committee in 1995 with the support of Majority Leader Raggio (who, incidentally, was a member of Paul Lowden's board of directors). This marked the first time in Nevada history that a major casino executive (and practically a co-owner) had chaired the committee that decided the state's gaming and mining taxes—a dangerous precedent largely ignored by the state's print and electronic media.

Despite the tremendous growth of the casino industry, especially in Las Vegas, the gamers' contribution to overall state revenues actually declined in 1995. In the 1993–95 biennium, they accounted for 43.8 percent of the state's General Fund revenues (including the 2.5 percent Casino Entertainment Tax). However, revenue projections for 1995–97 put the figure at 40.8 percent, and less than 35 percent in 1999.[17]

Clearly, in the booming 1980s and 1990s, the big gaming corporations used Nevada, and especially Las Vegas, as a bank to finance their gaming campaigns and projects in other states and foreign countries, many of which compete directly with Nevada for gaming tourists. Despite their expressed willingness to pay substantially higher taxes in Louisiana, Iowa, Missouri, Indiana, and elsewhere, resort makers in Nevada, especially those in Las Vegas, have successfully used their clout in Carson City to pay lower rates. In 2000, Nevada still had the lowest gaming tax in the United States. For example, the Silver State's gaming tax is 6.25 percent of gross proceeds plus fees, compared to New Jersey's 8 percent and fees. The Garden State also collects an additional 2.5 percent to fund city improvements and bond issues for future municipal projects and levies both corporate and personal income taxes, which Nevada lacks. Other states charge even more (ranging up to 20 percent in Iowa, Illinois, Missouri, and Indiana), but this has not driven off some Las Vegas casino owners, who know that, despite the high taxes, they can still make significant profits there.[18] In none of these states do the gamers exert the kind of control they now enjoy in Carson City.

There has been a sort of informal agreement since 1989 between the casino and mining industries in Nevada to respect each other's interests regarding tax policy. In 1989, however, when the population boom forced more state spending, mining interests sought to amend the state constitution to cap their taxes at 2 percent of net proceeds, and the two groups clashed. Unwilling to bear more than a half percent increase in the gaming tax (to 6.25 percent), the casino industry, led by Wynn, opposed the move. Anxious to resolve the conflict, Governor Miller proposed a mining tax of up to 5 percent on net profits. Assemblyman Marvin Sedway, however, produced figures to show that a 6 percent tax on *gross* proceeds, or even a $16.50 severance tax on each ounce of gold mined, would not drive the industry away. Miller's plan was designed to satisfy both sides. In the end, faced with the determined opposition of the state's casino interests and their ally, Governor Miller, the mining industry and its rural supporters backed off. As the governor noted reassuringly, his plan would still give Nevada the lowest precious metals tax in the nation. It did, and production continued to boom.[19]

Into the mid 1990s, Nevada led all states in gold and silver production. In 1994, it produced 61 percent of America's gold and 20 percent of its silver. Moreover, Nevada was the fourth-largest gold producer *in the world*. The other nine members of the top ten were countries, such as South Africa, that derived significant revenue from their mining taxes. Under Governor Miller's plan, as before, mining companies have been able to use their undertaxed Nevada profits to fund mining operations in other states and nations. Despite the shortage of funds in the past two bienniums, Governor Miller never proposed increasing the state's mining or gaming taxes. He justified this by arguing that any tax hike would cost the state jobs. But Colorado and other western states with higher precious metals taxes than Nevada in 1994 experienced no significant drop in mining activity until the price of gold on world markets reached a twenty-year low in 1997. Despite significant production in 1995, the cash-strapped Silver State collected only $113 million in taxes on well over $2.2 billion in *net* profits.[20] So, even in boom periods, Nevada has profited little. Obviously, the mining industry's political contributions have been a wise investment.

One of the governor's major contributors, Barrick Gold, a Canadian corporation, earned $250 million in *net* income in 1994, but paid only a 5 percent tax. For cities such as Las Vegas, facing problems caused by casino-driven growth, this has resulted in less state funding. Nevertheless, the conservative *Las Vegas Review-Journal* has applauded these events, crediting the state's tax policy with creating lots of "$40,000 a year jobs for miners," while at the same time ignoring the billions in profits that out-of-state and foreign mining corporations have been hauling out of Nevada.[21] The situation is a replay of the 1860s and 1870s, when the Comstock kings bought off state politicians and diverted fortunes derived from Nevada's mineral wealth to California. No one is stopping their modern-day counterparts either, and gold from Barrick's Nevada mines is going to build up Canadian properties. To be sure, Las Vegas gamers, anxious to maintain friendly relations with their rural allies in both houses, have made no effort to encourage the state's urban representatives (the overwhelming majority in both houses) to challenge the mining interests.

These taxation policies have been disastrous for state government as well as Las Vegas, reminding one of John Kenneth Galbraith's famous warning about public sector poverty and private sector affluence.[22] While new casinos sprang up on the Strip virtually every year and blueprints for future ones were announced almost monthly, state employees were given a cost-of-living increase for 1995–97 of only 8 percent (Governor Miller had pushed for 7 percent). Although hundreds of clerks, secretaries, and custodians (many of whom earn less than $25,000 a year) had endured wage freezes for the previous three years, Miller (who gave generous raises to his staff) insisted on a cost-of-living increase that amounted to only a little over 1.5 percent per year for 1993–97—even though the cost of living rose 16.6 percent during that period. Then in 1999, Miller's Republican successor, Kenny Guinn, the casino candidate, pushed for no cost-of-living increase until July 2000, and then an increase only for some state workers. This seems almost heartless when one considers that, during the mid to late 1990s, the Las Vegas gaming business continued to earn record profits and paid, as the local headlines put it, "No New Taxes!"[23]

As Diane Nassir has demonstrated, the effects of these policies upon the state's social programs have been destructive.[24] One glaring example, and one of the most unfortunate episodes in recent legislative history, occurred in 1995, a boom year with a healthy revenue surplus, when lawmakers rejected the plea of Las Vegan Vikki High, a 31-year-old Medicaid recipient and mother of three, who desperately needed a heart transplant. She lobbied them to amend the state's Medicaid law to provide the $100,000 required to fund the operation. Legislators walked past her wheelchair every day for over a month. In the end, they rejected her request, with Assembly Ways and Means Co-Chair John Marvel (R–Battle Mountain) coldly suggesting to reporters that "maybe the private sector can do a fund-raiser." One prominent physician glumly observed that "this state's health policy is . . . draconian. The state has a very healthy surplus and a healthy economy and is behind the rest of the country in paying for this." Lawmakers, however, estimated that her transplant and those of other poor people might add $1.3 million annually to the state's $2.5 billion biennial budget. So, despite its booming casino and mining industries, Nevada remains one of only eleven states that does not fund heart or liver transplants for adult residents.[25]

The casinos' increased power in Carson City negatively affects not only state employees and Medicaid recipients who live in Las Vegas, but the metropolis itself. In the late 1990s, the Las Vegas Valley experienced crises in water, schools, public services, and higher education spawned by the town's casino-driven development and worsened by the political economy of gambling. Thanks to its skyrocketing growth, Las Vegas today faces an infrastructure crisis of major proportions. Despite the construction of thousands of homes at Sun City Summerlin, Los Prados, and other large master-planned communities in the far western suburbs, county officials are just now planning the freeway routes and scrambling for funds. Thousands of commuters stranded in daily gridlock have finally awakened leaders and media to the city's infrastructure crisis, which has been twenty years in the making. And similar problems afflict public services such as police and fire protection.[26]

But the water crisis dwarfs them all. Reluctant to advocate higher taxes, local politicians waited until the 1997 state legislative session to push the Southern Nevada Water Authority's request for a quarter percent increase in the sales tax to fund a second pipeline from Lake Mead, with additional pumping stations and expanded mains to accommodate growth. In February 1997, the need for these improvements became obvious when a computer malfunction flooded the district's water treatment plant at Lake Mead, threatening the entire metropolitan area's water supply. Crews had only three days to fix the problem before the valley and its million people ran out of water, an emergency that would have shut down the Las Vegas Strip! "[W]hat this shows is how close we're living to the razor's edge, that we have no reliability as we start today. The community has outgrown the system," the Water Authority's general manager, Pat Mulroy, observed.[27]

Fortunately, the water district has powerful allies in the tax fight. Las Vegas casino owners have endorsed a sales tax increase to enlarge the water system. They had to, because their future depends on it. The Nevada Resort Association's president, Richard Bunker, who served on an advisory committee for new water and sewer lines, warned legislators that $5–6 billion in new casino projects would have to be shelved without an expanded water system. Bunker sidestepped any suggestion that the casinos should lead the way in paying for it with a higher gaming tax, observing that the state treasury currently boasts a $250 million surplus, thanks largely to casino-driven revenue growth.[28]

Governor Bob Miller, like the casinos, approached the infrastructure crisis reluctantly. Although concerned about the need for more roads, schools, and expanded water and sewer systems, Miller nevertheless announced in early 1997 that "we are preparing a budget without any new taxes on the general public. Infrastructure is a local government issue." Claiming that he lacked sufficient information "to determine how real and immediate the infrastructure need is," Miller hinted that he might support a local infrastructure tax "if one county wants to impose a tax increase and the Legislature wants to support it." Nearing the end of his term in office, and not wanting to jeopardize his political future by antagonizing powerful conservatives, much less his casino patrons, he was remarkably slow to recognize what the engineers have been trying to tell everyone for years: Las Vegas's infrastructure is currently lagging a decade behind the metropolitan area's growth.[29] Eventually, timid state and county politicians put the water tax to a vote of the people, who, prodded by the *Review-Journal* and other anti-tax forces, defeated the measure at the polls in November 1998.

Despite its rhetoric, the gaming industry has been doing relatively little about the infrastructure crisis. As one political insider anonymously confided to a local newspaper, the creation of the Assembly Committee on Infrastructure before the opening of the 1997 state legislature came at the behest of gaming lobbyists trying "to avoid any chance that the Assembly Taxation Committee would seek an increase in casino taxes" during the session. At the same time, the gaming industry, like the real estate industry, supports more growth. In Las Vegas as in state government, the casino moguls and land developers largely control city and county politicians. Don Schlesinger, a former county commissioner and an advocate of managed growth, put it bluntly: "[I]f you want to get re-elected, you need their money." Indeed, the home builders and commercial developers often rival the resort owners in power and influence.[30]

It has long been axiomatic in Las Vegas that new housing and commercial developments are rubber-stamped if builders have their paperwork in order. Even former Clark County manager Pat Shalmy observed, "[I]t's a first-come and first-served type of approach." The *Las Vegas Sun*'s political editor, Larry Henry, goes further, noting that "in Las Vegas, the overriding perception is that politicians are puppets, with developers and casino owners pulling the strings."

Unfortunately, Las Vegas's problems are not limited to freeways and water lines. The city's rapid development has also created a school crisis of significant proportions. In this case, it is the obsession with low taxes, rather than political fragmentation or belated planning, that is fueling the crisis. As growth continues unabated, money for new construction continues to be an issue. Brian Cram, former superintendent of the Clark County School District, estimated that 12,000–14,000 new students annually would enter the system in 1997 and for the next four years thereafter. In effect, this would require the district to open a new grammar school every month for the next five years. At the same time, Governor Miller tried to lower the student-teacher ratio to 16:1 in grades 1–4 *without* raising taxes, in a state that already enjoys one of the lowest tax rates in the nation. Not surprisingly, even with a bond issue approved by voters in November 1996, Cram expected to run out of construction money in three years and struggled in 1999 to find the money to hire enough teachers.

Much of the problem lies in Nevada's antiquated policy for funding new schools. Cram felt that school districts should not have to appeal to voters every few years for more bond issues. He argued that state legislators need to dedicate a portion of sales and property taxes to schools in order to ensure stable funding. "If the state is going to benefit from this great locomotive of an economy," he declared, "then the state is going to have to pay the price of the byproducts of the locomotive." But Miller and resort owners were less convinced.[31] Finally, at the end of the 1997 legislative session, they supported a bill under which voters would decide whether to fund school construction for four more years— another stop-gap measure. After a determined campaign by Cram and others, Clark County voters in 1998 once again supported bonds for new school construction, thus postponing the crisis for a few more years.

Casino control of the state, county, and city political systems has only worsened the infrastructure crisis. Although some large developers, such as the Howard Hughes Corporation, have supported new laws that will increase user and real estate transaction fees to fund parks, schools, and other infrastructure needs, Las Vegas casinos have been reluctant to do their part. In February 1997, after much prodding from desperate city and county politicians, the Nevada Resort Association finally supported a 1 percent increase in the room tax, which along with some Convention and Visitors Authority revenues, would pump about $30 million into the pot, plus some additional money for schools. Of course, this is far less than what could have been realized if the state gaming tax had been raised, but effective lobbying by the gaming and mining industries has kept their tax rates unchanged.

Following the meager room tax concession and other political maneuvering, resort industry leaders argued that developers, other businesses, and the public had "to do their share." Within two weeks of endorsing the new room tax, casino executives were already moaning about its effects. Although conceding that tourists and not the resorts themselves would bear most of the cost, the industry nevertheless emphasized a recent survey predicting that visitors would offset the increased tax by cutting back on gambling and other spending during their stay. In other words, in a city beset by growth-related problems largely created by the casino engine itself, the casinos projected the image of an industry sacrificing profits to preserve their employees' and other residents' quality of life.[32]

Given the reluctance of casino executives, developers, and politicians to endorse new taxes, the 1997 legislature responded half-heartedly to the growth issue. Ultimately, state and local officials in Las Vegas agreed to a watered-down version of growth control that pleased developers. County and some city officials refused to endorse a so-called "ring-around-the-valley bill" offered by State Senator Dina Titus (D–Las Vegas), which would have prevented the subdivision of land beyond the immediate metropolitan area.[33] Even in a crisis, local politicians and taxpayers may be slow to act. In a casino city like Las Vegas, market forces hold the trump card on infrastructure. Strangely enough, it may be the tourists who finally break the impasse. As Jeff Van Ee, a local environmentalist, observed, "[I]f casino owners sense that tourists are afraid to come here, they'll lean on politicians to impose a moratorium on new-home construction or to develop other dramatic measures." In April 1998, under pressure, the Clark County commissioners finally compromised with Titus and established a regional planning board to make recommendations concerning new development projects.[34]

Besides infrastructure, the baneful effects of the political economy of gambling and the state's reluctance to raise gambling and mining taxes also extend to higher education in Las Vegas. The only real university in what was the fastest-growing city in the United States for most of 1990s is the University of Nevada, Las Vegas (UNLV). During that same period, Nevada has been the fastest-growing state. Moreover, in 1995, it had the somewhat dubious distinction of enjoying the third-lowest state and local taxes and eighth-highest per capita personal income among the states and District of Columbia. In fact, by summer 1995, Nevada ranked first in the nation in the growth of per capita personal income.[35] The net results, while helpful to the economy, have put a harmful squeeze on university education, primarily because state support has not kept pace with Las Vegas's growth-driven needs.

Because the percentage of state funding for UNLV's operating budget has declined steadily from 54 percent in 1986 to 42 percent in 1996, students and their families have been forced to help close the budget gap by paying higher fees. But revenues from these regressive taxes have not been able to maintain the dramatic growth that the university experienced in the 1980s, when funding, especially for new faculty positions, was more forthcoming. While Governor Miller supported reductions in class size for the early grades of elementary school, his record in higher education, especially at the university level, was weak.[36] The deteriorating condition, particularly at UNLV, dates from his tenure as governor. In 1993, Miller ordered 10 percent across-the-board budget cuts in all state agencies. These spending reductions hit every department at UNLV; however, the president was able to offset these losses with subsidies from the university foundation. But the school's crisis was not over. Despite the Strip boom, national prosperity, and a new legislative biennium, Miller's new budget forced UNLV to make another 10 percent cut for the 1995–96 school year. Throughout the early 1990s, UNLV was forced to hire hundreds of temporary instructors (often lacking the necessary degrees) to cover classes. It was done because there were no *new* tenure-track faculty positions between fall 1993 and spring 1997![37]

The excuse given for the failure to hire full-time faculty members was "failure to meet growth projections." This presumed that the young university had been adequately staffed before the recession, which was not the case.[38] The school had never been granted enough faculty positions to catch up with the enrollment boom of the 1980s, much less to offer the courses needed for a respectable university curriculum. After gaining more than 10,000 students in the 1980s, UNLV saw its enrollment flatten out in the early 1990s and actually drop in 1994. Enrollment declined even more at the state's other university campus in Reno, a city that also grew in the 1980s and 1990s.[39] And both schools have suffered destructive budget cuts. The increases in enrollment since 1996 have resulted primarily from Las Vegas's growth and measures undertaken by President Carol Harter and her provost rather than from any state actions.

But if UNLV is the only university in America's fastest-growing city, why has enrollment growth dramatically slowed? The political economy of gambling is again the problem. To a large extent, lack of state funding to support basic services and programs has forced UNLV to raise tuition and fees, which has done little to help enrollment. But there is a deeper problem that stems from Nevada's low gambling and mining taxes. Under pressure from some state politicians anxious to please the casino elite, mining industry, and others with no tax increases, higher education officials have been forced to consider less expensive options. In the past few years, the Nevada Board of Regents and Chancellor's Office have been discussing new policies to make better use of the state's community colleges, whose tuition is almost half that of the universities and where many instructors lack terminal degrees. Already the old Northern Nevada Community College in Elko has been renamed Great Basin College and is granting some four-year degrees. Considering that northeastern Nevada has no university campus, this is understandable. But other community college presidents, including the president of the one in Las Vegas, proposed that their schools also be allowed to grant bachelor's degrees in some subjects.

In December 1995, Richard Jarvis, then chancellor of the University and Community College System of Nevada (UCCSN), raised the issue with the Board of Regents. After attempting to reassure them that "the idea of establishing a baccalaureate program at a two-year institution is *not without precedent in this country* [emphasis added]," he outlined his proposal. Despite insisting that he had "no plans to consider *at this time* [emphasis added] the wholesale transformation . . . of one of the UCCSN community colleges into a 4-year baccalaureate institution," he nevertheless endorsed "exploratory discussions of . . . possible baccalaureate degrees at community colleges." Obviously concerned about the budgetary pressures exerted by Carson City, he observed that "during times of strongly competing claims upon the state treasury, the UCCSN must be committed to cost-effective academic planning." No one, of course, would deny that cost-effective planning in education and all departments of government is always desirable. And no one would deny that each community college has some respected scholars teaching some subjects. But should one resort to the dubious practice of awarding baccalaureate degrees at community colleges just to shave a budget, especially in a booming state that already ranks near the bottom nationally in per capita spending for higher education?[40] To their credit, the Board of Regents rejected the proposal.

But the pressure to make more use of the community colleges remains strong. Aside from awarding four-year degrees at cheaper facilities, there is also a program in effect that allows several hundred high school students in Las Vegas to finish their senior year at community college and then begin work on their degree at the school. There is, however, no specific provision to encourage the academically talented students in the program to apply to the university upon graduation. Still another plan would have forced the two universities to accept the community college core requirements as their own, which would have surrendered university autonomy on curriculum in an effort to encourage more Nevada students to spend more time at community college. This is a serious problem when, for instance, some community colleges have in the 1990s compressed three-credit English composition (English 101) courses into just two weeks. To their credit, community college officials have recently been working to tighten academic standards.

Recent proposals that the state fund intercollegiate athletic programs at the community colleges in Las Vegas and Reno drew the wrath of the respected former governor Mike O'Callaghan. A onetime teacher himself, O'Callaghan declared that the purpose of a community college is "to meet the needs of local people wanting to improve their job skills, bring their academic grade up to a level [where] they can enter UNLV or some other four-year college, improve their quality of life or seek an associate degree in some field or skill." But it was to no avail. State officials approved the athletic programs. This action, like others, reflects the fact that many politicians quietly want to enhance the prestige of the community colleges and discourage traditional university students from attending UNLV or UNR exclusively for their four years of course work.[41]

There have also been proposals to build a state college (not a university or a community college) in Henderson. At this campus, faculty would teach a four-course load each semester but would not face a strict publication requirement. This would allow the state to pay the faculty lower salaries than at UNLV and eliminate the potential stigma associated with offering baccalaureate degrees at the community college level. At the same time, it would divert enrollment from UNLV, cut into the university's share of the higher education budget, and slow the costlier expansion of UNLV's programs and faculty. In 2000, the Board of Regents hired a president and city and business groups donated land for a campus. The 2001 state legislature is expected to fund initial construction.

Driving this movement, of course, is the desire of some state legislators to restrain spending on higher education, especially at the university level, and the subtle pressure on them and the governor comes from the gamers, mining companies, and other special interests anxious to keep their tax rates low. Even though Nevada currently enjoys the eighth-highest per capita personal income in the United States, it ranks an embarrassing forty-first among the states and District of Columbia in per capita spending on higher education.[42] So the fourth-largest gold producer in the world, and a state whose casino profits have run into the billions during the 1990s, is investing relatively little of its enormous wealth in the academic advancement of its people, especially its youth.

Ironically, this situation directly affects residents of the state's major revenue producer, Las Vegas, which in 1995 generated $1.02 billion of the state's $1.28 billion in *net,* pre-tax gaming profits.[43] Despite Las Vegas's spectacular growth since 1970, UNLV has historically been even more underfunded per student than its counterpart in Reno. One can clearly appreciate the cost savings if thousands of Las Vegas students can be lured to the local community college, where roughly 65 percent of all teaching positions are part-time (and the pay is $525 per credit), and where even tenured faculty earn a lower average salary than their UNLV counterparts.[44] Today in Las Vegas, some high school advisors are actually on the community college payroll, and even academically talented seniors hear the reasons for not attending the university directly after graduation.

While few members of the state's political and casino elite would consider sending their own children to community college for a degree, they seem less concerned about those of others. Indeed, the policy trend is obvious. In his 1995–97 biennial budget, Governor Miller proposed a 25.8 percent funding increase for the Community College of Southern Nevada. At the same time, UNLV received only a 12.4 percent boost—most of which went to upgrade equipment and offset inflation.[45] The subtle pressure to divert Nevada students away from their own universities and perhaps convert the community colleges into a sort of state college system is already having its effects on enrollment at both university campuses. This raises an important question: in a prosperous state like Nevada, should not all qualified residents be *encouraged* to attend their state university, where the faculty, libraries, laboratories, and other facilities are available for advanced learning and research?

Only in his final (1997) legislative session as governor did Miller submit a budget that adequately funded the state's two university campuses. After shorting them for nearly a decade, he could hardly have done it again, with a whopping $250 million surplus sitting in the state treasury. He approved UNLV's request for a badly needed library, appropriating $38 million for it—but only after university administrators had raised $15 million on their own for the project. Then, after initially omitting a long-awaited law school from his budget, Miller, himself a lawyer and former Las Vegas district attorney, succumbed to community pressure and allocated $4 million for it—but only on the condition that UNLV's new president raise another million dollars in matching funds.

As noted, in 1999 Dr. Kenny Guinn became the new governor of Nevada, thanks in part to heavy casino support for his campaign. Guinn, a former superintendent of the Clark County School District and interim president of UNLV for a year, announced that he would oppose any new taxes. In addition, he rejected cost-of-living raises for university professionals. And while he added money at the last minute to fund staff positions that were essential for UNLV's new library to even open, other shortfalls forced library officials to trim the acquisitions budget to the point of asking faculty to "adopt" (donate the subscription money for) major journals in their fields. Despite receiving a $2.2 billion windfall from Nevada's settlement with the tobacco companies, Guinn earmarked none of that money for desperately needed buildings, parking garages, and staff at the university, whose growth-related problems he knew so well. Nor did he even consider raising the gaming tax—even though an independent accounting firm clearly demonstrated that UNLV and the community college in Las Vegas had been grossly underfunded in the higher education budget approved by lawmakers. In the end, he made up less than a third of the gap for UNLV by taking money from other sources, while the community college received a satisfactory allowance.[46]

The fabulous growth of Las Vegas since 1970 and especially in the 1990s stands as a point to the counterpoint of its casinos' increased political power. The root of the city's problems in higher education and infrastructure lies in the corporate control of Nevada government at virtually all levels. In 1993, State Senator Matthew Callister, later a Las Vegas city councilman, boldly declared that the state was seriously underfunded, a situation whose effects continue to extend directly to the Las Vegas Valley.[47] In 1989, state politicians largely ignored the recommendation of a blue ribbon committee to impose a broad-based business tax to help pay for the expensive public works that continued urban development would require. In 1997, state and especially county politicians again failed to address the problems facing Las Vegas adequately.[48]

Clearly, political leaders must be more responsible. While non-gaming businesses and the general public must assume part of growth-related costs, the gaming and mining industries must pay their fair share, too. Although both industries have donated generously to Nevada institutions of higher learning over the years, *many* millions more could be realized each year through slightly higher taxes. Even with a flattening of gaming revenues in 1997–98, a 1 or 2 percent increase in the state's gambling tax would hardly weaken a casino industry whose profits have helped to fund many of the 300 casinos built outside of Nevada since 1989. And although gold and silver prices remain depressed, higher tax rates could be designed to kick in or phase out when they exceed or fall below given thresholds.[49]

In the 1999 state legislative session, Senator Joe Neal (D–Las Vegas) courageously proposed a bill to increase the gaming tax to 8.25 percent, which would have raised an estimated $113 million in additional revenue. MGM Grand's chairman, Terrence Lanni, responded by complaining that, after federal taxes (and one might add, a lot of creative accounting) most casinos netted only a 5 percent profit, and therefore could not afford the tax increase. In the end, virtually no lawmakers rallied to Neal's cause, and his bill died in committee. Later, in fall 2000, Neal's efforts to obtain a voter referendum to bypass the legislature and amend the state constitution to raise the gaming tax to perhaps 10 percent or more suffered a setback when he failed to obtain enough signatures for his petition in the face of determined opposition by Governor Guinn and Nevada's gaming community. He argues that even a 12 percent tax would not hurt the casino industry. The gamers and their minions have already begun their effort to marginalize Neal, who, as an African American representing constituents whose average income is less than the average Las Vegan's, will be vulnerable to the "big spending liberal" charge. But certainly a gaming tax of 8–9 percent on the major casinos would hardly put them out of business, although it might curtail some of their planned investments out of state.[50]

For the past decade, the powerful gambling interests and their various allies, concerned about their own taxes being raised first, have quietly opposed most of the fiscal proposals needed to cope with state and local growth. Governor Miller noted that, thanks to his policies, Nevada remained "the third lowest-taxed state" during his ten years in office—a position that largely ignores the demands for services resulting from Nevada's chaotic growth during that period.[51] Today, paradoxically, while gambling continues to create new jobs and attract new residents to Las Vegas, the political economy of gambling threatens the city's future as well as the state's. Polls indicate that residents want their elected representatives to do more about the crises in higher education, infrastructure, and public services. Unfortunately, the people of Nevada may not have the influence in Carson City to achieve this, because the real power lies in Las Vegas, not in the metropolitan area as a whole, but rather on the Strip.

NOTES

1. *Las Vegas Review-Journal*, May 20, 1999, 1D, 2D; November 27, 1989, 1B, 4B, 5B; June 20, 1990, 1A; October 10, 1993, 1A; December 26, 1993, 15D–16D; October 24, 1993, 1B; November 26, 1995, 1A, 12A; January 14, 1996, 14E, 16E; City of Las Vegas, *Downtown Las Vegas: Come Home to the Dome* (May 1995); *Las Vegas Review-Journal*, October 20, 1995, 1B, 2B.

2. *Las Vegas Review-Journal*, October 2, 1995, 1A, 3A; November 3, 1995, 1A; *1995 Las Vegas Perspective* (Las Vegas: First Interstate Bank, Nevada Development Authority, *Las Vegas Review-Journal*, 1995), 40.

3. *1995 Las Vegas Perspective*, 42, 44.

4. Ibid., 43–44.

5. Ibid., 43.

6. The service sector comprises 47.4 percent of the metropolitan area's economy, and hotel, gaming, and recreation account for 60.4 percent of this figure; see ibid., 47, 50.

7. R. Keith Schwer, "Demographic and Economic Profile for Southern Nevada" (Las Vegas: UNLV Center for Business and Economic Research, August 21, 1995); "Indexed Las Vegas Gaming Activity: 1980–1994," *Las Vegas Perspective*, 73.

8. *Las Vegas Review-Journal/Sun,* September 12, 1993, 6D; July 1, 1995, 1B.

9. *Nevada Business Journal* (October 1995), LLV 4–11; *Las Vegas Review-Journal,* November 3, 1995, 1A.

10. *Homebuyers Guide* (November 1995), 4–5; *Homes & Living* (November 1995), 24; *Las Vegas Review-Journal,* July 9, 1997, 1B, 5B.

11. James Hulse, *Forty Years in the Wilderness: Impressions of Nevada, 1940–1980* (Reno: University of Nevada Press, 1986).

12. *Las Vegas Review-Journal/Sun,* March 16, 1997, 1D, 6D.

13. Confirmed by State of Nevada Employees Association to author by telephone, January 29, 1996.

14. *Las Vegas Review-Journal/Sun,* March 14, 1993, 4D.

15. Ibid., August 4, 1994, 1B; March 20, 1994, 3D. One editor even declared that Steve Wynn runs the state; see ibid., April 10, 1999, 12B.

16. Ibid., December 24, 1995, 6K; July 4, 1995, 1B.

17. Compare Schwer, 18, with State of Nevada Legislative Counsel Bureau, Fiscal Analysis Division, "Nevada General Fund Revenues: Economic Forum Revised, 1995–1997 Biennium," *Las Vegas Review-Journal,* January 19, 1999, 1A, 6A.

18. Ibid., December 28, 1993, 7B; February 11, 1996, 13E.

19. Ibid., February 3, 1989, 1A, 17A; February 8, 1989, 7B. In 1989, the casino industry managed to keep the gaming tax increase to only one-half percent.

20. Nevada's rank confirmed by Mineral Policy Center, Washington D.C., by telephone, February 1, 1996. *Las Vegas Review-Journal,* March 7, 1993, 1E; *Las Vegas Review-Journal/Sun,* December 10, 1995, 5L–6L; *Las Vegas Review-Journal,* July 11, 1995, 7B.

21. Ibid., May 18, 1994, 8B.

22. John Kenneth Galbraith, *The Affluent Society* (New York: Mentor Books, 1958), 198–211.

23. Confirmed by State of Nevada Employees Association by telephone, January 29, 1996; *Las Vegas Review-Journal,* May 2, 1995, 3B; July 4, 1995, 1A; May 31, 1999, 1A.

24. For a good introduction to Nevada's failure to fund social programs adequately, see Diane E. Nassir, "Last in the Nation: Social Welfare in Nevada" (paper delivered in Las Vegas at the Fourth Biennial Conference on Nevada History, May 24, 1995), and id., "Nevada Welfare Assistance Caseloads and Gaming: A Cautionary Tale," *Nevada Historical Society Quarterly* 37 (Summer 1994): 115–41; *Las Vegas Review-Journal,* June 11, 1995, 8B.

25. Ibid., June 3, 1995, 1B, 3B; June 30, 1995, 1B, 3B; July 3, 1995, 2B. Nevada funds corneal, kidney, and bone marrow transplants for adults when strict eligibility criteria (as defined in the Medicaid Services Manual) are met.

State of Nevada, Department of Human Resources, Welfare Division, memorandum to author, February 8, 1996. The state funds transplants of all types for children.

26. With regard to police, for example, even with 450 new hires, the Las Vegas Metropolitan Police Department will have only 1.8 officers per 1,000 residents, compared with a national average of 2.9. See *Review-Journal*, June 5, 1996, 1B, 5B.

27. *Las Vegas Review-Journal*, February 23, 1997, 1A, 12A.

28. Ibid., January 12, 1997, 1B, 3B.

29. Ibid., 3B; *Las Vegas Review-Journal/Sun*, April 6, 1997, 1A, 18A, 19A, 22A.

30. Ibid.; *Las Vegas Sun*, January 12, 1997, 4D.

31. *Las Vegas Review-Journal*, January 12, 1997, 3B.

32. Ibid., March 3, 1997, 1D, 2D.

33. The *Las Vegas Review-Journal* already has indicated its opposition to hiking the sales tax; see ibid., July 9, 1997, 10B.

34. *Las Vegas Sun*, January 12, 1997, 5D; *Las Vegas Review-Journal*, April 17, 1998, 1A, 5A.

35. See *Las Vegas Review-Journal*, December 29, 1993, 1A, for the growth rate. Only Alaska and Wyoming had a lower average annual state and local tax burden than Nevada. The figures are based on a two-income family of four; see ibid., December 28, 1993, 1A, as reported in *Money* magazine, January 1994. For Nevada's income rank as computed by the U.S. Department of Commerce, Bureau of Economic Research, see *Las Vegas Review-Journal*, April 30, 1996, 1A.

36. UNLV Office of Institutional Analysis, *Selected Institutional Characteristics, Fall 1995,* 9, 96. To calculate the declining percentage of state support for UNLV between 1985/86 and 1994/95, divide the state appropriation figures on p. 96 with the total operating budgets on p. 9. *Las Vegas Review-Journal*, March 15, 1993, 7B; May 14, 1995, 1B, 7B.

37. UNLV Office of Institutional Analysis, memorandum to author, January 10, 1996.

38. Ibid.

39. *Las Vegas Review-Journal*, November 30, 1995, 1B–2B; *Selected Institutional Characteristics,* 29, and see earlier editions for earlier enrollment counts. UNLV's enrollment has improved since 1996 thanks only to the extraordinary efforts of the school's new president and provost.

40. Memorandum from Chancellor Richard S. Jarvis to the UCCSN Board of Regents, December 26, 1995.

41. *Las Vegas Review-Journal/Sun*, May 9, 1998, 14B.

42. *Chronicle of Higher Education*, October 19, 1994, A-45, A-46 uses 1994 figures for Nevada's 40th rank in lump sum spending. Nevada's per capita rank of 41st (the most recent figures are 1992) confirmed by U.S. Bureau of the Census, Education Division, by telephone, February 1, 1996.

43. *Las Vegas Review-Journal*, February 1, 1996, 1A, 2A. Statewide gross gaming profits for 1995 totaled $7.37 billion, ibid., February 10, 1995, 1A, 5A.

44. For the emerging crisis with part-time instructors at the Community College of Southern Nevada, see *Las Vegas Review-Journal/Sun,* March 30, 1997, 5D.

45. *Las Vegas Review-Journal,* January 19, 1995, 1A.

46. *Las Vegas Review-Journal/Sun,* May 15, 1999, 1A, 2A; June 2, 1999, 1A, 2A.

47. Ibid., May 13, 1993, 15B.

48. *Las Vegas Review-Journal/Sun,* March 16, 1997, 1D, 6D.

49. *Las Vegas Review-Journal/Sun,* February 15, 1998, 4E.

50. Ibid., April 25, 1999, 1B, 6B.

51. Interview with George Knapp, KLAS TV–Channel 8, November 1998.

JAY BRIGHAM

Lighting Las Vegas
Electricity and the City of Glitz

From that moment I associated the "Glory of Light"
with Las Vegas. I could see far in the future a city
glowing with the glory of light. But such a city as we
see today one could not imagine.

> Charles P. Squires, one of the founders of
> Nevada Power, recollecting the sunrise
> on the day he arrived in Las Vegas
> in February 1905

Every night the Las Vegas Strip is ablaze in a kaleidoscope of surreal electrical imagery, volcanic eruptions, and pirate battles. In an attempt to revitalize and draw tourist dollars back into the city's downtown area, the multimillion dollar Fremont Street Experience opened in 1995, complete with an illuminated awning capable of producing a multitude of images for weary gamblers. Advertisements for the Experience boast that more than two million lights make up the awning. The beam of the Luxor Casino, projecting upward into space, is so bright that pilots report seeing it soon after takeoff from southern California airports. Pilots have also complained that the laser lights from Strip hotels and casinos occasionally cause disorientation on the final approach to McCarran International Airport. Las Vegas is, in a sense, out of this world. Astronauts tell of seeing the city from their orbiting space craft. In an area otherwise devoid of many natural resources, electricity makes these and many other images in Las Vegas—and even the city itself—possible.

Since World War II, Las Vegas has emerged as a Sun Belt city dependent on energy-consuming tourism and gaming, and during the Cold War, on the federal government, for its economic livelihood.[1] At the outset of World War II, U.S. Senator Patrick "Pat" McCarran (D–Nev.) helped locate the Basic Magnesium plant and what would become Nellis Air Force Base on the city's outskirts. Several new casinos opened in the city during the war years, including El Cortez, El Rancho Las Vegas, and the Golden Nugget.[2] After the war, both defense money and tourism fueled southern Nevada's growth. The tremendous growth of Las Vegas in the postwar years has resulted in an ever-expanding need for electrical power. To meet that need, Las Vegas has reached beyond its borders to tap into the resources of adjacent southwestern states.

Historians often refer to the American West as a colony of the East.[3] Ever since Lewis and Clark, people have seen the region as rich in natural resources. Even before the Gold Rush, the hide and tallow trade forged a significant West-East commercial link, tying California to eastern markets. San Francisco's early dominance in the region manifested itself in the location of California's and Nevada's state capitals in Sacramento and Carson City respectively, both close to the mineral-rich Sierra Nevada mountains.

For a long time after the United States gained control of the West in 1848, the region functioned as a colony of the East, sending lumber, minerals, grain, livestock, and a host of other commodities eastward over the country's expanding railroad system. Refrigerated train cars made shipments of western beef to the East possible. At the turn of the century, southern California citrus growers shipped trainloads of fruit to eastern markets. However, federal spending during the New Deal, World War II, and the Cold War, and the accompanying economic and demographic growth, allowed the West to break many old eastern colonial ties. Even before the Great Depression, a new form of colonialism started to develop in the American West, which continues to shape the region. Although the West's products and wealth flowed east, the dramatic growth of San Francisco since the Gold Rush, and then of Los Angeles and all of southern California in the twentieth century, resulted in a reorientation. At the start of the twentieth century, Los Angeles began to exert an ever-increasing influence in the West. By the 1920s, it had surpassed San Francisco as the West Coast's major city, thanks in no small part to the federal financing of Los Angeles Harbor and the transfer of federal land for the Los Angeles Aqueduct. The most important manifestation of Los Angeles's influence involves water and energy. Thirsty southern California obtains water from the Owens Valley, central California, and the Colorado River. In taking water from the Colorado River, Los Angeles reaches into the seven Colorado River basin states from where the river's water flows. Transmission lines throughout the West deliver power to Los Angeles.

Especially since World War II, Las Vegas and Nevada have become part of the Los Angeles colonial system. The colonial system may be seen as a series of interrelated concentric circles with resources flowing toward the middle. Los Angeles is at the center. The first circle is the rest of southern California, the second circle is San Francisco and the remainder of California. The two outer most rings are Las Vegas and the rest of the West. This model is especially relevant to the generation and distribution of electricity in the region.

Las Vegas receives power generated at numerous power facilities in the West, although most goes to Los Angeles and southern California. Despite the short distance between Las Vegas and Hoover Dam, steam plants burning coal mined in Utah or Arizona, natural gas from the Southwest, or power bought on the open energy market are the city's primary sources of electricity. Electricity has made Las Vegas a tourist boomtown, a form of colonization, in that economic forces beyond its borders determine much of the city's prosperity. In the late twentieth century, Las Vegas is both a colony and a colonizer. The city reaches into bordering states to import electrical energy or fuel to generate electricity. Simultaneously, however, electricity generated in Nevada is exported to California.

Las Vegas and the Nevada Power Company, the private utility that serves much of southern Nevada, had humble beginnings. At the turn of the century, amid high expectations that the San Pedro, Los Angeles, and Salt Lake City Railroad would make the city a boomtown, local businessmen began to consider the idea of bringing electricity to Las Vegas. Although more than twenty years had passed since Edison first tested the electric light, gas lamps continued to be the major form of illumination in many parts of the United States. Las Vegas's business leaders lived in constant dread of a fire engulfing the city. A local merchant, Charles P. Squires, led a group of early Las Vegas businessmen in constructing the town's first generation and distribution system, powered by a ninety-horsepower gas-driven generator. In 1906, the founders of the Consolidated Power and Telephone Company incorporated their business, and electricity had officially arrived in Las Vegas. The company dissolved itself in 1929, splitting into Southern Nevada Power and the Southern Nevada Telephone Company.[4]

As did most electrical utilities, Nevada Power continually searched for additional sources of electricity in its earliest years. The demand soon outstripped the original ninety-horsepower generator, "Old Betsy."[5] In 1914, to meet increased demand, Nevada Power began buying all the electricity it marketed from the railroad. Forty-one years passed before the company began to generate its own electrical energy. During that time, Nevada Power became the first utility to distribute power generated at Hoover Dam when it went on line in 1937.[6]

Nevada's congressional delegation successfully amended the Swing-Johnson bill to increase the state's allocation of the electricity generated at Hoover Dam. Edward W. Clark, president of Nevada Power and a member of the original Colorado River Commission, reportedly played an influential role in the passage of the Nevada Amendments.[7] Hoover Dam quickly became the city's sole source of power, which it remained until 1955, when postwar growth and the Cold War increased demand and forced Nevada Power to develop other sources of electricity. In February 1949, after several adjustments to the original Hoover Dam power allocations, the Federal Power Commission set Nevada's allotment of the dam's firm power at 18 percent.[8] Hoover Dam today supplies energy to various southwestern communities, but little to Las Vegas.

Under the Hoover Dam agreements, most of the electricity generated—approximately 64 percent—goes to California, with the remainder being divided between Nevada and Arizona. Nevadans have long been sensitive to the fact that the state receives such a small share of the total output. A 1976 *Las Vegas Review-Journal* article asked the rhetorical question "Will California Always Get 64 Per Cent?" Acknowledging that power allocations were not likely to change, the paper suggested that California had originally received 64 percent because the authors of the legislation, Congressman Phil Swing and Senator Hiram Johnson, were both Californians, as were prominent people in the Department of the Interior and Bureau of Reclamation. The writer depicted Los Angeles as having avariciously demanded all the Hoover Dam power, whereas the "less greedy" Southern California Edison requested only half. Los Angeles city officials claimed that LA had received the first Hoover Dam power, not Las Vegas or Nevada Power, as the power company maintains. Financial arrangements for repaying the government for the dam's construction also favored California because of its large population.[9]

World War II profoundly affected the West and transformed Las Vegas and Nevada, along with the rest of the region, placing new demands on the region's electrical systems. In 1940, the state's population numbered 110,247; eight years later, it stood at an estimated 141,000. Mining had long dominated the state's economy, and that continued for much of the war. Basic Magnesium required a tremendous amount of electrical energy. In 1943, for example, the state's wartime power requirement reached 1,618 million kilowatt-hours, with most of that power being used for magnesium production. Ten years earlier, the Depression low for electrical power consumption in the state was 62 million kilowatt-hours. By war's end, electrical requirements had dropped nearly 75 percent after magnesium production reductions. Not all of the power went to wartime industries. In the mid 1940s, per capita use of electricity by nonfarm residential customers in Las Vegas was among the highest in the United States. The lack of other energy sources for heating and cooking and "the almost universal use of air-conditioning equipment" further contributed to the high levels of electrical usage.[10]

The end of the war brought only a temporary reduction in the city's power demands. Several events of very different character forever altered the electric power situation in Las Vegas. Las Vegas and Nevada continued to grow as the nation's population moved westward. Gambling took on a new face in 1946 when Benjamin "Bugsy" Siegel came West and opened the Flamingo Hotel, marking a new phase in Las Vegas history. The Cold War soon engulfed the world, and Nevada played a unique role in that conflict, because the Nevada Test Site served as the proving ground for the country's expanding atomic arsenal. In 1956, Nevada Power built the 64-mile Mercury transmission line to serve the Atomic Energy Commission's complex at Mercury and the Indian Springs Air Force Base, both northwest of Las Vegas.[11] These factors all made unprecedented demands on Nevada Power to provide more electrical energy. Within a few years, the Las Vegas Chamber of Commerce symbolically tied together tourism, gambling, and atomic weapons when it started to print calendars showing test days. Soon afterward, Las Vegas casinos began sponsoring trips so that "tourists could experience the blast and watch the rising mushroom cloud," before the ban on atmospheric tests in 1963.[12]

Reports filed with the Nevada State Public Service Commission, which regulates electrical utilities, reflect the growing demand for electrical energy in Las Vegas and southern Nevada during the immediate postwar years. In 1945, Nevada Power reported that customers used 77 million kilowatt-hours of electricity; by 1949 the amount had more than doubled, to nearly 160 million kilowatt-hours.[13] Demand soon outpaced supply, forcing the city and Nevada Power to search for additional sources of power. A major impediment was Nevada Power's fiscally conservative president, Sam Lawson, who took charge in 1946. He opposed expenditures for steam-driven generating plants, believing the cost too high. That policy soon resulted in a power shortage so severe that Nevada Power pushed for a ban on electric space heaters. By 1950, Las Vegas needed more power than the area's allocation of Hoover Dam electricity could supply. Removing Lawson so as to permit the development of steam-generated power was the first step in resolving the energy shortage. Lawson finally retired in 1953 and sold his financial interests in Nevada Power.[14]

Reid Gardner succeeded Lawson as president, marking a symbolic shift in company history. Previous company presidents, including Lawson, had been Las Vegas "pioneers." Gardner moved from California to take control of Nevada Power. It seems ironic that a Californian became company president, given the relationship of California to the remainder of the West.[15] Gardner quickly recognized the dire energy situation and took immediate steps to increase the company's power supply. The company made its first purchases of power generated elsewhere soon after Lawson left the company. More important, under Gardner's leadership, the company embarked on an energetic program to build a series of steam plants to generate electrical power, because no undeveloped hydropower sites existed in the area.

Investment in new plant construction in 1955 exceeded the total amount spent for construction during the company's entire history. Constructing steam plants that burned either oil or natural gas helped the company meet growing demand. The first such plant, Clark Station, went on line in December 1955. During planning for Clark Station, the company canceled its initial order for a thirty-megawatt generator and replaced it with a sixty-megawatt unit.[16] By 1961, three generators operated at Clark Station, with a combined potential output of 190 megawatts of power.[17] Nevada Power's completion of the first Clark unit represented a milestone in Las Vegas's energy history. For the first time in more than forty years, Nevada Power generated part of the power it sold. In subsequent years, Hoover Dam power provided an ever-shrinking percentage of the electricity that Nevada Power marketed. In 1995, exactly forty years after the first Clark generator went on line, hydropower accounted for only 4 percent of the total energy that Nevada Power sold.[18]

During the 1950s, Nevada Power first looked beyond Nevada for energy. In 1949, the Nevada Natural Gas company started to take the necessary steps to build a 114-mile natural gas pipeline between Las Vegas and Topock, Arizona, on the Colorado River. The Topock facility received natural gas via a 433-mile El Paso Natural Gas pipeline that originated in the company's natural gas fields in eastern New Mexico. The pipeline, completed in 1953, furnished gas for all three of the Clark Station generators and for Sunrise Station, completed in the mid 1960s.[19]

By 1960, a complex energy situation had emerged in the Southwest. Los Angeles and southern California received most of Hoover Dam's power. To meet its growing demand for electricity, Las Vegas tapped into the natural gas fields of eastern New Mexico. Arizona received power from Hoover Dam and the Salt River Project. El Paso Gas had been supplying Phoenix and Tucson with natural gas since the 1930s. The region's power system became even more complex in the 1960s, when electrical utilities turned to coal-burning plants. Generators using coal and then nuclear energy raised a new set of issues in the context of the social and environmental concerns of the 1960s and 1970s. Worries over the environmental impact of coal mining, air pollution caused by coal-burning plants, growing concern over water, issues related to Native American control of energy resources, the energy shortage, nuclear waste, and, finally, the ever-expanding Sun Belt population created an enormous set of challenges for electrical utilities and the public.[20]

Las Vegas first received power generated from coal-burning plants in 1965. Construction of Reid Gardner Station in Moapa, fifty miles northeast of the city, marked the beginning of Nevada Power's reliance on coal. The first Reid Gardner plant generated 113 megawatts of power. Three additional plants went on line in 1968, 1976, and 1983; the last generates 250 megawatts of power. Coal for Reid Gardner Station originates in underground mines in Carbon and Emery counties in Utah, 450 miles to the northeast. At the time that the plant started generating electricity, it burned 1,050 tons of coal a day. Nevada Power collected the fly ash, the unburned coal particles, and shipped it to the Nevada Test Site for use in well casing. When the first Reid Gardner unit started operating, the company reported that its three steam-generating plants, Clark, Sunrise, and Reid Gardner produced 85 percent of the company's power. In line with pro-growth ideas of progress in the 1950s and 1960s, a company brochure said the Reid Gardner plant added "a spectacular landmark to historic Moapa Valley."[21]

In the 1960s, Las Vegas was well on its way to becoming the nation's gambling playground. Electricity had become part of the popular image of Las Vegas because of the neon signs adorning the town's hotels and casinos. An *Electric West* article commented that Fremont Street "was the most electrically lighted street in the world." Electricity dominated the development of the region. Las Vegas power users continued to exceed the rest of the nation in per capita electrical consumption by nearly 300 percent, although the cost per kilowatt-hour was half the national average.[22]

Las Vegas was very much an electrical city in the 1960s, and air-conditioning led the way. In 1960, 38.7 percent of all Las Vegas homes had either central air-conditioning or at least one room air conditioner, well above the national level of 12.4 percent. Given the extreme summer heat, the large number of units is not surprising. Electricity was the most widely used type of energy in Las Vegas, where 51 percent of all homes used it for heating, 60.2 percent for water heating, and 74.4 percent for cooking, as against national figures in 1960 of 1.8 percent for heating, 20.4 percent for water heating, and 30.8 percent for cooking. In 1980, 94.6 percent of all Las Vegas residences had air conditioners, as compared to 53.9 percent nationally.[23]

Las Vegas's high per capita use of electricity, coupled with its expanding population and energy-intensive tourist industry, soon forced Nevada Power to seek additional sources of electricity. In June 1967, construction began on Mojave Generating Station, located in the congressionally declared "Fort Mojave Development Area," near the tip of southern Nevada. Unlike in the case of Moapa Station, Nevada Power originally shared ownership of Mojave Station with utilities in Arizona and California. Nevada Power's share has always been 14 percent, the Salt River Project at first owned 10 percent, and the Los Angeles Department of Water and Power controlled 20 percent. Under the original plans, Southern California Edison was to control 56 percent of the output, but by 1980, SCE, which operated the station (and Hoover Dam), owned 86 percent, with Nevada Power retaining ownership of its original 14 percent. The first two generating plants at the station provided 790 megawatt units.[24]

Mojave Station typifies the interdependence of the West and the prominence of Los Angeles and southern California in electrical distribution. The plant burns coal strip-mined at Black Mesa on the Navajo Reservation in northeastern Arizona. Peabody Coal Company of St. Louis originally contracted to provide coal for the station's estimated 35-year life. Whereas Moapa Station is supplied by trains, pipelines deliver coal to Mojave Station. Pumps send a slurry of pulverized coal and water 275 miles to the plant, twice crossing the Colorado River. The slurry requires three thousand acre-feet of water per year from Navajo and Hopi Indian land in Arizona and New Mexico. The original price was $5 per acre-foot, but in 1987, under a new contract, the cost increased to $600 per acre-foot. Energy generation had used so much water by 1990 that the water table had already dropped between 10 and 70 feet. The worst-case scenario is that the water table will drop 175 feet by the year 2032.[25] Mojave Station, located less than a mile from the Colorado River, uses water drawn from the river for cooling purposes.[26]

A second coal-burning station, of which Nevada Power owns 11 percent, is Navajo Station at Page, Arizona, on the Navajo Indian Reservation. Plans for Navajo Station began to take shape in the late 1960s. The plant required Colorado River water, and its planning became entangled in legislation authorizing the Central Arizona Project. The chairman of the House Interior Committee, Colorado Congressman Wayne Aspinall, feared that the Navajo's Colorado River water rights could cut into his state's allocation of the river. Aspinall pressured the Bureau of Reclamation and the Salt River Project to persuade the Navajo to relinquish most of their Colorado River water before he would let the Central Arizona Project legislation out of committee. The Navajo, worried about the loss of potential jobs, signed over nearly 70 percent of their Colorado River water for use at Navajo Station.[27] With the water issue resolved in their favor, the utilities completed construction of the station's first generation plant in 1974.[28]

Electricity generated from coal continued to be the primary energy source for Nevada Power and Las Vegas in the early 1980s. A breakdown by generation type shows that in 1980, electricity from coal accounted for 69 percent of the company's total power, while 27 percent came from natural gas or oil-fired plants, and 4 percent was hydropower.[29] To meet the growing demand, Nevada Power began to contemplate construction of two more coal-fired plants, the Harry Allen plant northeast of Las Vegas and the White Pine Power Project near Ely, Nevada.[30]

Although downsized considerably, early plans for the Harry Allen Plant included four 500-megawatt units, each burning more than 2.2 million tons of coal per year. The White Pine Power Project was to be a 1,500-megawatt coal-fired station.[31] Although not yet built, the White Pine Power Project has already generated intense controversy. Essentially, the Los Angeles Department of Water and Power (DWP) was to build the plant to meet the power needs of southern California, with most of the plant's capacity going to the DWP. Nevada Power would receive part of the energy if it helped finance the project. Part of the controversy in the late 1980s surrounded the giving of federal land to Los Angeles for the plant site and transmission lines. The proposed transmission lines would have crossed the Sunrise Mountain area east of Las Vegas, which some wanted set aside as wilderness. Environmentalists said that they would drop their opposition if the federal government proclaimed 731,000 acres of new wilderness area elsewhere in the state. Senator Chic Hecht (R–Nev.), who tentatively supported the project, opposed tying the plant to wilderness area politics. Lobbyists for Los Angeles claimed that the plant would create 2,200 construction jobs and 550 permanent jobs, an appealing notion to people in Ely, who had long suffered economic doldrums since the region's copper industry bottomed out.[32]

Currently, the White Pine Power Project is in limbo. In recent years, the Los Angeles DWP has lost some interest in the plant, because of new California state regulations regarding power sales. Additionally, concerns over air pollution have dampened ideas for new coal-fired plants. The Los Angeles DWP still holds title to more than 50 percent of the proposed power, and Nevada Power to 25 percent. Both companies continue to contribute money to maintain their rights in the project.[33] Although plans are dormant, the debates surrounding the proposed White Pine Power Project show the continued complexity of the relationship between Los Angeles and the region. Los Angeles depends on the rest of the West for its energy and continues to reach out to meet increased demand. Simultaneously, the rest of the West receives some benefit, such as the potential jobs that new projects create. Los Angeles has not been the only city to need additional electricity.

One word summarizes Las Vegas in the 1990s: growth. The population growth of the city and southern Nevada are nearly unparalleled in the United States. To date, Nevada Power has met the challenge of providing more power to the region. Instead of building more generation stations, the company is buying electricity on the open market. In 1995, of all the energy Nevada Power sold, it bought more power on the open market (45 percent) than it generated at its coal-burning plants (44 percent). The company's total hydroelectric power remained at 4 percent, while natural gas or oil accounted for 7 percent. This is significant, in that most of the power used in Las Vegas comes from out-of-state sources: either coal from Utah or Arizona, natural gas from New Mexico, or energy bought from other utilities. Only the hydropower comes from Nevada itself, and that is a product of the seven-state Colorado River basin where the river's water originates.

The gaming industry is a major customer of Nevada Power. In 1995, it bought 1.9 million megawatt-hours of electricity from Nevada Power, 15.6 percent of the company's total energy sales.[34] Gaming industry power demands have caused headaches for the power company. In 1995, Nevada Power and Mirage Resorts, owner of several major Las Vegas casinos, reached an agreement to lower Mirage's rates by an undisclosed amount. At the time, Mirage's management threatened to construct a 25-megawatt natural-gas-fired generation plant not far from the Las Vegas Strip. Fearing the loss of a large client, Nevada Power agreed to lower Mirage's rates. Concerned that a domino effect might develop, in that other businesses also would try to negotiate lower rates, Nevada Power sought to keep the exact amount of the rate reduction a secret. In July 1995, the State Public Service Commission ruled, however, that the public's right to know required that the parties reveal the terms of the contract. In defending the agreement, Nevada Power argued that loss of Mirage Resorts would result in higher rates for other customers, because a smaller group of customers would pay the utility's fixed costs. Grass-roots organizations such as the National Council of Senior Citizens and the Nevada Senior Coalition objected to the agreement. Representatives for each group argued that the agreement discriminated against residential users and maintained that small users subsidized large users. A Nevada Power spokesperson stated just the opposite and said that large users made lower residential rates possible.[35] Regardless of who subsidizes whom, the salient issue is that electricity remains a vital energy source that is politically, economically, and socially volatile.

Shortly after agreeing on the contract with Mirage Resorts, Nevada Power asked the Public Service Commission for permission to lower rates. The utility said that lower coal and natural gas costs, and cheaper power on the open market, made the reduction possible. When company officials first announced the reduction, they were unsure of who would receive rate cuts, big consumers such as casinos or small residential users. Finally, the utility decided that residential users would receive a reduction amounting to less than 1 percent—for the average consumer, about a dollar a month during the high-use summer months. The reduction for small to medium customers would be about 2 percent, while big users, including casinos, would see their rates cut by 6 percent. The cut for large customers came close to what the power company had offered Mirage Resorts in the once secret agreement.[36]

The State Public Service Commission did not delay in announcing its decision on the legality of the Mirage Resorts–Nevada Power contract. Toward the end of July 1995, the commission unanimously voted to dismiss the contract, citing lack of legal authority to authorize a rate reduction for a single user. Mirage Resorts immediately announced plans to build a generation plant as it had threatened to do and estimated that it would go on line in eighteen months. Company spokesmen said that the Mirage, Treasure Island, and the then unfinished Monte Carlo and Bellagio resorts would use power generated at the plant.[37]

In January 1996, the Clark County Commission approved Mirage Resorts' request to build the power plant. During the hearings, rate and usage information became public. The Mirage and Treasure Island used enough power to electrify 14,000 homes. To compensate for the loss of revenue, the rest of Nevada Power's customers saw their monthly electric bills increase by 36 cents on average. Perhaps in response to the Mirage situation, Nevada Power's president, Charles Lenzie, told members of the state legislature that despite what the public thinks, an enormous amount of cheap and unused power does not exist. Lenzie urged the legislators to move cautiously before deregulating the state's energy market. In the end, Lenzie warned, California may be the big winner. A rate decrease in California may mean an increase in other western states.[38] The history of energy generation and distribution in the Southwest suggests that Lenzie's concern that California might emerge the winner has merit. Historically, California has long been the big winner, as resources have flowed from the periphery to the center. Despite the growth of southern Nevada's electrical demands, they remain small compared to California's. In an unregulated market, the biggest customer may get the most power at the best price.

Mirage Resorts' quest for cheaper electricity shows the importance of electricity to the city's continued growth, and city boosters feature cheap electricity in attempts to attract new residents and businesses. Several business interests finance *Las Vegas Perspectives,* the city's self-proclaimed yearly "report card," which publishes the findings of researchers at the University of Nevada, Las Vegas. In 1994, *Perspectives* reported that an average of 3,000 people moved to Las Vegas each month. In the previous year, forty-three industrial concerns had either been started in or moved to southern Nevada, and all, needless to say, required electrical energy. A hypothetical company could expect to pay $102,000 less for electricity in Las Vegas than in San Francisco, $71,000 less than in Los Angeles, and $73,000 less than in San Diego. Residential customers also could expect cheaper utility rates. Tourism had become a $15 billion industry, and the city had more hotel rooms than any other city in the world.[39] The energy-intensive gaming and hotel industry accounted for 30 percent of the city's jobs.[40]

The concern that Nevada Power's President Lenzie expressed about California being the big winner in a deregulated energy market is surprising. Las Vegas holds a paradoxical position in terms of its relationship with California and the West. California receives enormous amounts of energy from sites throughout the region, plants that it either operates or partially owns. Hoover Dam and Mojave Station are two prime examples. The energy needs, and water needs in the case of Hoover Dam, of southern California were the determining factors in the construction of those projects. Southern California's wealth and influence helped make the projects possible and in doing so contributed to the growth of southern Nevada. The ability of Nevada Power, and by extension Las Vegas, to tap into the region's energy resources makes the city's constant growth possible. The paradox of electricity in Nevada is that the state both imports and exports electrical energy. Power generated at Mojave and Hoover Dam flows out of the state, while Nevada Power buys energy on the open market or generated from Utah coal or New Mexico natural gas. Las Vegas is both a colony and a colonizer in the energy-intensive American West.

Tourism and gaming, two electrically intensive enterprises, are enormously important to southern Nevada's economy. Construction of new casinos continues unabated, and each new casino will require large amounts of power. Comparing an event in the early 1950s to the Mirage controversy of the mid 1990s puts the city's growth and need for energy into perspective. To ease the town's energy shortage in the early 1950s, Nevada Power originally ordered a thirty-megawatt generator, only five megawatts more powerful than the plant Mirage Resorts planned to construct. Las Vegas is a city dependent on energy-intensive businesses for its economic health, and out-of-state sources provide most of that energy. Only the future will tell if this system of generation and distribution will be enough to provide energy for southern Nevada's continued expansion.

NOTES

Epigraph: Charles P. Squires, "The Glory of Light: Half Century of Service" (MS [1955]), 1, University of Nevada, Las Vegas [henceforth cited as UNLV] Special Collections.

1. Las Vegas's postwar growth is examined in Eugene P. Moehring, *Resort City in the Sunbelt: Las Vegas, 1930–1970* (Reno: University of Nevada Press, 1989).

2. Ibid., 31–72, as cited in Michael S. Green, "Understanding Nevada Today: The Southern Shift," *Halcyon* 16 (1994): 182–83.

3. See, e.g., William Robbins, *Colony and Empire: The Capitalist Transformation of the American West* (Lawrence: University Press of Kansas, 1994); Richard White, *It's Your Misfortune and None of My Own: A New History of the American West* (Norman: University of Oklahoma Press, 1991); and Patricia Nelson Limerick, *The Legacy of Conquest: The Unbroken Past of the American West* (New York: Norton, 1987). For the impact of the New Deal and World War II on the West, see Richard Lowitt, *The New Deal and the West* (Bloomington: Indiana University Press, 1984); and Gerald Nash, *The American West Transformed: The Impact of the Second World War* (Bloomington: Indiana University Press, 1985).

4. The early history of electricity in Las Vegas is discussed in Charles P. Squires, "The Glory of Light" and "Nevada Power Company," *Livewire, Diamond Anniversary Edition, Seventy-Five Years of Service, 1906–1981* (Las Vegas, 1981), UNLV Special Collections. "Southern" was dropped from the companies' names in 1961. For the sake of clarity, "Nevada Power Company" is used throughout this essay.

5. In the first decades of the twentieth century, electricity was commonly measured in horsepower instead of kilowatts. One horsepower of electricity equals 746 watts of electricity, or .746 kilowatts. Electrical consumption is normally measured in kilowatt-hours; a kilowatt of power equals 1.34 horsepower. One kilowatt-hour of electricity is required to burn ten one-hundred-watt light bulbs for one hour.

6. *Livewire* (cited n. 4 above), "Power and Telephone Split."

7. Ibid. Edward W. Clark was not related to the William Clark for whom Clark County is named.

8. Federal Power Commission, Bureau of Power, San Francisco Regional Office in Cooperation with Colorado River Commission of Nevada, *Power Market Survey, State of Nevada* (n.p., 1949), 66, UNLV Special Collections. The term "firm power" refers to the amount of energy that is always available from a generator. Generators rarely produce at full capacity. Reduced turbine speed at hydroelectric dams due to low water can influence power production, as can decreased pressure at steam plants. Some energy loss is also inherent in electrical systems.

9. "Nevada's Power Needs and Hoover Dam," *Las Vegas Review-Journal,* October 24, 1976. Although the article does not mention it, Herbert Hoover and Secretary of the Interior Ray Lyman Wilbur had been classmates at Stanford.

Wilbur had also spent part of his youth in Riverside, California, and later in life, he became chancellor of Stanford.

10. Federal Power Commission, Bureau of Power, San Francisco Regional Office in Cooperation with the Colorado River Commission of Nevada, *Power Market Survey, State of Nevada* (n.p., 1949), xiv–xv, UNLV Special Collections.

11. *Livewire* (cited n. 4 above), "Las Vegas a Tourist Attraction" and "Clark #1 Goes On Line."

12. A. Costandina Titus, *Bombs in the Backyard: Atomic Testing and American Politics* (Reno: University of Nevada Press, 1986), 93–94.

13. State of Nevada, *Biennial Report of the Public Service Commission of Nevada, 1949–1950* (Carson City, 1950), 28.

14. Moehring, *Resort City in the Sunbelt,* 218–21; and *Livewire* (cited n. 4 above), brief biography of Lawson.

15. Barbara Chulick, "How Electrified Las Vegas Got Its Juice," *Las Vegas Review-Journal,* November 14, 1982, 7L.

16. *Livewire* (cited n. 4 above), "Las Vegas as a Tourist Attraction."

17. Nevada Department of Energy, *Energy in Nevada: A Summary of Historical and Projected Energy Uses* (Carson City, 1980), table III.6 "Steam Electric Generating Plants," 39, UNLV Special Collections. See also *Livewire* (cited n. 4 above).

18. The Nevada Power Public Affairs office generously provided this information.

19. Moehring, *Resort City in the Sunbelt,* 222–23. El Paso Gas was already supplying Phoenix and Tucson with natural gas, a further indication of the region's interlocking energy system.

20. See, e.g., Martin Melosi, *Coping with Abundance: Energy and Environment in Industrial America* (Philadelphia: Temple University Press, 1985); Marjane Ambler, *Breaking the Iron Bonds: Indian Control of Energy Development* (Lawrence: University Press of Kansas, 1990); and White, *It's Your Misfortune and None of My Own,* esp. pt. 6, "The Modern West."

21. Nevada Power Company, *Reid Gardner Station, Moapa Valley* (n.p., 1965), UNLV Special Collections.

22. *Electrical West,* 129 (1962): 143–61, copy in UNLV Special Collections.

23. U.S. Bureau of the Census, *Census of Housing, 1960,* vol. 1: *States and Small Areas,* pt. 5, *Michigan–New Hampshire* (Washington, D.C., 1963), table 16, "Type of Fuel, and Selected Equipment, for SMSA's, Constituent Counties, Places of 50,000 Inhabitants or More, Urban Balance, Rural Total, and Urbanized Area: 1960," 30–15, and table 13, "Type of Fuel and Selected Equipment, for the United States, inside and outside SMSA's, Urban and Rural, 1960," 1–44; id., *1980 Census of Housing,* vol. 2: *Metropolitan Housing Characteristics, Las Vegas, NV* (Washington, D.C., 1983), table A-7, "Year Structure Built for Owner- and Renter-Occupied Housing Units: 1980," 214–17; and id. *1980 Census of Housing,* vol. 2: *Metropolitan Housing Characteristics, United States Summary* (Washington, D.C., 1984), table A-7, "Year Structure Built for Owner- and Renter-Occupied Housing Units: 1980," 1–7.

24. *Mojave Generation Station Units 1 and 2* (n.p., 1971), 1–4, UNLV

Special Collections; and Nevada Department of Energy, *Energy in Nevada,* 39. SCE continues to operate Hoover Dam and the Mojave Plant.

25. Ambler, *Breaking the Iron Bonds,* 222–23. See also Hal K. Rothman, *Navajo National Monument: A Place and Its People* (Santa Fe: National Park Service, 1991), and "Pokey's Paradox" in *Second Opening of the American West,* ed. id. (Tucson: University of Arizona Press, 1997).

26. *Mojave Generation Station Units 1 and 2,* 4.

27. Ambler, *Breaking the Iron Bonds,* 174, 222. The Navajo had controlled 50,000 acre-feet of water before the deal.

28. Nevada Department of Energy, *Energy in Nevada,* 39.

29. *Livewire* (cited n. 4 above), "Challenges in the 1970s."

30. Ibid. When it finally went on line, the Harry Allen plant had been scaled back to a 72-megawatt oil and natural gas burning plant (Nevada Power, Public Affairs Office).

31. Nevada Department of Energy, *Energy in Nevada,* 43–44.

32. *Las Vegas Review-Journal,* August 13, 1988.

33. Information provided by Nevada Power and the White Pine Power Project county office, Ely, Nevada.

34. In 1995, Nevada Power sold a total of 12,190,353 megawatt-hours of electricity (Nevada Power Public Affairs Office).

35. *Las Vegas Review-Journal,* July 7 and 21, 1995.

36. Ibid, July 7, 1995.

37. Ibid., July 21, 1995.

38. Ibid., January 18 and February 21, 1996. And see ibid., May 12, 1996, for more on energy deregulation.

39. *Las Vegas Perspective* (n.p., 1994), 1, 30, 32.

40. The Greater Las Vegas Chamber, *Here Is Las Vegas* (Las Vegas, 1995), 11.

JON CHRISTENSEN

Build It and the Water Will Come

At the end of the twentieth century, Las Vegas faced a water crisis: the city would not be able to continue to grow into the new millennium on its existing water supply. By the late 1980s, planners at the Las Vegas Valley Water District could see that even with the most conservative estimates of growth rates and the most optimistic projections for conservation, Las Vegas would run out of water soon after the turn of the century. Estimates as to exactly how far the water supply could be stretched differed, depending on the variables planners used in their computer models, but a few things were certain. Las Vegas was growing at a steady pace, adding roughly 5,000 new residents each month, year after year, putting it among the fastest-growing areas in the country. The aquifer underlying the Las Vegas Valley was already overtapped.

The ground under parts of the city was slowly subsiding. And the city was reaching the limits of Nevada's allocation of Colorado River water, which was negotiated in the 1920s, when fewer than 5,000 people lived in Las Vegas. With the 1990s looming and the population of the greater Las Vegas metropolitan area quickly approaching 1 million, with no sign of slowing, Patricia Mulroy, the hard-driving general manager of the Las Vegas Valley Water District, knew something had to be done.

Western water has attracted a lot of practical visionaries, like William Mulholland, who brought water to Los Angeles, and Floyd Dominy, who engineered the mighty dams of the Colorado River. These were the men who imagined and built the plumbing of the West. Patricia Mulroy was a practical visionary for the postreclamation era. She saw where reform of western water was headed: away from new dams and water-importation projects and toward more efficient management of rivers and ecosystems. And she knew what she needed to get from this change: more water for Las Vegas. That may sound paradoxical. Her genius lay in realizing that it was not. Mulroy was reviled at times as the "Water Witch of the West" because of her obstinate advocacy on behalf of a city that still suffered from a sinful image, especially when people wanted to thwart its objectives. But Mulroy not only managed to barge her way into the old boys club that controlled water in the West, known affectionately as "water buffaloes," she also went on to play out a pivotal transitional story of water in the West.

In 1989, Mulroy proposed one of the biggest urban water grabs in western history—claiming all the available underground water in almost half of Nevada—only to turn around and use it as a bargaining chip for her real goal: more water from the Colorado River. She stuck her foot in the sluice gates of the Colorado River by claiming water in the Virgin River, and then she enlarged that opening with one of the first water banking deals on the Colorado River. She persuaded voters to build a new $2 billion pipeline to the river. By the turn of the century, Mulroy had staked the future of Las Vegas on reform of the Colorado River, the key lifeline of the American West. Mulroy's success occurred in the context of a changing of the guard in western water, an era that saw the end of dam building proclaimed by the Bureau of Reclamation and the rise of political and financial deals to move water within the West's existing infrastructure, rather than build massive new dams and water projects. Mulroy's strategy was essentially to parlay money, which Las Vegas had in great supply during the greatest gaming boom in the history of the world, into water, which has always been in short supply in the Mojave Desert. But pulling this off would require astute political organizing both internally, within Las Vegas and Nevada, and externally, with federal agencies and other states on the Colorado River.

Early in the 1990s, Mulroy negotiated mergers with several competing water districts to form the Southern Nevada Water Authority and organized politically to consolidate southern Nevada's power on the state's Colorado River Commission. As Las Vegas boomed, the power of her agency grew. By the end of the 1990s, the water agency served nearly 1.6 million people, more than two-thirds of the state's population, and proved itself a regional powerhouse. Mulroy also took her crusade to Washington, D.C., as the first chairman of the Western Urban Water Coalition, a new lobbying group for cities seeking a greater share of water in the West. Mulroy put Las Vegas in the center of the action of reforms changing the way water is managed in the West. That this story started with a water grab more reminiscent of the Old West than the vaunted New West is one of the twists that shows what a jam Las Vegas was in and how savvy Mulroy was in playing her cards to get out of it.

In the dusty outback of Nevada, there is little love lost for Las Vegas. Although it is the economic engine of the state, the rest of Nevada looks down on the city. But they never turn their backs on it. The rural cow counties of Nevada suspect that Las Vegas is just out for itself. All the proof they needed came at the end of 1989 when the Las Vegas Valley Water District filed claims on every drop of available ground water in a 20,000 square mile area, covering most of the southern half of the state. The district claimed 805,000 acre-feet of ground water in twenty-six valleys as far as 250 miles north of the city, as well as the Virgin River, a tributary of the Colorado River that flows through the southeastern corner of Nevada. Mulroy announced that rural Nevada could not stand in the way of the state's economic engine. "Nobody wants to wipe out rural Nevada," she said. "But they have a lot more water than they need. It's there. It should be available to use elsewhere. You can't take a community as thriving as Las Vegas and put a stop sign out there. The train will run right over you."

In rural Nevada, the battle cry became "Remember the Owens Valley!"—the West's first and best-known raid on rural water by a booming metropolis. Once a fertile home to orchards, farms, and ranches just east of the Sierra Nevada, Owens Valley was virtually dried up by Los Angeles. The bitter conflict broke out in pipeline bombings in the 1920s and again in the 1970s, when ground water pumping peaked in Owens Valley. Owens Valley veterans advised rural Nevada neighbors on how not to lose their water to an ever more thirsty city. County officials in Nevada said they would fight Las Vegas with every legal weapon at their disposal. Some residents spoke cryptically about vigilante groups that would not hesitate to blow up pipelines if Las Vegas dared to "steal our water." Steve Bradhurst, a consultant hired to co-ordinate opposition to the water grab, said Las Vegas was "foreclosing" on the future of rural Nevada by tying up all the available water rights in four huge counties. "We're fighting for our future," said Floyd Lamb, a rancher and former state senator from Alamo, a small town 100 miles north of Las Vegas in the scenic Pahranagat Valley. "Nothing infuriates people like messing with their water. These ranchers get worked up, they don't even take their hats off. It's going to get bloody," Lamb predicted.[1]

The plan seemed a bold blast from the past. Its scale—over 1,000 miles of pipeline—would dwarf the Owens Valley pipeline to Los Angeles. In the early 1990s, the fight seemed likely to become a classic Western water war. The district spent millions of dollars on hydrologic and engineering studies to give its gambit some credibility. But within just five years, Mulroy was saying the grandiose water importation project was the "singularly most stupid idea anyone's ever had."[2]

David Donnelly, the chief engineer for the water authority, was openly disdainful of the project, which he had helped design. "Frankly, it doesn't make any sense," he said. "We don't want to build any more dams, reservoirs, or construction projects. We want to do things that cost less and that are politically, socially and environmentally acceptable."[3] Suddenly, it seemed as though Las Vegas had discovered water in the New West. Mulroy offered to abandon the controversial quest to pipe underground water from rural Nevada, but only if Las Vegas could get more water from the Colorado River. Mulroy laid out her new strategy at hearings before the Nevada state water engineer on the Southern Nevada Water Authority's applications for water from the Virgin River, which originates in southwestern Utah, flows through Zion National Park, and then through the northwestern corner of Arizona and into Nevada, where it joins the Colorado River in Lake Mead. Because it flows through largely barren red rock canyons, the Virgin River is not fully appropriated like most western rivers. And it is not part of the Colorado River Compact or any other interstate agreement. Nevada claimed that the water that reached Nevada was therefore up for grabs by whoever could first develop it.

On paper, the agency's development plans called for building a dam and reservoir on the river and a pipeline to Las Vegas. But it turned out that the Southern Nevada Water Authority did not really want to build the dam and pipeline. The agency would rather let the river flow into Lake Mead and take the water from there, Mulroy said. Environmentalists who opposed the damage and disruption the dam, reservoir, and pipeline would cause were blindsided. They also favored letting the water flow into Lake Mead. In one bold move, Mulroy thus won over many opponents and sidelined others. She persuaded towns along the Virgin River in Nevada to drop their protests against the Las Vegas applications by cutting them in on the water and offering them a seat on the Southern Nevada Water Authority. She got the Interior Department to drop protests by the U.S. Fish and Wildlife Service, Bureau of Land Management, and National Parks Service by promising that the agency would comply with all required federal studies and permits. And the remaining opponents of the Las Vegas ground water importation plan—the rural counties and environmentalists—supported what the district wanted: more water from the Colorado River so that the city would not have to drain rural Nevada.

By the mid 1990s, Mulroy had consolidated her southern Nevada power base, placated most of her opponents in the state, and found a common agenda with other urban centers and the Bureau of Reclamation. But, she added, by way of reminding anyone who would listen of the millennial stakes in the game, the new water regime had to be ready by the year 2000. This high-stakes game required bold moves, which naturally raised the question of whether the rural water grab was essentially a bluff. Mulroy practically acknowledged as much. "I don't think we would have gotten attention to southern Nevada's needs without the outpouring of concerns on those applications," she said. If Nevada could add "200,000 to 250,000 acre-feet" to the state's current annual allocation of 300,000 acre-feet from the Colorado River, she would recommend dropping the agency's claims to rural Nevada water. In the meantime, she would negotiate with rural counties to allow them to develop the water if they needed it. Mulroy said the water needed to supply the next century of growth in southern Nevada was "not a major amount," given the allocations to other states on the Colorado River. "But to get there," she acknowledged, would require "major rethinking" up and down the river. That, however, would require loosening the "law of the river" to allow "wheeling" water through Lake Mead. That could ultimately require changes in the "law of the river," an interstate compact that was ratified by Congress in 1922 and has governed the Colorado River ever since. And that was the prize that Las Vegas was playing for. "The Virgin is the linchpin to the rest of the Colorado River," said Mulroy. Getting more water through Lake Mead, including water from the Virgin River, would require negotiations with Utah and Arizona, and agreement from other states, especially California, which holds priority rights on the lower Colorado by virtue of a 1963 Supreme Court ruling.[4]

The 1922 Colorado River Compact—a major strand in the web of interstate compacts, legislation, regulations, and court rulings collectively known as the "law of the river"—allots 7.5 million acre-feet of water annually to the upper-basin states of Colorado, Wyoming, Utah, and New Mexico, and 7.5 million to the lower basin states of Nevada, Arizona, and California. Of that, California gets 4.4 million acre-feet, Arizona gets 2.85 million acre-feet, and Nevada 300,000 acre-feet. In California and Arizona, farms use most of that water, but over time more and more of it is being transferred to urban and suburban uses. In contrast, southern Nevada, an overwhelmingly urban area, has essentially no agriculture around it to buy and then dry up. Mulroy delighted in pointing out that one large hotel in Las Vegas employs more people than all the farms and ranches in Nevada. The Southern Nevada Water Authority already controlled Nevada's share of Colorado River water. The "law of the river" presents a formidable obstacle to Mulroy's quest—an obstacle rooted in the traditional West, much like the laws and traditions governing mining, logging, and grazing. The 1922 Colorado River Compact was designed to protect the other six compact states from the economic power of California. The theory was that states like Colorado and Wyoming and Arizona needed time to develop their economies and put their Colorado River water to use. If money and population had been the only measure, all the Colorado River water would have immediately flowed to southern California, rather than remaining in Wyoming and Utah and Arizona to raise alfalfa and cotton. Not much has changed since 1922. From the perspective of a Utah or New Mexico or Wyoming, still awaiting further urbanization, watching their compact water flow away from marginal farms and toward buyers in Las Vegas is no different than watching it flow toward buyers in Los Angeles. Officials in those states were reluctant, however, to let Las Vegas push too far too fast.

Mulroy did not take on the upper basin states of Colorado, Wyoming, Utah, and New Mexico. Her goal was to change how the lower basin states—California, Nevada, and Arizona—apportion water among themselves. Until Arizona, Nevada, and California had their house in order, she said, it did not make sense to talk to the upper basin states about water transfers. In an era when irrigation districts across the West were having trouble paying for their water, Las Vegas had what they needed: cash. And Mulroy found that allies in high places shared her vision of a changing region that needed to change some of the rules of water.

Before he became secretary of interior, Bruce Babbitt had advised the rural Nevada counties fighting the Las Vegas ground water importation plan. Once in office, Babbitt became a self-described "advocate" for southern Nevada. "I'm trying to find a way for Nevada to get an increased share of Colorado River water," he announced. "Las Vegas needs an expanded water supply from the Colorado River." Betsy Reike, the assistant secretary of interior for the Bureau of Reclamation, explained plans for reform to an annual gathering of high-powered water managers and attorneys at the University of Colorado's Natural Resources Law Center. "The Colorado River has been locked up in the chains created by the law of the river," Reike said. "It is time to figuratively melt those chains." The Department of Interior, which manages most of the river, would "patiently leverage change" on the Colorado River, starting in the lower basin, Reike said.[5] That was just what Mulroy, who was sitting in the audience, wanted to hear. The Bureau of Reclamation was drafting rules and regulations to provide for voluntary transfers of water between states on the lower Colorado River. "This is something that does not require fundamental changes in the law of the river or tampering with the basic apportionments among and between states," said Ed Osann, an assistant to the Bureau of Reclamation's director, Dan Beard. But it would be "a big step forward in encouraging the marketing of water in the lower Colorado."[6] The Southern Nevada Water Authority had already opened a small crack in the Colorado River with a three-way deal Mulroy had put together with the Metropolitan Water District in southern California and the Arizona Water Conservation District. The California and Nevada urban water districts agreed to pay the financially troubled Arizona irrigation district, which operates the Central Arizona Project, to store up to 100,000 acre-feet of Colorado River water in depleted groundwater aquifers under farms served by the aqueduct. Essentially, the cities paid the farmers not to pump groundwater and instead store that water for future use. During droughts, the cities could take that amount of water from Arizona's allocation on the Colorado River. "It's a first chip away at water marketing" on the Colorado River, said Donnelly, chief engineer of the Las Vegas water agency. "It's significant and precedent setting that both California and Nevada now have water stored in Arizona."[7]

Las Vegas hoped to use its growing muscle to enlarge that crack and nearly double its supply from the Colorado River. That would require negotiations with the other Colorado River states. The Southern Nevada Water Authority created computer models that showed that the Colorado River could provide a more reliable long-term supply, through water banking and leasing, even if Nevada cannot increase its permanent allocation from the river by amending the compact. They showed that Las Vegas could get by with leasing water from farmers in Arizona well into the next century.

However, to bring more water from the river, Las Vegas would need a bigger pipeline from Lake Mead. The water agency produced plans for a 12-foot-diameter pipeline that would double the city's capacity to suck water from Lake Mead and pump it four miles uphill to an expanded drinking-water treatment plant. The new pipeline was designed to bring more water from the Colorado River immediately to meet peak demand and as a backup for the existing pipeline. It would also be big enough to carry water banked or leased in the future. The total cost was more than $2 billion—roughly the same as projects for the rural ground-water importation project. When Mulroy had agreed to lay off the rural water grab, environmentalists had agreed not to challenge the pipeline. The issue came to a head when the Southern Nevada Water Authority asked the Nevada Legislature to put a measure on the ballot to raise the local sales tax by a quarter of a cent to pay for the expansion. Mulroy had played her cards so well that the only opposition came from a wild card group of senior citizens.

Larry Paulson, a retired biology professor with the University of Nevada, Las Vegas, and Ken Mahal, the president of the Nevada Seniors Coalition, a group of about three hundred, attacked the Southern Nevada Water Authority's plans to provide water for future growth from a populist angle. The coalition wanted to defeat the measure and instead raise taxes on gambling and new development. "The gaming industry and developers have reaped the lion's share of the benefits of growth," said Mahal, "while they have dumped the costs and negatives of growth on the general population. The gambling moguls and developers are being subsidized. And who pays? Poor people, families, people on fixed incomes."[8]

Paulson and Mahal saw themselves as Davids up against a nefarious web of Goliath developers, politicians, agencies, and even some go-along-to-get-along environmentalists involved in a conspiracy that made the plot of the movie *Chinatown* seem simple. Paulson said that the pipeline was bigger than it needed to be, and that the water was destined to benefit fat-cat developers like Summa, the corporation once owned by Howard Hughes, and the Arizona-based developer Del Webb, which were building sprawling suburbs on the fringes of the Las Vegas Valley. When the Interior Department released water from Glen Canyon Dam to create floods in the Grand Canyon to restore beach habitat, Paulson called it an ecological "masquerade" for a water grab that moved 700,000 acre-feet of water from the upper basin to the lower basin states on the Colorado River.[9]

But the loudest alarm that Paulson and Mahal sounded was their claim that Southern Nevada Water Authority was ignoring a potential public health disaster by putting a "second straw" into Lake Mead just six miles downstream from the city's sewage treatment plant. Paulson said the city's existing pipeline already sucked up polluted water from a treatment plant that discharges effluent into the lake at Las Vegas Wash, which drains the Las Vegas Valley. He charged that the effluent plume flowed directly toward the city's intake pipes, 150 feet below the surface of Lake Mead, especially in late winter and early spring, when there is less mixing in the reservoir, which moves like a sluggish river in slow motion. Paulson said that people had already died from drinking the water and that the second pipeline would increase the danger. In fact, in 1994, thirty-seven people infected with HIV had died in Las Vegas from cryptosporidiosis, an infection produced by *Cryptosporidium parvum*, a microscopic one-celled protozoan, commonly called "crypto," that causes diarrhea, fever, and vomiting. Healthy individuals are able to fight off infections, but scientists said that ingesting just one crypto spore could kill a person with AIDS.[10] An investigation by the Centers for Disease Control concluded that the most likely source of crypto in Las Vegas was tap water, where it was probably present in such minute amounts that it could not be detected.[11] "We monitor for crypto and we've never detected it in our water," said David Donnelly, the water agency engineer. Paulson and Mahal were "trying to create public outcry because our intake is downstream some six miles" from the sewage treatment plant outflow in Las Vegas Wash. "But that's the case throughout the United States. On the Mississippi, one city discharges and another takes it in. Whatever river system you're on, you always monitor it. Lake Mead is one of the most pristine systems in the United States. We've never detected any problems with this plume," Donnelly said.[12] Mahal and Paulson mounted a public relations campaign that inundated public officials and the media with statements, protests, and electronic news. And they threatened to expand the campaign. "If this community doesn't want to shape up, we're going to broadcast through the world what you should expect when you come here," said Mahal. "We have 30 to 40 million visitors from all over the planet. They bring bacteria from all over the planet. And we're dumping this in Lake Mead in the same back bay where we pump water." For Mahal, an architect who had moved to Las Vegas when it was "a fun quirky town 15 years ago," it was a battle against the "gambling hall operators and developers" who are "destroying the community" and "giving nothing back."[13] For Paulson, it was "a vindication for my life and career."[14] Paulson had studied Lake Mead limnology as a field biologist for twenty years before being asked to teach biology to pre-med students at UNLV. He quit instead to campaign against the water agency's plans.

Ultimately, their campaign was quixotic. Even Howard Hughes had found it impossible to prevent Lake Mead water from flowing out of Las Vegas taps. In 1968, when he was holed up on the thirteenth floor of the Desert Inn, Hughes urged Governor Paul Laxalt to kill the project that put the first Las Vegas straw in Lake Mead. "If it becomes known that our new water system is nothing but a closed circuit loop, leading in and then out of a cesspool," Hughes wrote, "our [competitors] will start a word of mouth and publicity campaign that will murder us."[15] But bad publicity has never fazed Las Vegas for long. In the end, Paulson and Mahal managed to raise a significant stink, but they were unsuccessful in slowing the Las Vegas water machine. During the campaign, Mulroy worried publicly that if opponents kept the new pipeline from being built, the Las Vegas Valley would need to ration water to existing homes and casinos and to shut down new construction by 1999. That encouraged Paulson and Mahal. Their ultimate goal was to stop growth, a goal many Las Vegans shared, at least in spirit. Their immediate goal, however, was to stop the agency from building the new pipeline, designed to bring more water from the Colorado River to meet peak demand and as a backup for the existing pipeline. And in that they were up against the political power structure of the entire state of Nevada, which was lined up solidly behind the Southern Nevada Water Authority. Paulson and Mahal joined a chorus of people who publicly voiced concerns about growth in the Las Vegas Valley over the course of the 1990s, from local environmentalists to city planners, Mayor Jan Jones, and even Steve Wynn. The casino mogul told the Chamber of Commerce that Las Vegas was in danger of losing its allure because of unregulated growth. But no one else called for stopping the new pipeline, which was a key to solving the city's long-term need for water from the Colorado River. In November 1998, the voters overwhelmingly approved the tax increase to pay for it.

By the turn of the century, Las Vegas had a new pipeline, the expanded capacity, and water banking and leasing plans that tied the future of Las Vegas to the Colorado River. Many of the financial and political details of water deals with neighboring states on the river remained to be worked out, but Mulroy seemed to be on a winning streak. She had taken Las Vegas from being a minor pariah to being a major player on the river. She spoke optimistically of creating a community of common interests among the states that share the Colorado River. "Our future is part of their future," she asserted.[16]

Although Las Vegas was still seen as an urban cancer in some circles, Mulroy had effectively averted the crisis. Las Vegas could continue to build.

The water would come.

NOTES

1. Jon Christensen, "Troubled Waters: Rural Counties Map Plan to Dash Las Vegas' Pipe Dream," *Nevadan: The Sunday Magazine of the Las Vegas Review-Journal,* April 15, 1990.

2. Jon Christensen, "Las Vegas Wheels and Deals for Colorado Water," *High Country News,* February 21, 1994.

3. Ibid.

4. *Arizona v. California,* 373 U.S. 546 (1963).

5. Christensen, "Las Vegas Wheels and Deals."

6. Ibid.

7. Ibid.

8. Jon Christensen, "Las Vegas May Shoot Craps with Its Water," *High Country News,* June 23, 1997.

9. Ibid.

10. Peggy A. Roefer, J. T. Monscvitz, and David J. Rexing, "The Las Vegas Cryptosporidiosis Outbreak," *Journal AWWA,* September 1996, 97.

11. Susan Goldstein, M.D., "An Outbreak of Cryptosporidiosis in Clark County, Nevada: Summary of Investigation," Centers for Disease Control and Prevention, National Center for Infectious Diseases, Division of Parasitic Diseases, Epi-aid #94–45–1.

12. Christensen, "Las Vegas May Shoot Craps with Its Water."

13. Ibid.

14. Ibid.

15. Donald L. Bartlett and James B. Steele, *Empire: The Life, Legend, and Madness of Howard Hughes* (New York: Norton, 1979), n. 306.

16. Jon Christensen, "Learning from Las Vegas," *High Country News,* April 3, 1995.

ROBERT E. PARKER

The Social Costs of Rapid Urbanization in Southern Nevada

etween 1950 and 1990, Nevada's population grew by 651 percent, more rapidly than that of any other state, easily outdistancing Arizona's gain of 389 percent during the same time.[1] The fastest-growing state throughout the 1980s, Nevada shows no signs of slowing its rapid expansion. Most of this growth occurred in southern Nevada, where Las Vegas and its surrounding communities surpassed 1.3 million residents by 2000. Key actors in the city and the majority of ordinary citizens have heartily embraced the unbridled expansion of recent years. While many of those in the "urban growth coalition," particularly those in the hotel/gaming/recreation sector, have had cause to celebrate, the area's rapid growth has left a trail of serious social costs that are borne by local residents.

LOCAL AND NATIONAL BOOSTERISM

In part, Nevada's population explosion can be traced to the mostly favorable treatment the state has received in the electronic and print media, particularly from popular and business periodicals. For example, in 1995, *Money* ranked Las Vegas as the ninth-best city in the United States in which to live, up from forty-third in 1994, and the fifth-best community among mid-sized cities, and in November 1998, *Fortune* listed Las Vegas as the best place in the country to have any kind of business.[2]

Other national publications have couched the area's rapid growth in glowing terms. In 1994, *Time* magazine made Las Vegas, "The New All-American City," its cover story, and *U.S. News and World Report* featured the city prominently.[3] The 1995 edition of *Retirement Places Rated* selected Las Vegas as the nation's most desirable retirement destination. *Your Money* and *New Choices* magazines have also listed Las Vegas as among the best retirement locations.[4] Earlier in the decade, *U.S. News and World Report* carried two highly favorable articles on the University of Nevada, Las Vegas, calling it "one of the top up-and-coming universities in the West."

Virtually without exception, these media accolades bombarding the national consciousness have focused on the "good business climate" and have failed to consider quality-of-life factors. The following provides a brief sketch of the concept of "local growth coalitions" and identifies key pro-growth actors in Las Vegas.

THE LOCAL GROWTH COALITION

John Mollenkopf and Harvey Molotch have used the term "local growth coalitions" to describe business elites who actively promote development at the local level.[5] Molotch suggests that virtually every U.S. city is dominated by a "small, parochial elite whose members have business or professional interests that are linked to local development and growth."[6] Typically, such coalitions consist of industrialists, bankers, and developers and are supported by real estate agents, the legal establishment, and the news media.

Business leaders are at the heart of most local growth coalitions. They and allied political leaders consistently espouse a pro-growth, pro-development ideology. Urbanists like William Angel have underscored the importance of local "boosterism" in generating corporate development in cities.[7] Cities of all sizes are aggressively advertised by their local growth coalitions as being "business-friendly." Roughly 15,000 cities, towns, counties, states, and other political jurisdictions have marketed themselves nationally. Some organizations, such as the Urban Land Institute, a developers' think tank, are formal and nationally based. Specific examples of organized local growth coalitions include the Dallas Citizens Council, the Greater Philadelphia Movement, and Civic Progress in St. Louis. In many cities, the local growth coalition is anchored in the chamber of commerce, and it often represents the city's private-public partnership, as with the Houston Economic Development Commission. In still other cities, the growth coalition is characterized by a looser structure, surrounded by few formal organizations.

Todd Swanstrom distinguishes between two types of local growth coalitions.[8] In some cities, "conservative" growth officials place city planning squarely within the private domain and discount the social welfare needs of citizens. In contrast, other urban political leaders practice "liberal" growth politics where social service programs are provided along with private economic development efforts. In Sunbelt cities, such as Miami, Houston, Phoenix, and Las Vegas, the tendency has been for the conservative variant to emerge. In these cities, few local politicians are independent of business linkages.

Molotch argues that the organized effort to generate city growth is the focus of local government as a political force. Local politicians, on behalf of private interests, work hard to provide public support for business-oriented growth, including financial assistance for material infrastructure, such as water, sewer, and utility facilities. Regardless of the composition of the coalition, the general objective of these groups is to transform cities into "growth machines" where private owners can maximize profits on industrial and real estate investments.[9]

In the southern Nevada area, the local urban growth coalition has popularized the gospel of unregulated urban growth. Businesses perceive growth as profitable, most citizens and members of organized labor believe growth creates more and better jobs, and most of the local press sees benefits in terms of enhanced advertising revenues. Consider this excerpt from a recent "news" article in the city's leading circulation newspaper:

> Las Vegas' sizzling economy, bolstered by a strong gaming industry, sustained population growth and business development, was the envy of the nation in 1995. The metro area's job growth, low taxes, booming tourism market and growing retirement base made headlines in a slew of national media reports. When all the numbers are gathered for 1995, Las Vegas will show strong growth in employment, gaming revenue, business sales, home sales and population.[10]

Beyond the local media, the Nevada Resort Association, a powerful group of thirty-two hotel-casino operators, local chambers of commerce, the Nevada Development Authority, the Las Vegas Visitors and Convention Center, the airline industry, and allied "pro-growth" public officials are integral to the local growth coalition in southern Nevada.

Most in the coalition engage in unrestrained boosterism, hailing the good business climate and defending growth at all costs. In contrast, few members engage the local citizenry in a dialogue about managing or controlling growth in the rapidly sprawling region. Though the number is growing, there are few grassroots organizations actively resisting growth. One exception is Citizen Alert, an environmental and anti-nuclear group founded in 1975, which claims over 7,000 members in Nevada. The group has drawn attention to the deteriorating physical environment in southern Nevada and the importance of conservation. Its former local spokesman says that while Citizen Alert does not have a formal policy on urban expansion, there is a "sentiment within the group to have what you'd call 'managed growth.' "[11]

Bob Miller, Nevada's former governor, also played an active role in promoting the development of the Vegas Valley, traveling nationwide to tout the advantages of corporate relocations in the state. Miller stressed the job creation record of southern Nevada and the "good business climate" companies can anticipate upon relocation. In Las Vegas, there is no dearth of development proponents. Don Schlesinger was one exception. The Democrat won a seat on the Clark County Commission in the early 1990s by running on a "managed, controlled" growth campaign. But Schlesinger was largely alone. His victory was, by all accounts, an upset. Schlesinger's opponent contended that restricting growth would harm the economy, and that it was essential for southern Nevada to "keep on with the pro-growth ideas." Ultimately, the popularity of the pro-growth sentiment led to the defeat of Commissioner Schlesinger and his advocacy of managed growth in the 1994 primary elections. To summarize, the southern Nevada region has undergone a rapid period of demographic and economic expansion. But these changes did not occur naturally. Instead, the growth was initiated and shaped by pivotal economic actors, such as real estate developers and resort operators who were starting and expanding facilities at an unprecedented pace, creating a demand for a large, mainly unskilled low-wage workforce. The growth has been fueled by local boosters and a considerable amount of free publicity in the national media. But this confluence of factors has led to social costs that threaten to destroy the quality of life to which the multitudes of migrants now resident in the region were initially drawn.

SOCIAL COSTS: THE BOOM'S UNDERSIDE

The unreflective pro-growth position described above glosses over serious social problems directly associated with rapid urbanization. Many urban problems associated with rapid development affect everyone, such as air pollution, while others, such as the lack of affordable housing and strained public facilities, are experienced disproportionately by specific segments of the community, especially low-income and minority groups.

AIR POLLUTION

The contamination of Southern Nevada's air is a severe problem that threatens the health of the region's inhabitants. It is an "externality" amplified by an overreliance on automobiles, a culturally based wariness of government, and the absence of strict zoning regulations. According to a 1990 report by the Environmental Protection Agency (EPA), Las Vegas and New York City tied for fifth among the nation's metropolitan areas with the highest carbon monoxide pollution levels. It marked the fourth consecutive year that Las Vegas ranked no better than sixth in carbon monoxide emissions, the main component in the region's smog. A 1996 EPA report shows Las Vegas still in fifth place, as well as having the fifth-highest levels of dust particles among all U.S. cities.[12] And the Natural Resources Defense Council, a nonprofit environmental group, found that Las Vegas was tied for eighth among 238 U.S. metro areas in the rate of people who die prematurely from illnesses linked to air pollution.[13]

Unhealthy air is not a new phenomenon in southern Nevada, but the problem has become increasingly acute with the heavy population influx. In the early 1990s, the number of days in which the valley experienced unhealthy air pollution levels, as measured by the Pollution Standard Index, was growing by one-third annually. Carbon monoxide is emitted directly from vehicle tailpipes and poses a significant public health threat. Persons with chronic respiratory disease, the elderly, and victims of anemia are particularly at risk.

Michael Naylor, director of Clark County's Air Pollution Control Division, maintains that the region's continued high pollution ranking stems from southern Nevada's rapid growth and the influx of more vehicles.[14] Many residents complain of a type of air pollution known as "brown haze." Until recently, it mainly appeared during winter months, but it has increasingly become a year-round phenomenon. Brown haze is aesthetically odious and has detrimental health consequences. Cases of throat irritation and sinus problems are common on mornings when brown haze is visible. While automobile emissions contribute to this phenomenon, other factors include wood-burning fireplaces, stagnant air patterns in winter, and new construction. The Health District attempts to minimize automobile-caused pollution through a "clean fuels" oxygenated fuel program. Of the remaining contributors to air pollution, new construction and wood-burning fireplaces are the most important.

So far, only piecemeal reforms, which at best may stabilize the valley's air pollution problem, have been attempted. To reduce pollution significantly and keep it at acceptable levels would require more drastic political and economic measures, and the leaders of this free-enterprise Sunbelt boomtown have so far lacked the political courage to deliver that message.

Developers, who have generally benefited from the city's expansion, have also directly contributed to the air pollution problem. Many are heavily invested in commercial and residential real estate. In 1994, Clark County issued more than 44,000 residential building permits and 2,725 commercial permits to developers. Unmistakably, this intensive pace of development has contributed to southern Nevada's air pollution problem. The unrelenting construction, coupled with high winds, creates conditions that literally make Las Vegas air unsafe to breathe. On bad air days, residents are advised to stay inside, particularly if they belong to a high-risk group. Exacerbating the construction-generated air pollution problem are the unwillingness of developers to abide by air pollution regulations and the underenforcement of existing standards. According to Naylor, on any given day, there may be fifty complaints about dust and only one available enforcement officer. Many construction contractors view pollution citations as a business expense. Naylor suggests that "on high wind days, contractors should just shut their projects down, but they usually don't until an officer comes by."[15] In mid 1999, an air-quality report said that construction-site dust pollution was on the rise in the Las Vegas Valley.[16] In short, the current system of controlling pollution from construction sites is ineffectual. Whatever the ultimate cause, Las Vegans increasingly confront health risks from breathing growth-generated polluted air.

Indeed, the carbon monoxide problem has reached a sufficiently severe level that local control over air pollution efforts will now be monitored much more closely by EPA officials. During the first three weeks of 1996, Clark County exceeded the number of allowable days a city can violate the established carbon monoxide level for the entire year. The Las Vegas Valley had also tallied a high number of bad air days, and the EPA informed local officials that the agency would declare Clark County a "serious nonattainment area." And, indeed, in 1997, the county moved from a "moderate nonattainment" to a serious nonattainment designation by the EPA.[17] Independent studies suggest that southern Nevada's air quality problems continue to worsen. A report released by the U.S. Public Interest Research Group (PIRG) stated that the Las Vegas Valley violated new standards for ozone (a pollutant formed when sunlight mixes with car and truck exhausts) thirty-three times at twelve monitoring stations in the summer of 1998.[18] In late 2000, after a clean-air plan was rejected by the EPA in 1999, Clark County again submitted a plan to federal officials. Hanging in the balance are the loss of highway funds and the authority of Clark County to write its own air quality plan.[19]

Beyond the profound health implications, the worsening haze precludes an uninterrupted view of the mountainous natural beauty that surrounds the Las Vegas Valley. Between the aesthetic and health costs, air pollution is clearly eroding the very quality of life that initially attracted many to the region.

AUTO-DEPENDENCY IN LAS VEGAS

Several factors are responsible for the social costs surrounding southern Nevada's transit system. Most fundamentally, Las Vegans are heavily auto-dependent. Private taxis and a limited bus system are the only alternatives to private automobiles. A significant increase in the number of cars on southern Nevada's roads has worsened auto-related problems. The number of vehicles registered in Clark County rose from 298,000 in 1980 to 609,137 in 1993 and to more than 800,000 in 1998.[20] In turn, this growth has produced several negative repercussions, including, as suggested earlier, an increased likelihood of contracting a respiratory disease. Despite the all-too-visible airborne pollutants in the valley, air pollution officials downplay the problem, attributing high carbon monoxide levels in part to a 42-foot-tall Aleppo pine tree growing near one of the monitoring stations. The air control director is also on record as stating that despite the routine occurrence of unhealthful days, air pollution is not generally a threat to runners as long as they run during the day, avoid particularly polluted neighborhoods, and do not breathe exhaust fumes.[21] To reiterate, Las Vegas Valley residents suffer from a lack of formal planning on the part of public transportation officials and the absence of a comprehensive mass transit system.

Higher taxes to pay for public roadways are another consequence of rapid population growth. A study released in the early 1990s by The Road Information Program (TRIP), a nonprofit organization based in Washington, D.C., which is funded by companies in the highway construction industry, indicated that Nevada would need to double its spending on transportation infrastructure over the next ten years to avoid safety problems. The report documented 161 bridges and nearly 26,000 miles of roads in the state that needed immediate improvement.

Bob Miller, Nevada's former governor, said that the transportation infrastructure in southern Nevada was under so much stress that it was beginning to fail, and that in some areas, the road and highway network was in a state of collapse. He and other officials have expressed concern that tourist trade from California will be lost as a result of the dilapidated roads.

Another cost directly associated with rapid population growth is increasing traffic congestion. Many residents have experienced a doubling in the length of their daily commutes in recent years. Whereas all roads have become more crowded, some key roadways are nearing gridlock, particularly those that intersect Las Vegas Boulevard. For example, at peak times, it can take up to thirty minutes to travel the two blocks from Tropicana Avenue to Flamingo Road on the Strip.[22] The redevelopment of the "Spaghetti Bowl" intersection of I-15 and U.S. 93/95 has created disastrous conditions.

Studies have documented the magnitude of traffic problems in the region. For example, according to the consulting firm BRW, Inc., the city would need to spend $25 million over the next two decades to alleviate downtown gridlock. Another study, by the engineering firm of Parsons, Brinckerhoff, Quade & Douglas, examined parking problems downtown, another symptom of unchecked growth.

Regional Transportation Director Kurt Weinrich says that Clark County is paying the price for eighteen years of inadequate planning. As he explains it, there are several growth-related factors creating southern Nevada's traffic problems, including substantial numbers of young drivers on the roads and the growing number of women workers. Weinrich also notes that the length of an average motor trip is increasing, along with the number of cars per household. Furthermore, vehicle miles traveled are increasing faster than the population. "We have the longest per-person, per-trip, per-day ratio in the country . . . [and] we also have the lowest vehicle occupancy rate in the country," claims Weinrich.[23]

Some local leaders do not view traffic congestion as a significant social cost of rapid urbanization. Many citizens are sanguine about the situation, relieved that they are no longer battling even more congested conditions in southern California. Nonetheless, traffic jams present an imminent threat to the economic prosperity and the quality of life in southern Nevada. Traffic tie-ups are frustrating and ultimately detrimental to the well-being of local residents. One obvious implication is an ever-enlarging amount of otherwise productive (or leisure) time that is spent simply idling in overcrowded streets. Nick Pavlica, a local journalist and social critic, quantifies the congestion problem this way: an additional ten minutes a day means that we get stuck in traffic for an extra two and a half 24-hour days each year, or over seven and a half work days annually in all. Yes, you are working an additional one and a half weeks of unpaid overtime a year in heavy traffic because of our uncontrolled growth. And that's based on only ten minutes a day.[24]

While rapid growth may boost the economy, it clearly creates costs that are borne by local residents. Other types of costs directly endanger residents' health by exposing them to increased chances of accidental injury and death. Ultimately, unregulated rapid growth maims and kills people. While the national roadway traffic fatality rate has declined from 2.23 fatal accidents per 100 million miles driven to 1.92 since 1986, the rate in Nevada has increased from 2.52 to 2.81. In 1995, the upward trend in highway fatalities continued: more than 313 traffic fatalities were recorded in the state, making it the fourth consecutive year of increased fatalities.[25] The trend continued in 1996, when 348 people lost their lives in traffic accidents, and reached a new state high of 361 fatalities in 1998.[26] In 1999, the dangers associated with pedestrians navigating wide roadways in Las Vegas was revealed when 70 pedestrians lost their lives, a rate of 3.7 pedestrians killed per 100,000 people. According to Federal Highway Administration figures, Nevada was first in the rate of pedestrian fatalities in the nation, with more than double the national rate of 1.8 fatalities per 100,000 people.[27] High numbers of vehicular collisions and auto-related fatality rates typically accompany rapid urbanization. The carnage on a short stretch of Highway I-95 provides corroboration for that generalization in the case of Las Vegas. This section has been the key artery facilitating the population boom along the city's northwest corridor. Between 1980 and mid 1990, there were 2,100 accidents there, which killed or injured 960 people.

Labeling it a "bloodthirsty bit of pavement," Rick Healy, a journalist for the *Las Vegas Business Press,* draws attention to key actors instrumental in the highway's construction: "The cancerous urban explosion that's making so many of our builders, bankers, gamers and, yes, elected officials so wealthy, so quickly, would not have been possible without it." He characterizes the controversial stretch of highway as a "manmade disaster that . . . suggests that innocent lives were readily sacrificed in order to turn a profit."[28]

Finally, because of growth and traffic accidents and fatalities, the average Nevadan is required to pay hefty automobile insurance premiums. In 1996, the average Nevada motorist spent $913 on auto insurance, the eleventh-highest rate in the nation (the national average in 1996 was $774). Nationwide, auto insurance rates increased 2.02 percent between 1995 and 1996, but in Nevada, the advance was 4.14 percent.[29]

HEALTH IN SOUTHERN NEVADA

Many barometers indicate that southern Nevada is not a healthy place to reside. Not all health problems can be traced to the population influx of the past decades, but clearly some illnesses are linked to rapid changes. According to United Health Group, a Minneapolis-based health maintenance organization, Nevada ranked forty-fifth among all states for the health of its residents. The 2000 study (the latest in eleven annual reports) cites the high prevalence of smoking, lack of health insurance, and incidence of infectious diseases and premature death as major factors contributing to the relative ill-health of Nevadans. For the past decade, the state has led the nation in the number of smokers relative to the population. The state's poor health ranking is also attributable to the low percentage of women who receive prenatal care and the nation's fourth-highest teen pregnancy rate.[30] This study highlights the connection between poor prenatal care and the state's high infant mortality rate, which ranks fifteenth nationally. Not to be overlooked among the more severe health-related problems are the nation's highest suicide rate and fifth-highest rate of fatal car accidents per capita in 1998.[31]

Within the overall health picture, one group in particular—those suffering from emotional problems—have seen their health and the resources available to them decline with the rapid population influx. Advocates estimate the number of Nevadans with serious mental illnesses at 50,000, although the state provides services for fewer than 15,000. Despite the growing population, the state legislature cut spending for the mentally ill, severing services to 10,000 persons suffering from emotional ailments.[32]

Nevada ranks first in another health-related category—the number of children who die as a result of inadequate care. According to the *Archives of Pediatric and Adolescent Medicine,* Nevada has the highest child-abuse death rate among children four years and younger in the nation. Rapid urbanization does not create problems like these, but it does tend to exacerbate them. Southern Nevada's growth has been so rapid that it generates a sense of rootlessness and a lack of community. Friends, families, and neighborhoods are seldom cultivated in a fast-paced, rapid-growth area.[33]

Moreover, southern Nevada's rapid growth has created a generally "stressed-out" population. The hectic pace of everyday life in Las Vegas engenders many negative emotional effects. Using fifteen stress variables, Arnold Linsky and Murray Straus rated Nevada the most stressful state in the nation in 1986. The high percentage of the population who had been resident in the state for less than five years was an important reason for this ranking. The same study identified Las Vegas as the second most stressful city in the country, behind Reno, in which to live. Stress is a significant but largely unquantifiable social cost of rapid urbanization.[34]

Finally, overburdened public services impede the delivery of health care—another problem commonly associated with rapidly growing urban areas. Many Sunbelt cities, such as Houston and Phoenix, have struggled to adequately treat wastewater, maintain quality education systems, and staff hospital, fire, and police departments. Southern Nevada contends with similar problems.

RECREATION AREAS

In addition to strained educational and water resources, the area's recreational facilities are also becoming inundated. Many residents of southern Nevada see access to parks and green space as central to their quality of life. But with rapid urban development, the amount of park and green space in Las Vegas per person has dwindled. Park professionals consider ten acres of park space for every 1,000 people as ideal. With the past decade's rapid influx into the area, the city's ratio has steadily declined to below two acres for every 1,000 residents. As with pollution-marred vistas, it is impossible to quantify the social harm implied by growing numbers concentrated on a diminished amount of recreational land.

Another recreation-related social cost emerging as a result of the region's rapid growth is the danger of urban sprawl foreclosing "an escape hatch from urban life." Environmentalists and others believe that Las Vegas's "crown jewel"—the Red Rock Recreation Area—will soon join the list of other major urban parks as residential, retail, and commercial developments edge ever closer to the popular site a few miles from the city. The population growth means that the Red Rock area is becoming host to hordes of cyclists, rock climbers, and others, including vandals who have used the 1,000-year-old Native American rock art there for target practice. The problem is intensified by the absence of urban parks in Las Vegas.[35] The erosion of psychological and physical breathing space is an unanticipated result of rapid growth and signals a diminished quality of life for inhabitants of southern Nevada.

OTHER SIGNS OF SERVICE STRAIN

Beyond the serious service strains considered above, Clark County faces a multitude of additional growth-generated social problems. One involves an overextended criminal justice system. Researchers studying the Clark County Detention Center claim that the jail is at a crisis level. The population of the jail increased 100 percent during the 1980s. By 1994, it was increasingly common for the jail to be operating at double capacity.[36]

Between 1975 and 1995, the incarceration rate in Nevada grew by 325 percent.[37] The swelling population helped give the state the highest incarceration rate in the country between 1986 and 1992. In 1997, Nevada, with 518 people incarcerated per 100,000, easily outdistanced the U.S. average of 445.[38] Clearly, the growing population, particularly among young people, is more responsible than the police force for this ranking.[39] National assessments corroborate the strain on the criminal justice system. According to studies released in early 2000 by Morgan Quitno Press, because of crime, Nevada is the third most dangerous state in the United States in which to reside. Morgan Quitno Press, which specializes in reference material comparing U.S. states and cities, uses just six major crime factors—murder, rape, robbery, aggravated assault, burglary, and motor vehicle theft—in arriving at its ranking.[40] According to FBI statistics, the number of major crimes reported to police in Nevada increased 13 percent between 1993 and 1994—the fastest increase in the nation.[41] According to Department of Justice data, the growing prison population in Nevada means that the state system is holding 42 percent more prisoners than it was designed for, a visible implication of the volatile region's rapid growth.[42] Official crime statistics collected by the FBI since the mid 1990s show that crime in Nevada stabilized, though at a high rate. For example, the FBI's Uniform Crime Report (an index of seven major felonies) showed that despite the demographic expansion, the overall number of crimes per 100,000 declined 2 percent from 1996 to 1997.[43] In 1999, the FBI's Uniform Crime Report was mixed. Although it showed small declines for most of the index crimes, the number of rapes in Las Vegas increased, from 501 in 1998 to 532 in 1999, a 6.2 percent rise.[44] Although Nevada had the highest per capita incarceration rate for much of the 1980s and 1990s, the state ranked sixth nationally in 1999. The improved ranking, however, was not attributable to a lowered incarceration rate in Nevada (which edged upward to 542 inmates per 100,000 in 1999) but to the fact that other states, such as Louisiana (736 per 100,000), were imprisoning people at a much higher rate. North Las Vegas, traditionally ranked among the most violent mid-sized cities by the FBI, has been adding more officers and saw a drop of 7 percent in serious crimes between 1994 and 1998.[45] Nonetheless, North Las Vegas's rate of 24.2 violent crimes per 1,000 residents was precisely twice as high as that of adjacent Las Vegas.[46] Another sign of growth-generated complications in southern Nevada has been a steadily rising homicide rate, a development at odds with national trends for three consecutive years. Police officials attribute the escalating homicide rate to the population boom, which has greatly exceeded the growth of the city's police homicide unit.

For much of the 1990s, homicides increased at a record-setting pace each year, both in number and as a percentage of the population. In 1995, 148 people died in the city of Las Vegas alone, then an all-time record. Another 150 people died violently in other parts of Clark County, just five homicides shy of the previous year's mark.[47] In 1996, another record number of homicides (168) was recorded in Las Vegas.[48]

In short, like other southern Nevada institutions pressured by rapid urbanization, the law enforcement infrastructure is insufficient both to contain criminal activity and to adequately process the growing number of perpetrators apprehended.

THE ALLURE OF BOOMTOWN GROWTH AND ITS SOCIAL CONSEQUENCES

A pivotal social cost created by rapid urbanization can be seen in the growing numbers of individuals who migrate to Las Vegas in search of well-paying, permanent jobs, but who instead fall victim to dead-end employment, underemployment, or unemployment.[49] Persistently high poverty levels, a fluctuating welfare caseload, and the difficulty of locating affordable housing are facts of life for growing numbers of working southern Nevadans.[50] According to the U.S. Census Bureau, the percentage of Nevadans living in poverty increased from 8.3 in 1980 to 11.3 in 1999. At the same time, the U.S. rate was declining from 13 percent to 11.8 percent (a 20-year low).[51] Again, we see that not all of the population are beneficiaries of unfettered growth.

It may seem ironic that with every new wave of resort development, such as the one the city underwent in late 1998 and 1999, the unemployment, poverty, and welfare caseload rates expand. But that has been the general trend for the past two decades. In late 1993, when the MGM Grand Hotel and Casino, Treasure Island, and the Luxor Hotel opened within weeks of each other, the overall economic condition for most rank-and-file workers actually worsened. To comprehend how the quality of life suffered in southern Nevada amid the creation of approximately 14,000 new jobs, it is key to recall the context of Las Vegas within the broader U.S. economy.

When the managers of the new resorts prepared to staff their new facilities, they drew not only on local labor markets but also on regional and national ones. Gaming corporations recruited nationally and advertised extensively to potential tourists across the United States about the opening of the city's new gaming destinations. News of job openings in southern Nevada alerted a large pool of idle workers nationwide. Many headed to Las Vegas at that time with virtually no information about the local occupational structure or the labor requirements of employers there. As Curtis Wilke, a journalist for the *Boston Globe*, has written, "Las Vegas calls to the rootless."[52] The tremendous influx of jobless workers meant that the proportion of those seeking but not finding work increased, rather than declining, as did the poverty rate and the welfare caseload.[53]

During the 1993 expansion, employers exercised great control over the hiring process. This left tens of thousands of workers scrambling for work elsewhere. For example, the biggest employer among the three new resorts in 1993—the MGM Grand—eventually hired nearly 8,000 workers, but screened more than 100,000 potential employees.[54]

Similarly, the Luxor interviewed 1,000 workers every day in the first two months that its employment office was open.[55] Treasure Island was swamped with applicants as well.[56] Clearly, even with three major new employers creating thousands of jobs in the context of a generally booming economy, an economy the size of southern Nevada's simply cannot absorb the 3,000–6,000 additional job seekers corporations there attract monthly. Enticing large numbers of potential employees when relatively few will actually find stable, full-time employment puts downward pressure on the wages and working conditions of all employees in the Las Vegas metropolitan area.

The local population is surging with hopeful job seekers, straining public services available to resident Nevadans, including welfare for under- and unemployed families. In February 1995, the number of Nevadans receiving food stamps passed the 100,000 mark for the first time. Yet the 3.1 percent increase in the number of food stamp recipients during the previous twelve months was dwarfed by the 12 percent advance in the ADC caseload during the same time.[57] Later in the year, the number of Medicaid recipients also crossed the 100,000 threshold for the first time, climbing to 100,460, nearly 12 percent higher than for the same month the previous year. Although welfare reform began sharply reducing the number of Nevadans receiving these forms of public assistance after 1995, the rapidly growing population in southern Nevada is again pushing the number of recipients upward. In the spring of 2000, enrollment in Nevada's welfare (cash assistance), Medicaid, and food stamp programs were all increasing. Even with a local and national economic expansion, the region simply lacks enough opportunities to prevent many from turning to public assistance programs for help.[58] The Medicaid caseload has expanded as more working poor and unemployed individuals needing health care migrate to the state.

Despite the robust job creation rate, the vast majority of jobs in the Las Vegas economy are low-paying, putting home ownership out of reach for many southern Nevadans. Rapid growth has exerted upward pressure on all types of housing in the area's real estate market. Without a second income, or other supplemental funding, many Clark County residents are simply shut out of the American dream. Interestingly, one of the advantages touted by the pro-growth coalition is that virtually anyone can afford to purchase a home. In fact, Las Vegas is one of the least affordable areas in the nation for workers earning the median income or less. According to a mid-1995 National Association of Home Builders survey, Las Vegas was identified as the 139th least affordable housing market out of 175 metropolitan areas canvassed.[59] Beyond the upward pressure of the growing population, an ever-widening gap between workers' "real" wages and housing prices makes home ownership an even dimmer possibility. In 1994, the average wage per person in the Las Vegas area was $25,528, one-quarter of 1 percent, or $68, more than the average had been two years earlier. Meanwhile, between February 1994 and August 1995, the overall cost of living rose by more than 6 percent, and the median price of a new home increased by 8 percent, to just under $122,000.

In the late 1990s and into the new century, housing prices continued to outpace the overall rate of inflation and workers' wages. In November 1999, the median price of a new home in the Las Vegas Valley was $144,000, or 6 percent higher than a year earlier.[60] Prices of existing homes offer little encouragement to those in search of home ownership; in 1999, the median price of existing houses in Las Vegas was $124,100, a 6 percent increase over the previous year.[61] The mismatch between decent-paying occupations and affordable housing increased the estimated number of homeless people from 2,000 in 1990 to more than 18,000 in 1999, one-fifth of whom hold regular part- or full-time jobs.[62] In short, despite the hyperbole, ordinary southern Nevadans earning the median income find it difficult to buy their own homes, owing in no small part to the rapidly growing population.

Most migrants to southern Nevada have discovered that permanent, well-paying jobs with fringe benefits are becoming increasingly rare. In Las Vegas, the most plentiful jobs are in the largely unskilled, low-paying hotel/gaming/recreation sector of the service economy. For thousands of cashiers, porters, and support personnel, the jobs that show up in southern Nevada's glowing job creation figures are too often pathways to substandard living conditions, or even homelessness.

For many new arrivals to the city, securing stable employment is hindered by structural factors most local residents seldom consider: the lack of a permanent address, reliable transportation—particularly critical in a city with inadequate mass transit—a home phone number, and local references. Even among the fortunate ones who find stable work, wages are often inadequate to afford median-priced housing and other necessities. The occupations that make up the greatest number of jobs seldom pay much above the minimum wage. For example, in 1999, waiters/waitresses, maids, retail clerks, general office clerks, and janitors were among the top ten occupations that employed the greatest number of workers in Las Vegas.[63] Some service workers receive tips, but the amount received is closely monitored by the Internal Revenue Service.

The types of jobs being produced and the available housing stock are substantial obstacles for those who hope to settle in southern Nevada. A disproportionate amount of housing construction in Clark County is for the middle and upper middle classes, whereas most of the jobs being produced in the service sector are relatively low-paying positions. In short, residential construction and income trends in recent years have conspired against southern Nevadans, sharpening social divisions between the prosperous and impoverished in the process.

Growth means more jobs and more money for some, but a very dear price is paid by others. Growth also means more crime, more pollution, more traffic, more taxes, more unemployment (when boom jobs evaporate), and, in general, more of the bad things of life and less of the good. All Las Vegans are paying for this growth with our tax dollars, with our health, and with our quality of life, while a few developers and hotel owners are profiting from the community's sacrifices.[64]

NOTES

1. Kathleen Morgan et al., *State Rankings, 1993* (Lawrence, Kans.: Morgan Quitno Corporation, 1993), 395.

2. Marguerite T. Smith and Sheryl Nance-Nash, "The Best Places to Live Today," in *Money*, Sept. 1995: 126; "Boom Town Stats," *Fortune*, Nov. 23, 1998: 147.

3. *Time*, January 10, 1994; *U.S. News and World Report*, January 31, 1994, 61.

4. *Las Vegas Review-Journal*, November 12, 1995, 1M.

5. John Mollenkopf, *The Contested City* (Princeton: Princeton University Press, 1983); Harvey Molotch, "The City as a Growth Machine," *American Journal of Sociology*, vol. 82 (September 1976): 309–32.

6. Molotch 1976, p. 309.

7. William D. Angel, "Beggars in Velvet Gowns" (Ph.D. diss., University of Texas, 1977).

8. Todd Swanstrom 1985.

9. Molotch 1976, p. 313; Feagin and Parker, 1990: 18.

10. Caruso, 1995: 5K.

11. Healy, 1990: 5.

12. Rogers, 1996: 1B.

13. "Pollution a Killer in Vegas," *Las Vegas Sun*, May 9, 1996.

14. Papinchak, 1990: 1A.

15. Splawn, 1989: 6.

16. Art Nadler, "Construction Sites Raise More Dust," *Las Vegas Sun,* June 23, 1999.

17. Adrienne Packer, "EPA Gets County's Air Quality Report," *Las Vegas Sun,* August 16, 2000.

18. "Las Vegas News Briefs," *Las Vegas Sun,* October 13, 1998.

19. Packer, "EPA Gets County's Air Quality Report."

20. *Nevada Statistical Abstract* (online: www.state.nv.us), "Transportation and Crashes," table, "Motor Vehicle Registration in Nevada by County–1998."

21. Rogers, 1996a: 1A; Feour, 1995: 5D.

22. LaGanga, 1994: A1.

23. McKinlay, 1990: 11.

24. Nick Pavlica, editorial, *Las Vegan City Magazine* (Summer 1990), 11.

25. Whaley, 1996: 1B.

26. "State's Traffic Deaths Increased in '96," *Las Vegas Sun,* May 7, 1997; "Traffic Fatalities Down Slightly from 1998," *Las Vegas Review-Journal,* January 4, 2000.

27. Launce Rake, "Nevada Tops in Rates of Pedestrian Fatalities," *Las Vegas Sun,* October 21, 2000.

28. Healy 1990a: 4.

29. Sean Whaley, "Insurance Rates Driven Higher," *Las Vegas Review-Journal,* March 4, 1998.

30. Launce Rake, "Nevada Again Rates Near Last in Health," *Las Vegas Sun,* November 15, 2000.

31. "Nevadans Are among the Nation's Most Unhealthy," *Las Vegas Sun,* November 23, 1999.

32. Whaley, 1995: 1B.

33. Green, 1994: 1B.

34. Arnold S. Linsky and Murray A. Straus, *Social Stress in the United States: Links to Regional Patterns in Crime and Illness* (Dover, Mass.: Auburn House, 1986).

35. Woyski, 1990: 8T.

36. Hynes, 1994: 1B.

37. Levy, 1995: 9K.

38. State of Nevada, *Nevada Statistical Abstract,* 2000 (online), "Crime and Corrections," Table "Incarceration Rates of Prisoners in State Institutions."

39. Vogel, 1992: 1b.

40. Launce Rake, "Study Says Nevada Is Unhealthy, Dangerous," *Las Vegas Sun,* April 24, 2000.

41. Ostrow, 1995: 1A.

42. Jerry Fink, "Fewer Landing Behind Bars," *Las Vegas Sun,* August 25, 1999.

43. Jerry Fink, "Despite Battles Downtown, Crime Rate on Decline in Valley," *Las Vegas Sun,* December 22, 1998.

44. Keith Paul, "FBI Report Shows Crime Rate Falling as Population Grows," *Las Vegas Sun,* May 11, 2000.

45. Ibid.

46. Riley, 1996: 1A.

47. Keith Paul, "Las Vegas Homicide Rate Holds Steady," *Las Vegas Sun,* July 5, 2000.

48. Friedman, 1996: 1B.

49. Jobs: Jeffrey Libby, "Low-Wage Earners Struggle Below the Poverty Line," *Las Vegas Sun,* December 16, 2000; Mike Husted, "Where I Stand—Vegas Must Limit Vulnerability of Its Working Poor," *Las Vegas Sun,* August 8, 1998; Robert E. Parker, "Underemployed," *Las Vegas Citylife,* June 24–30, 1999, 16–17; Martin Kuz, "Working, Yet Homeless," *Las Vegas Sun,* March 21, 1999; Brian Seals, "Study Says Most New Nevada Jobs Don't Support Families," *Las Vegas Sun,* December 11, 1998; Cy Ryan, "November Unemployment Up," *Las Vegas Sun,* December 21, 2000.

50. Michael Weissenstein, "State Poverty Rate Up," *Las Vegas Review-Journal,* September 27, 2000, 1, 4A; Robert E. Parker, "Less Isn't More," *Las Vegas Citylife,* December 7, 2000; Kiley Russell, "Economic Slump Could End Nevada Welfare Caseload Decline," *Las Vegas Sun,* February 25, 1999; "LV Homes 87th in Affordability," *Las Vegas Sun,* August 22, 1996.

51. Joseph Dalaker and Bernadette D. Proctor, *Poverty in the United States* (U.S. Census Bureau, Current Population Reports P60–210, September 2000); Weissenstein, "State Poverty Rate Up"; Parker, "Less Isn't More."

52. Curtis Wilke, "Las Vegas Calls to the Rootless," *Boston Globe,* March 9, 1995, A4.

53. Vogel, 1993: 4B.

54. Burbank, 1993: 1B.

55. Moskowitz, 1993: 1.

56. Palmero, 1993: 1B.

57. Vogel, 1995b: 1B.

58. "After Steady Decline, Nevada Welfare Roles Increase," *Las Vegas Sun,* May 21, 2000.

59. *Las Vegas Review-Journal,* 1995: 8E.

60. Launce Rake, "Valley Home Prices Heading Upward," *Las Vegas Sun,* January 23, 2000. See also "LV Cost of Living Posts Rare Decline," *Las Vegas Sun,* April 18, 2000.

61. Rake, "Valley Home Prices Heading Upward."

62. Robertson, 1995: 1B; Martin Kuz, "Working, Yet Homeless," *Las Vegas Sun,* March 21, 1999.

63. Robert E. Parker, "Underemployed," *Las Vegas Citylife,* June 24–30, 1999, 16–17.

64. Nick Pavlica, "Is the Boom a Bust?" *Las Vegan City Magazine,* Spring 1990, 12.

Rise to Power
The Recent History of the
Culinary Union in Las Vegas

The story of the Culinary Union's rise to power in Las Vegas is a dramatic tale in which workers battle mega-resorts and wealthy casino families in the most unlikely union town in America. In the past decade, the casino economy and its enviable standard of living have been responsible for Las Vegas's explosive growth. Thousands of people move to the Las Vegas Valley each month because good jobs are being generated in the gaming industry. The jobs are part of a growing national service economy, but here they come with middle-class wages and benefits. That standard of living, which allows a hotel maid to own her own home, has been established through years of struggle by the Culinary Union, an affiliate of the Hotel Employees and Restaurant Employees International Union (HERE) and representative of many of the city's casino workers.

Since a brutal citywide strike in 1984, when some gaming companies undertook an unprecedented effort to destroy the union, the Culinary Union and its members have fought a series of strategic battles leading to the union's revival. These struggles were instigated by factions of casino owners who bet that they could break the only organization in the state not controlled by their wealth and influence in a grab for absolute power. Instead, the union charted a course through these battles that took advantage of a power struggle within the industry: gaming's founding families, who were used to dominating the power structure, were losing economic and political ground to emerging casino corporations. These corporations had in mind the transformation of gambling into a subset of the booming entertainment industry.

The Culinary Union has doubled in size since 1984, to 40,000 members, in stark contrast to the general decline of trade unions in the United States, which have lost members and clout steadily for the past fifteen years. One in ten residents in greater Las Vegas is covered by the HERE Health and Welfare Fund, the best health insurance plan in the state, because someone in the family is a Culinary Union member. In 1996 alone, the union added 10,000 more members when four mega-resorts opened with union agreements. The union's remarkable growth, in a right-to-work state no less, has been achieved through a smart battle plan, creative leadership, and, supporting it all, a resilient union membership. The Las Vegas experience is now being looked at as one model for reviving the national labor movement. Here, the Culinary Union has become the counterbalance to gaming's consolidation of power, and in the context of Las Vegas's wild and chaotic growth, the stronghold of the middle class in this newest of American cities.

A decade of labor disputes that would inadvertently challenge the power structure in the city began in 1984. The Culinary Union, which had grown alongside the industry as its supplier of casino workers, represented approximately 20,000 workers on the Las Vegas Strip and in downtown's casino center. The Nevada Resort Association (NRA), an employer organization that represented half of the union casinos and also served as the lobbying arm of the gaming industry, took an aggressive approach to contract negotiations. As the citywide agreement expired in April 1984, a schism developed in the industry over labor relations. Members of the NRA, many of which were corporations, provoked a strike (with the noted exception of Circus Circus casinos), while eighteen nonmember casinos, many of them privately owned operations, settled contracts. In hindsight, this division revealed the beginning of a power struggle between the emerging corporate gaming industry and established family-owned casinos.

Gaming corporations like Hilton Hotels and the MGM Grand led the NRA to provoke a bitter, two-month-long strike that year at many Strip and downtown casinos. The association demanded control of the union health insurance fund, elimination of the 40-hour work week, and reduced tip guarantees, along with offering minimal wage increases. In this respect, the corporatization of the industry had a lot to do with its changing labor relations policies. Corporate-owned casinos were instituting new accounting and operational policies to satisfy the demands of public investment. One such change targeted the old practice of treating the food, beverage, and hotel departments as "loss leaders," allowing those departments to generate losses as long as they attracted profitable gambling results. Those departments were generally labor-intensive, while generating lower revenues than the games. Loss-leading was embedded in Las Vegas's operating style, because it was a key to the city's reputation as one of the most affordable vacation spots in the country: room, food, and entertainment prices were artificially low because they had always been subsidized by gambling profits. While attempting to make each department profitable, the corporations turned to labor costs for concessions, seeing the 1984 contract negotiations as their opportunity.

In contrast, many of the privately owned casinos, like the Barbary Coast on the Strip and Binion's Horseshoe downtown, did not make that shift in operational emphasis, and they did not provoke a strike by their workers. These casinos were at odds with the NRA on a range of issues because of the corporations' growing dominance in policy making. Michael Gaughan, owner of the Barbary Coast, was by no means pro-union, but his negotiating position stemmed mostly from disenchantment with the association. In an interview about the labor negotiations, Gaughan told the *Las Vegas Sun* on March 19, 1984: "I didn't care to be involved [in the NRA] with the bigger Strip hotels because their needs and my needs are different." Illustrating this split, the Nevada Hotel and Casino downtown, a noncorporate casino, published advertisements supporting the strikers and challenging the NRA's motivation. Don Pulliam, the hotel's representative, was quoted as saying: "It seems like giant resorts like the MGM, Hilton and Caesars want to monopolize on the gaming market and force smaller casino operators out of business. When it is all over the workers pounding the pavement will either have a strong union to maintain their living dignity . . . or there will be corporate monopoly. That's what is at stake."[1]

While the split between corporate and family-run casinos was not absolute in this dispute, this industry fissure would go on to dominate casino politics and labor relations over the next decade. At this juncture, the independent casinos pursued a unique strategy of positioning the Culinary Union on their side to check the increasing dominance of the corporate gambling interests.

The NRA's dual role as negotiator and lobbyist was evidence that the exercise of gaming's political power and its economic power were convergent. In pursuit of its goal of breaking the union, the NRA used political power as its primary weapon. At the behest of the NRA, District Judge Charles Thompson issued an injunction against picketing, prohibiting strikers from walking within thirty-five feet of one another on the public sidewalks around the hotels. District judges in Nevada are elected officials who rely on campaign contributions to remain on the bench. The elected sheriff of the Las Vegas Metropolitan Police Department, who also relied on contributions from the industry, was in charge of enforcing the court's order. Under the injunction, the resorts were required to pay for the police officers who were stationed at their hotels, an obvious blurring of the lines between law enforcement and hired guns. Despite a federal judge's ruling that the arrests made for violating the injunction were unconstitutional, the state legislature later codified the restrictions in legislation, which the union dubbed the "Thompson Law."

Picketing continued throughout the dispute, and more than nine hundred strikers were arrested. The injunction and law enforcement's actions to uphold it were excessive responses, intended to shut down the picket line. Instead, such a clear-cut reaction reinforced workers' instincts about the strike: that it was about power, and they asked themselves whether they would have any in an otherwise casino-controlled world.

Stories of the arrests were broadcast nationally, and the industry emerged from the strike with a black eye. In the end, the industry's escalation of the dispute had hurt the casinos by damaging Las Vegas's image as a tourist destination and disrupting their ability to make money. The combination of lost business and a sullied image forced the corporations to negotiate a settlement after two months. There was an irony inherent in the corporations' choice to pick this fight: corporate casinos were driving the industry to expand its market, a move dependent on Las Vegas's public image, and they were susceptible to the concerns of public investors about lost cash flow. The experience of these companies in 1984 would inform their labor relations for the rest of the decade, as the industry's evolution into a casino entertainment business magnified the importance of image and public investment.

There were a few casino owners who followed the lead of these corporations into battle but decided not to settle the strike. One of them was the Boyd Group, which at that time owned the California Club downtown and Sam's Town Hotel and Gambling Hall in a southeastern Las Vegas neighborhood. The Boyd Group would come to epitomize the transition from family-owned casino company to corporate player. In 1984, the company was one of the more sophisticated and profitable private casino companies, with layers of stockholders and executives. Bill Boyd, the company's chief executive, had just inherited his position from his father, Sam Boyd, who had built the company and was also one of the city's founding fathers. The Boyd Group's role in this strike would foreshadow the company's desire to be one of the industry's leading corporations. It also captured the new division between corporate and family ownership philosophies. When Bill Boyd forced his workers to strike, Sam Boyd joined them on the picket line. This largely symbolic act signified the end of the era in Las Vegas when casino owners treated their workers as part of the family.

Bill Boyd did not settle with the union when much of the industry did in June 1984, prolonging the strikes at both properties for more than a year. He had hired permanent replacement workers, who petitioned for a decertification election—an election in which the striking employees could not vote—and voted out the union a little more than a year after the strike began. Unlike the corporations he admired, Bill Boyd did not then have public investors to answer to or an image to maintain. His ability to accomplish what the corporations set out to do made him an inspiration to other family operators who had not engaged in the anti-union campaign of 1984.

Another company that rebelled against the citywide settlement was Elsinore Corporation, owner of the downtown Four Queens Hotel and Casino. Under the leadership of Robert Maxey, Elsinore Corporation endured the strike for fifteen months, sacrificing its financial health on the altar of anti-unionism. Maxey was successful in decertifying the union in July 1985, but the Four Queens lost money doing it. Between a $2.8 million loss at that casino in 1984 and a $33.6 million loss in 1985 at Elsinore's other casino, the Atlantis in Atlantic City, the company was hemorrhaging. Elsinore filed for Chapter 11 bankruptcy protection one month after Maxey's resignation from the company in October 1985. It remained on the ropes more than a decade later. Elsinore ignored the business reasons that forced the majority of the industry to resolve the labor dispute, putting ideology before the operation's viability. It would not be the last time this happened in Las Vegas.

The June 1984 settlement provided for a five-year contract with small increases in wages and contributions to the health insurance fund and an 80 percent new-hire rate for the first year of employment. Union members had beaten the casinos' plan to bust the union overall, keeping their contracts largely intact, but it was a costly victory; there were four casinos lost to the union in the wake of the 1984 strike. For the Culinary

Union, that loss created a powerful legacy: 1984 forced the union to fight for its very existence, and in doing so, set in motion the decade-long development of a more potent organization than any non-casino entity in the state.

For the family-owned casinos, which had not fought the union as a group in this last round of negotiations, the strike taught them that it was possible to become union-free operators. That belief was reinforced when a group of casinos with strong ties to Jackie Gaughan, Michael Gaughan's father, a Las Vegas patriarch and active NRA participant, began to follow Bill Boyd's lead. Jackie Gaughan had reluctantly settled the 1984 strike. After the Boyd Group and Four Queens' decertifications in 1985, Jackie Gaughan led six downtown casinos, the El Cortez, Western, Union Plaza, Las Vegas Club, Golden Gate, and Showboat, to freeze wages and ignore contract increases in health insurance payments. The union filed unfair labor practice charges with the National Labor Relations Board, prompting Jackie Gaughan's El Cortez and Western to honor the contracts. A seven-year legal battle ensued with the remaining "Downtown Four," as they came to be called. The union eventually won the litigation, but for two years these casinos thought they were union-free.

In 1987, in an effort to stem its disintegration, a new leadership was elected to run the Culinary Union. Jim Arnold, the union's new secretary-treasurer, requested organizing help from its parent organization, HERE, and its general president, Edward T. Hanley, who responded by sending a team of organizers and researchers to assist in the long-term plan for rebuilding the union. The Las Vegas team included seasoned organizers, rookie activists, and even Yale University graduates, who worked with the local union leaders in reviving Las Vegas's largest union.

Their experience was used to build an organizing committee of rank-and-file leaders who would resurrect the union inside their casinos. The organizers recruited committee leaders in various departments at all of the union properties who would participate in the union's decision-making process, attend negotiations, and lead their co-workers to back the union up on the job. It took guts on the part of members to stand up for their union after the losses of 1984, but they knew better than anyone that workers did not stand a chance against the innate power of the gaming industry without a strong union. This rank-and-file organization was democratic in nature, but disciplined in its leadership development, because day-to-day demonstration to managers of the union's real power, collective action, could only happen on the casino floor. This new, diverse leadership returned the union to its members and inspired a new generation of union leaders in Las Vegas. Included among them was Hattie Canty, an African-American maid and mother of ten, who had become Culinary's president based on her pure instincts as a leader and through many years of hard work.

In December 1987, early in the organizing process, a federal judge ordered the Downtown Four to honor their collective bargaining agreements and pay millions of dollars in back wages and benefits, a decision appealed for years by the hotels. That ruling jump-started the union's campaign to make these hotels live up to their contracts, starting a battle with downtown casino owners that climaxed during the 1989 contract negotiations. In spring 1988, union members picketed the resorts, delivered petitions to management, and advertised the disputes to tour groups and travel agencies. The union program was called "The American Way to Play Is Fair," a challenge to the Las Vegas Convention and Visitors Authority's nationwide campaign advertising Las Vegas as "The American Way to Play."

The union also addressed the shareholders of Showboat, Inc., owner of the Showboat Hotel and Casino. That spring, Showboat's management wanted shareholders to pass eight anti-takeover measures designed to protect management from corporate raiders targeting undervalued companies. Analysts were estimating that Showboat's stock, which was trading around $10 per share, might be worth $18 a share in a takeover attempt that ousted the current management. At the shareholders' meeting on April 26, 1988, the company did not receive enough votes to pass the measures and continued the meeting to May 24, 1988. The union, which opposed the existing management team, obtained permission from the Securities and Exchange Commission, which regulates public companies, to solicit proxies from stockholders opposing the measures. On May 24, 1988, the union presented proxies representing 1.8 million shares to be voted against the anti-takeover measures. Showboat announced a week after the meeting that one million of those votes were not counted and the anti-takeover measures passed by an extremely small margin. Shortly thereafter, Showboat settled the labor dispute, on the eve of the 1989 citywide negotiations. The other three casinos did not settle, and their contract disputes were folded into the labor war brewing downtown.

Between 1985 and 1989, while the union focused on rebuilding its organizational strength, the industry was expanding rapidly. This was the start of the era of "junk bonds," and such high-yield instruments fueled new casino construction throughout southern Nevada. The development of the industry during these years aggravated the split between corporate casinos and the established family-owned gambling halls, with the majority of new capital and expansion opportunities available to the corporations. Gaining unprecedented access to capital, publicly owned casinos like the Golden Nugget, Circus Circus, Caesars Palace, the Hiltons, Ballys, and the Tropicana built 1,000-room hotel additions and expanded their gaming space, generating record gaming revenues for Las Vegas.

The privately held Boyd Group also took part in this race to expand dominated by corporate casinos. In 1985, shortly after Boyd Group casinos bust the union, the State Gaming Control Board chose that company to act as supervisor for two casinos whose licenses had been suspended, the Stardust Hotel and Casino on the Strip and the Fremont Hotel and Casino downtown. Despite the company's labor relations problems that year, the Control Board considered the Boyd Group a model gaming operator and granted it the lucrative job of running these establishments. Months later, the company negotiated agreements to purchase the properties, giving it a strategic foothold on the Strip. The company was one of the first private companies to have access to junk-bond financing, using that market to raise the $135 million needed to buy these two casinos.

Both the Stardust and the Fremont were subject to union contracts like the ones from which the company had just escaped, and successor owners were bound by their terms. The very purchases that brought the Boyd Group closer to its goal of being one of the corporate players in Las Vegas ironically forced the company to re-fight its union battle. Bill Boyd would spend the next five years with one foot in the camp of the established casino families, acting as their leader in the anti-union movement, and the other in corporate gaming territory, building a corporate structure that could take advantage of public financing and expansion possibilities. Boyd's labor relations prevented the Boyd Group from fully breaking with the family-owned casinos and becoming a corporate leader until after 1990.

Steve Wynn, chairman of Golden Nugget, Inc., used capital from the bond markets to become one of the industry's dominant corporate players. In 1988, Wynn borrowed $623 million in junk bonds to build the Mirage Casino-Hotel, next door to Caesars Palace on the Strip. The Mirage led the entertainment revolution in the gaming industry with its emphasis on must-see attractions like an erupting volcano and a white tiger display, radically changing the way Las Vegas made money. Wynn ushered in an era of Disney-esque performance entertainment designed to broaden the appeal of Las Vegas and gambling to a new generation of consumers.

The Mirage was scheduled to open shortly after the citywide contracts with the Culinary Union expired in June 1989, bringing growth into sharp focus at the negotiating table. By then, the NRA was no longer the negotiating agent for the industry, and groups of casinos aligned themselves on one side or the other of the corporate divide. Generally, the corporate casinos were highly leveraged, again with the exception of Circus Circus Enterprises, and as a result, they were dependent on uninterrupted cash flows to service their debt. Even national hotel companies like Holiday Corporation and Hilton Hotels produced as much as 40 percent of the cash available to meet debt obligations from their casinos. Against this backdrop, the corporate industry had to think hard about provoking another large-scale labor brawl.

Leading the corporations, Golden Nugget, Inc., negotiated a groundbreaking five-year agreement with the Culinary Union that included significant work-rule changes in exchange for language allowing the union to organize workers at the Mirage without opposition. The contract also provided for increases in wages and health fund contributions that would maintain no-cost insurance for the workers, and it halved the duration of the 80 percent rate for new hires to six months. At the heart of this landmark agreement with Golden Nugget was the notion of a partnership between labor and management that would grow as the company expanded. It took vision on both sides of the negotiating table to craft this partnership.

From the union's perspective, the contract's provisions for organizing new casinos were its most innovative aspect. Under the contract's "organizing language," the union agreed to exchange its right to take economic action against new casinos in exchange for the employer's agreement not to oppose union organization at its new operations in Las Vegas. The language included a formal provision for recognizing the union if a majority of its employees signed union authorization cards. It was designed to create an alternative to the National Labor Relations Board election process, which as a rule leaves workers vulnerable to nasty anti-union campaigns and years-long appeals processes. The organizing language was strategic to the union's goal of preserving its majority on the Strip in the face of unprecedented, if underestimated, periods of casino development. The Golden Nugget contract set the standard for the 1989 negotiations, and it was followed by similar agreements from the Big Six, a loose-knit negotiating group including Circus Circus, Caesars Palace, the Las Vegas and Flamingo Hiltons, the Tropicana, and Bally's. This group included some of the aggressors in the 1984 strike, like Caesars and the Hiltons, who shifted away from that role primarily because they recognized that a better national image was valuable to gaming's future. That image was important to the customer market, a lesson learned in 1984, and to the legislative issues facing the industry, ranging from legalization of gaming on Indian reservations to taxation of gambling winnings. The benefits of a labor-management partnership in all of these arenas outweighed the financial incentive to play hardball in these negotiations for the corporate sector of the industry.

Although it ultimately accepted the pattern agreement, the Holiday Hotel-Casino on the Strip resisted the organizing language for some months, until it was persuaded that its workers would not settle for a substandard contract. This dispute would test whether the new organizing language would be applied industrywide or just to the leading corporate casinos. The Holiday Casino, owned by the Holiday Corporation (now Harrah's Entertainment) has for years exhibited anti-union behavior, even in its unionized casinos in Las Vegas and Atlantic City. Arguing that it had no plans to operate another casino in Las Vegas, the company agreed to all of the other terms of the Strip contract save the organizing language. The negotiating committee, made up of Holiday workers of various classifications, rejected the second-class proposal, and over 95 percent of the employees signed an open petition to management demanding the Strip contract. The demonstration that an overwhelming majority of employees would stand up for the whole contract was bolstered by an alliance between the Culinary Union in Las Vegas and its sister local in Atlantic City, whose contract with the company's Harrah's Manna Hotel and Casino expired in September 1989. Those two casinos generated approximately 40 percent of Holiday's cash flow, a critical proportion of the amount needed to pay interest on $2 billion worth of long-term debt. After engaging in picketing demonstrations and a trip to Laughlin, Nevada, to see firsthand how Holiday treated nonunion employees—the bus was greeted by police cars and paddywagons lining the only highway into the city—the workers called Holiday's bluff. The company agreed to meet the terms of the Strip contract rather than subject itself to sustained labor action.

The real fight in this contract round came from the family-held casinos that sought to pick up where they had left off in 1984. The Boyd Group recruited Binion's Horseshoe, Michael Gaughan's Barbary Coast, Jackie Gaughan's casinos, and the Elardis' Frontier into an alliance by arguing that they were not in the same league as the large Strip resorts and deserved a less demanding contract. Their position was based on the growing division between corporate mega-resorts and old-style gambling halls. This opposition group believed it could regain position in the economic battle between family- and corporate-owned casinos by cutting labor costs. This short-sighted view did nothing to address the real problem facing these operations: that the corporate casinos were setting a new standard of entertainment and service on the Strip and at the Golden Nugget downtown that demanded renovation and innovation from the older operations. While the corporations transformed the industry, the family-owned gambling halls chose instead to foment labor troubles.

Although the Boyd Group was clearly leading this alliance, Binion's Horseshoe downtown became the center of the dispute when it illegally fired the union's rank-and-file negotiating committee after they opposed the casino's contract offer. On January 19, 1990, after filing numerous unfair labor practice complaints with the NLRB, the union struck. The casino had been built by Benny Binion, one of the city's most politically astute casino owners, and had been inherited by his son Jack. The Binion family was a political powerhouse in Nevada, backed by elected officials from the Sheriff's Department to the governor's office. During the strike, Jack Binion hired John Moran, Jr., son of the long-time sheriff, as one of the casino's lawyers. The younger Moran and Binion gloated as they watched strikers being arrested for violating noise restrictions along Fremont Street, always noted for its revelry.

The Horseshoe was also one of the most profitable family-owned casinos in Las Vegas. The company had approximately $100 million in retained earnings, made anywhere from $20 to $40 million annually, and had almost no debt. The Horseshoe accepted any bet, no matter how large, and displayed $1 million in a giant glass horseshoe at the casino's entrance. It was best known as the home of the World Series of Poker, one of the Old West's highest-profile gambling tournaments. The Horseshoe's clientele was an intensely loyal mixture of local residents and Texas cowboys, none too sympathetic to the strikers. Nevertheless, after months of picketing the casino, groups of customers began going elsewhere, especially locals, who had an increasing selection of neighborhood casinos to patronize. Despite Binion's money, political clout, and strong business, the strike hurt.

A combination of factors, not the least of which was the tenacity of the strikers, who persevered for nine months in the face of Binion's raw power, drove that success. The remaining Culinary Union members doubled their monthly dues to pay $200 a week in strike benefits, which helped mitigate the financial impact on strikers. Another critical factor was the union's legal strategy of pursuing violations of federal labor law to protect the strikers' jobs. The NLRB issued a collection of complaints alleging unfair labor practices, including the illegal firing of union activists and threats of retaliation from security guards. The breadth of the complaints formed the basis for a declaration from the NLRB that the strike was an "unfair labor practice strike," not an economic dispute, which effectively prevented the Horseshoe from hiring permanent replacement workers and holding a decertification election like the ones that had voted the union out of Boyd's casinos in 1985. These two factors combined meant that this strike would not free Binion's Horseshoe of a union.

The Culinary Union also became involved in other states with other groups that were opposed to Binion's interests. The union's strategy of broadening the dispute outside of the workplace, and often outside of Las Vegas, was becoming its trademark. One effort in this vein was the distribution of videos telling the story of a federal indictment handed down against the Horseshoe for alleged racketeering activities. The indictment was later dismissed. These activities, combined with a picket line that cut the casino's business by an estimated $16 million during the strike, prompted Binion to settle the dispute in November 1990.

Binion's political and financial power made the settlement that much more important for the union. The local owners had believed that the restraints on public investment and image, which led the corporate casinos to settle in 1984 and 1989, were not applicable to them. But if the union's new strategies succeeded with Binion, the remaining casino owners would be far less likely to prevail in a war of attrition.

The success of the Horseshoe strike also revived striking as a viable tactic, and the remaining unsettled downtown casinos were vulnerable to job actions focused on their market. The Horseshoe strike had aggravated the decline of downtown Las Vegas as a thriving casino market. The growth of Strip resorts coincided with the emergence of neighborhood casinos and satellite gaming markets in Stateline and Laughlin, which siphoned off a significant portion of downtown's low-budget gamblers. The compact layout of Glitter Gulch helped to widen the impact of the Horseshoe strike by driving some of those customers into new markets.

With the Horseshoe strike settled, the Boyd Group was next. That company's anti-union campaign had begun at the Stardust and Fremont shortly after their purchase and pursued the goal of decertifying the union in 1989. The union began preparing workers at the Boyd properties for this fight in 1987 by building a strong organizing committee of rank-and-file leaders throughout the two casinos to counter management's campaign. The union's organizing was not taken lying down. The Boyd Group sought to divide the local union from its parent organization by barring union representatives who were on the payroll of HERE from its premises. The rank-and-file committee became the only presence of the union inside the Boyd casinos, making committee members stronger union leaders in the end.

The union also began studying the Boyd Group's financial condition and business plan. Analysis of the company's financial condition revealed a strategic fact to the union: the Boyd Group was no longer one of the most profitable casino companies in Las Vegas. The company owed almost ten times more in debt than it had in 1984, when it had had a 13 percent profit margin, high enough to withstand a year-long strike. By September 1990, having borrowed heavily to buy the two casinos, and borrowing another $100 million to add 1,500 rooms to the Stardust, the company was overleveraged, and its profit margin had shrunk to almost nothing. Armed with these facts and the success of the Horseshoe strike, the organizing committee was confident that the Boyd Group could not weather a strike this time around.

Another part of the union's strategy was to build an alliance with the company's lenders in this dispute. The union had spent years communicating with the company's junk-bond holders and other lenders about the dangers associated with the Boyd Group's plan to borrow a mountain of money, while it simultaneously provoked a costly labor dispute. In 1989, the union also investigated the company's partners in its Sam's Town Gold River casino in Laughlin, revealing their questionable character to that project's investors. When the Gold River partnership filed for bankruptcy protection in 1990 as a result of its huge debt load, the Boyd Group's lenders could see how risky the company's course actually was.

During spring 1991, the union prepared to strike the Stardust and Fremont casinos with two thoughts in mind. First, a strike after the opening of the Stardust's new tower would have the most impact on the company's ability to meet its debt obligations; second, the condition of the downtown casino market was so fragile that the threat of a strike at the Fremont might cause all of the unsettled downtown casinos to negotiate, which was exactly what happened. After years of being leaders of the anti-union movement, the Boyd casinos agreed to a union contract without a strike and corralled the remaining downtown properties, including Jackie Gaughan's, into a settlement.

This contract settlement was a milestone for the Culinary Union. The company that had bust the union in 1985 and led the family-owned casinos in their quest to be nonunion made a strategic decision not to provoke a strike in 1991 in order to implement its business plan to become one of the more successful, multi-property gaming companies in Las Vegas. Assured of labor peace, the Boyd Group made the leap over the next few years from a family-owned casino company to a public corporation with a national gaming presence, now known as Boyd Gaming Corporation. The Boyd settlement signaled the end of an older attitude and was an early indication that companies that wanted to take advantage of public financing and the industry's expansion opportunities could not afford to provoke their workers.

On a more subtle level, the settlement of the downtown contracts was recognition that the corporate casinos had the right business strategy and labor relations policies. While battling the union, the family-owned casinos lost valuable time in which to make the changes necessary to keep up with gaming's evolution. A January 10, 1991, *Wall Street Journal* feature entitled "Las Vegas Clans Hope Cards Will Turn," run months before the downtown settlement, addressed this division:

> While the old-line gaming families retain substantial power and wealth, their clout has been shrinking. Corporate players now dominate political giving in Nevada as well as much of the state's political agenda. . . . The current round of casino-industry labor talks illustrates the town's changing power balance. The corporate players all quickly reached agreement with the Hotel Employees and Restaurant Employees International Union. But the family casinos rejected the deal as too onerous. . . . Mr. Binion concedes his family operation has been "losing ground" to the corporate casinos. But neither the Binions nor the other families intend to simply fade away. "We'll outlast the corporate guys," vows Michael Gaughan, a leader of his gaming family.

The downtown settlements meant that family-run operations would not gain a financial advantage over the corporate industry by cutting labor costs and were compelled to find a more proactive solution to the competitive decline of their casinos. Once the labor disputes were resolved, the downtown casinos tackled their dilemma together, forming a partnership to develop the Fremont Street Experience, a $70 million light and video canopy and street that opened in December 1995. The Fremont Street Experience increased overall revenues and capital improvements after its debut and marked downtown's integration into the entertainment revolution in gaming.

Meanwhile, the Culinary Union kept getting stronger, with the addition in 1989 and 1990 of 5,000 new members from the industry's newest casinos, the Mirage, Excalibur, and Hilton's O'Sheas' on the Strip.

With the Boyd settlement came a perceptible shift in the balance of power, which became visible during the now five-year-old Frontier strike. Margaret Elardi and her two sons, Tom and John, had bought the Frontier and its neighbor, the Silver Slipper Casino, from Summa Corporation, Howard Hughes's casino holding company, in 1988. Margaret Elardi had been involved in gaming since the mid 1970s, when she was part owner of the Pioneer Club in downtown Las Vegas. Her anti-unionism first surfaced there when she bust the Culinary and Bartenders Unions in an apparently unprovoked challenge to the highly unionized state of the industry, with a strikingly similar strategy of bargaining in bad faith and litigating into oblivion. In the early 1980s, Elardi sold her first casino to buy the Pioneer Hotel and Gambling Hall in the tiny Colorado River town of Laughlin, Nevada. The nonunion Pioneer in Laughlin, which generated roughly $20 million annually in profit, made most of her money. In 1988, shortly before buying the Frontier and Silver Slipper on the Las Vegas Strip, she sold the Pioneer to Sahara Gaming Corporation for approximately $100 million more than she had paid for it. The family was cash rich, but it was out of place on the Strip.

Upon buying the Strip casinos, the Elardis tore down the Silver Slipper, "an odd fixture of Nevada politics," made famous by Howard Hughes.[2] From 1968 to 1971, Hughes had financed Nevada's political races to the tune of $858,500 from the tables of the Silver Slipper. The Elardis' demolition of the Silver Slipper reflected the family's lack of participation in Nevada's political process. This political standoffishness, uncommon among casino owners, was one of the factors that isolated the Elardis. The Silver Slipper site is now an empty parking lot. The Desert Inn Superarterial roadway, a major east-west corridor, runs through it.

The Elardis then took a number of steps to turn the Frontier into a "grind joint," a casino with few amenities, no entertainment, and little emphasis on anything but slot machines. They closed the showroom, which had been home to the magicians Siegfried and Roy, who went on to gain top billing at the Mirage at $85 a ticket, and focused their marketing of it on the same customers who frequented their Laughlin casino: low-budget gamblers from Arizona and southern California. The Elardis even refused to book rooms to conventioneers, ignoring the growing convention market in Las Vegas. These changes were in stark contrast to the innovations of the Mirage and Excalibur, which created a new level of nongaming amenities designed to enhance the entertainment experience in Las Vegas. As one corporate casino executive told the *Wall Street Journal,* "You are going to need more than a slot palace . . . run by the seat of your pants."[3] Simply put, the Elardis, who had waited so long to make it on the Strip that they named their company Unbelievable, Inc., were battling the transformation of the industry.

On September 21, 1991, over 500 workers from four different unions struck the Frontier Hotel and Gambling Hall on the Strip in response to a slew of unfair labor practices by management. In addition to retaliating against union members, as had the Horseshoe, the Frontier had illegally implemented some of its contract proposals, such as the elimination of pension contributions and implementation of new work rules without negotiating with the union. The Elardis also switched to an inferior health insurance plan that made approximately 100 workers ineligible, slashed wage rates by up to $4 per hour, and gutted the grievance procedure that regulated compliance with the contract. The proposals were designed to eviscerate the collective bargaining agreement and force the union to strike. They were also motivated by the family's desire to lower its operating costs to gain an advantage over the booming corporate casinos, a strategy proven unsuccessful during the downtown disputes.

The Elardis had no intention of operating a union casino, and even though the family had watched the union's recent successes, they thoroughly underestimated the resolve of Frontier workers and their union. When the strike ended in 1997, almost six years later, it was the longest in American history. Not one striker crossed the picket line to work at the Frontier during this strike, a remarkable testament to their courage and conviction.

The family's lack of political involvement and its opposition to the now-dominant corporate wing of the industry isolated the Elardis from the power structure even before the strike began. By contrast, the union had succeeded in battles with the most powerful patriarchs in Las Vegas, increasing the organization's influence throughout the city. Those two developments made this strike different from previous disputes. The political forces that had lined up against the union in past strikes, the courts, the Metropolitan Police Department, the state's politicians, and the local newspapers, had little affinity for the Frontier. There were no nightly arrests on the picket line, and the newspapers editorialized about the need to resolve the strike.

The Frontier aggravated its isolation by trying to drag the rest of the Strip into its dispute. During the early months of the strike, the hotel placed advertisements in the *Los Angeles Times* headlined "Culinary Union Strikes the Strip," infuriating the managements of other Strip casinos, who had settled union contracts in part to avoid publicity like this. Not until this false advertising was referred to the district attorney by the Clark County Commission, a casino licensing authority, did the Frontier desist. The Frontier's lawyer, Joel I. Keller, who had been suspended from the Washington, D.C., bar for masquerading as a neutral arbitrator in a case involving one of his associates, became the unwelcome public face of the hotel when he appeared on local news insulting conventioneers who supported the Frontier picket line. The Frontier's slash-and-burn approach to this dispute was making some powerful enemies.

One was Circus Circus's powerful chairman, William Bennett, who had a history of union contracts and offered to feed the strikers out of pure generosity. Bennett's food truck visited the picket line three times a day to feed the strikers in what was the most unique display of the division between corporate and family-owned casinos. "Las Vegas has enough of an image problem without the Frontier making it worse. We [Circus] just had a record quarter, and we're unionized," Bennett told *Fortune* magazine.[4] The Frontier strike also inspired government involvement in a different way than in the past.

On May 19, 1992, Nevadans for Labor Peace, a group made up of political leaders at the state, county, and city levels, held a press conference calling for both sides to agree to mediation or binding arbitration of the Frontier strike. The Frontier would not agree. It was the first time that a group of public officials in Las Vegas had pressured a casino to resolve its labor troubles. In July 1992, Governor Bob Miller facilitated negotiation between the two sides, which ended without progress but demonstrated the state's interest in ending the strike. By April 1993, nineteen months into the strike, Miller announced that he was appointing an independent fact-finder to recommend ways of resolving the dispute, and that the Frontier would be obliged to cooperate. While the appointment was welcomed by the unions and supported by a bipartisan group of thirty-nine legislators, the Frontier agreed to participate only "under duress." Sam Kagel, the governor's fact-finder, who had fifty years of mediating experience, issued his report on March 1, 1994. Kagel blamed the Frontier for the failure of the negotiating process. The governor's willingness to intervene in this dispute, although not yet successful, highlighted the shift in the balance of power that has occurred since the Horseshoe and Boyd settlements.

Despite the Frontier's cavalier attitude during this dispute, the strike cut business at the casino by an estimated 40 percent in the first year. The strikers also received tremendous support from union members throughout the country. On December 5, 1991, approximately 12,000 union members from every labor organization in southern Nevada marched up the Strip to support the Frontier strikers. In December 1992, the striking unions invited union members from around the country to a march called "Desert Solidarity: Our Line in the Sand." With help from the AFL-CIO, the December 5 rally attracted 20,000 participants, closed the Strip for four hours, and attracted national media attention. The Frontier strikers found themselves leading the rebirth of American unionism.

In the meantime, the NLRB processed scores of complaints by the union. Case after case was tried before federal judges, and every major ruling was favorable to the union and appealed by the company. These rulings both vindicated the union's actions and started assigning financial liability to the Frontier. Judges decided that the Frontier had violated the law when it halted pension contributions and changed the employee handbook outlining the hotel's work rules without negotiating the changes. Reimbursing employees for these unilateral changes cost millions, and the liability grew daily. In addition, a federal labor judge declared the strike an "unfair labor practices strike," like the Horseshoe strike, preventing the Frontier from hiring permanent replacement workers and decertifying the unions. The Elardis could ignore the judges' decisions, choosing to appeal, but they would not be able to rid the Frontier of the union.

In 1993, Michael Gaughan's Barbary Coast gave the Elardis an inkling of what might happen. The Barbary Coast had employed the same lawyer as the Elardis, intending to become a nonunion operation. Unlike in 1984, when he had fought the NRA's strike-baiting proposals,

Gaughan now had a highly successful nonunion casino, the Gold Coast Hotel and Casino, located in a southwestern neighborhood. Gaughan was also still fighting the corporate casinos on legislative issues. For some time, his desire to "outlast the corporate guys" made reaching agreement with the union almost impossible.

The Barbary Coast made the same negotiating mistakes that the Frontier did, halting payments to the union health insurance fund and implementing work-rule changes without going through the negotiating process. Gaughan also lost ruling after ruling. When faced with an estimated $11 million liability in 1993, which grew during any appeal, he settled a labor agreement. This settlement left the Frontier alone in its fight against the union. Gaughan has gone on to merge the Barbary Coast and Gold Coast into a quasi-public corporation with publicly traded debt. Instead of outlasting them, he has become one of the corporate guys.

While the Frontier strike continued, workers from a newly opened neighborhood casino, the Santa Fe Hotel and Casino, called the Culinary Union. The Sahara Gaming Corporation, which also owned the unionized Sahara and Hacienda casinos on the Strip, launched the Santa Fe in February 1991, and given its Culinary Union contracts, the workers had expected the new casino to be unionized too. The Santa Fe was part of Sahara Gaming's plan to expand its nonunion operations, however, and the company joined the Elardis in defiance of the changing balance of power.

Although Sahara Gaming was a public company and had fully participated in the use of public financing to fund its growth, a majority of the company's stock was controlled by Paul Lowden. In truth, Sahara Gaming was a family-run operation behind the façade of a public company. Lowden borrowed millions from the company, even though it generated bottom-line losses, and he paid insiders substantial fees to perform services for the company. Its corporate structure was complex, with public stockholders, public limited partners, and public bondholders, all investors with no say in the direction of the company. Lowden's myriad financial transactions maintained his absolute control, while obscuring a company that was borrowing too much money and producing constant losses. In 1992, the company lost $9.4 million, having spent $39.6 million on interest payments alone. Lowden's obsession with control colored his business decisions, from labor relations to financing arrangements, and locked him out of the lucrative changes sweeping the industry.

In the fall of 1992, over 75 percent of Santa Fe employees signed union cards and demanded recognition based on a card check, the same process by which the Mirage and Excalibur had recognized the union. The workers at the Santa Fe wanted parity with their co-workers at the Sahara and Hacienda: on average, they made $2 per hour less in wages, had to pay for their health insurance, if they were eligible (many full-time workers, like most of the maids, were classified as temporary workers, who were ineligible for insurance), and had no job security. Santa Fe management refused to consider a card check, insisted on a cumbersome and time-consuming election, and launched a vicious campaign of retaliation and delay that continued until 2000, when the Santa Fe was sold to the Station Group, another nonunion local casino chain.

The dispute between Sahara Gaming and the union had obvious political overtones, because Lowden's wife, Sue, had been elected to the state senate in November 1992. One of her first acts after taking her seat as state senator was to fire a Santa Fe union member who had testified before her labor committee on the casino's health and safety problems. In February 1993, a Santa Fe cook was fired just three days after giving testimony, but was rehired after a firestorm of negative publicity about the senator's retaliation. Sue Lowden's action set the tone for a nasty, long-running fight over the unionization of the Santa Fe.

The Santa Fe was eager to use the NLRB's election process, because it routinely allows employers to delay the results of any election for as long as six years. Despite that risk, the Culinary Union, the Teamsters, and Operating Engineers filed a joint petition with the NLRB in the summer of 1993 for a union election at the Santa Fe. Confident of the workers' support, the union's strategy was to demonstrate the abuses of the NLRB process, while being able to tie an election victory into the 1994 contract fight with the company's two union casinos. On the night of October 1, 1993, despite a string of labor law violations by management, the unions won the election by 300–241. The Santa Fe predictably contested the results, calling the election a "close vote," even though the union had received the same percentage of votes as Senator Lowden had in her election to the state senate. The Santa Fe's challenges to the election were overruled in their entirety in April 1995, but the company continued to appeal.

During this dispute, Sahara Gaming was desperately trying to take advantage of the rapid legalization of gaming outside of Nevada by developing casinos in emerging jurisdictions. This was a company that mostly considered how it would buy or build its next casino. Sahara

Gaming had doubled in size since 1988, buying the nonunion Pioneer Hotel and Gambling Hall in Laughlin from Margaret Elardi—unwittingly providing her with $100 million with which to fight the union at the Frontier—and building the Santa Fe, all with borrowed money.

In 1993, Sahara Gaming wanted to refinance the company's outstanding loans and borrow additional funds for riverboat projects. Bear Stearns, a leading investment bank for gaming companies, was hired to do a "global refinancing" that would lower the company's interest payments and provide expansion funds. There was a catch: bond buyers wanted stock warrants to sweeten the deal. Lowden refused to issue additional stock, because it would lower his holdings below 50 percent, the threshold of absolute voting control. Instead, the company leveraged the successful Santa Fe casino, issuing $115 million in junk bonds in December 1993. Lowden was willing to bet his last hand in order to preserve his absolute control over the company's stock.

Cash flow from the Santa Fe casino paid the interest on that debt rather than being used to improve the wages and benefits of the casino's employees; in essence, the company's expansion plans were being financed by the Santa Fe's workers. The Santa Fe could afford to meet those interest obligations at the time because it had a monopoly in its northwest neighborhood, but overall the company was highly leveraged and gambling on its ability to generate higher and higher revenues. In contrast, the bulk of the industry was expanding through stock offerings, a more financially stable source of funding, but one that required power-sharing. Lowden's obsession with control led the company into a financial quagmire.

Consequently, the union chose to oppose Sahara's new riverboat plans actively. There was Moline, Illinois, where Sahara lost the last of ten state casino licenses to what is now the highest revenue generating riverboat in the state; Parkville, Missouri, a small bedroom community on the Missouri River, which endured four public referenda on the issue of gaming and emerged deeply divided and without a casino; and Mississippi, where Sahara managed two riverboat casinos for Treasure Bay Gaming and Resorts, which filed for bankruptcy and ejected Sahara management late in 1994. The union submitted testimony to gaming regulators in all three states and distributed information about Sahara's record to Parkville's voters in that town's three successive gaming elections.

By July 1995, Santa Fe had to write off $25 million spent on the failed Missouri and Mississippi riverboats, while it desperately held on to one last expansion project. Addicted to debt, the company had taken out a one-year loan of $15 million in March 1994 to buy a piece of vacant property in the Las Vegas suburb of Green Valley on which to build a neighborhood casino modeled on the existing Santa Fe. In the fall of 1994, Sahara attempted to raise $75 million in the bond market to finance the project, called Santa Fe Valley, but the offering was unsuccessful. With its $15 million loan coming due, the company negotiated a sale of the Green Valley property to Players International, a riverboat company looking for Las Vegas operations. After the union informed Players about the "organizing language" in its existing union contracts, Players terminated the agreement to purchase the Green Valley property. Sahara Gaming sued the Culinary over its letter, but the case was dismissed and appealed. Shortly thereafter, Sahara Gaming sought a buyer for its Hacienda and Sahara casinos on the Strip in part to repay the Green Valley loan.

Meanwhile, the union's citywide contracts came up for renewal in June 1994. By then, the Strip looked very different than it had five years earlier. In fall 1993, Mirage Resorts opened Treasure Island, another mega-resort, near the Mirage, and Circus Circus Enterprises opened the pyramid-shaped Luxor Hotel and Casino next to the Excalibur. Both were highly themed resorts, pushing Las Vegas casinos to the next level of entertainment. They also recognized the Culinary Union and agreed to the Strip contract under the same process used at the Mirage and Excalibur. Those two casinos increased the union's citywide membership by another 5,500 workers months before the 1994 labor negotiations began.

The corporate landscape was also transformed. Most casino companies had issued public stock, taking advantage of Wall Street's fascination with gaming in the early 1990s. The Boyd Group went public, changing its name to Boyd Gaming; Jack Binion from the Horseshoe set up a new public company called Horseshoe Gaming to pursue riverboat casino projects, while keeping the Las Vegas casino in the family's hands; and many of the privately held and nonunion neighborhood casinos, Palace Station, Arizona Charlie's, and the Rio, issued public stock in one form or another. The division between corporate and family-owned casinos had shifted: the new divide was between the entertainment-oriented mega-resorts and the older, second-tier gambling halls.

The new resorts were joined by the $1 billion, 5,000-room MGM Grand Hotel, Casino and Theme Park, which opened on December 17, 1993. The Wizard of Oz–themed resort was developed by MGM Grand,

Inc., a public company 73 percent owned by Kirk Kerkorian. A multi-billionaire with forty years of experience investing in gaming, Kerkorian had built the International Hotel, now the Las Vegas Hilton, and the first MGM Grand, now Bally's. The new MGM Grand's chairman was Robert Maxey. Maxey had survived the Elsinore disaster, reemerging years later with a reputation for opening casinos on time and within budget. His management style was still driven by ideology, and he waged a highly public and costly campaign to prevent the union from organizing MGM Grand's employees. Long before the casino was completed, the defining union battle of the 1990s was launched.

MGM Grand became the first mega-resort since 1984 to risk its public image and public investment on an anti-union crusade. In 1992, when MGM Grand was putting the project's financing together, the union warned the investment community of Maxey's operating and labor relations record. It was the beginning of a campaign by the union to educate stock analysts and bond buyers that the most successful operations in Las Vegas embodied the spirit of a labor-management partnership, and that the MGM Grand would be managed with the goal of preventing unionization, not making the highest profit. The union also pointed out that companies with active union opposition, like MGM Grand, would face difficulties when competing for projects in the new gaming jurisdictions, because many were in cities with historically strong unions.

Part of Maxey's plan was to counter Culinary's growing political power before the casino's opening. Unlike most gaming companies, which as a matter of course give to both parties, sometimes in the same race, Maxey decided to contribute almost exclusively to Republican candidates for office. This alienated the state's Democratic party. MGM Grand also hired Black, Manafort, Stone and Kelly, a Washington-based lobbying firm known for representing dictators like Ferdinand Marcos of the Philippines, to forge a political agenda and a high-tech anti-union campaign. MGM Grand even had a "war room" from which executives and consultants directed their union-busting program.

The key to that program was MGM Grand's *union-scale* wage and benefit package. The company advertised the best wages and benefits in Las Vegas, highlighting the casino's on-site medical clinic, flex-time instead of vacation days, an in-house grievance procedure, and the University of Oz. It was a clear example of who set the standard of living among casino workers: in order to be nonunion, MGM Grand had to beat the union standard. Amid the greatest employment hype ever seen in Las Vegas, 100,000 people applied for 8,000 jobs. Included in the orientation program was a Wizard of Oz video in which Dorothy says that MGM Grand employees won't need outside representation. The tactic was anything but subtle.

On MGM Grand's opening night, 5,000 union members from Culinary and other service trades picketed the VIP celebration, causing a majority of the state's politicians not to attend. The governor and a host of state legislators, commissioners, and council members honored the picket line; it was the first time the governor had not attended the opening of one of Las Vegas's mega-resorts. Politically, a real tug-of-war ensued. Unlike the Elardis, MGM Grand was by nature a leader in the powerful corporate wing of the industry, not to mention being backed by a billionaire. But in the 1992 election season, the union had defeated Doc Pearson, a county commissioner supported by gaming, who had crossed the Frontier strike line to take contributions from the Elardis. The 1994 elections were around the corner, influencing politicians' choices that opening night.

After the opening, Maxey began searching for expansion opportunities outside Las Vegas. The stock market rewarded gaming companies that could expand into new jurisdictions, and after the casino's opening hype, MGM Grand's stock price was falling. The company chose China for its proximity to the Asian gambling market. MGM Grand negotiated an agreement with a resort town on the pristine island of Hainan, China, to develop a mega-resort. However, the Chinese central government was fundamentally opposed to gambling and had reacted schizophrenically to recently opened tourist-oriented casinos. The union investigated the difficulties and uncertainties affecting plans for gaming operations in China, and Hainan in particular, and reported them to gaming companies and investors.

MGM Grand's nonunion status became the centerpiece of labor negotiations that spring, making the union's rally on December 17 the first step in an ongoing battle. On May 26, 1994, days before the citywide agreement was set to expire, another 5,000 union members rallied, this time under threat of arrest. In a tactic reminiscent of a 1930s company town, MGM Grand laid claim to private ownership of the sidewalk and enlisted county bureaucrats to subvert the normal process of dedicating public sidewalks in a construction project, allowing the hotel to retain private property rights over them. MGM Grand then filed an easement granting pedestrians use of the sidewalk on its terms. No union activity was permitted. A showdown followed.

Defiantly asserting their constitutional rights, 500 union members were arrested that night for trespassing on the MGM Grand's sidewalk. They had not retreated in 1984 when arrests were used to squash union activity, and they would not back down in 1994. In response, the Culinary Union filed a civil fights lawsuit against MGM Grand, Clark County, and County Manager Pat Shalmy. The union argued that the three had conspired to deprive union members of their free speech rights in violation of the U.S. Constitution. The district attorney refused to prosecute the charges against the sidewalk picketers pending the litigation's outcome. The union casinos watched.

The MGM Grand situation dominated contract negotiations throughout the city. Across the board, companies proposed three-year agreements, instead of the standard five, because of uncertainty about whether the union would succeed in organizing their nonunion competitor. Most union casinos wanted labor peace, so that they could focus on their booming business and the myriad expansion opportunities outside of Nevada. They were also mindful of the tenacity of the Frontier strikers, who had demonstrated that the union would not give up.

Generally speaking, the casinos grouped themselves by size, with the mega-resorts negotiating together, the second-tier Strip casinos as a group, and the downtown casinos as another group. A number of casinos negotiated independently, like the Mirage casinos, the Sheraton–Desert Inn, and Harrah's. Among the mega-resorts, the toughest issue was subcontracting, or outsourcing, as it is called in manufacturing, the emerging practice of contracting out union work to nonunion employers. MGM Grand led the industry in leasing casino restaurants to independent restaurant companies. Resorts like Caesars Palace, Bally's, the Hiltons, and Harrah's wanted to attract similar restaurateurs by allowing them to hire nonunion workers. In turn, the union wanted to protect the jobs of its union members, as well as maintain the union standard in the industry. After members held mass meetings with managers in each of these casinos and picketed Harrah's over the issue, the mega-resorts agreed to language requiring that subcontracted work be done by union members under the collective bargaining agreement. The settlement also provided for 25 cents an hour in raises each year, continuation of the organizing language, and preservation of no-cost health insurance for workers and their families, making the union's the only no-cost family plan in the industry.

Two Strip companies, Sheraton–Desert Inn and Sahara Gaming, fought the agreement. Sheraton–Desert Inn proposed to open a 5,000-room Desert Kingdom next door and did not want to agree to language that facilitated unionization. Sheraton, a subsidiary of ITT Corporation, had recently purchased the Desert Inn, a luxury casino on the Strip. Despite being a newcomer to gaming, ITT attempted to undercut the industry standard. The Desert Inn became the focus of the union's membership, which held a variety of demonstrations at the resort and communicated the Las Vegas dispute to union members at other Sheratons. In addition, the same planning lawyer who had helped privatize the MGM Grand sidewalks represented ITT. The union protested Desert Kingdom's planning approval before the County Commission, demanding that the sidewalks remain public. The union's protests delayed the project's approval by two months, after which the company put its plans for Desert Kingdom on indefinite hold. After a six-month campaign that also raised questions about ITT's insurance business and risky derivative investments, Sheraton–Desert Inn accepted the Strip contract with an agreement not to fight unionization at the new project.

The second-tier Strip companies, including Sahara Gaming, formed their alliance in the belief that the smaller properties deserved a less costly contract, a position staked out by the Frontier. Their proposals were similar to downtown's. These groups made proposals such as lowering the number of hours in required shifts from eight to four, abolishing the 40-hour work week, and not extending the organizing language. The proposals were met with a fierce reaction by workers in those hotels, causing most of the casinos to drop out of the second-tier alliance and ultimately settle on the Strip contract. That left the Sahara and Hacienda casinos, owned by Sahara Gaming, alone with the Frontier.

Sahara Gaming was overburdened with debt and vulnerable to a job action at any of its casinos, especially the Sahara Hotel. The Sahara and Hacienda workers negotiated for over a year alongside the Santa Fe employees, picketing and boycotting the company's convention business. Instead of agreeing to the Strip contract, the Lowdens decided to sell the Sahara and Hacienda, its only Strip casinos. In an affidavit given late in 1995, Paul Lowden said: "The inability to reach agreement with Culinary for successor agreements was a major factor in my decision to seek a buyer for the Sahara and Hacienda and to sell those properties."[5] The new owners of the Sahara and the Hacienda signed the same union contracts as the rest of the Strip.

On April 20, 1995, Administrative Law Judge David Heilbrun issued a sweeping decision on the Santa Fe's challenge to the union election. He dismissed every charge brought by the Santa Fe against the union, discredited every witness who had given testimony on behalf of the Santa Fe, and ordered certification of the unions. Senator Lowden, who was by now the president of the Santa Fe, and her husband appealed that decision too. The irony was poetic: Senator Lowden, who sat in the legislature as the result of the electoral process, was ignoring the results of the union election because she did not like the outcome.

On April 29, 1995, 1,500 union members picketed the Santa Fe, launching a neighborhood boycott of the casino that over the next year would utilize tactics like placing yard signs in union members' front yards saying, "Stay Away from the Santa Fe," systematically calling customers, and appearing on radio talk shows. The union also contacted business customers like the Ben & Jerry's Scoop Shop, which planned to open inside the Santa Fe. In that case, the union obtained an unprecedented agreement that Ben & Jerry's would delay its opening by five months in support of the union boycott. The boycott roughly coincided with the opening of two new casinos in the Santa Fe's marketing radius: the Fiesta Hotel and Casino, which opened in December 1994, and Texas Hotel and Gambling Hall which followed in July 1995. The Santa Fe's cash flow dropped 40 percent after it lost its monopoly, and the casino no longer generated enough cash to pay the interest on the debt it borrowed for its failed riverboat projects.[6]

The Santa Fe's labor dispute also has a growing liability now. Despite the company's appeals, the union is certified as the employees' representative. As a result, all changes in working conditions must be negotiated with the union before the hotel implements them, just like at the Frontier. The NLRB has issued complaints over unilateral changes in the health plan, schedules, and work hours, for which every worker must be made whole under the law. That liability could be more than the Santa Fe can absorb in its current condition. The Santa Fe has been fighting unionization for three years, following in the footsteps of the Frontier, both facing the same bitter end.

In September 1995, the Ninth Circuit Court of Appeals made the final ruling that the Frontier's changes in working conditions, implemented four years earlier, were illegal, that Frontier workers were entitled to be made whole for those changes, and that the strikers were entitled to their jobs back. The total liability was estimated at between $10 and $60 million, a record decision in the history of labor relations in Nevada and an embarrassment to the gaming industry in this state. The dispute still lingered on. The strikers have been vindicated at every step of the process, but ultimately, the system has failed them. The Frontier broke the law, and the strikers are the only ones who will hold the casino accountable. In the end, union action brought the Elardis to their knees. In 1997, they sold the Frontier to Paul Ruffin, an out-of-town investor, who immediately settled the strike. It was a tremendous victory for the union and a defeat for the mentality represented by the Elardis. Stuck in the low-budget, nonunion mentality, the Elardi family fought and lost the entertainment revolution, of which the union is a growing part, now taking Las Vegas by storm.

In December 1995, the MGM Grand, which provided leadership for the Elardis and Lowdens from the potent corporate wing of the industry, resolved its union conflict. The company agreed to halt its anti-union campaign and recognized the Culinary Union as bargaining agent for 3,500 workers. In addition, New York New York, MGM Grand's joint venture with Primadonna Resorts, located across the Strip from the MGM Grand, agreed not to oppose unionization and to recognize the union based on a card check.

After MGM Grand's first year of operations, its revenues were flat. Operating income fell. Additionally, under Maxey's direction, the company had failed to execute any of its plans to expand outside Nevada, partly as a result of the union's campaign. Under mounting pressures to refocus the company's operations and end the labor dispute, Maxey resigned in June 1995 as MGM Grand's chairman and was replaced by J. Terrence Lanni, a former CEO of Caesars World. In the quarter ending March 31, 1996, nine months after Lanni took over operations, the MGM Grand produced a record 525 percent increase in net income and announced a refinancing plan to fund expansion into the coveted Atlantic City market. MGM Grand's stock price doubled during the first years of Lanni's reign.

Since the agreement with MGM Grand, the union tide has turned. Stratosphere Tower, Hotel and Casino, which opened on April 30, 1996, with 1,300 union workers, recognized the union based on a card check and agreed to a union contract substantially similar to the Mirage contract. Stratosphere is majority-owned by Grand Casinos, an emerging gaming company that manages Native American casinos and owns riverboat casinos in Mississippi. It was the first company without a pre-existing labor contract to agree to an amicable process for unionization in Las Vegas. It did so after careful observation of the Frontier strike and the MGM Grand agreement. On June 17, 1996, the new Monte

Carlo Hotel-Casino, a joint venture between Mirage and Circus Circus, recognized the union in a similar manner, as did downtown's Main Street Station and New York–New York, the newest entertainment superstore, or mega-resort, later that year. These four casinos added approximately 5,000 workers to the union fold. Most of the mega-resorts on line on the Strip have been developed by companies with union contracts and are union, including Mirage's Bellagio and Hilton's Paris.

Further evidence of the union's rise is the appointment of John Wilhelm, Culinary's chief negotiator and general secretary-treasurer of the HERE International Union, to the National Gambling Impact Study Commission, a congressionally mandated commission charged with studying the nationwide growth of gaming. He was appointed by Congressman Richard Gephardt to represent the point of view of the industry's workers, an appointment supported by many in the Las Vegas industry familiar with his keen understanding of the business.

The success of the Culinary Union's organizing efforts during this decade prompted the newly elected leadership of the national AFL-CIO to commit substantial resources to new organizing in Las Vegas, in a pilot program aimed at revitalizing the country's labor movement. Since the election of John Sweeney, Richard Trumka, and Linda Chavez-Thompson to its top three offices, the AFL-CIO has funded projects by the Building Trades and Service Employees Unions to organize construction and health care workers throughout Las Vegas, as well as supplementing Culinary's program to unionize the rest of the casino industry in Nevada. In Sweeney's words, Las Vegas has become the "heartbeat of the American labor movement."

The Lowdens and the Elardis were the last of the old-style casino families who had desperately held on to their ideological opposition to power sharing—the very heart of a partnership between labor and management. Senator Lowden sacrificed her position as the rising star of the state's Republican party to such ideology in 1996's most closely watched local election. Hundreds of union members volunteered for months to elect a political novice in Lowden's district, sending shock waves through the power structure on the November 5 election night. Her campaign was financed by the industry, and she was defeated by its workers.

As her company faded from the gaming scene in Las Vegas, Senator Lowden has become a good example of the old style of Las Vegas politics, where the casino-political complex was unchallenged. Her style was growing increasingly out of sync with the new balance of power, with respect not only to the union's deep and broad-based roots in the community but potentially to the influx of new residents, who are forever changing the one-industry, small town politics of Las Vegas. Arguably, the Lowdens and Elardis lost their place in the new Las Vegas, although it seems safe to say there will in the future be the occasional casino owner who, like them, puts ideology above better business and challenges the distribution of power.

The Culinary Union will continue to be a partner in Las Vegas's development, striving to ensure that gaming jobs provide a middle-class standard of living. That role was challenged by the emerging corporate gambling interests in 1984 and then by the family-run gambling halls. Those disputes forced the union to defend itself during the most tumultuous time in gaming's history. As Las Vegas's old-line families were consumed by the entertainment revolution of the corporate casinos, the union wove a path through the changes to emerge as one of the more powerful organizations in the state.

The Culinary Union has earned its place as the counterbalance to gaming's wealth and clout, securing its future in the industry's growth by being innovative, focused, and disciplined, just like the industry itself. In contrast, Las Vegas is expanding at an explosive rate and is enveloped in an unsettling sense of chaos. Unfettered construction, a haphazard infrastructure, and regressive policies for using the desert's scarce resources are the results of a laissez-faire approach to growth, an approach that is contributing to an unmanageable future. Las Vegas's boom recalls the early growth of Los Angeles, another western city overcome by chaos. As this desert city grows to an estimated 2.5 million residents in the next two decades, the Culinary Union's drive to unionize the rest of the industry will play a pivotal role in determining whether Las Vegas's working class, its economic foundation, will keep up with the rising cost of living. In the end, Las Vegas's hope of being different from Los Angeles and other sprawling southwestern cities lies in the fact that it is graced by a strong union movement with a unique ability to improve gaming's middle-class standard of living and maintain the new balance of power.

NOTES

1. Don Pulliam quoted in "Hotel Exec: Corporations Strangling LV Economy," *Las Vegas Review-Journal*, April 10, 1984.

2. Michael Drosnin, *Citizen Hughes* (New York: Holt, Rinehart & Winston, 1985), 131.

3. *Wall Street Journal,* January 10, 1991.

4. *Fortune,* September 21, 1992.

5. Affidavit of Paul Lowden, December 11, 1995.

6. Santa Fe's cash flow, or EBITDA, for the March quarter for 1996 was 43 percent lower than in the March quarter 1994, before the competition was open.

Class Struggle in Oz

The eighty-eight-foot lion that guarded the entrance to MGM's Emerald City casino looked unusually glum on the eve of the Memorial Day holiday, 1993. As dust devils chased early evening commuters down Tropicana Boulevard, Las Vegas police strapped tear-gas masks to their gun belts. Sullen resort security men in blue blazers stood sentry behind hastily improvised little signs declaring the adjacent sidewalk, probably the busiest section of the casino Strip, "private property." Earlier in the day, the management of Kirk Kerkorian's $1.1 billion Oz-themed family gambling complex had warned employees about "dangerous chaos," while a police spokesman had fretted that "someone might be killed."

For months, southern Nevada had been anxiously awaiting this dramatic rematch between the world's largest casino-hotel and the nation's biggest private-sector local union. The year before, the MGM Grand Hotel and Theme Park had broken ranks with the other new mega-resorts—Luxor, Excalibur, Treasure Island, and Mirage—and refused to bargain with Culinary Workers Local 226, the 40,000-member affiliate of the Hotel Employees and Restaurant Employees International Union (HEREIU). Robert Maxey, MGM's famous union-busting CEO,

This chapter was originally published as "Armageddon at the Emerald City: Local 226 vs. MGM Grand" in *The Nation*, vol. 259, no. 2 (July 11, 1994). It appears here in slightly modified form.

had announced that "in the best interest of our employees" the 5,005-room resort, whose hyperbolic but mundane architecture encloses the biggest single concentration of cash-points on earth (3,500 slot machines and 150 gaming tables), would open without a union contract. When 4,000 union members and their families mobilized in December to picket the resort's opening-night extravaganza, the police prevented them from assembling on the sidewalks. Invoking the fine print of its deal with Clark County, MGM claimed ownership of the pedestrian easements around its property. Outraged union leaders cried, "The sidewalks belong to the people" and promised to return in 1994.

So, on May 29, thousands of culinary workers, tiny American flags in hand, again gathered outside the gates of Oz. "We Get What We *Take*. We Keep What We Have the Strength to *Hold*," their banner declared. In a brief preliminary rally, State Senator Joe Neal from Las Vegas's largely black Westside urged demonstrators to become "lion killers," and Local 226 secretary-treasurer Jim Arnold reassured them that "Bob Maxey, like the Wizard, is just a greedy fake."

For the next three hours, as union loudspeakers blasted out Bruce Springsteen's "Born in the U.S.A.," the trespassers were arrested in groups of forty. Above the demonstration, the electronic ghost of Sinatra periodically materialized out of the digital fog of the MGM sign. The high-spirited pandemonium of the culinary workers—more than half of them black and Latino, maids in blue uniforms and bartenders in Hawaiian shirts—amazed the crowds of tourists who gawked, uncomprehending, from behind police barricades.

But the police seriously underestimated both the scale and militancy of the demonstration. After the first 500 busts, police commanders threw in the towel. Hundreds of unionists, having waited hours to be arrested, demanded their place on the police bus. A weary officer quipped back, "Next time, you guys should make reservations." Thus ended the biggest mass arrest in Nevada history.

THE LAST UNION TOWN IN AMERICA?

"No contemporary labor movement in the country, with the possible exception of the Mine Workers, has endured longer, more bitter strikes, or faced such constant repression," said Glen Arnodo, the ex-machinist from Cleveland who led the team of crack organizers assigned to the MGM Grand. Yet the culinary workers fought back with astonishing success, doubling their membership between 1984 and 1994. For this reason, Arnodo and others like to refer to Las Vegas as "the last great union town in America." This is not the ordinary image of Sin City, and Local 226's surprising ability to survive the Darwinian swamp of Reagan/Bush–era labor relations, as well as the corporate restructuring of the gaming industry, demands an explanation.

The gene for class struggle, after all, was not part of the local's heredity. For a quarter century until 1977, the culinary workers were dominated by their charismatic but roguish secretary-treasurer, Al Bramlett. Although Nevada became a right-to-work state in 1951, Bramlett negotiated a de facto union shop with Las Vegas's invisible government. In what many older workers still fondly recall as "the good old mob days," the godfathers recognized Local 226 in exchange for labor peace and a reliable supply of skilled workers. They also provided Bramlett with the "comps" needed to sustain his ostentatious lifestyle of fast cars, Italian suits, and beautiful women.

This sweetheart deal lasted until the mid 1970s, when Howard Hughes's Summa organization—the vanguard of the corporate succession that sent the Mafia into retirement—began to pressure other casino owners into taking a hard line against the union. At the same time, according to allegations before a Senate racketeering subcommittee, Chicago gangsters were attempting to seize control of Local 226's lucrative health and dental plan. When Bramlett reputedly resisted them, he was kidnapped at McCarran Airport, taken out into the desert, and shot three times in the heart and once in each ear. Horrified rockhounds later found his partially visible, decomposing face leering back at them from a hastily dug grave.

The back-slapping union machine and passive rank and file that Bramlett left behind were ill prepared to fight the giant corporations that were transforming Las Vegas's "green felt jungle" into a mass-market family resort. The first defining clash took place in 1984. Against the background of a local recession and the new competitive threat of Atlantic City, the Nevada Resort Association attempted to crush Local 226 and allied unions during a bitter, often violent sixty-one-day strike. For the first time in memory, strikebreakers were imported to keep the Strip operating, while a local judge enjoined mass picketing and the Metro Police filled the jails with 900 unionists. One strike veteran recalled the situation as "a literal Marxist paradigm—from judges to cops, the state was completely aligned with the casino owners."

On the brink of catastrophe, Vincent Sirabella, director of organizing for HERE, parachuted his best young organizers into the battle. Linking up with the most dogged rank-and-filers, they rallied the 17,000 strikers to keep the struggle going through the 100-degree heat of early June. The eventual settlement, covering forty-six hotels and casinos, was hailed by the AFL-CIO's president, Lane Kirkland, as a "major victory."

From the perspective of labor's national debacle in the early 1980s, it certainly was. But as D. Taylor, one of Sirabella's original commandos, explained to me: "The culinary workers also suffered grave wounds. Six casinos, led by Bob Maxey [then CEO of Elsinore Corporation], kept their scabs and decertified the union. Despite our public bravado, we knew that our members were demoralized and that the rest of the industry was simply biding its time until the next contract expiration to administer the coup de grâce."

The subsequent five years, according to Taylor, were "a desperate race against time to rebuild the union. Our highest priorities were restoring belief in the efficacy of the strike weapon and convincing old members that organizing new members was more important than higher wages." The young turks from the International, including a "whiz kid" research team set up during HERE's famous clerical workers' strike at Yale University, made common cause with the 400 to 500 picket captains under Jim Arnold who had been the backbone of local militancy in 1984. When contract time came up in 1989, they mounted such impressive demonstrations that the Resort Association backed down from new union-busting attempts.

Local 226, moreover, won unprecedented contract language that year guaranteeing employer neutrality in organizing drives and immediate union recognition if a majority of workers signed union cards, eliminating the need for costly and bruising elections. The first such agreement was negotiated by Steve Wynn, the Strip's wunderkind, and applied to the Mirage, the first of the mega-resorts. "In essence we brought the more progressive Canadian system of union recognition to Las Vegas," says Taylor. The 1989 contract also created a split between the giant gaming corporations and an increasingly virulent group of traditional family-owned casinos.

The notorious Five Families (the Binions, Boyds, Gaughans, Engelstads, and Elardis) still retain great political clout in Nevada, although economically overshadowed by the Fortune 500 mega-casinos. Since the 1984 strike, they have tried to undermine union gains by demanding givebacks and firing union supporters without cause. Cowboy capitalism, of course, has always been inclined to fascism. Literally so in the case of the Imperial Palace's bizarre proprietor, Ralph Engelstad, who glorified the Holocaust in a huge private suite decorated with swastikas and floor-to-ceiling portraits of prominent Nazis, collects human soap and skulls from death camp victims, and in April 1988 threw a lavish birthday party for Hitler.

Although Local 226, with the decisive help of Jesse Jackson and the city's black community, beat the most powerful of these families, the Binions, in a ten-month strike against the Horseshoe Casino in 1990, workers were locked in deadly combat with the Elardis at the Frontier. Beginning in 1991, the Frontier strike projected extraordinary scenes, including a demonstration by 20,000 union supporters and a 300-mile march across the Mojave Desert to Los Angeles by twelve strikers. Not a single Frontier striker has crossed the picket line, but the Elardis, despite the estimated loss of 40 percent of their gross revenue, remained intransigent. In a war of attrition carefully monitored by the entire industry, Local 226 was grimly determined either to win or to close down the Frontier and sow salt on its ruins. In the end, in 1998, the union won a major victory.

THUNDER FROM THE BACK OF THE HOUSE

The union hall of Local 226 is surrounded by pungent symbols of this city's greed and despair. For most of the day, it is in the shadow of casino owner Bob Stupak's mad phallic fantasy, the Las Vegas Stratosphere. Just south of the hall are the stucco tenements and converted motels that house the working poor who serve the city's nonunion employers. Meanwhile, a colony of homeless men has established itself across from the union parking lot. Some of them are what Las Vegans contemptuously refer to as "reverse Okies"—refugees from southern California's structural recession.

A few days before the assault on Oz, the 1,000-member Citywide Organizing Committee, the union's "rank-and-file engine," met to discuss strategy and demands. D. Taylor had just given a familiar sermon on why the union must reinvent itself as a social movement, in which each member is an organizer, when the local's president, Hattie Canty, stepped forward to speak. Scanning the room for the tired faces of African-American and Latina women, she said: "Housekeepers! This is your time. You hold the keys to the 1994 contract. In order to be a true union, all departments must have a place at the table. This year you must be at the fore."

Local 226, reflecting the revolution in the size and composition of the work force, is in the midst of a profound transition. In the Bramlett era, the union was led by white men who primarily articulated the needs of high-paid tipped employees from the "front of the house"—doormen, bartenders, bellboys, waiters, and cocktail servers. The maids and kitchen helpers (then largely black, now majority Latino) were frequently ignored. With the coming of the mega-resorts, however, the "back of the house" contingent has soared. Nine of the world's ten largest hotels are now in Vegas (the tenth is in Moscow), and each depends on several hundred housekeepers per shift. Indeed, some 9,000 maids and cleaners constitute the second-largest occupational category (after table-waiting) in the city's booming economy.

The election of Canty, a black woman who raised ten kids while making beds in Maxim's, has given new prominence to the exploitation of housekeepers. According to the *Monthly Labor Review,* maids and housemen—exposed daily to back strain, falls, and toxic cleaning chemicals—suffer 60 percent of the disabilities in the lodging industry (which, in turn, has among the largest number of occupational injuries). Housekeepers I met at contract meetings argued passionately that killer quotas—having to clean as many as eighteen rooms per day in some hotels—must ultimately become a strike issue for the whole union.

Empowering the "back of the house" also means enfranchising a new union majority: 25 percent Latino, 22 percent black, and 7 percent Asian. And this extends beyond the union hall. For example, a union-run job-training center established in 1992 was to provide young blacks from the West Side and North Las Vegas with the skills to enter previously white-only domains such as cocktail serving and specialty cuisine. Yet some union activists frankly acknowledge that Local 226 must be more aggressive in the face of persistent discrimination by the large casinos.

Black workers, moreover, frequently express their fear of "creeping Miami-ization." Latinos, an almost negligible stratum in 1960, are now the largest minority in the city. Unlike African Americans, however, they have almost no political clout, and their poverty rate is considerably higher. As Hattie Canty emphasizes, the union is the major melting pot for the city's increasingly diverse ethnicities, and it must struggle ceaselessly to reinforce their solidarity inside and outside the workplace.

Local 226 is also the dike holding back a deluge of minimum-wage labor. Thanks to the downsizing of defense industries in southern California since the end of the Cold War, the supply of labor far outstrips the demand. When the MGM Grand began hiring in 1993, it was overwhelmed by more than 100,000 applicants, 30 percent of them former residents of the Los Angeles area. Evidence of a new immiseration—homelessness, crack addiction, youth gangs, even malnutrition—can be easily discerned on the side streets of the Strip. Unionized workers are becoming acutely conscious that the survival of their middle-class standard of living (two-thirds of Local 226 members own their homes) is strictly dependent on their fighting strength in the workplace.

THE YELLOW BRICK ROAD

With MGM, particularly, there's no underestimating the enemy. "Make no mistake," Glen Arnodo told me, "MGM Grand is a brilliant template for deunionizing Las Vegas. Unlike the smaller grind joints and scab casinos, its hourly wage structure is comparable to the union contract, and it provides an in-house medical clinic for employees, who also enjoy a flextime vacation scheme and company pension plan. It has even semantically abolished the subordination of labor to capital. From dishwasher to housekeeper, everyone has been transformed from employee into 'cast member' with a 'part' and indoctrinated with an anti-union video."

Meanwhile, the privatized sidewalks and an elite security force, recruited from veterans of the Metro Police intelligence squad, keep organizers at a distance. Maxey has also imported the Washington, D.C., firm of Black, Manafort, Stone and Kelly to coordinate anti-union public relations. As Arnodo points out, "Their past clients have included such progressive causes as George Bush, Jesse Helms, Ferdinand Marcos, and President Mobutu!"

Yet he is confident that Local 226 will eventually recruit a majority of the 6,000 MGM workers (out of a total "cast" of 8,000) who are eligible for union membership. "Maxey cannot provide the three S's that workers crave: security, seniority, and solidarity. It will take time for green employees—including the refugees from L.A. and the kids fresh from McDonald's—to appreciate this, but hundreds of former culinary workers now working at MGM already understand the difference." Indeed, at the end of May, a group of MGM workers risked their jobs to attend one of the union's huge precontract rallies. "I've worked at MGM since it opened," Barbara Bickson, a hotel porter and single mother of four, told the crowd, "but recently my hours were cut from eighty every two weeks to twenty-seven. There was nothing I could say about it. We need a union to protect job security and guarantee us a voice of our own."

Local 226's strategy for organizing Oz is a fascinating combination of CIO fundamentalism and high-tech anticorporate guerrilla warfare. Arnodo, whose grandfather fought in the ranks of the bloody "Little Steel" organizing drive in the late 1930s, admonishes his MGM contacts that the burden of the struggle will be borne by the internal cadre. Members of the (inside) MGM organizing committee are being recruited solely on the basis of their willingness to risk their jobs and more. At the same time, 40,000 other culinary workers are being trained as a disciplined street army. The May 29 protest was just a dress rehearsal. (Nevada's deputy attorney general, Chuck Gardner, made a close legal analysis of MGM's sidewalk dictatorship, writing that the state has no authority "to 'deed away' fundamental constitutional rights" like free speech and assembly.)

The union's research department has also been transformed into an offensive weapon. When MGM offered Barbra Streisand $20 million for two New Year's performances, for example, the department sent female members of Congress videotapes of waitresses at a casino formerly run by Maxey (the nonunion Rio) who denounced him as "among the worst offenders of women's rights" and described how they had been sexually harassed and made to wear degrading uniforms. A dozen congresswomen urged Streisand to meet with union women. Although the liberals' godmother and the world's wealthiest voice (an LA TV station calculated that Streisand would earn $1,390 per second from the gig) ignored their request, the ensuing publicity drove Maxey into a daylong tantrum against Local 226's "corporate terrorists."

Focusing on Maxey rather than on the owner, Kirk Kerkorian, is deliberate strategy. Whereas Oz's CEO is renowned as a die-hard antiunion ideologue, Kerkorian, its 73 percent owner, with whom the culinary workers eventually hope to negotiate a contract, has a reputation as a business pragmatist. In the next stage of their campaign, union researchers put Kerkorian's bottom-line sensibility to the test by concentrating pressure on his highly leveraged corporation's access to capital. HERE contributed political muscle around the country to block proposed MGM Grand expansion plans.

If organizers like Arnodo and Taylor have a vision of Las Vegas as the "Detroit of the postindustrial economy," which will establish a high-wage standard for service-sector workers across the country, they also have a nightmare that the MGM Grand ("the River Rouge of gambling") may be the beginning of the end for Local 226. As the old saying goes, the culinary workers don't need a weatherman. . . . In D. Taylor's words: "This is the defining struggle for Las Vegas labor. It will be a very long, nasty campaign that could easily become the catalyst to a gigantic strike in this town."

PART III **VOICES**

"Squeezing the Juice Out of Las Vegas"
Reflections On Growing Up in Smalltown, USA

Having "juice" was everything when I was a kid growing up in Las Vegas in the 1970s. Juice was not a tangible thing. You couldn't actually see it, but you knew when someone had it. If you had juice or access to someone with it, you could get into any show or restaurant on the Strip—without paying. The joy of having juice lay only partially in the fact that you didn't have to pay. The real joy was knowing that *you had* the juice. Having juice also meant that you didn't have to wait in a line to see a show. Waiting in lines was only for the chump tourists. When I was twelve years old, I loved being able to go to a Las Vegas showroom and have the maitre d' walk my family and me to the head of the line and watch the look on tourists' faces as they wondered what was so special about us that we didn't have to wait like they did. The pleasure came from the fact that they knew we had juice. The free flow of juice provided locals with perks and privileges and, most important, with a degree of respectability. Being Italian and from Las Vegas was a difficult predicament for a kid going to college in Los Angeles. I don't know how many times I defended my birthplace with the refrain "Growing up in Las Vegas is like growing up in Smalltown, USA." The entire time I lived in LA, I defended my hometown—more times than I can count. As time passed, I began not only to appreciate the town's outlaw image (which, by association, became my own) but actively to cultivate it. When someone asked where I was from, I instantly snapped, "I'm from Las Vegas and, yes, I live in a hotel, and, yes, my mom is a hooker, and, yes, we have a roulette wheel mounted on the wall above our fire-place." My Italian ancestry only added to the image. Once I found out where the questioner was from, I dug the knife in deeper by asking, "Is it true that people from Anywhere, USA, really like wearing concrete shoes?" While I fashioned myself as a renegade, I genuinely believed that my experience was no different than anyone else's. I began to con-sider that this might not be the case as I reflected upon how juice influ-enced my life as I was growing up.

Those who had the power to do favors because of their juice did not become arrogant. Part of the obligation of having juice required the possessor to be generous. In fact, most of those who actually possessed juice took pleasure in taking care of friends. An Italian immigrant who worked in casinos his entire life, my grandfather had numerous contacts with those with juice. He dealt cards in "illegal" gambling halls in the Midwest until the police decided to stop taking bribes. Grandpa and many of his European ethnic co-workers moved to Las Vegas in the late 1950s to work where gambling was legal. I remember the countless times I walked into casinos with him or my mother and was introduced to someone who worked there whom they had known for years. It was somewhat uncouth for a person with juice to wait for a friend to ask for a favor. If the person with the juice had real class, he took the ini-tiative to ask first if you were hungry and wanted to eat in the hotel restaurant or see a show. "I want you to meet my grandson," my grand-father would say to one of the pit bosses watching over the tables. "I've known your grandfather since before you were born," the pit boss would reminisce. As a token of his affection and tribute to his longtime relationship with my grandfather, he would then ask, "Are you hungry? Why don't you go have something to eat?" That night dinner was on the hotel.

While kids throughout the country played baseball and went to sum-mer camp at the end of the school year, my friend Robbie and I rode our bicycles to the Aladdin Hotel on the Strip, where my mom worked, and where her juice enabled us to partake of a free lunch in the hotel restaurant. This was a spectacular outing for two twelve-year-old kids. Because my mom worked on the fourth floor as an executive secretary for the casino brass, she was well equipped with the juice necessary to ensure a pleasant day. The first leg of our adventure involved riding our bicycles down Las Vegas Boulevard, commonly known as the Strip. It was tradition for Robbie and me to stop on the sidewalk in front of Caesars Palace, where at the base of the hotel's marquee were life-size statues that included everyone from Caesar himself to his Roman servants. As tourists walked by gawking at the Roman "art," Robbie and I involved ourselves in conversations with Caesar and his retinue. Without cracking a smile, we asked Caesar for directions or if he had the time and proceeded to yell at him for ignoring us when he refused to answer. Out of the corner of my eye, I looked for the puzzled expression on the tourists' faces as they tried to make sense of the entire affair. Most passersby quickly understood that two kids were having fun at their expense, but occasionally some walked away with a look of disgust, holding firm to the conviction that they had beheld what happens when children grow up in Sin City.

After finally arriving at mom's hotel, the first privilege we enjoyed was carrying our bicycles to the gaudily decorated executive offices, where we stored them so that they wouldn't get ripped off. Our minds at ease with the knowledge that our bicycles were safe, we started the day by lying out at the pool, basking in the hot desert sun among the many pale-skinned midwesterners in search of a good time. After cooling off from the long bike ride and "accidentally" splashing tourists trying to relax on their vacation, we headed back to mom's office to get the obligatory complimentary ticket, or "comp slip." The word "comp" functioned as either a noun or a verb. You could receive a comp, which meant you ate for free, or someone could comp you. Theoretically, comps functioned as an incentive to appease gamblers by keeping them in the casino to ensure that they continued betting. The longer a patron gambled, the more likely it was that the house would come out on top. Without batting an eye, my mom's boss comped my friend and me for lunch in the hotel restaurant. Like everyone with the power to comp, he understood the reciprocal nature of the relationship between himself and those for whom he did favors.

With comp slip firmly in hand, Robbie and I headed to the hotel's gourmet restaurant to feed our faces or, as grandpa used to say, get the wrinkles out of our bellies. We were in heaven! After starting with a shrimp cocktail for an appetizer, we had the waitress bring on the New York steak. We topped off our lunch with the dessert of our choice and usually washed it down with a milkshake. Although as minors we couldn't legally gamble, we entertained ourselves with the crayons and keno tickets available at our table by blackening a selection of numbers. Waiting with anticipation to see if the numbers lighting up on the keno board corresponded to those we had selected, we fantasized about the things we'd have bought if we had really placed a bet.

With bellies unwrinkled, we headed back upstairs to mom's office. She introduced my friend and me to the executive who supervised hotel security, and I'm not talking about a security guard who threw out the occasional loud-mouthed drunk who lost control at one of the tables. No, mom's friend was The Eye in the Sky, the guy in charge of camera surveillance to ensure that employees weren't stealing and that players weren't cheating the house. He took us upstairs to his headquarters and showed us the panel of dials and switches he used to control the numerous television monitors throughout the casino that provided him with a bird's-eye view of the tables. Robbie and I were amazed. I remembered thinking that anyone would be crazy to cheat under those circumstances. The Eye in the Sky also showed us his newest piece of equipment, a lie detector.

The polygraph machine was a fairly new invention at the time, and the hotel had just acquired one. Mom's friend was in charge of administering the test to anyone suspected of cheating or stealing. Contained in a metal suitcase with a number of wires, paper readouts, and knobs, it was an ominous-looking contraption. He offered to show us how it worked, and my friend and I took turns trying to out-lie one another. He showed us a playing card and instructed us to lie in response to every question he asked. When he asked if the card was between one and five, we said no. When he asked if it was red, we said no. By gauging our responses to each of his questions, he was able to determine which card we had picked. "Man," my twelve-year-old mind thought, "if you take money from this place, you'll be one sorry sucker."

Hearing the stories my college friends told of growing up in other cities, I began to consider that maybe my Las Vegas wasn't as typical as I liked to think. For instance, when I was thirteen, a classmate and I decided to take the day off school after we'd missed the bus. We were faced with the predicament that all kids cutting class face once they've made the fateful decision—"What do we do now?" Although ditching school was and continues to be practiced by ornery little cusses throughout the country, growing up in Las Vegas provided us with some additional options. Since we were in a town that offered few distractions for children, we figured our only option was the Las Vegas Strip. Kids who cut school in Las Vegas did not regularly go to the Strip. Because we understood that we were going to a place where children stood out like a sore thumb, we headed for the one hotel where kids were common— Circus Circus. Although a gambling establishment like any other Vegas resort, Circus Circus was the first hotel to offer minors some form of entertainment. On the second floor overlooking the casino, kids could enjoy a number of circuslike games for a few quarters and try their luck at winning a stuffed animal or glass figurine. Of course, when we arrived at 8:00 A.M., all the games were shut down for the obvious reason— most kids are in school at this time. As it turned out, we didn't care that we never had the chance to play any of the games. Without a hoard of children to supervise, the security guards were absent from the entire second floor where the games were located. We took advantage of the silly fools who underestimated our cunning by proceeding to help ourselves to four-foot Wile E. Coyotes and Pink Panthers. We didn't feel that we were actually *stealing* the stuffed animals. Having experienced the privilege of receiving comps for all of my thirteen years, I grew up with the understanding that locals received certain entitlements. Unlike tourists, we shouldn't have to pay for such amusements.

With our animals grasped firmly in hand, we went on to another adventure. We hadn't got very far from Circus Circus when we noticed the Hollywood-style camera crews in front of the Desert Inn Hotel. After spotting the 1950-something fire-truck-red Ford Thunderbird under the hotel canopy, we instantly knew what was going on. They were filming *Vegas*, the cheesy television drama starring Robert Urich as Dan Tanna, a private detective who fights crime and always gets the girl. My friend and I instinctively headed for the action, for we both knew that excitement lay ahead.

We stood for hours waiting to see Dan Tanna jump onto a craps table, pull out his revolver, and shoot it out with a Vegas bad guy. Unfortunately, we were sorely disappointed. Despite missing school, we received an education that day—in the not-so-magic world of movie-making. We were shocked to discover that Robert Urich was nothing like the character he played on television. Absolutely *nothing* exciting happened! We waited for hours, only to hear Urich repeat some stupid cliché over and over again, something like "When the dice roll, that's the way it goes in Vegas." That's the way *what* goes? What dice? What the hell did Robert Urich know about Las Vegas anyway? He was just some phoney baloney actor from Hollyweird.

Desperate for excitement, we gave up on the pretty-boy actor and walked out front to fuel our fascination by peering at the Ford Thunderbird, which my brother and I used to swear we'd own one day. To add insult to injury, the security guards barked at us to stay away from the car. I snapped back, "What do you think we're gonna do, steal it? I can't even reach the gas pedal." I didn't care about Dan Tanna's stinking red jalopy anyway. In my thirteen-year-old mind, I wondered who could get excited about a car with phoney license plates that read VEGAS in stick-on letters. Needless to say, watching the television show after that day was a very hollow experience.

While I was growing up, Las Vegas was still a relatively small town. The population was roughly 300,000, and people usually bumped into someone they knew wherever they went. Intimate social ties created an atmosphere that gave locals the feeling they had a stake in the town. Kids like myself who had grown up in an atmosphere where certain privileges were available to locals eventually began to see a change.

Corporate gaming squeezed the juice out of Las Vegas, at least this was the impression among family members who worked in the casinos—and, for that matter, the only impression that mattered. The idea that "things were better in Vegas when the mob ran the town" has now become a popular refrain among longtime residents. Because I experienced life there before and after this change, I can't help but wonder if it's true.

Many "credit" one of Nevada's current senators, Harry Reid, with "cleaning up" the town. Early in his political career, as head of the Gaming Control Board, Reid initiated a campaign to run the mob out of Las Vegas. To outsiders, Reid was a clean-cut good guy who rode into town wearing a white hat, with six-shooters strapped to his hips, determined to run the black-hat-wearing bad guys out of town by sundown. The Aladdin was the first hotel to be closed in Las Vegas because of ties to organized crime. The Gaming Control Board charged that the licensed owner was really a front man covering for mobsters who profited from the hotel. As a result of Reid's missionary zeal, my mom lost her job and significant economic hard times hit our family. Thousands of others also lost their jobs as a result of the hotel's closure. I'm not an apologist for organized crime, but I can't help wondering if Reid ever considered the working-class people who suffered while he carved out a name for himself as a "get tough" politician on the way to his current position as a U.S. senator. Hard-working people like my mother who lost their jobs didn't know or care who owned the hotel. Almost twenty years later, I remember the anxiety in our home for the prolonged period of time my mother remained unemployed. In our house, Reid wore the black hat.

My mom's boss at the Aladdin eventually rehired her after he had moved on to another hotel, but her experiences there revealed that the juice in Las Vegas was beginning to dry up. In the late 1970s, Steve

Martin had been hitting it big as a comedian across the country and was going to be playing at the hotel where my mom had begun to work. My friends and I listened nonstop to Martin's comedy albums and laughed till our sides hurt as we watched him on television dance around the stage wearing those stupid rabbit ears that made him so famous. Having worked in casinos for so many years, my family never had a problem getting into any show, but the fact that Martin was such a hot commodity altered the equation. Mom told my brother and me not to get our hopes up, but that she'd drop a hint to her boss that we'd like to see the show and he would probably provide her with a comp. When my mom came home that day, my brother and I were the envy of our entire block after telling our friends that we were going to see Steve Martin. Our status instantly skyrocketed when they realized we had the juice.

My mom, brother, and I got dressed up, went to the showroom, and sat down at the table on the night of the show, but we never got to see Steve Martin. It wasn't until we were seated that the waiter pointed out to my mother that, although we had a reservation for the show, her boss had not signed a complimentary pass, and that the $150 admission charge was due in full. This amount of money for a two-hour show was not in our family budget. The same man who comped two little kids to the hotel restaurant had become reluctant to go out on a limb in the new corporate climate by comping someone who was not a hotel guest. It was an embarrassing situation, both for him and for us. Rather than spend money we didn't have, the three of us looked at each other with disappointment and headed for the door. What had made Vegas acceptable to locals had been the acknowledgment that they were different from tourists. Those with the juice took care of those without it. Reid effectively ran the mob out of Las Vegas, opening the door for corporate gaming and altering a way of life that locals had come to expect and enjoy.

Locals don't matter anymore in Las Vegas. When I was eight years old, my mom took me to see Elvis at the Hilton Hotel. As we were waiting for the showroom doors to open, a hotel employee wheeled a rack of rhinestone-studded white leather costumes past us toward the stage. I was amazed. "Wow! Those are the King's clothes!" These were the very clothes that he wore later that night as he performed his famous karate moves on stage and handed out scarves embroidered with his signature to the pretty women sitting up front. I can still see one of Elvis's white leather jumpsuits and cape, but to do so I have to go to the Hard

Rock Hotel where they are preserved behind glass. Corporate establishments like the Hard Rock are changing the town, making Las Vegas respectable to the mainstream, but without having to court locals in the process. Las Vegas is no longer the small town where I grew up and where locals experienced the intimacy that made possible a chance encounter with Elvis's clothes.

SHANNON MCMACKIN

I Didn't Know Anybody Lived There

I cringe whenever someone asks, "So, where are you from?" I know the next few minutes of conversation by heart. "Las Vegas? Oh, I didn't know anybody lived there." I shrug my shoulders. But the second question always follows, "So what was it like growing up in Vegas?" I never know what to say. I could bring up stories people want to hear, of my sister Sukey baby-sitting me backstage of a Liberace show in between her dance numbers, or how I went to school with the mob's offspring, or the tacky grass shack bar with its blue rainwater fountain we had in our living room. Maybe people just want me to entertain them with a discussion of the conceptual *meaning* of Vegas.

Instead, hoping to end the conversation, I finally come out with: "Growing up in Las Vegas was, well, normal." Then I change the subject, because the Las Vegas imagery that comes to most people's mind is far removed from the barren landscape I remember.

Besides, it depresses me to be reminded that the desert where I collected lava rocks as a kid has since sprouted into four exclusive golf courses; that the mesa where coyotes howled is now condos; or that corporate kings stuffed dynamite into the Dunes Hotel and Casino, destroying the site of my senior prom. It is only since my hometown has become a worldwide phenomenon, and since people have started chuckling when I tell them where I was born, that I have realized that most people think there is something peculiar about growing up in Las Vegas. The fact is, I didn't know it was any different. I think my family expe-

rience in Las Vegas could have been anywhere in the Southwest; my family settled a desert plot and grimaced at suburban growth. The difference was that we happened to dwell on the fringe of a town with an unusual industry.

SUBURBAN INCORPORATION

Suburbia came to us in this time of running out of space. Dried worms on the sidewalk crawl out from the grass while the sprinkler blasts. The sun bakes the pavement in the desert heat. Swamp cooler rattles. Coming up for air with no time to duck back into the pool to shield my ears against the sonic booms of jets overhead.

I was born in 1967, the year the first mall in Las Vegas, the Broadway, was erected next door to our house. The area was remote, with the exception of our street of homes. This pocket along Maryland Parkway was important because until then most locals, like my family, had lived in apartments directly off Las Vegas Boulevard, known as the Strip. My brothers and sisters rode the school bus down the Strip to Las Vegas's first school on Fourth Street; like every other American schoolchild, they practiced A-bomb drills every morning after the Pledge of Allegiance.

Then, in 1969, we were surrounded when Las Vegas's first master-planned community, "Spring Valley," was built around our house. So, we moved deeper into the desert—onto the edge of a mesa—to get away from the development. Only dirt roads led past a cattle ranch and horse corrals to our new house, which sat with two others around a Bermuda grass golf course. That is, until they built Las Vegas's second master-planned development, "Green Valley," around us. It seemed as though my family's strategic moves to "nowhere" always found us somewhere in the middle of development.

All by ourselves, my brother and I tried to stop it. With orders from Mom, we tore through graded desert plots—me on the back of my brother's scooter—pulling up subdivision marker stakes, orange plastic ribbons blowing behind.

But our childhood eco-terrorist acts were to no avail, and what Mom dubbed "instant city" moved in. From then on, my parents made it their intent to disregard these intruders and live life as we had before the encroaching condos. When the developers decided to widen and pave the road, taking out our circular driveway in the process, Dad decided to leave the five-foot cliff that had once been our drive until we were adequately compensated. Eight years later, the developers finally tired of looking at the unsightly overhang in the middle of what had become fancy, custom-home lots, and paid us a bundle. Dad installed air-conditioning soon afterward, so I guess he won that battle.

The funny thing is that the developers' arrogance just made my parents do everything they could to "white-trash" our house. It started when they sent notices soliciting homeowners dues for the privilege of living in our new neighborhood. Apparently, they wanted us to pay for paving our roads, plowing our driveway, intercepting our natural spring to pump in city water, and installing those hideous yellow street lights that ruined our family's after-dinner star-gazing ritual.

Well, my Dad would have none of that. He started hauling as much junk as he could find to deposit on our three lots. There were the fire-ravaged 40-foot mobile home; beat-up old cars; tractors; piles of useless, rusting stuff; and, of course, the enormous cement mixer that has long been a fixture in our front yard. The war escalated. We continued our crusade against the Homeowners Association and their demand for dues. They mailed us the minutes of their meetings detailing the newest homeowner rules; these were typically an accounting of everything in our yard. If they mentioned anything we didn't have, such as live farm animals, Dad was sure to go out and get some goats.

The developers' most devastating blow came when they staked out a

property line we thought was ours and graded over our pet cemetery. It was the area under the oleanders behind the house where, on those sad occasions, we slowly marched in the hot sun, tears flowing, as Mom read Psalm 23: "He maketh me to lie down in green pastures. . . . Though I walk through the valley of the shadow of death." My brother Corby dug a grave in the caliche where we put our rag-wrapped beloved pet in a shoe box, sprinkled sand, which the wind helped blow over the grave, decorated the plot with lava rocks shaped into a peace sign, topped it with a creosote bush cross, and placed a peanut butter jar of freshly cut garden roses at the base.

These weren't green pastures being developed. It was arid land. We fought to keep it ours because cementing over the desert was death to my family's way of life. So we kept moving away from civilization and attempted to live off the barren land as primitive desert rat settlers. Unfortunately, everyone followed, with their own backyards. Our vision of paradise was open space, while others were migrating to Las Vegas to chase a paradise they'd heard was an oasis with clean air, and without traffic and violence, all eroded advantages that haven't existed in Las Vegas since I was a kid.

DESERT LANDSCAPE

I had the desert around my house memorized. I walked for miles into the low brush, always able to find my way home from a familiar rock, sand, bush, or pattern on the desert floor; this was my stomping ground. I wandered through the thick creosote brush along the sandy sides of alkali washes using scattered lava rocks as my footpath; the game was to avoid scarring the sandy crust.

Sometimes, though, my best friend Eris and I made a game of seeing who could pick up one of the whole crusted, clay tiles that patterned the wash beds. I gently eased my fingertips under the corners that curved up from baking in the sun. Then, I lifted the tile out of its place, leaving a soft spot in the cracked surface of the wash. The trick was keeping the tile from disintegrating to dust.

I busied myself with hunting expeditions under the canopy of wires draped between wooden telephone poles in search of fallen green or purple glass conductors. I also conducted thorough treasure hunts through the desert dumps—kicking up rusted cans and rummaging around discarded mattresses. The Union Pacific railroad tracks offered curious finds. Empty rifle cartridges were so common, I pretended they were the clam shells of the desert.

Not all of my entertainment came from the desert. The abandoned

golf course was our park. At dusk, when there was a degree of relief from the heat, my brothers and sisters descended onto the turf to play football and toss Frisbees for the dogs.

During summer thunderstorms, the golf course became a water park when flash floods caused storm drains to empty a gushing river onto the grass. My brother boogie-boarded on the slick surface while I rafted down the green grass. I remember how the golf course swelled into a swift current during the summer storm of 1975 that dropped nearly the entire annual rainfall within minutes. The newspaper ran a photo of cars floating down the Strip.

The desert's extreme nature didn't dissuade my parents from their romantic notion of living off the land. Once we moved into our second attempt at a "country house," my parents immediately mapped out a garden in a maze of railroad ties. One of the first chores was to make rock-hard dirt into fertile soil. My brother and I spent our summer sifting piles of stone from the sandy beds. After we had hauled in pure cow manure, our garden grew genetically defective vegetables and so much sun-tanned lettuce that we had to eat a leathery salad every night. Commenting on the absurdity of our desert garden never got me excused from the table without having to eat all of my vegetables.

Planting a garden and digging in our family roots gave us no more rights to this land than anyone else. We homesteaded, sort of, but we

weren't pioneers who could scribble a deed and put it in a Prince Albert can under a pile of rocks to mark our claim to the land. Essentially, we trespassed and became attached to something that wasn't ours just because it was in our sight.

It's no wonder we became possessive of our unencumbered 360-degree view of the mountains. No trees and cinder-block-gated communities. With the exception of the howling coyotes, train whistles twice a day, or a funnel of wind auctioning loose sand, the air was still. It was a place where I could see the shadow of a cloud lying silhouetted over the flat land. With such simplicity, I could feel the landscape. Now that landscape has been obliterated, and I feel claustrophobic. There is no room to breathe.

THE STRIP

Dad booked lounge acts on the Las Vegas Strip. Mom jokes that she changed more diapers in showrooms than at home. She also tells the story about the time we made a rare appearance at church for my baptism; after the choir finished their hymn, my brother Casey leapt to his feet, started clapping and whistling just as he would for an encore of a snappy rendition of "Tie a Yellow Ribbon."

Going to see Dad's variety acts was just one occasion for visiting the Strip. Every Sunday we paid our reverence to the champagne brunches held in the showroom of a large casino where feathers from the previous night's chorus line flocked the floor. This was followed by a drive down Las Vegas Boulevard to admire the plaster figures that once lined the Strip: the camel figure statues at the Sahara, the molded plastic clown at Circus Circus, the Victorian era figurines boarding a paddle boat at the Holiday Casino, the massive papier-mâché cutout of a water fountain at the Tropicana, and, my favorite, the grand sultan statue with his billowed cape that guarded the Dunes. I always blew him a kiss, vowing that someday I would marry him.

Our Sunday drives ended with a cruise of the custom home development near Wayne Newton's ranch, Casa de Shenandoah. Past the communities of tan tract homes blending with pink stucco shops and mini-mall churches, we arrived at Newton's gated estate. A fountain sprinkled green and blue.

Back home, we had indoor and outdoor fountains too. They came on with the flick of a light switch. The living room fountain was the perfect backdrop for the shows I performed as a kid. I'd flick that switch then emerge from behind the hidden door; my little tip-tap on the terrazzo barely audible over the gushing waterfall behind me.

As I got older, the Strip became an amusing baby-sitter. While my parents saw a show, my brother and I would be left to play air hockey at the old MGM arcade. Sometimes they dropped us off at the upper level of Circus Circus, where we played carnival games while waiting for the live trapeze act to begin. Towering above the center of the casino, with the net stretched just over the slots, the performances were breathtaking to watch. Whenever a fishnet-stockinged performer accidentally slipped on her swing, I held my breath, waiting for her to crash through the net and onto the green-felt 21 tables below.

In high school, my friends crowded into the white Naugahyde back seat of my '75 Cadillac Eldorado and we cruised the Strip. We pulled into a casino, tossed the keys to a valet, and headed for a late-night 99 cent breakfast in the coffee shop.

Gambling never crossed my mind until I returned home from college and a friend pointed out that if I pretended to put a nickel in the slot just as the waitress passed, I could get a free drink.

When someone asks where I am from, the Strip doesn't immediately come to mind. Instead, I first remember the composed rock garden of the desert floor and that holler that came near dusk when someone called the rest of the family to watch the sunset against the silhouetted purple-hued mountains.

The Las Vegas Strip was a distant landscape, far removed from the empty desert that encircled our house. Yet we went into town and utilized the amenities of the Strip—we swam in nearly every hotel pool, dined at the buffets, and played in the arcades—just as any family uses Main Street in Anytown, USA. That's what these places are for!

This isn't an option for locals anymore. The new mega-resorts have made the Strip inaccessible. It is impossible to cruise the Strip and toss your keys to a valet without getting into traffic jams and lines. And I thought the town was humbled by the oil crisis that forced it to put its lights out at midnight?

CORPORATE BOOMTOWN

Descending into the Las Vegas Valley each drive home from college, I've watched a ring of lights exploding like a bomb toward the mountain edges; a mushroom cloud of construction dust diffuses the glare. The golden track lights of the city are like the glistening fruits of the Gold Rush. People, hearing there are well-paying jobs, migrate in a modern-day *Grapes of Wrath* to a dust bowl of construction.

I know about the sad lives of these migrant workers from working for my Dad's contracting business. He started this business after he sold 160 acres of the mesa where we grew up to Metropolitan Homes. After years of fighting development of the desert, he cashed in and adopted an "If you can't beat 'em, join 'em" attitude.

This is how the Desert Sands R.V. Park and Mini-Market came to be. Unfortunately, the Desert Sands is home more to permanently parked trailers housing down-and-out migrant workers than to senior snowbirds touring the Southwest.

While it seems the rest of my family had glamorous jobs—my oldest sister Sukey danced and sang in the big production shows, my brother

Corby was a lifeguard at the old Marina Hotel, my sister Cary designed
bell bottoms for a store on the Strip, and my other brother Casey played
guitar in the lounges—I worked at Dad's R.V. Park in Henderson to
help pay for school. It's tough to be the college-bound kid in a Las Vegas
family.

It was a shock returning home from my first year at a women's college
to my summer job selling cigarettes to the workers' wives—who sat
hypnotized at the slots gambling away their husbands' measly paychecks, distracted only long enough to buy their crying children Twin-
kies. On payday, the workers settled their debts at the mini-market and
bought Budweiser. The next day, after hitting the casinos, they drank
Schlitz. Hoping to ease graduate school debts, I went home again to help
my Dad build his dream, a little neighborhood casino with his own
lounge.

The Roadhouse Casino & Lounge sits on the Boulder Strip, where
small casinos have lined the highway since the days when workers from
Boulder Dam stumbled into Henderson to gamble their week's wages.
The area's clientele is still working-class—nonunion construction workers who haven't been lucky enough to get a job building the mega-
resorts, workers at the smaller casinos and bars, and others who can see
the Strip from where they are but never seem to land there. Still, they
earn enough to make blue-collar slot joints like my Dad's profitable.

My job at the Roadhouse was to help supervise the construction crew of migrant workers. This was quite a task, which entailed arranging their accommodations—ushering them across the street to the R.V. Park and unlocking a trailer, fielding phone calls from their parole officers, and scheduling their drug tests. Taking in ex-cons, Dad boasted that he was an equal opportunity employer. We were the last stop of third and fourth chances to a host of colorful and quirky characters. I learned more from the odd tales of these down-on-their-luck drifters than I ever did at school.

My duties for the casino also included helping with the gaming application process. The Gaming Control Board has cleaned up Las Vegas by conducting intense investigations of gaming applicants, which required our family to deliver carloads of paperwork to their offices. I asked our Gaming Control Board investigator many questions between his inquiries into the accountability of nearly every cent my Dad ever made and spent. I was stunned to learn that although there had once been rules limiting games to back rooms and prohibiting people from making bets that would jeopardize their families, there now were no restrictions stopping major casinos with bowling alleys and movie theaters from building within a mile of a mall or a high school. There isn't a single regulation limiting the number of new casinos either. Every slot and poker machine, played or not, pays hefty city, state, and federal taxes. I was beginning to understand why states across the country were pushing to legalize gaming; it's a panacea for withering economies. Finally, I discovered the only gaming restriction, the only rule to be abided by before handing over a gaming license, is that the owner not have an "unsavory background." You see, if you have been really bad, you're banned from town, and your mug winds up in the Black Book with those of the mobsters. While I sat at the gaming hearings, I watched a man being denied a license because he had once run a 900 number and a topless bar. Our application to build a blue-collar slot joint was granted without question. Within hours of our casino opening, the same construction workers who had labored for a year were begging me for an advance because they had already lost their wages.

LOOSE CHANGE

Just as I had watched my Dad do for years, I neatly folded my tip so that the numbers on the bill jutted toward my palm. As I smiled broadly and shook the maitre d's hand, I inquired if there were any seats by the stage. He kindly returned my crisp $20 and informed me, "No, there is only assigned Ticketmaster seating." "When did this silliness start?" I demanded. "Since Steve Wynn got to town," he responded. "You can blame him."

Back at my assigned seat, I was flustered in disbelief that the entire monetary structure in Vegas was in shambles. Greasing palms, slyly passing a few bucks, that was Las Vegas! Not any more. The "cha-ching" of coins has been subverted by a bigger payoff at the corporate level. What's the difference between paying off the maitre d' or the city? The passed buck is still ingrained in the town. But it no longer works for the individual. As the curtain fell, the maitre d'—in an apparent act of old-timer comradeship—came to escort my friend and me to ringside Tom Jones seats, where we got a closer look at the cheap panties the ladies threw on stage. At least some things don't change.

Vintage Vegas is gone. I knew this for sure when I did my Valley High senior class presidential duty and scoured the town for our reunion location. Finding a place that was familiar to the class of 1986 proved impossible. The Dunes had been imploded, the Landmark had been leveled into a parking lot, and the home of the Rat Pack, the Sands, had closed. From my hotel room, I had a view of the Sands marquee, announcing an auction of its fixtures. Its tower stood small-scale, like a dollhouse toy, against the new mega-resorts and building cranes that littered the skyline. Fanciful papier-mâché figures have been replaced with ominous porticos. Ridiculous attempts at refined tastefulness have painted the town beige. It's bland, for God sakes!

As baffled as I am by the demise of local history and color, I guess I understand the motivation behind bulldozing Bugsy's rose garden at the Flamingo and imploding the mob associations of the Dunes. I can even comprehend blasting, not preserving, the Landmark Hotel, with its Jetson motif celebrating Vegas's atomic testing roots. Gangsters and A-bombs just don't fit the new corporate town, except as nostalgia. Besides, private enterprise has come to control native nostalgia. Locals' voices are lost among those of packs of rootless newcomers who don't remember the old Las Vegas.

Sad as I am about the development of the desert and the corporate takeover of Las Vegas's glitzy glamour, I can't ignore the ironic changes to which my own family succumbed. We changed from desert rat renegades into conspirators of big daddy development. In the position of our nemesis, we are now prey to destructive acts of the kind we once directed at desert developers. Unfortunately, violence has supplanted our childhood vandalism. In an armed robbery attempt at the Road-house, a disgruntled employee charged the casino cage, cut the electric-ity, grabbed the manager by her hair, and held a gun to her head, while shouting at everyone to hit the floor. The kindly security guard, a dis-abled old veteran, shot him dead. Blood soaked the carpet I had helped pick out.

I remember Las Vegas as piecemeal landscapes: desert, Strip, suburbs. Now a piece is missing. The desert has disappeared. The remaining el-ements are enmeshed, and gaming is bleeding onto the streets, soaking into suburban neighborhoods. Working at the casino, I've had a glimpse of this brew and see it intoxicating the town. It's a lethal risk when I think of what's at stake when people move out of all those cheap first-time homeowner tract homes and leave behind a valley of wagering ghettos. The goal of my games as a kid was to avoid scarring the desert's crust. When I lifted a clay tile from a dried wash bed, I left behind a sandy spot in the cracked surface—a piece of a pattern missing. The game wasn't over; the winner was the one who could carefully fit the clay tile back into its spot. No one ever won. The clay tile disintegrated to sand—its imprint left behind.

In the delicate composition of the desert, every piece serves a purpose. In Las Vegas, the space of the desert functioned as a buffer between gambling and the suburbs. Like the clay tile, once the desert is removed, it is impossible to wedge a piece of space back into place. Unlike a chip of clay taken from a wash bed, there is no spot remaining to indicate the desert's removal. When a place vanishes, nobody wins.

Everyone remembers nuances of their hometown landscape—ravines of cattails, natural washes, a boulder since removed that originally caused the curve in the road—but what is remarkable about Las Vegas is the speed and greed with which the natural imprints of the land have been obliterated. In this decorated desert, there are no remains of what once was; there is no lingering sense of place.

WILLIAM N. THOMPSON

How I Became a Native

1 980: My little girl said casually: "Did Mom tell you about Kristen?"
I said, "No." "Well," she said, "You know, I kinda asked Kristen
if she was going to Lisa's Halloween party. When she said, 'No,' I
asked her if she had been invited. She said she had been. Then she said,
'I really can't go to parties, because, well, I shouldn't talk about it, but
I have like a housekeeper who brings me to school and picks me up. He
really isn't a housekeeper. He is a bodyguard. There are some bad people
who told my Dad that they are going to get us.'" Kristen's father was
the president of a leading casino in Las Vegas.

A couple of years earlier, such a conversation with my daughter
would have sent chills up and down my spine. But then I was just another innocent midwesterner, new to Glitter Gulch and the Strip, a ne-
ophyte to the tinseltown known as Las Vegas. I have settled in, however.
I have a Nevada driver's license, I am registered to vote, and I have had
my call for jury duty. I am a native.

As soon as I got my job teaching at the University of Nevada, Las
Vegas, I started reading about my new hometown. I hungered for and
absorbed the likes of *The Green Felt Jungle, The Last Mafioso, Easy
Street, The House of Cards, The Girls of Nevada,* Hunter Thompson's
Fear and Loathing in Las Vegas, Hank Greenspun's *Where I Stand,* and
Ralph Pearl's *Las Vegas Is My Beat.* I read all the local tourist guides,
and I ran to get the paper each morning. I had an insatiable need to
know, to learn. The books painted the picture of a quaint desert railroad

stop that had been transformed in the 1940s into a haven for gamblers with unsavory reputations elsewhere.

Benjamin "Bugsy" Siegel led the group that sought to operate "legally like" in the small oasis town whose name means "The Meadows." And they settled in. And they "fit in." They founded the country clubs and social clubs. They started the first synagogue and a number of churches, and, of course, private schools. They became good Joe Citizens. They were the Joneses next door with whom everyone kept up. The stories were quaint in a menacing sort of way, like a murder mystery on television. But I knew things had to have changed. Las Vegas had grown into a metropolis. It was in the fastest-growing region in the United States. I was sure that the older professors would be able to tell me stories about the unsavory characters I had been reading about. And I did thrill at the stories that real natives—who can actually be found—told me. But, for me, the characters would be just names in the papers or names in the local history books. So I thought.

For my first few months in Vegas, the papers didn't give too much attention to its notorious inhabitants. They had other stories to report. The MGM fire took eighty-four lives, the Hilton fire eight more. These tragedies had hit corporate casinos, not mob hangouts. No unsavory characters, just good ol' American enterprise, corporations after a quick buck, willing to cut corners on building codes in order to get their profits a little faster. Las Vegas seemed more typical every day.

The first hot gaming story involving the city's "new solid citizen" types concerned Tony "The Ant" Spilotro. The local press introduced me to the famous Nevada Black Book, the official list of unacceptable characters who were not permitted on the premises of any of the 216 establishments that held Nevada gaming licenses. Spilotro, allegedly the contact man in Las Vegas for the Chicago mob, took some friends out to dinner at Diamond Lil's Restaurant in Sam's Town Casino. The police were tipped off and swooped in for the catch. But as they arrived, Spilotro drove off. He was later found innocent of the Black Book violation after claiming that the person at Sam's Town had really been his brother. Witnesses could not positively establish his presence there. Tony has two brothers in Las Vegas, Bobby and Fred. I first heard about Fred in the papers too. In 1981, he was sentenced to seven months in federal prison for income tax evasion. My little girl also brought the story home from school. She told me that her friend's father was going to have to go to jail.

Gunshots were fired into the homes of Bobby and Fred later in the year. The parents of another of my daughter's friends told us how they wouldn't let their little girl play at Shirley Marie's house any more. They were just afraid of what might happen there. A few months later, all the girls spent the night at Shirley Marie's birthday slumber party. There really wasn't anything to fear, and the girls could not get over just how nice Shirley Marie's parents were.

We knew that they must have brought their kids up right. On Awards Night at Orr Junior High, their little girl trotted up to the stage time after time to accept this academic award and that citizenship award. Nevada's attorney general, Richard Bryan, later governor of the state, and now a U.S. senator, presided at the honors ceremony. I wondered if a stray thought or two about organized crime was running through his mind at the time. Probably not. He has been a native all his life.

That first Vegas summer, we sent our daughter back to the Midwest to be with her grandparents and old friends. It was a time of great happiness for her. She had not adjusted well to Las Vegas. But the departure did have one sour note. Her friend Laurie was upset because her father had disappeared. The kids at school were sort of worried over Laurie.

We kept the news from our daughter over the summer, but she found out when she came back in the fall. The father—a wonderful family man who really loved his children—had been "wasted" gangland style. His head was found by a dog in the desert near Needles, California. Laurie is doing well now. She is a good student. I took the girls to the high school football game a few weekends ago. They seemed to have a good time.

The start of summer 1981 also brought our introduction to the Paradise Valley Little League. First came the tryouts. Would our boy make the majors or be sent to the minors? It's a Little League parent's nightmare. The non-native parents did a double take as the loud speaker read the names of the players making the tryouts. Little Anthony Spilotro stepped to the plate. It didn't matter how well he did—in fact, he got a decent hit—when it was announced that he was coach's choice for a major league team. He was Fred's boy. My kid made the minors. In fact, they had to expand the league to make room for him and other kids. His expansion team was sponsored by Rumba Pools. They were called the Rumba Bears, but they played like the Bad News Bears. In the quickly arranged expansion, the league officials grabbed anyone who wanted to coach. The Rumba coach was an unkempt young man of about twenty, with shabby clothes and a totally unwashed, unshaven face. He seemed friendly, so the parents thought it was probably OK. But we certainly became apprehensive when he was delivered, always late, to games and practices by his grubby friends in junky-looking "low rider" cars. His younger brother was assigned to the team, and somehow this kid became the permanent pitcher. His stepmother became the team mother, but as they didn't have an address or phone, no one knew where to call to remind them that they had called a practice or that there was a game scheduled. When they did get to the games, things were worse. They couldn't keep the kids' names straight, lineups were constantly messed up, and several kids wouldn't get into the games, in violation of league rules. Many parents, myself included, were especially angry over this latter fact. The anger peaked when the coach appeared at a game stoned. The time to speak out had arrived. I reluctantly called Tommy Gazela, the league's vice president, and asked if my kid could be on another team. He asked me if the problem I had was with the Rumba Bears. I said it was. He relayed the fact that I was not the first to call; I was the last. I had actually been the most patient of the parents. I wasn't yet a full-fledged native. The league officials called a meeting of all the parents. For some reason or another, one parent, Peggy, wanted me to be a critic. When I showed up at the meeting, she was delighted. She later told me that my presence had made all the difference, that the other parents knew that if the cool-headed professor was concerned, action had to be taken. I protested that I had kept my mouth shut at the meeting. She reiterated that my silence made my presence even more meaningful. But I had kept my mouth shut because I didn't want anyone to think anything about me at all. I was there only because Peggy had leaned on me. At the meeting, I remember nudging Peggy and saying, "Who is that presiding?" She said, "Oh, that's Bobby." I said "Bobby?" She put her finger up to her mouth, and uttered a noticeable "Shhhh!" Then she whispered, "Bobby Spilotro. He's the league president." I whispered, "Who is sitting next to Tommy Gazela taking notes?" Peggy whispered, "That's Tommy's wife. She is the league secretary." I said quietly and with a chuckle: "At least the mob didn't elect all the league officers." She laughed and whispered, "She's Bobby's sister." "Oh," I replied. And I determined, once again, to keep my mouth shut. The more vocal parents let their tirades fly, and the coach hadn't bothered to show up to defend himself. So, bowing to the pressures of the crowd, the league officials agreed to replace him with one of the parents, who was quite willing to tackle the job. "We took on the Mob and we won," I thought. "And we lived to tell about it." At the next game, Gazela and

Brother Bobby went around to all the parents almost apologetically, saying, "Hey, yeah, everything is OK." Peggy kept telling me that I had made the difference. "No way, Peggy. No way, Tommy. No way, Bobby." But then, the FBI just may be reviewing my telephone conversation with the Little League vice president today.

John Moran was elected sheriff of Clark County and chief of the Metropolitan Police Force in 1982. During the campaign, he was accused of taking political contributions from Tony the Ant. He was also accused of associating with low-life mob types, among them Vince Rubano, who had been the MC of a fund-raising rally and barbecue for the candidate. Indignantly, Moran denied the charges and took a lie detector test to prove his innocence. The Moran forces were up in arms about their opponents defaming Rubano, a well-liked local philanthropist. I wondered.

A few weeks later, a nice-looking car pulled up to my house to drop off my little girl after school. The car had personalized Nevada licence plates reading RUMBA. I asked her, "RUMBA?" She said, "Yes, my friend's father owns Rumba Pools." I said, "What's his name?" "Oh, that's Mr. Rubano." Follow-up stories in the press indicated that this Little League team sponsor had quite a long FBI file. Just friends and neighbors.

How friendly, how neighborly? I wondered as I pulled into the drive one Saturday night about 1 A.M., just wanting get into the house and get some sleep before church. "What is that?" my wife said. I looked and there was a man standing beside a car right in front of our house. "I don't know, but let's get into the house," I responded. Watching the man apparently talking to someone in the car, I grew more concerned. He looked big and ugly. I kept peeping out the window. I did feel a little better when I saw a police car pass by, but it would have been nicer if the police car had stopped. It didn't. The man stayed there. Then there was a loud knock at my door. "What the hell is this?" I thought. "Yeah," I yelled through the door. "Police," the man said. I said, "Go to the window." He did, and he showed me a badge. He said he could tell that I was concerned, and he just wanted me to know he was going to be there all night, and it didn't have anything to do with me. I took him at his word.

On Friday night I had gone to Safeway for some milk at about 8:30. The Saturday news reported that a man had been abducted from the parking lot next to the Safeway at 9 P.M. Friday and taken to Sunrise Mountain, where his body was found, "done-in mob style." The Sunday *Las Vegas Review-Journal* told the rest of the story. The poor fellow was a house guest of Moe Valzano's. The two were spending Friday with some friends at Moe's house, and they decided to have some ice cream. The guest went out to get it in Moe's fancy car, but he didn't come home. The police speculated that the abductors were after Valzano and had been watching his house. They grabbed his guest by mistake. The paper went on about how Valzano was a past partner of Sal Albino, Laurie's father, in the Crazy Horse Saloon and was in a struggle with the Chicago mob over control of topless joints and porno bookstores in Los Angeles and Las Vegas.

All during that Saturday night—with the police watch in my front yard—I was awake, wondering which of my neighbors was in trouble. Could it have been the neighbor who had had an accident and was facing over $30,000 in hospital bills? Could he have robbed a bank? Perhaps it was the neighbor who owned Chicago Al's restaurant, a name that would seem to invite trouble? The twenty-one dealer who had just gotten a divorce? Maybe the settlement hadn't been all that amicable. Or maybe the trouble came from the empty house that had used to headquarter the rock band. All night I worried and wondered. The Sunday paper relieved me of my suspicions about my immediate neighbors, all except one. The paper gave Moe Valzano's address. He lived next door to the residence directly behind my own. He lived on my block. The stakeout was protective. The police wanted to be sure that the murderers of Moe's house guest didn't come back to try again.

Neighbor Moe is now trying to sell his house. He doesn't need it. He has another home, Terminal Island Federal Prison. Moe gladly pleaded guilty to minor drug charges in exchange for joining the federal witness protection program. If he survives, he is expected to live to testify about the activities of Tony the Ant and his friends. Moe won't be seen at the local Safeway for a long time.

The case of Valzano and the mistaken identity problem worries me. But I am a native, and I am sure I shall adjust. In the meanwhile, I'll keep driving my Toyota Corolla, thank you. Just a safety measure.

I tell all my unemployed friends in the Midwest to come out to Vegas. It sure is a neat place to be: good schools, lots of churches, good concerts, good parks, fabulous weather, and nice scenery. Any native can tell you, Las Vegas is a good family town.

Inside the Glitter
Lives of Casino Workers

MAXINE ERNST SHOWROOM USHER

I come from a large Mormon family. We came over with the pushcarts. My people came across from England, and were converted back east in the days of Joseph Smith. My kids were raised within the church and they're raising their children that way.

I came to Vegas from Utah when I decided that marriage was no longer right. I was twenty-six and I had three kids to support. My mom said, "Well, the waitresses here seem to do pretty good with tips, so why don't you come on down?" My dad was here on a construction site. I found a little place of my own and with the help of a baby-sitter, I've been here ever since.

I have been a showroom server since the year I came to Las Vegas forty years ago. I worked at the Sahara, the Thunderbird, the Sands in its heyday, Caesars Palace, the Hilton. I've seen so many stars. Judy Garland, Mae West, Elvis, of course, Sammy Davis, Jr., Wayne Newton. Ann-Margret was a favorite, and Liberace. I loved the dancers—Donald O'Connor and Debbie Reynolds always put on a good show. I've never

This chapter forms part of *Inside the Glitter: Lives of Casino Workers,* by Kit Miller (Great Basin Publishing, 2000). It has also been published as "Inside the Glitter," in *Change in the American West: Exploring the Human Dimension,* edited by Stephen Tchudi (Reno: University of Nevada Press, 1996). It appears here in slightly modified form.

interacted with the stars. Oh, I've been whistled at a couple of times—
Tom Jones, Frank Sinatra, Harry Belafonte.

Now I am in charge of a VIP area. It's a pleasant job. I go to work
at 5:00, have my dinner, then I go downstairs and seat people. I talk
with them, help them enjoy the show, cheerlead for their side. I watch
the show twice every night. How many people would love to have that
job!

In days gone by, the VIPs were the high rollers, and your local people
who are high in politics. The VIPs as we knew them are long gone. Some
say that because they've taken service out of the showroom, they won't
be back. They like being catered to. Now they're sitting in theater seats,
not dining tables. Back then, the average John Doe did not come to
town with his family. You had people coming to get away from family.

I'm making about $9 an hour, and there are no tips. I've got hospi-
talization, fantastic health benefits. And four weeks a year vacation. But
working conditions have changed tremendously. Before, the owners
knew you. If you ever got into a really tight spot, you could always go
talk to him, and he would help you out financially. The hotels have
become so big they don't seem to have time for us. All we are is another
cog in the wheel. Even though I may have been in this hotel twenty-four
years, I doubt if the bosses know us. We're just another face in the
crowd.

I've always been union. My dad was a crane operator and a miner,
he was always union. When there was a student strike, my dad said,
"You're not going to school." I spent the day on the picket line. Consequently, I will never cross a picket line, regardless of who's picketing.
When I came to Las Vegas, first thing my dad said was, "There's the
union hall. Go join up." I went in that day, they sent me out to the
coffee shop at the Riviera, where I worked for three months.

In those days, the union was Al Bramlett and a few of his agents. He
was a good ole boy. He knew me as a union member who would get
out there and fight for the average working person. I remember when
he said we were gonna get a health program, then a pension program.
We all stood up and said, "Hurray!" We more or less idolized him. Who
knows why he was killed. They were trying to start the dealers union
and were having a tough time. Dealers have never been unionized in this
town, as much as they want to try.

There's no church edict against casino work. I'm working to make a
living. Just because I'm serving liquor, doesn't mean I'm drinking it.

Maxine Ernst, showroom usher.

Maxine Ernst.

Because I'm working in a casino doesn't mean I'm gambling. My family standards are as high as they would be up in Salt Lake City.

My mother's family numbered fourteen children. And they were always very proud of me. No one has ever said I should not go out and make a living for my children in the best way I know how. I'd go home and I was making as much as my brother who was a schoolteacher. I raised my family. I was able to buy a home. Everyone says, "Here's Maxine from Las Vegas! How is it down there? We're so proud of you, you've done so great!"

CINDY TRUDELL SERVING WENCH

Family entertainment has ruined Las Vegas. These families are on a budget. They have three or four kids on their laps. When you ask if they want a cocktail, the first thing they ask is, "How much?" and you want to kill them. It's lost the glamour. Now it's just baby strollers everywhere you go.

I'm a food server in the showroom at the Excalibur. The women are "wenches," the men are "serfs." The show is medieval jousting, fighting, horses. It's very loud. People are screaming for their knight to win.

I work a 4–10 P.M. shift. When I get to work, I go down to wardrobe and get my uniform, change into my peasant girl blouse and skirt. I clock in at the showroom and set the room up. We take our break and eat. Then we come back and do cocktail service and dinner. At the show, everybody eats with their hands. Cornish game hen, broccoli spears, roll and soup. I serve sixty-seven people with a partner.

I make about $2,400 a month after taxes. My little girl and I can live pretty good on that. We live in my mom's house with my brother and his wife and two kids and our elderly great-aunt.

Ashley has a nanny. She's from Poland, but Ashley understands her. I offered her the job when I was three months pregnant and she came over from Poland. She cleans houses in the morning, then comes over to watch Ashley at 3:00. It's expensive, but I want her to have someone's full attention. I don't want her to get lost in the shuffle.

I grew up in Las Vegas. When I was fifteen I got my first job in the casinos. I was a coffee girl during the summer at the Union Plaza. I've been a coffee shop waitress, a cocktail waitress, a gourmet food server, a banquet and a showroom server. I've worked at the Stardust, the Golden Nugget, the Dunes, the Marina, and in Reno at the MGM, the Nugget, the Sands. I'll probably stay in gaming all my life.

Cindy Trudell, serving wench.

Cindy Trudell.

When the mob was running Las Vegas, everyone made money. I could make $300 a night in tips. They were strictly interested in gambling. They comped the shows, the meals. Now people only get comped if management screws up and has to make good. It's gone down the drain. The corporations have ruined it. They want every room to make a profit. It was a safer place to live when the mob was here. You'd never see bank robbers come in and try to rob a cage. The mob would blow their brains out right there.

I got pregnant at thirty-seven. My boyfriend didn't want a kid. I said, "Fine if you don't want to be a part of her life. But I'm gonna go ahead and have my baby." He said, "Then you do it on your own." I had insurance and a steady job. I worked until the day I had her. My three girlfriends supported me all through my pregnancy, and they were at the birth. There are a lot of single mothers out there.

I spend all my free time with Ashley. On my free days we'll go out for breakfast, go grocery shopping, go to visit someone. She's my little buddy.

GLORIA HARRIS COCKTAIL WAITRESS

Cocktailing is like self-employment. If you stand in the station, if you don't go out and take care of your customers, you're not gonna make a decent salary.

The Golden Gate is the oldest casino in Nevada. It used to be called the Sal Sagev, that's Las Vegas backwards. We've all been here a lot of years. Everybody's friendly, that's how we keep our customers. We give them our undivided attention and let them know we appreciate them being here, just have fun, hang loose. Downtown is down to earth. We're just a big caring family. When one of us hurts, we all hurt.

A lot of our customers are elderly, locals. In the winter we get our snowbirds that come for six months. Some of them get rooms here at the hotel. Or they get their little apartments because they have animals. This is their hangout. Sure they lose money. But we accommodate them with meals, and the drinks are free. The house gives a lot away, and we take care of them. If one of our customers goes into the nursing home or the hospital, we send them cards or go see them.

The Golden Gate is a "break-in" casino. The kids get out of dealer's school and then they come here and they get hands-on. Working with real money, real people. After six months, they might go to the Strip, where they're dealing with much more money and the stakes are higher.

Gloria Harris, cocktail waitress.

Gloria Harris.

I wouldn't want to work on the Strip. Here I'm closer to home. I don't have to hustle bustle with the traffic, no thank you. I'm used to downtown. I've been here so long I'm part of the furniture.

I've been at the Golden Gate twenty-two years. I spent ten years as change girl and cashier and twelve years in cocktails. We take a class to get an alcohol awareness card. You learn how to identify a drunk, when to serve him and when not to. Everyone that seems drunk isn't always drunk, they could be on medication, they could be old or crippled. Alcoholics—you can smell them before you get to them. They stink.

I work swing shift. I come on at 5:45, sign in, go downstairs, get my tray, let the girl know I'm here and her time's up. I make $6 an hour and I pay $65 a night in taxes, that's taken from my paycheck. How do you tell the IRS you're not making that? I make $75 dollars a night in tips now. Before the Fremont Experience redevelopment I was making $35. I was in favor of the Experience—heck, yeah, do something! Or I was gonna have to learn how to belly dance real soon.

Downtown Las Vegas was dead, almost a ghost town. We were hurting the last five years because of the mega-hotels. They was killin' us, like when the big gas companies come in and kill the little-bitty gas stations. They had more to offer. Then they started putting hotels in the neighborhoods. After that, why should you come downtown?

I get about four hours of sleep. I'm off work at 2:00 in the morning, then I go home and lay out my daughter's clothes. She's fifteen. I check her diabetes. I turn on the news and see what's happened while I was at work. I lay down from 3:30–6:30. Then I get up and take my daughter to school at 7:20 and I stay up all day. Lots of days I watch my grandbabies while my kids are working.

I'm originally from Shreveport, Louisiana. I don't gamble. I prefer the mall.

MARYANN RODRIGUEZ HEAVY EQUIPMENT OPERATOR

I prepare the ground for these cranes that are building the Stratosphere Casino. I'm good. I know just what you need for compression, moisture. Getting the right mix is like baking bread. I don't read a recipe. I do it by feel. This loader is an extension of my thoughts—it does what I think.

I did my apprenticeship at the Nevada Test Site. I applied three times before I got in. It was very competitive. I met my husband there. He was a crane operator. I think it's good to help women and minorities get into

Maryann Rodriguez, heavy equipment operator.

Maryann Rodriguez.

these jobs. Otherwise they don't get much of a chance at this work. But once you're in, you've gotta be good to stay.

Last week I worked eighty hours. I'm really enjoying it. My husband's been gone for a year and a half, working in Oregon. He was thinking I got a piece of cake here, running the kids. Now he's back and he has to run the kids, pay the bills. He sees how hard it is.

I was raised Seventh Day Adventist in Tennessee and Oregon. We lived in the mountains. We had no TV, no radio. I heard my first country western song when I was eighteen. I didn't get a formal education. I was home-schooled from eight to eighteen. At a certain point, my mom sat me down with the Bible, and within two months I was reading. Then she left my education to me. We would go to junk stores and I could get any book I wanted as long as it was nonfiction. I read thousands of *National Geographic*s.

At school you get a lot of peer pressure about who you should be, what you can do. No one told me I couldn't do this or that. When I was a kid, I skidded seven cords of wood a year on horseback. I was an artist with a chain saw, I liked to figure out the hardest way to cut a tree. When I was eighteen I left home and worked on ranches.

The way I deal with the guys on the crew is a little unusual. I just give it right back to them. When I first worked at the Test Site, I went through some hazing. Every inch of the walls was covered with center-folds. One guy put up a real explicit one, just to throw me. I tacked up one of my own, of the male variety. His came down real fast. Did I gain their respect? Yes. Did he lose face? You bet.

If I keep working overtime, I could make $100,000 this year. But I won't be able to ride these machines forever. Now I'm trying to figure a way to stay in this field, but do something else as I get older. My boss is teaching me to read plans. He doesn't look like Einstein, but he is.

Bronc, my husband, and I have a seven-year-old son and a nine-year-old daughter. My mom lives with us too and helps a lot with the kids. We'd like to live on a little ranch we have in Oregon. But my daughter's really good in gymnastics, and here in Vegas she has the chance to develop that. I think she could make it all the way to the Olympics.

MARIO BRUN COOK

Today I became an American citizen. It's nice, I feel I'm part of something. Now I can get arrested at union demonstrations. I can get full benefits for the taxes I pay. I'm grateful to the U.S. for opening the door, and maybe saving my life.

I grew up in Uruguay. My grandparents went there as farm workers. Italy was overpopulated, and they were looking for land. We were a very close family. The main thing in my childhood was playing soccer.

I left home when I was fourteen to go to work. My first job was in a casino, the Parque Hotel, in 1954. It was owned by the City of Montevideo. I ran the elevator and was a bellman, cashier, cook. I learned to cook by hanging out with the cooks the casino brought in from Italy. On days off, we made barbecues on the beach. Then the public workers went on strike—60,000 members, including our casino—and I started working with the union. The casino switched me to graveyard shift.

In 1962, Che Guevara came to the Parque Hotel. He was defending Cuba at a meeting of the Alliance for Progress, President Kennedy's Latin American plan. They were voting to expel Cuba from the Organization of American States. He would wake up at 4:30 in the morning, I brought him his maté tea, and we talked. He was a brilliant man, a doctor and a great leader. I was very sad when he was killed.

In the 1960s and 1970s, I helped the United Nations with refugees coming in from other dictatorships, Bolivia, Brazil. I was living in Brazil when Uruguay became a dictatorship. I came back to fight it. Clandestine work. We'd paint signs in the street, take out all the lights in the city, bang pots and pans. We helped the families of people in jail, raised money. It was dangerous—if you leafleted in a bus and somebody saw you, you'd go to jail. There was a big demonstration, the tanks were waiting for us. We threw stones. They gassed us. A lot of people were killed.

The military took me to jail. They tied a hood around my head, filled it with water, suffocating me. They wanted names. I thought, "I'm going crazy, maybe I'm giving names unconsciously." I threw myself through a window, got all cut up.

I knew I had to leave the country. I went to Argentina, Costa Rica, Mexico, the United States. I worked as a cook in New York, New Jersey, Florida, Texas, often with no job security, no vacation.

Here in Vegas I've worked in the Stardust, the Mirage. I work swing shift. I get to the Mirage at 3:30, put on my hat and coat, get my station ready. From 5:30 to 11:30, I'm cooking. I prepare 70 to 100 meals per night. They let me use the best ingredients—olive oil, meat. I make about $13 per hour. Now I'm getting very tired and looking forward to retiring in Mexico. If I stay here, I'll be poor.

Mario Brun, cook.

Mario Brun.

A few years ago, I married Natividad, a Mexican woman. She's a maid at Treasure Island. She has two teenage boys. She's raising them old-fashioned. They go to church, come back, watch TV, no go out, no games. She's very Catholic. I respect it, but I am not. We're a happy family. On my day off, I make barbecue for everyone. Barbecuing is a religion for Uruguayans.

BERNICE THOMAS MAID TRAINER

I organized the maid's school for the Culinary Workers Union. The training is free. I've had all nationalities, all over the U.S., policemen, teachers. Lotta people come to Las Vegas thinking money grows on trees. You can get a job, but it might not be in your classification. So they'll always fall back on housekeeping.

I'm from Tallulah, Louisiana. I was young, doing farmwork, when I had this, I guess you could call it a vision. I said, "I want a white house. I want a husband and a daughter. And I want a nice car." There were no jobs there, just farm laborer. I got married. His grandparents was coming to Las Vegas and we came too.

I started out as a guest room attendant, a maid, twenty-five years ago. I was a GRA about five years and I told myself, "I want to be an inspector." Back in those days it was almost impossible to get an inspector job. But I always had faith and confidence in myself, so I got an inspector job. I did that about fourteen years. Then I was promoted to assistant executive housekeeper. I always was flexible and willing to work. I had eight children in the meantime, and I worked every day.

When I was hired to organize the maid's school, I had been in hotels all my life, so this is something I just knowed with my eyes closed. We talked to the housing authority and found a place. It's a suite of rooms that we set up like hotel rooms. My three instructors set things up, I direct them.

We mess up the bed, put dust and makeup on the floor, lipstick messages on the mirror, McDonald's packages, beer bottles, it be really trashed. We train them how to make a bed nice, dust the entire room, don't miss a lick of nothing! Now maids have to worry about needles, blood, all kinds of things. We show them how to use gloves, put that linen in a special bag. We also have a class where they can learn English.

We train thirty-three students every two weeks with a full class. They graduate if they can work up to hotel standards. When they get that certificate, the hotels usually will hire them. Sometimes they hire them

Bernice Thomas, maid trainer.

Bernice Thomas.

right there at graduation. At the hotels, the maids clean fifteen, sixteen, even eighteen rooms. The starting wage is $8.20 per hour. They get vacation time according to how many hours they've put in.

It's a goal out there. But it's not easy. You have hard days, you get real disgusted. But the main thing is to do the best you can, keep a positive attitude and you will make it. That's what I teach the people here. I say, "Just think about how nice it's gonna be when you go out there and make that check. Think about that new car, the wardrobe." They'll get a job and come back and thank me for it, show me their new car. That makes me proud to feel that I done help somebody.

I reached all my goals. I got a white house, a car, a husband, and a lot of kids and grandkids. Most of my kids live in Las Vegas. And I'm blessed that my mother and auntie live here now. On my off days, I drive them places, shopping, to church. Some hot days we just sit here in the shade and watch TV.

HIPOLITO CHARLES POT WASHER

People don't really notice the work a pot washer does. It's like being a garbage man. No one pays any attention to him, but they sure would if he stopped picking up their garbage!

I've been at Jerry's Nugget for a year. I was working at the Fremont Hotel, washing pots, dishes, cleaning floors. One day I just came in here and applied. That day I had an interview and I got hired. Got lucky, really.

In the mornings I'm here at 7:00. I ride my bike 'cause it's the only transportation I've got right now. I get to see the sun rise over the mountains. First thing, I cut vegetables for soup, cut up the snack bar, salad and sandwich stuff. You just go from there, wash your pots and dishes all day. That's basically it. We get one 30-minute break. From 12 to 1:30, it's our lunch rush, we're usually just slammed. Sometimes it goes fast and sometimes you're just draggin'.

I picked up technique from a guy who worked here. You rinse 'em all off, put the worst ones to soak for a coupla hours. Two sinks have hot soapy water, you use some sanitizer. You get faster at it. These guys make the day easier, they're always joking around, singing Spanish music. In a year's time I learned more Spanish here than I've known my whole life. We teach each other.

I'm making $8.43 an hour, that's 100 percent after working a year at 80 percent. We have full benefits, dental, medical, eyes. We can eat

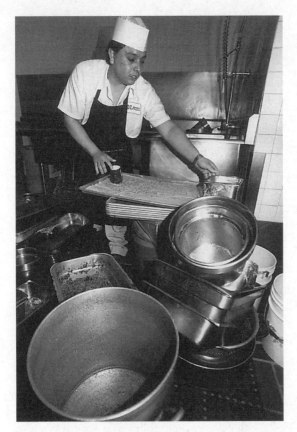

Hipolito Charles,
pot washer.

Hipolito Charles.

two meals here, but I usually just eat one. Getting fat is an occupational hazard.

I had an uncle who was a cook here for twenty-seven years. He had a stroke right over there by the stew pots, and he had to retire. I'll try to become a cook. But it's hard to get on, and I don't wanta change to graveyard shift.

I'm from Vegas. My mom's folks first came here in the 1940s. They sold vegetables from a truck. My dad's from San Antonio. He was in the Air Force at Nellis, a jet engine mechanic.

When I was a little kid we had to stand near the door while my parents gambled. That was the life here. Now Security gets a hold of 'em and calls you on the intercom, "Come get yer kid!" Sometimes I like to gamble, when I have money for it. Otherwise I'll just stick a quarter here and there and see if I hit anything. I never played the tables.

I got a wife and a dog, two cats—that's my family. No kids, yet. We met at the Fremont. She was a waitress. We'd go out drinking and gambling and stuff, the Las Vegas life. Now I mainly like to be home, play with my dog, watch football. This weekend I've got ten bucks on the Cowboys.

ROY DUNCAN ARCADE MANAGER

I'm a child of the projects. I can go over there today and see guys I grew up with, still right there. Still getting high, sleeping all day and runnin' around all night. That puzzles me that they haven't tried to take their minds past that little area. I've always looked for training opportunities.

My degree is in hotel management. I've been interested in it since I was a kid. I'm a supervisor at the Cotton Blossom at the MGM theme park. The boat is a replica of the one in *Show Boat*. Since I started here, we've changed from being a Cajun Restaurant to a deli to a casino-deli to an arcade-deli.

I'm responsible for basic repairs on the machines. I collect numbers from the meters, put it in a bank bag and return it to cast member control bank. I order the food. I'm also a team leader. We get our people together and say, "It's real important to smile." I'm getting my Ph.D. in Think-ology at the University of Oz. They offer classes on management, computers, scheduling, speech.

I do think a lot of kids are addicted to these machines. They have three bucks, they play the games, then they come to me and say, "That machine took my money!" A lot of times they're out of money and they

Roy Duncan, arcade manager.

Roy Duncan.

just want to play the game. The most popular ones are Mortal Kombat. Killer Instinct is also hot. Mostly boys play them. I think we're over-exposing our kids to these types of things. They need to have themes that cater to kids, that are less violent, less sexy. Once it's in your mind, it's something that's always there.

My mama came from Louisiana. She left a lot of unpleasant things behind, she would never talk about them. She was getting fifty cents a day down south. When she came to Vegas in the sixties, she made $8 a day cleaning houses. Then $17 in the hotels. She raised us kids on her own. I was very fortunate to have a strong mother.

But children nowadays don't have anybody. Parents are whacked out on something. The grandparent ends up taking care of the kids. When I was coming up, there was still some respect for the parents and grand-parents. But there's no respect for nobody no more.

This generation now is a crack generation. It's a cycled poverty that recycled itself into a worse situation. It's gonna take an intense effort from within the community to bring that back into balance. You get caught on drugs and you can't compete. People are shutting themselves out of jobs.

Family is the most important thing. That's one of the reasons I went to the Million Man March. I took an oath to do whatever I can to help myself, my family, and my community, economically and spiritually. I never met so many beautiful men in my life. It was profound. I shook hands with people from all over the world, the Caribbean, South America, the Middle East. I came home with a great feeling of brotherhood.

I want one day to own my own business. That's where you get ultimate freedom, doing what you want to do, not what someone's telling you to do. I could do pool cleaning, maintenance, floors. My sister makes beautiful jewelry that's been exhibited all over. Maybe we'll go into business together.

My wife works in housekeeping at the Stardust. My daughter Libra is nine and I'm involved with her school. We like to go out in the wilderness around here—Red Rock Canyon, Valley of Fire. Ever since I went to camp as a kid I loved being outdoors.

MARIO BASURTO SIGN MAINTENANCE MAN

It's possible to get electrocuted up there. You gotta have your meters, always test the wires. You can get shocked pretty bad, 480 volts. You just take your time so you don't slip or fall.

Mario Basurto, sign maintenance man.

Mario Basurto.

I work for the Young Electric Sign Company. We maintain the lights for the Fremont Experience. It is a five-block-long canopy of lights where they run a light show every hour. There are 2.1 million bulbs up there, each one is only as big as my baby fingernail. There's thirty sections and thirty computers up on top. The life expectancy of the bulbs is about 20,000 hours. They're new now, but when they run out we'll have a lot to change all at once.

My shift is graveyard, 11 P.M.–7 A.M. We come to the office, grab our radios, and get set up. When the last show's over, we get out there and start work. Three of us take turns riding the lift 110 feet up, running computer tests and changing any bulbs that are out. It takes a week to check the whole Experience.

I've been at YesCo about six months. I was going to welding school when I heard they had job openings. I went down and they hired me right away. I'm an apprentice. I make eleven bucks an hour, half what a journeyman makes.

Graveyard was hard to get used to. I don't see my friends anymore. We used to go out to casinos, movies, clubs. I stopped having time for my girlfriend, so we broke up. In a couple of months I'll go back on day shift at the shop. I'll be working on all kinds of signs, changing neon and fluorescent lights, for banks, casinos, tennis courts. I like the work. I put my mind to it, and I learn all I can from these guys. They take the time to teach me.

I was born in Las Vegas, I've lived here all my life. My mom grew up here, my dad's from Juarez, Mexico. He works at Timet, a plant where they make titanium. She works at an elementary school. I got one brother, one sister.

When I get off work I usually work on my car. It's a '79 Corvette. I like the Corvette cause it looks cool, the girls notice you and it goes real fast. Next month I'm getting another car so I can overhaul the engine and restore it to keep as an antique. Then I'll enter it in car shows.

I learned about cars from my dad. He used to fix them up to sell. Since I was six I helped him. He'd say, "Give me a 5/16 wrench," and I'd have to figure out what it was.

I think I'll stay in Vegas. YesCo is in eight states. If there's an opening, I could move. But I doubt it. Las Vegas is the best place to live because of all the lights.

LILO DISTLER PICKET CAPTAIN

The casinos won't hire older people. But if you're in the job, they can't terminate you. We've got a union. But they can make it really rough on you. They want only young ones. If you go to the nonunion hotels, you won't find a cocktail waitress over thirty.

I came to the U.S. from Germany in the 1940s and married an American. In 1955 I made my citizenship. I've been at the Frontier since 1967. At that time, you needed 1,000 hours' food service to get into cocktails. I served food at the Tip Top Drive-in, the Pussycat a Go-Go, and worked banquets in all the hotels. I never called in sick, and I was never late. I worked graveyard twenty-two years. It gave me time to go to college and study politics and computers.

Now I'm on the picket line. We're striking for a contract. Pension, good wages, insurance. We're the oldest strike in the country. I work the line swing shift. I sign people in and out and see that everything's OK. I talk with people to keep up morale. We have 350 people picketing. They come thirty hours a week, after their shift or on their days off. If they have full-time jobs, they do fifteen hours. The Sahara sends a free food truck, really good food!

It's been hard. Summers it's very hot. You have to drink water, get shade when you can. I keep up morale. I say, "What would you have if you go back in? You've only got one choice, stick with the union or go with management." They say, "I'm gonna stick with the union." I say, "So don't cry about it." We are a community. We have our Gray Panthers, a group of older men who all picket together. We have our strike shack.

The Frontier is being kept open with scab labor. They make $4.25 an hour. The scabs come from the street, they don't stay very long. When they settle the strike, I will go back just for spite, to get rid of the scabs. I want my shift back, and I want that scab out of there.

Under Howard Hughes the Frontier was 100 percent better. You could be elected employee of the month, get a free vacation, a $500 bonus, free dinner. They gave a Christmas party for all the children in the big showroom. You got a turkey or a ham, an extra day's pay. After so many years on the job, you get a gold watch, a ring, diamond bracelet.

We had several uniforms over the years. One was taffeta with a big full skirt. Another was a Hawaiian dress. Customers dressed up too, in dresses and high-heel shoes. Back then they came with a lot of money.

After awhile in the business, you know how to handle people. They

Lilo Distler (left), picket captain.

Lilo Distler.

get drunk and say, "Bring me a double. Bring me a triple." I used to tell them, "Yes, there's a double in there." But there was no booze in there.

My daughter is a cocktail waitress at the Horseshoe, studying to be a social worker. Cocktailing is not such a good job anymore. You've got more of a family crowd now. People don't tip like they used to.

I'm very interested in politics. I don't like Republicans. It's for the rich, and I'm not rich. I'm pro-choice, to each his own body. Like affirmative action, the more you think about it, you have to have it. Otherwise people will never move up, they'll be pushed down all the time. I register voters. I've been pushing the Spanish people in the union to register to vote, to get citizenship.

My neighborhood wants me to run for office. They're all senior citizens. I'd like to run for county commissioner, or state assembly, but it takes a lot of money.

When I'm not on the picket line, I'm home reading, or making dolls. I visit my daughter. I've been married fifty years, same person. My husband was with the police department. We don't go on vacations. We stay in town, go out to eat, watch TV together. I like to crochet and knit. I have made dozens of these dolls. Please take one to each of your daughters!

MARK ZARTARIAN ROOM SERVICE

The interesting thing about this job is when you knock on the door, you never know whether the person on the other side has got a gun, it's a naked woman, or both.

At the Sahara on swing shift, there are three guys running 2,100 rooms. It is much better than being a dining room waiter. I don't have those classic waiter nightmares anymore. You know the one. You've got a hundred people in your station and you can't remember anyone's order. In room service I can pour a $100 bottle of wine without some kid tugging on me going, "Mister, I want some more butter!"

Sheri and I ended up in Vegas when we were attempting to walk across country. We walked across New Hampshire, Vermont, into New York and got heat stroke, water and food poisoning all at once. We ended up in the hospital and decided to get a van so we could see the country.

We were in Vegas on our way to go camping in California, and I took one look at the Strip and said, "Whoa, I could make money there!" Being a waiter I just knew it was the kind of place the tips would be

Mark Zartarian, room service.

Mark Zartarian.

flowing. And I was right. As far as the restaurant business goes, it's probably the best money in the world.

We had jobs inside a week. We went down to the union and basically bought a job. It cost a hundred bucks a head to sign up, get your sheriff's card, health card, TAM card.

Once we were in, it was so worth it. The wages and benefits were beyond anything I'd ever imagined. I had worked in states where the dining room waiter would make the subminimum of $2.25 an hour plus tips with no benefits at all, not even a meal. Here they were paying $7.50 an hour plus full health, paid vacation, guaranteed break, two meals a day, can't be fired unless you're really screwing up. We were just gonna stay for six months at the outside. That was almost seven years ago.

People who order room service don't want to stand in line. They've had a long day at a convention or they've been gambling all night and they've got a hangover. Sometimes they just want to argue. You go into a room and there's four guys all bigger than you and they're in a bad mood because they just spent half their life's savings on the tables stupidly. You gotta keep your eyes open.

Then there's the porno convention. They answer the door and there'll be five naked people standing there. They like to see the shock on your face. For us the idea is not to get in trouble. Just give them their order and leave.

One night we saw a magic show on the Strip, and the next day I blew a bunch of money at the magic shop. I do parties and I'm building a show. I have stage illusions and animals. Odin the boa, the iguana, the doves. My goal is to do it six nights a week for a casino.

People say, "Oh, love at first sight doesn't exist." Well, it does. First day of high school in Alaska, I was at my locker and I turned around and there was Sheri. It was kind of like the movies. The background just faded out and everything was kind of hazy except her face.

Now we've got Nicole. Our main concern is working to make the environment better for her.

PART IV **SHAPING LIFE**

JOANNE L. GOODWIN

"She Works Hard for Her Money"

A Reassessment of Las Vegas Women
Workers, 1945–1985

When I received my first academic position at the University of Nevada, Las Vegas, I thought the fates were having a little fun with me. I am a feminist. History is most interesting to me when interpreted with a gender analysis. My familiarity with Las Vegas amounted to a brief glimpse years earlier while on a cross-country trip. Unlike the millions of visitors, who flocked to the city to experience its constructed fantasies, I preferred the tangible beauty of the area's high deserts and canyons to the amusements of "Glitter Gulch." In fact, as a young progressive adult in the 1970s, the images of the city presented through the media ran counter to my views on social justice and equal opportunity. To be specific, I found the tourism industry's use of the female body to promote the city's economy an obstacle in the path to women's equality. I found the "job opportunities" of sex work, which I perceived to be the main lucrative occupation for women in Las Vegas at the time, degrading and hardly a choice. As I packed my things to move, I wondered how a feminist would fare in "sin city."

Twenty years later, not only had I changed but so had Las Vegas. Gambling and tourism still provide the economic base for this rapidly growing metropolitan area, but gambling is no longer unique to this desert town. Communities across the country now seek to enhance their local economies through gambling and entertainment tourism. The organization of the gambling industry also changed. Corporations bought out many of the individually owned properties and the pooled interests associated with organized crime. With the flow of capital stringently regulated, the postwar casino culture died. Job seekers still migrate to the area, but now retirees are joining them. The packaging and marketing of the female body continues unabated in Las Vegas, but the power relations that sustain it appear far more complex than I once thought. My move to this city, known worldwide for its commodification of marriage, divorce, sex, and entertainment, became for me not only an odd twist of fate but an opportunity to investigate its international popularity and its development during the postwar years.

I came to Las Vegas because of a job; however, it was not to work in a casino but to teach U.S. women's history at the university. It may not surprise the reader to learn that the history of women in Las Vegas is in an early stage of development. We are still discovering where and how women participated in the area's growth, as well as their significant contributions to the region's history. Locals refer to women's activity in the development of the area since its earliest days, yet little of that history has been written. To further complicate the process of retrieving a past that includes women, too few traditional historical resources exist. Despite these obstacles, my initial interest in finding local sources for graduate student seminars rapidly grew beyond those borders. I now understand that the histories of working women in Las Vegas offer a new perspective on the interaction between postwar gender systems and the consumer economy of the post-1945 era.

Americans' popular conceptions about women in Las Vegas in the years after World War II came from casino public relations departments and Hollywood screenwriters' imaginations. Aside from these sources, we know little about them. Las Vegas business leaders experimented with several images to promote the gambling resort town during the 1940s and 1950s, but the image that persisted was that of the glamorous "showgirl." Created during the same era as the Hollywood starlet, this female icon became a standard in public relations material.

Dancers and showgirls worked without additional pay to model for photos that went to newspapers around the country to promote the attractions of a Las Vegas vacation. Such pictures—usually posed near the hotel swimming pool, with the casino sign in the background—represented the glamour, excitement, and leisure available in Las Vegas even to "average" Americans. No mystery surrounds the popularity of these images. "Pretty girls sell," Al Guzman, a veteran of the Las Vegas publicity business, told a journalist. "You need to do something to get people's attention. A pretty girl will get an editor's attention . . . then

Miss Houston.

maybe you've got some free publicity."[1] The significance of selling Las Vegas through the glamorous image of a showgirl went beyond free publicity, however. It was part of a larger plan, initiated by Benjamin (Bugsy) Siegel with the Flamingo Hotel and by Wilbur Clark with the Desert Inn, to develop luxury resort casinos in the desert. The "glamour girl" replaced "Vegas Vic" and the western theme used by early properties to portray Las Vegas as a wild, no-holds-barred frontier town.[2] By the early 1950s, Las Vegas's image had more in common with Hollywood than with Dodge City. Promoters wanted Americans to think of Las Vegas as a vacation destination "with something for everyone" while the casinos consumed their discretionary income.[3]

Hollywood also played a role in constructing the public's image of women in Las Vegas. Movies with a Las Vegas theme or setting dichotomized female characters as either an innocent or evil. Ann-Margret's role in *Viva Las Vegas* provides an example of the innocent, while Sharon Stone's character in *Casino* starts out as a prostitute and proceeds to slide into a morass of addictions. While casino promoters scrupulously avoided references to mob ties, Hollywood satisfied the public's infatuation by mixing danger with glamour. The importance of organized crime to early casino financing is well known. Periodic government inquiries into organized crime and gambling have kept this part of the city's past alive in the public's imagination.[4] However, the organized crime version of the Las Vegas story has a male-only cast. When women appear, they are typically portrayed as marginal stereotypes.

The glamorous showgirl became the best-known image of women in the marketing of Las Vegas. The prototypical white, All-American "feminine beauty" aroused admiration and respect from female as well as male viewers. The image was highly sexualized, although not yet nude; public and conceivably available. Publicists, as well as the women who participated in creating these images, capitalized on a new consumer market.

This essay moves beyond an interpretation of women's experiences in Las Vegas as either glamour girls of a bygone era or pawns of a larger power system. It includes individual women's choices within a paradigm that recognizes sexism and racism. Taking these power relations as a starting point, it explores the tension between the representation of women's bodies and the experiences of women's lives. This essay is a first step toward a larger synthesis that examines the ways in which many women took charge of their opportunities and used them to their best advantage despite the existing inequitable systems of power.

The essay challenges the popular assumptions about women's work with an analysis of the patterns of women's employment in Las Vegas between 1945 and 1985. Sex work is not included, because of the difficulties involved in acquiring historical material on the topic. I focus instead on the areas of work that occupied the majority of women and discuss the patterns of their work over time. Census data document the types of jobs women took and make national comparisons possible. Women who worked in the hotel-casino industry during those years fill out the census data with their own words. They make the case that many women workers exercised far greater self-determination in their wage earning than has been acknowledged. Furthermore, they did so at a time when their alternatives in wage work would have been in less well paid jobs in offices, cafeterias, and private homes.[5] Finally, this historical account of Las Vegas's working women changes what we know about women's history and the history of the American West in the twentieth century by challenging the thesis that domestic containment typified postwar American women. It builds upon research that finds women received conflicting messages regarding gender roles, family responsibilities, and sexuality. Rather than adopting any one model, postwar women followed many, varied paths.[6] The Las Vegas story contributes to this revisionist literature by illuminating the way in which gender and race operated to create both restrictions and opportunities.

Las Vegas changed from a small desert town created by the railroad to an international tourist destination during the forty years discussed in this survey. The incorporated town of Las Vegas had fewer than 8,500 residents in 1940, yet it accounted for more than half of the population of the entire county. In 1931, when the state legislature relegalized gambling, that enterprise made up only a small part of the local economy. Federal spending for Boulder Dam in the 1930s and the military during the 1940s proved far more important for local businesses.[7] With people moving into the area in search of jobs, the population doubled several times during the next two decades. The net in-migration declined slightly between 1960 and 1980 as the incorporated city's population increased 1.5 times.[8] Women did not make up a significant part of the labor force until the casino expansion of the 1950s. They numbered slightly over 1,000 and accounted for only 16.5 percent of the civilian labor force in 1940. That would change dramatically as the city's economy expanded with gambling in the years following the war.

The influx of newcomers did not significantly alter the racial composition of the area. Most of the residents were white, and the combined total of African Americans, Native Americans, and Asian Americans remained under 10 percent of the population until 1970. The most dramatic change occurred with African Americans. Only 178 blacks lived in Clark County in 1940, but those figures increased to 11,005 between 1940 and 1960, to make up 8.6 percent of the county's population. Many came from southern states as part of the second great migration during the war years. In general, male African-American migrants took jobs in the area's wartime industries and later in the hotels. Women worked in the housekeeping departments of the Las Vegas hotels, in personal service, and, by the 1970s, in offices.[9]

The postwar expansion brought women of all backgrounds to Las Vegas because of the jobs the city offered.[10] Las Vegas Standard Metropolitan Statistical Area (SMSA) figures show that women and men were evenly distributed in the population across most racial and ethnic groups. Yet the rate at which women entered the workforce grew faster than the rate of increase in the number of women in the overall population. For example, between 1940 and 1950, the number of working-age women increased 196 percent in the general population while their participation in the labor force increased 413 percent. That trend toward wage earning by women continued through the next decade, slowed between 1960 and 1970, and then resumed again by 1980. The narratives of women who moved to Las Vegas for work in the hotel-casinos give us some indication of their motivations.

Las Vegas provided plenty of work for women who wanted or needed to earn money. In fact, the rapid expansion gave service workers the mobility to move from job to job. Eileen Noreen came to Las Vegas in the late 1940s from California to work briefly as a dancer, then as a cocktail waitress. She grew up taking dancing lessons near her home around Los Angeles and danced with a group called the Fanchionettes as a teenager. When the managers of the troupe decided to move their operation to New York City, she quit. After that, "I danced independently in different clubs. Then I was asked to join the Dorothy Dorbin dancers and I came to Las Vegas with them. They had a short engagement for two weeks at the Hotel Last Frontier. When that ended, I got acquainted with the cocktail girls at the Last Frontier and found that they made a lot more money than I did. So I applied for the job and, thankfully, I got it." Eileen came to town at the beginning of development on the Las Vegas Strip. The only major properties were the El Rancho Vegas and the Hotel Last Frontier. The entertainment scene had not developed to the extent it would within twenty years, and the qualifications for talent varied from property to property. Although her career in dancing was erratic—she returned to California periodically to take jobs in small clubs—her work as a cocktail server offered a steady job, with lucrative tips, in a town with considerable excitement.[11]

Essie Jacobs and her husband came to Las Vegas because of the bright lights and, more important, because they hoped to find better opportunities for themselves and their family. They were two among thousands of African Americans who left the South during the war years. After they moved from Fordyce, Arkansas, her husband started to work, while Essie spent time with their children. Although she did not plan to take a job immediately, Essie mentioned women's employment when discussing the differences between Fordyce and her new home. "It wasn't mandatory [for me] to work down there [in Fordyce], 'cause mens didn't

Dunes Hotel cocktail staff.

believe in womens working. But when I come to Vegas, with the cost of living and things . . . well, for two to make ends meet, two had to work. So, I decided to get me a job. So, I went to work at the Aladdin [Hotel and Casino] in December 1963."[12] A friend of her sister's, who also lived in Las Vegas, helped her find a job working as a maid in the housekeeping department of the hotel. The work in housekeeping was much easier, she said, than the nursing home work she had done in Fordyce.[13]

Eileen Noreen and Essie Jacobs came to the city from different sections of the country. They both worked in service sector jobs, yet those jobs were segregated on the basis of sex as well as race. The separation of their work environments mirrored the segregation of the workplace and the social milieu of Las Vegas. Eileen was visible in the showroom and on the floor of the casino serving drinks to guests in the bar. After work, she socialized in the city's bars and casinos with co-workers and friends. Essie worked in the "back of the house"—an area of the hotel-casino that remained invisible to the tourists, yet provided the infrastructure for the hotel. Segregation policies restricted Essie from socializing in the casinos, but the African-American community developed its own area for clubs and entertainment in the city's Westside neighborhood. According to both women, the unofficial income from tips made these otherwise traditionally female jobs more appealing.

Close ties between Las Vegas and Hollywood brought many performers to the casino showrooms. Betty Bunch's career on stage and in the movies shared several characteristics with those of other white entertainers. She came to Las Vegas in 1956 as a member of the chorus line with the Moro-Landis Dancers. "I came over here to work. When that job was over, I went back to Los Angeles and auditioned for another show that was coming to Las Vegas. Finally, I realized that all the work was in Las Vegas, so I moved over here to stay." The dancers opened the show at the Sahara for a headliner. They worked two shows a night, seven nights a week. The hard work was worth it for a variety of reasons, the salary among them. "We made $95 a week, which was a fortune at the time. We considered that being very well paid. The average secretary at the time made $45 a week."[14]

Betty Bunch fitted the mainstream standards of racial and gender beauty promoted in the postwar United States. Until the mid 1960s, Las Vegas showgirls were not only white but frequently European. African-American entertainers had a parallel system for producing icons of African-American beauty. All-black acts, black clubs, separate performance circuits and popular publications played to predominantly black audiences. Similar networks existed in Latino communities. Asian women not only worked as featured groups of entertainers but were occasionally found "integrated" into chorus lines. The segregation practiced in most American cities, whether de facto or de jure, also existed in Las Vegas. Entertainment venues maintained a policy of race segregation until the 1960s. Headliners such as Lena Horne played in Las Vegas casino showrooms, but she did so to all-white audiences. The Las Vegas African-American community, through the local branch of the National Association for the Advancement of Colored People, worked continuously to end race discrimination in all areas of community life.

Eileen Noreen, Essie Jacobs, and Betty Bunch came to Las Vegas during the early days of the casino boom to take advantage of openings created by the expanding tourist economy. Sex and race discrimination existed in labor practices, yet each woman maneuvered her way around

them. By the 1970s, labor patterns began to change as the successes of
the civil rights movement and sex-equity legislation lowered the barriers
to employment across the nation. The same economy that fostered gender and race stereotypes and maintained segregated labor practices continued to attract a diverse group of working-class women and men to
the service-sector tip economy of casinos, hotels, motels, and restaurants.

Women increased their workforce participation nationally during the
1960s and 1970s, yet Las Vegas had higher rates of female participation
in the labor force than the nation as a whole. Nearly half (44 percent)
of all women of legal working age in Las Vegas held jobs in 1960, compared to slightly over one-third nationwide. (These percentages are ag-
gregate figures and do not account for differences in marital status, race,
or ethnicity.) By 1970, the gap had closed, but Las Vegas still had a
greater portion of women in its workforce than the nation (47 percent
to nearly 43 percent). The pattern of higher employment rates held true
irrespective of a woman's marital or parental status. Women generally
worked less after they married, *if* their husbands lived with them and
the family income could support it. This was the case nationally for
married women, too, at the time. Nevertheless, a higher percentage of
married women worked in Las Vegas, particularly as shown in the 1960
census.

The most significant influence on women's employment in Las Vegas
proved to be the presence of young children in the home. Half of all
women worked for wages when no children under eighteen lived at
home.[15] This included young single women, "empty nesters," and the
elderly. However, when children under the age of six years were present,
the rate dropped to 28 percent. This employment rate was still ten percentage points higher than the national average in 1960. Las Vegas and
the nation had similar rates of employment of mothers with young children by 1970. It reached approximately 30 percent in both cases.[16]
When children reached school age (6 to 17), the proportion of mothers
who went out to work jumped to 50 percent. Single mothers with children (but no husband present in the home) had the highest employment
rates. The ages of their children made little difference in terms of their
need to work. Seventy-five percent of single mothers with children under
six years were wage earners. When their children went to school, these
women stayed in their jobs and continued to support their families.[17]

Las Vegas does not appear to have offered any greater number or
variety of childcare alternatives than other parts of the country at the

time. Some workers found family members to help with the children during work hours. When that strategy failed, some sent children "back home" to be cared for by grandmothers. Women with more discretionary income placed their children with private families for the day. A few well-paid women workers hired nannies or housekeepers.

Employment figures from the federal census suggest strongly that wage earning played a central role in many Las Vegas women's lives, particularly when compared to the national average. What might explain these trends? One would need to conduct a more extensive analysis to answer that question fully. In the meantime, I propose the following hypothesis: no particular set of demographic, social, or environmental reasons created a situation in which a greater percentage of Las Vegas women worked outside the home. While it may be tempting to argue that liberal divorce and marriage laws weakened family structure, or that the 24-hour casino culture created stresses for families that led to separation and divorce, I propose a simpler alternative. Women (like men) came to Las Vegas for jobs. Working women held a higher percentage of jobs because the service tourism economy provided ample work in traditional lines of "women's work." They could serve drinks, type letters, clean rooms, or wait tables in a small city that offered better tips and more diverse forms of entertainment than they had back home.

Women worked in several industry categories, but the largest group—slightly over 40 percent of women workers—found jobs in those sectors most likely to be related to tourism: entertainment and recreation, hotel and lodging, eating and drinking establishments, and retail. Las Vegas's reliance on gambling and tourism created a narrow and unusual economic base, but the types of jobs women took within those industries varied little from those of women across the country in the decades before civil rights and employment opportunity legislation. A photograph published by *Life* magazine in a 1950 article on gambling in the United States shows the employees of the recently opened Desert Inn posed in a graphic illustration of the business's occupational structure. At the center stands Wilbur Clark, president and general manager of the Desert Inn. His all-male casino managers, floor bosses, and directors flank him on each side. A second tier of workers includes both mixed and same-sex groups. Desk clerks, office workers, and showroom personnel include both men and women. Women-only groups include cocktail girls, waitresses, and change girls. Men also stand in homogeneous groups of dealers, bellboys, and waiters. At the far rear of the photo, in light too dim for them to be identified, stand the porters and chambermaids.[18] In the hotel-casino, as in the majority of business settings until the mid 1970s, jobs had traditional sex typing, and the boundaries were rarely crossed.

The narrow range of jobs held by women, regardless of the industrial sector, illustrates the existence of sex-typed employment during the era. Half of all women workers in Las Vegas in 1940 took jobs in service, sales, or clerical work. Thirteen percent of women worked at professional jobs, such as teaching and nursing. Ten percent worked as proprietors, managers, or officials. Domestic service and operatives made up 10 percent and 9 percent of jobs, respectively, taken by women before the war. These occupational statistics for Las Vegas differ significantly from the national figures. Three of the four leading areas of employment at the national level—manual work, private service, and machine operators—did not figure substantively in Las Vegas. Conversely, sales work did not account for many positions at the national level until later.[19]

During the next twenty years, thousands of people moved to the area to work at wartime jobs and hotel-casino construction on Las Vegas Boulevard. The population of the county increased from 16,414 to 127,016. Women, once a small part of the workforce, made up 48 percent of the civilian service sector. A corresponding expansion of areas of employment for women did not accompany this shift, however. Two-thirds of the women employed in Las Vegas in 1960 worked in the same three occupational areas as they had in the 1940 census: service (excluding private homes), clerical work, and sales.

Most women (12 percent) worked as waitresses. Sales clerks and maids each made up 6 percent of the female workforce. A second tier of frequently held positions included domestics, secretaries, and cashiers (5 percent each). Professional services, which included nursing and teaching, still attracted a significant (12 percent) portion of the female workforce. The tourist economy of Las Vegas distinguished women's labor patterns from the national profile. Nationally, 29 percent of women workers held office clerical jobs. In Las Vegas, they worked as waitresses, saleswomen, and maids. Las Vegas likewise offered few factory jobs, which employed 16 percent of women workers nationally.[20]

Modest changes in women's work patterns began to appear by 1970. Most women continued to work in traditional jobs as waitresses, secretaries, cashiers, retail clerks, elementary school teachers, and nurses. Domestic service, on the other hand, dropped off the list of the top five jobs held by women. The shift out of domestic service indicated a broad-

Thunderbird staff.

ening of job opportunities, particularly for racial minorities. A second change in work patterns emerged in the 1980 census. Managers, an employment category parceled with other areas of work in 1940, surpassed clerical work as one of the top five jobs held by women. Cashiers, secretaries, waitresses, and maids followed it. A third change exists in the importance of a second tier of industries—finance, insurance, and real estate—as new areas of job growth for women. These industries did not appear independently in the 1940 census, but ten years later, they supplied jobs to nearly one-fifth of women workers, and by 1980, the ratio had increased to slightly over one-quarter.

Three elements contributed to the change in labor patterns. First, the organization of the gaming industry changed. The 1969 passage of the Nevada Corporate Gaming Act allowed corporations to invest in and own casinos. Restructured business procedures, as well as the expanding size of individual properties, created greater levels of administration than existed prior to the act. Second, the passage of the federal Civil Rights Act of 1964 made discriminatory hiring practices illegal and installed state equal employment opportunity offices. It took political mobilization, however, to bring the full force of the equity laws into effect. The Las Vegas chapter of the National Association for the Advancement of Colored People played a pivotal role in ending employment discrimination by race and obtaining a 1971 consent decree on hiring with casino operators. Ten years later, a similar decree opened up casino and hotel jobs regardless of sex or ethnicity. The third element to affect women's work opportunities was the Culinary Union. The consent decrees initially targeted the union as well as casino management, charging that it lacked initiative in opening all casino jobs regardless of sex or race. However, the union also played a significant role in maintaining job security and benefits for workers. Among the housekeepers interviewed, several placed the local union leadership alongside Reverend Martin Luther King, Jr., and President John F. Kennedy in promoting equal opportunities.

What does this reevaluation of wage-earning women tell us about postwar America and women's opportunities? The tourist economy of Las Vegas in the decades immediately following the war offered a variety of lucrative jobs relative to one's education and training. From the glamorous and well-paid entertainment jobs to the traditional occupations of waitress and housekeeper, women said they could make more money doing similar or easier work than they did "back home."

It is also clear that the women who came and worked in Las Vegas accommodated themselves to the commercialization of the female body. None of the interviewees to date has perceived the showgirl or dancer as either a pawn or a victim. They express quite the opposite view. As consumers of American culture, they saw a kind of power in the showgirl image; one available only to women, that could lead to wealth and social influence. They admired the image uncritically and wanted what it symbolized. The representation of the female body was a key element of the postwar gender system and the politics of consumption. As such, it signified power relations between the sexes, but it did not operate solely to disadvantage women. The sex-gender system that promoted sexualized portrayals of women and prevented gender equality for all women offered individual women great economic advantages. The power relations of race created a different yet related cultural paradox of inequality and opportunity. That many Las Vegas women accepted this postwar gender model does not invalidate the feminist critique of the commodification of the female body. Nor does it imply a false consciousness on the part of Las Vegas women. The power of an image rests, not only in what it embraces, but also in what it excludes. The image of the showgirl (or pinup or starlet) reinforced the status quo of sex and race relations in postwar America, while at the same time masking the wide range of values and behaviors experienced by women.

This essay raises numerous points to be explored in the next stage of research, and one with which to conclude this chapter. Sex, wealth, and power—the triumvirate ruling postwar American culture—are key components of the fantasies on which the Las Vegas tourist economy is based. Furthermore, it is Americans' contradictory responses to sex, wealth, and power that one sees in the public's attraction to and repulsion by Las Vegas. On the one hand, the city's particular mix of consumption and wealth fits squarely within many Americans' views of the economic opportunity and freedom of expression offered in the United States. On the other hand, the fantasies and illusions that casino owners and business leaders have capitalized upon in this part of the Mojave Desert also present an uneasy counterpoint to other cherished American values. For example, fortunes gained from gambling are considered suspect when compared to traditional capitalist enterprise. Licensing prostitution and gambling, as well as marketing easy divorces, are perceived to threaten the stability of social mores. Similarly, caricaturing women solely in terms of appearance and sexuality debases half of the population and seriously stalls advancement toward equal treatment. The tension between these competing systems has not hurt business in the city and may have expanded the city's appeal. As commentators struggle to explain the similarity and differences between Las Vegas and other American cities, Las Vegas has thus far been an anomaly in the American landscape, an outpost offering that which is forbidden elsewhere. Yet, looking at Las Vegas, one finds it thrives from the support of tourists from all backgrounds.

Women, as actors in postwar culture, have used those fantasies to create real material opportunities for themselves and their families. Although not feminist or protofeminist, studying women as actors making choices in Las Vegas sheds light on both the realities and fantasies of social relations in postwar America.

NOTES

This research was made possible through the support of the Nevada Humanities Committee and the Foundation at the University of Nevada, Las Vegas. The work has benefited from the comments of Carol C. Harter, Betsy Jameson, Gene Moehring, Hal Rothman, and Rickie Solinger, who have shared their ideas about this research with me. The history of women in Las Vegas is at the "contributory stage," a term coined by Gerda Lerner, a founder of the field of women's history. It defines an early stage of research that tends to be descriptive of individuals and activities as opposed to a later stage of analytical research that builds upon the early work.

1. Ned Day, "The Selling of Las Vegas," *Las Vegan Magazine,* August 1984, 78.

2. Two neon figures, Vegas Vic and Sassy Sal, welcomed visitors to Fremont Street, the original gambling area in downtown Las Vegas. Recent downtown revitalization efforts covered over the dramatic avenue of neon and lights with a computerized laser light canopy. In the renovations, Vegas Vic had his height shortened. Sassy Sal resumed her position atop a building that housed a nude show called the "Girls of Glitter Gulch."

3. During the 1990s, the image of the showgirl itself changed, and she no longer retains her former stature. Not only does she wear less, but her standing has, literally, declined. In today's adult Disneyland, where fantasies of wealth, luxury, and indulgence of all kinds can be had for a price, advertising portrays the showgirl reclining or kneeling, no longer standing upright.

4. In a performance in Las Vegas, the comedian Mark Russell suggested that business leaders capitalize on their past by using "the mob" as a theme for a new resort. Visitors would enter the hotel-casino through a giant automobile trunk. Dealers and floor men could assume the clothing and accents of "da boys." Different areas of the property would be designed to represent New York City, Chicago, Kansas City, Los Angeles, etc., during the 1930s and 1940s. The ideas for rides are endless.

5. The Las Vegas Women Oral History Project has conducted approximately thirty oral histories of women who worked in various areas of the gaming and entertainment industries between the years 1945 to 1985. Owners, managers, dealers, waitresses, housekeepers, and entertainers are included in the project. My search for historical sources on (non-brothel) prostitution in Las Vegas during the years of this study has been unrewarding to date. The research project, which is still in progress, has, however, fostered undergraduate and graduate research on the subject.

Oral histories are a vital component of the history of this new city. As a result of the city's age and preoccupation with future development, rather than the past, there are few collections for research. Consequently, individual narratives provide an important resource. Memory and personal reflection, however, are as vulnerable to relativity and reinterpretation as sources such as newspapers, diaries, or letters. These narratives are used with the recognition of the value of individual recollections, as well as in the knowledge that the narratives themselves are constructed entities.

6. For the thesis that domestic containment typified American women during the Cold War, see Elaine Tyler May, *Homeward Bound: American Families in the Cold War Era* (New York: Basic Books, 1988). For alternative interpretations of postwar gender systems, see *Not June Cleaver: Women and Gender in Post-War America,* ed. Joanne Meyerowitz (Philadelphia: Temple University Press, 1994). Few historical studies of working women in the postwar West

exist. Notable exceptions include Vicki Ruiz, *Cannery Women, Cannery Lives: Mexican Women, Unionization, and the California Food Processing Industry, 1930–1950* (Albuquerque: University of New Mexico, 1987), and Karen Anderson, *Changing Woman: A History of Racial Ethnic Women in Modern America* (New York: Oxford University Press, 1996).

7. Eugene Moehring, *Resort City in the Sunbelt: Las Vegas, 1930–1970* (Reno: University of Nevada Press, 1989), 2.

8. The census recorded the population of the Las Vegas region in three categories. The Las Vegas Standard Metropolitan Statistical Areas (SMSA) included all of Clark County. The Las Vegas Urbanized Area included both incorporated and unincorporated districts in proximity to the city. The final category covered the incorporated city of Las Vegas. The figures cited here are for the incorporated city of Las Vegas. U.S. Department of Commerce, Bureau of the Census, *Sixteenth Census of the United States: 1940, Population*, vol. 2: *Characteristics of the Population*, pt. 4, 756, 758; *Seventeenth Decennial Census of the United States: 1950*, vol. 2: *Characteristics of the Population*, pt. 28, 28–6; *Eighteenth Decennial Census of the United States, Census of Population: 1960*, vol. 1: *Characteristics*, pt. 30, 30–27; *Nineteenth Decennial Census of the United States, Census of Population: 1970*, vol. 1: *Characteristics*, pt. 30, 30–23.

9. *Sixteenth Census: 1940*, 747; *Seventeenth Census: 1950*, 28–36; *Eighteenth Census: 1960*, 30–40; *Nineteenth Census: 1970*, 50–59, 30–51. For a detailed account of African-American women workers in Las Vegas, see Claytee White, "The Roles of African American Women in the Gaming Industry" (M.A. thesis, University of Nevada, Las Vegas, 1997).

10. The 1960 and 1970 censuses pick up the changing patterns of women's labor participation as a result of migration and economic expansion. During the period of study, most hotel-casino development took place outside the city limits along Highway 91 (commonly referred to as the Strip). Only minor differences existed in the rates of employment for the three census areas. This is explained largely by the fact that 90 percent of the county population resided in Las Vegas and contingent communities. This section uses the figures for the Las Vegas Urbanized Area.

11. An Interview with Eileen Noreen McClintock, conducted by Joanne L. Goodwin (University of Nevada, Las Vegas: Las Vegas Women Oral History Project, Gaming and Entertainment series [hereafter referred to as LVWOHP], 1997).

12. The property was actually called the Tally-Ho until 1966, when it became the Aladdin.

13. An Interview with Essie Jacobs, conducted by Claytee D. White (UNLV: LVWOHP, 1997).

14. An Interview with Betty Bunch, conducted by Joyce Marshall (UNLV: LVWOHP, 1997).

15. In 1960, the census calculated the age at fourteen years and older. A decade later, it had increased to sixteen years.

16. U.S. Department of Commerce, Bureau of the Census, *Eighteenth Census: 1960, Census of the Population: 1960*, vol. 1: *Characteristics of the Pop-*

ulation, pt. 30, Nevada, table 33, 30–51; "Marital Status of Women in the Civilian Labor Force," in *Historical Statistics of the United States: Colonial Times to 1970* (Washington, D.C.: Government Printing Office, 1975), 133; *Nineteenth Census: 1970,* 30–130; "Married Women (Husband Present) in the Labor Force, by Age and Presence of Children: 1948 to 1970," in *Historical Statistics,* 134.

17. U.S. Department of Commerce, Bureau of the Census, *Nineteenth Decennial Census of the United States, Census of the Population: 1970,* vol. 1: *Characteristics of the Population,* pt. 30, Nevada, table 85, 30–130.

18. *Life,* June 19, 1950, 100–101. The extensive article appeared during Senator Estes Kefauver's national hearings on organized crime and gambling.

19. Jobs for men in the region were more widely distributed in construction, mines, railroad, utilities, government, and agriculture. By 1960, they would be concentrated in gaming. *Sixteenth Census: 1940,* 758; *Historical Statistics,* 182–232.

20. *Historical Statistics,* 140.

The Racial Cauldron

as Vegas's frenzied Memorial Day weekend in 1992 was winding down with the promise of a big storm. Spring lightning danced in the dark clouds above Charleston Peak and the Valley of Fire. As raindrops the size of silver dollars intermittently splattered the sidewalks outside, weary casino tellers counted a quarter-billion dollars in holiday revenue. Across the Mojave, 50,000 homebound revelers were strung out almost bumper to bumper, from Ivanpah Dry Lake to the outskirts of Los Angeles, 250 miles away.

In a small park in the northwest part of town, several hundred Crips and Bloods, ignoring the storm warnings, were merrily barbequing pork ribs and passing around forty-ounce bottles of beer. Earlier in the day, dozens of formerly hostile sets with names like Anybody's Murderers (ABM), Donna Street Crips, and North Town Bloods had joined at a nearby cemetery to mark a gang truce and place flowers on the graves of their homeboys (there were twenty-seven local gang-related deaths in 1991). Now these erstwhile enemies and their girlfriends were swapping jokes and new rap lyrics.

But gatherings of three or more people, however amicable, had been banned on May 17, 1992, by sheriff's order throughout Las Vegas's black Westside, as well as in the neighboring blue-collar suburb of North

This chapter was originally published in *The Nation*, vol. 255, no. 1 (July 6, 1992). It appears here in slightly modified form.

Las Vegas. To enforce this extraordinary edict, Metro Police pulled up in front of Valley View Park in three V-100 armored personnel carriers borrowed from a nearby Air Force base. When defiant picnickers refused to disperse, the cops opened up with tear gas and concussion grenades. The Las Vegas "riots" had resumed for the fourth weekend in a row since the Rodney King verdict had ignited a tinderbox of black grievances.

"THE RULES HAVE CHANGED"

I caught up with some of the casualties in the parking lot of a burned-out market an hour later. As a fascinated crowd watched, Yolanda, who said she was seventeen, exhibited the bloody gash in her leg, while her boyfriend, David, hopped around excitedly with a crumpled olive-green canister in his hand. "Check this out!" he commanded somewhat menacingly as he shoved the offending projectile in my face. I read the label out loud: "Model 429, Thunderflash, Stun Grenade."

"We were just having a picnic, a goddamn peaceful picnic," David repeated. Several kids stared hard, unblinking, in my direction. Someone lobbed an empty Colt 45 bottle into the sagebrush. Then a tall figure in a Georgetown sweatshirt grabbed my arm. "You better split, man. If you want an interview, come back tomorrow. I'll tell you anything you want to know about Lost fuckin' Vegas." I asked his name. He laughed: "Just call me Nice D, Valley View Gangster Crips. OK?"

I went looking for D the next day. West Las Vegas (population 20,000) is the antipode of the pleasure domes of downtown and the Strip—grit without glitter. It has no hotels, casinos, supermarkets, banks, or even regular bus service. Yet, like South Central LA, it scarcely resembles the Frostbelt stereotype of a ghetto. Its detached homes lack the verdant, Astroturf-like lawns and backyard swimming pools of the white neighborhoods, but they appear to be lovingly tended, with groves of shade trees to protect against the blast-furnace desert heat. Even the spartan public housing units in Gerson Park have a tidy ambience that belies their poverty.

I met up with D, who was twenty, near the ruins of Nucleus Plaza—the closest thing on the Westside to a shopping center. He recalled the night of April 30, the day after the LA verdict, when protest turned to riot and gang members looted and firebombed buildings, including the Korean-owned Super 8 Market in the middle of the plaza. "A young brother [high school senior Isaiah Charles, Jr.] went in to rescue a little girl. She managed to get out, but he was trapped when the roof collapsed. The fire department had already run away, so the fire just burned for a long time." He showed me the charred remains of an adjacent NAACP office and AIDS clinic.

Although the scale of arson damage in West Las Vegas ($5 million) was minute compared with that of Los Angeles (about $1 billion), the sheer fury of confrontation was, if anything, more intense. Accounts of that first day's events have a *Rashomon*-like ambiguity, only here no third party emerges to resolve the contradictions. Everyone agrees that rioting did not begin until about 7:30 on the evening of April 30, after police used tear gas to turn back several hundred young blacks trying to march from the Westside to downtown. From that point on, the stories diverge dramatically, from the local newspapers' version, almost totally reliant on police reports, to the street-level perspective of young African Americans like D.

According to Metro Police Lieutenant Steve Franks (who would shoot a teenager during the second weekend of disturbances): "Our intelligence was that if that group had reached downtown, they were ready to set fire to the hotels. Had it not been for our officers this town would have gone up in flames." D says: "This is total bullshit. We were only trying to demonstrate against the Rodney King verdict and apartheid right here in Las Vegas. The police just wanted an excuse to attack us."

Having broken up the march, the police cordoned off most of West Las Vegas and drew weapons on anyone who approached their barricades. Hundreds of young people, meanwhile, had regrouped near the Gerson Park Projects, where the local Kingsmen Gang was hosting an impromptu party for the various Crip and Blood sets, who had agreed the previous day—apparently influenced by news from LA—to stop fighting. According to D, a Metro squad car drove straight into the festive crowd. "People went crazy. They started throwing rocks and bottles; then one of the homies opened up with his gat [gun]." The angry crowd burned down a nearby office of the Pardon and Parole Board, while other groups attacked stores and gas stations with Molotov cocktails.

Lieutenant Franks claimed that snipers "hid in trees and rooftops, and used human targets when they came out in the open to fire. . . . These yellow-bellied rats stood with young children around them and then opened fire on police cars." Another police spokesman claimed that gang members tried to kidnap an infant from a white family living on a predominantly black street. I found no one who could confirm either of these lurid stories, which the city's two daily papers disseminated uncritically to a horrified white public. Nor were there follow-up reports of suspects in such crimes from among the 111 people arrested.

At the same time, the media, as in Los Angeles, studiously avoided any reference to police misconduct during the disturbances. D, however, has vivid recollections. "Me and my friends left after the shooting started," he said. "Our car was pulled over a few blocks later. When we asked what we had done wrong, a big redneck cop said, 'The rules have changed, nigger,' and hit me in the face with his pistol. I was held five days in jail for 'obstruction.' The cops threw away my ID and health card, so I lost my job at Carl's Junior."

D got out of jail just in time to witness the renewal of violence on Sunday, May 10. Once again kids gathered near Gerson Park to play softball and party. Metro Police called in an armored personnel carrier and began shooting wooden bullets at the crowd. The following week-end was a virtual rerun, as a gang picnic at the Doolittle Community Center disintegrated into a wild all-night melee between cops in their V-100s and hundreds of angry youths.

D thought that these now-ritual confrontations would only grow more violent over the summer. Like other black youths with whom I spoke, he believed that Clark County's Sheriff John Moran would "do anything, however extreme, to break up the [gang] unification process." Indeed, D and the others were convinced that a recent drive-by shooting that wounded four members of the Rollin' 60s (a local branch of the famous LA Crip set) was actually organized by the police. They also spoke derisively of the "reverse buy" program, in which undercover cops posed as drug dealers to entrap crack addicts, whom they then coerced into becoming police informants. D warned me that Las Vegas was on the verge of what he called "an underground holocaust." Why?

"MISSISSIPPI WEST"

Although Las Vegas's mythographers typically elide race, black entertainers and laborers played decisive roles in the transformation of a sleepy desert railroad town into a $14-billion-a-year tourist oasis. But the sensational rise of the modern casino economy went hand in hand with the degradation of black rights. Glitter Gulch was built by Jim Crow.

As exiled LA gamblers began to buy up the old Fremont Street casinos in downtown Las Vegas in the late 1930s, local black residents were barred from the blackjack tables and slot machines. When Tom Hull opened his El Rancho in 1941—the Strip's pioneer casino and resort hotel—restrictive covenants were being used to evict black families from downtown and force them across the Union Pacific tracks into West Las Vegas, a wasteland without paved roads, utilities, or fire protection. Thus, by the time Meyer Lansky's gunmen ruined Bugsy Siegel's good looks in 1947, segregation in Las Vegas was virtually total. Blacks could wash dishes, make beds, even entertain, like Lena Horne and Sammy Davis, Jr., but they could not work as dealers or bartenders, stay in a hotel, live in a white neighborhood, or go to a white school.

The all-white police department, which had a national reputation for brutality, enforced the color line in a town that African Americans began to call Mississippi West. When in 1944 black GIs guarding nearby Boulder Dam tried to defy the racist rules that kept them out of downtown bars and casinos, they were attacked by police. In the full-fledged riot that erupted, one soldier was killed. A quarter-century later, in October 1969, heavy-handed police tactics, together with disgust over continuing job discrimination, again ignited a riot. Two people died, and Governor Paul Laxalt called in the National Guard to seal off the Westside. For nearly a year afterward, Clark County's schools, only partially integrated, were rocked by battles between white and black students. While racism was building in the premier city of the Silver State, those with power could ignore its ugly features, but now racial turmoil was tarnishing its image.

The major hotels and their complicit unions reluctantly signed a consent decree in 1971 guaranteeing open employment. In the same year, the Nevada legislature passed a long-delayed fair housing law. Clark County schools followed a year later with an integration scheme that overrode white resistance to busing. After thirty years of wandering in the wilderness, black Las Vegans thought they could see equality ahead.

Like so much else in the desert, this has turned out to be a cruel mirage. Although token integration is the rule, the majority of blacks are locked out of Las Vegas's boom economy. In recent years, as the rest of the Sunbelt has slipped into recession, Clark County's population has increased at warp speed (1,000 new residents per week), and Nevada, the "most fortunate state in the nation," according to the local AFL-CIO, has repeatedly led in job creation (8 percent annually between 1987 and 1990). Employment on the Strip has soared with the construction of mega-hotels like the 4,000-room Excalibur and the MGM

Grand, the biggest hotel in the world, with 5,005 rooms—while the so-called South Nevada Industrial Revolution has seduced dozens of high-tech computer and military aerospace firms from California.

But only a handful of black families have found their way into afflu-ent new-growth suburbs like Green Valley. Despite the twenty-year-old consent decree, blacks remain vastly underrepresented in the higher-paying hotel jobs and construction trades, as well as in the new science parks. Although minorities make up 20 percent of Nevada's labor force (25 percent in Clark County), they hold only 14 percent of public-sector jobs, and Governor Robert Miller acknowledged the bankruptcy of the state's affirmative action efforts. Concurrently, the growth in the city's Latino population—from 5,800 in 1970 to 32,400 in 1990—and a huge influx of jobless whites from nearby states have severely crimped tra-ditional black employment in the low-wage service industries.

Not surprisingly, black Las Vegans of all classes worry about creeping "Miamization," with their community, despite impressive political gains, becoming more socially and economically peripheral. For too many native sons like D, the recent boom has been an embittering "pris-oners' dilemma," offering equally futureless choices between menial la-bor and the underground economy. As in Los Angeles, the shortfall between the spectacle of profligate consumption and the reality of ghetto life has been made up by street gangs and rock cocaine. The first Crip set, transplanted from Watts, took root in Gerson Park in 1978–79; crack hit the streets of West Las Vegas in 1984, shortly after its arrival in South Central LA. Now an estimated 4,000 Crips and Bloods (to-gether with 3,000 Latino and Asian gang members) are locked in a grim twilight struggle with police a few dozen blocks from the Liberace Mu-seum and Caesars Palace.

"LYNCHING, LAS VEGAS-STYLE"

Chan Kendrick is a scraggy, angular southerner with a jawline beard who might have stepped out of a Civil War daguerreotype. A veteran civil liberties activist, he headed the Virginia ACLU for many years be-fore moving to Las Vegas to run the organization's Nevada chapter. He makes no bones about which area is morally farthest below the Mason-Dixon line: "Police abuse here is worse than anywhere in the contem-porary urban South. In an average month I get more complaints about police misconduct in Las Vegas than I received altogether during twelve years in Richmond. The situation is just incredible."

According to Kendrick and other critics, the Metro Las Vegas Police Force, formerly headed by Sheriff Moran (whom a local reporter described as being "as accessible as the king of Nepal"), is little more than a mean guard dog for the casinos and the Nevada Resort Association. Kendrick is constantly challenging the use of nuisance, loitering, and vagrancy laws to keep "undesirables," especially young blacks and homeless people, off the Strip. Likewise, he fights to force the police, particularly its rogue narcotics squads, to respect the constitutional constraints on search and seizure.

In a notorious 1989 incident reported by the *Las Vegas Review-Journal,* ten policemen, presumably looking for illegal narcotics, raided the home of 58-year-old Barbara Melvin. They announced their arrival by tossing two powerful concussion grenades through her bedroom window, then broke down her front door. While her fifth-grade grandson cowered in terror, they called her "nigger" and "bitch," tore off her nightgown, knocked her to the floor, and kicked her between the legs. After trashing the house and finding nothing, they seized $4,500 in cash and left. Melvin was not charged with any offense. She filed a complaint with the police, but it was dismissed with a form letter. According to the *Review-Journal,* the cops also kept $4,001 of the confiscated money.

The case that most haunts West Las Vegas today, however, is the killing of casino floorman Charles Bush in July 1990. Bush was asleep when three plainclothes police, wanting to question him about the arrest of his pregnant girlfriend for prostitution, broke into his apartment without a warrant and choked him to death. The official police explanation was that Bush, surprised in his sleep, had fought with them. At the coroner's inquest, attorneys representing Bush's family were prevented from asking questions, and the strangulation was ruled "justifiable"—the forty-fourth time in a row since 1976 that the police had been exonerated in the death of a suspect.

Despite a storm of criticism over the coroner's verdict, the Clark County DA would not indict the three cops. Six months later the Nevada Attorney General's office brought them to trial for manslaughter, but the all-white jury deadlocked 11 to 1 for acquittal and the case was dropped. The local U.S. attorney ignored the ACLU's petition for prosecution under federal civil rights statutes. As Kendrick points out, "The legacy of the Bush case is even more disastrous than the Rodney King verdict. It shows that the Las Vegas police are allowed, on the flimsiest of pretexts, to break into black people's homes and kill them when they resist."

For D and his friends, meanwhile, the Bush case "is just another lynching, Las Vegas–style." They point to the hypocrisy of a new state law that doubles sentences for gang-related felonies while local law enforcement "plays patty-cake with the Mafia up on the Strip." They complain about the humiliation of being strip-searched in front of girlfriends and neighbors. And they acidly contrast the Feds' apathy in the Bush case with their zeal to crush "Killa" Daniel and the other ABM Crips from North Las Vegas—"really small-time hoods," according to D— who were recently indicted on federal conspiracy charges of distributing twelve grams of cocaine.

But their bitterest feelings are reserved for the politicians who think black Las Vegas's grievances can be swept under the rug with a few more token gestures, like liberal former mayor Jan Laverty Jones's grandiloquent promise of forty-two new jobs in the casinos, or Sheriff Moran's offer of "better communication" with the Westside. For D—who felt that the only people "telling the truth about radical-level reality" in America were rappers like Ice Cube and Chuck D—"things are already near the ultimate edge. The time for lies is past. We built Las Vegas for them, and without equality, we will tear this motherfucker down."

Inside Jean

G etting into prison the first time was easy. I was a stringer for a now-defunct trade publication, and enough people knew about my interest. So when the story came along, my editor at *Nevada Contractor* thought of me right away. Prison seemed an unlikely place to hold a job fair, but, as he explained, the construction business in Las Vegas is notorious for its transient workforce. Men fresh out of prison have an incentive to show up for work regularly—it's one of the conditions for probation. "And they couldn't be any worse than the people we hire right now who've never been to prison," one employer told me later.

"Remember who buys the ads," were the editor's final words. "Try to build up the employers."

My only goal was getting inside the prison. In November 1989, I was a graduate student at the University of Nevada, Las Vegas. Reporting for the newspaper was my part-time job. My real interest was doing research on the rehabilitation of convicted criminals. Looking back, it is amazing that anyone took me seriously; a first-year graduate student with little experience in research, much less with convicted criminals. The director of prisons laughed at me when I first presented him with the idea. We met in his office a few weeks after the job fair. I needed his approval to begin the study.

In 1989, much attention was being given to a set of educational theories and methods based on "Socratic questioning." The Greek philosopher Socrates used a style of teaching that relied on asking questions rather than simply feeding information to students. The idea was to teach them how to think rather than just memorize facts. Some people surmised that we could even teach people to make better life choices by following these methods. Many of the critical thinking courses now taught at universities were an outgrowth of Socratic methods revived and developed in the 1970s and 1980s. At the time of my research, little had been done to explore these methods in a prison setting. Admittedly, the notion that a course in philosophy could turn robbers and rapists into law-abiding citizens may have sounded flaky on the surface, but there was enough research to suggest that similar programs showed promise. The immediate benefit for me in teaching such a course at the prison was to collect data for a master's thesis. Still, I thought the methods had long-term potential for rehabilitation.

As I elaborated on the study, I was impressed with the way the director's deep tan set off the gold at his wrist and pinkie finger, just as his bronzed skin was shown off by a flashing white smile. My experience with prisons was more limited then. To my unschooled eye, his jewelry, expensive-looking shoes, and trim good looks proclaimed: *Las Vegas.* I would not have assumed that he was head of the entire state prison system.

Despite his initial reaction, the director okayed the project saying, "I don't suppose you could do any harm." He saw only one solution to crime. "Criminals get old, and they get tired of doing what they do," he told me. "Like anyone else, they want to retire. It's age that rehabilitates a criminal."

Age and gender, as it turns out, are highly correlated with crime. More than poverty, lack of education, poor upbringing, or any other factor, being male between the ages 14 to 35 (allowing for variations at the extremes) puts one in the demographic group most likely to commit repeated crimes. Females of the same age have yet to achieve equal representation.

The director's undue conclusion was that regardless of rehabilitative intervention, once a person is past the "age of crime," participation in illegal activities begins to taper off. The logical conclusion is that criminals should be locked up until they are thirty-six; a simplistic solution at best, because we can never tell who will be rehabilitated and who will continue to commit crimes long past that age. Nonetheless, the director seemed assured, and despite his somewhat disparaging remarks, I gathered that he was happy enough to encourage a novice researcher. "If your program helps even one person," he added, "you will have accomplished a great deal."

That such a study took place in Las Vegas is significant. Nevada has one of the highest incarceration rates in the United States. By 1989, the retributive mood of the American criminal justice system nationwide, signaling society's loss of faith in criminal reform, was well entrenched, having supplanted the rehabilitative models of the previous decade. Retribution seems always to have been the favored method of dealing with criminals in Nevada. "A lot of people would just as soon string 'em up and end the problem there," was an opinion voiced with troubling frequency. Surprisingly, the prevailing attitudes of average Las Vegans were not necessarily reflected by those responsible for running the prison. Although a recurring theme among Nevadans at large ("Take 'em out into the desert and let 'em die!"), frontier justice was seldom proposed in my conversations with the prison administration and staff.

It is also significant that what had begun as a six-week preliminary study developed over the course of two years into a well-respected program funded by UNLV at a time when an inordinate proportion of the school's funds were devoted to maintaining its basketball supremacy. Officials of the Department of Parole and Probation thought enough of the program to recommend expanding it to other institutions, even suggesting the possibility of legislative funding. In 1991, widespread budget cuts at the state level severely curtailed such hopes. Jean Prison closed in January 1992, and its inmates were dispersed to other institutions around the state. Lacking alternate means to support the program, I concentrated instead on my studies and home life. By then I had moved to Los Angeles to be with my husband, following a commuter marriage that had begun a year and a half earlier while I was attending UNLV. Leaving the prison was not as easy as I had expected.

"If you want to make a difference here," said one student, a longtime habitual offender named Ben, "stop talking about 'us' and 'them.' We are all participants."

An axiom of serving time observes that prison changes you; it's in the way you move through a room, the way you look at people when speaking to them. Once you've served time, you forever carry the prison inside you. In a different way, it was true for me. The prison followed me to Los Angeles. In the eyes of the inmates, the classes I taught at Jean were promises made, hopes proffered, expectations raised. They were not about to let me forget. Not long after moving to Los Angeles, I began commuting back to Las Vegas to continue the program on a part-time basis, first at Indian Springs, then at Jean Prison when it reopened.

Ben was right on many levels. Despite the guards, the fences, and barbed wire, the line between "inside" and "outside" will always be fuzzy. Over the course of a lifetime, everyone commits occasional, if insignificant, crimes—the intentionally misparked car, the stop sign we "didn't see," the purloined memento of a summer resort. Beyond these mundane crimes are the sad unkindnesses of daily life: feelings trampled, cruel words, "little" lies. What damages us most as human beings is seldom officially classified as crime.

More philosophically, society is in need of prisons. They are an object lesson—a means of dividing "good" from "evil," of separating "normal" from "deviant." Such divisions require the compliance of an entire society. Locking up criminals, some say, is only the excuse for building prisons. Ben's words took on particular meaning when an intruder broke into our home and murdered my husband, Edward, in February 1992.

"How would it feel if it happened to *you*—if someone *you* loved was killed?" This question often stands in the place of arguments defending a harsh system of criminal justice, advocating punishment rather than rehabilitation (read: leniency). It is intended to stall all discussion, to stop it cold; it's played like a high card that wins the hand.

"*How would it feel? What would you do?*"

The following account is taken from my journals covering the period from November 1989 to September 1992. If I have learned anything from my experience, it is that prison reveals far more about society and oneself than it explains why people commit crimes. Life, of course, is never so simple.

JEAN RESORT APRIL 10, 1990

From a distance, Jean Prison looks like a desert retreat: squat condominiums set against the hills just behind the Gold Strike Casino. In camouflage-sand, they arrest only the perceptive eye surveying the foreshortened landscape east of Interstate 15. If it were not for the sign announcing "Southern Nevada Correctional Center," one might mistake them for the quarters of casino employees.

Jean Prison, often referred to simply as "Jean," takes its name from the virtually nonexistent township in which it lies. The prison houses approximately 560 men, more than the rated capacity of 519. Many of the men have been convicted of sex crimes. Because sex offenders in Nevada receive comparatively longer sentences, they are represented in higher numbers than men convicted of other crimes. Even so, the system at large has no treatment programs targeted specifically at sex offenders, save for the informal group sessions conducted by one of the psychologists at Jean.

In preparation for the research project, set to begin in May, I have been given limited access to the inmates' records, including their criminal and prison histories. Of the forty-two men who are signed up for my class, more than one-third are serving time for crime-related sexual deviance. Today I was to complete my review of their files ("jackets," they call them) and to meet with the warden prior to beginning a series of interviews and pre-tests next week to lay the groundwork for the study. Today marks my fourth trip to the prison.

The twenty-six mile drive south from Las Vegas to Jean, mostly through empty desert, gave me time to reflect upon my earlier visits. During the November job fair, I wasn't able to see much of the prison. The event took place in the visiting room adjacent to the Administration Building. Parking my car, I could see the prison yard through the fence and barbed wire. My only frame of reference was a visit made many years earlier to Auschwitz. Angry coils of razor wire surround the compound at both sites, in each case raising the hair on the back of my neck as I imagine life within its confines. At Auschwitz, gaily colored flowers planted *in memoriam* belie past horrors. Likewise, the prison yard at Jean, visible through her imposing metal "veil," is jarringly peaceful in contrast to my imaginings.

The scene inside is less dramatic: voices, laughter, men passing from prospective employer to prospective employer. An area sectioned off near the entrance displays inmate-crafted leather bags, paintings, curio boxes, and other items for sale. Behind the guard checking my ID hangs a placard: Rules for Visitors of Nevada Prison System. The dress code for female visitors warns, "You must wear underwear," specifying, "panties, a bra, a slip (if wearing a dress)." Low-cut blouses, short skirts, sandals, and stirrup or stretch pants are not permitted.

As I pass through the metal detector into the visiting room proper, a young man steps up to greet me. Identifying himself as Inmate Parker, he offers me coffee and introduces me to some of the participants. Young and articulate, he is unlike any stereotype of "a convict" I can conjure. Where are his tattoos? Why is his English so perfect?

The remainder of the job fair is taken up interviewing employers

("How will hiring an ex-con benefit your company?") and trying to find some time alone with the man who organized the event, Parole and Probation Supervisor Don Peters. I am looking for an opportunity to pitch him on my research. In the end, I give him my card and extract the promise of an interview the following afternoon.

The next day, just after lunch, I meet Peters at the prison administration building. We pass through the metal detectors of the guard station and into the prison yard.

"Aren't you afraid to go there with all the *criminals,*" friends and family members have been asking. Despite outward signs of support my husband, Edward, has been expressing concern for my safety. Overshadowing any sense that I ought to be afraid, walking among murderers and child molesters, are my attempts to look like a serious scholar as I discuss my work.

Jean is a medium-security prison—it's the last stop in the system for many inmates before they "hit the gate" (prison lingo for being released, as opposed to "hitting the fence," or escaping). The prison, sometimes jokingly referred to as "Jean Resort," because it is a relative garden retreat compared to the other prisons in the Nevada system, was originally intended as a minimum-security facility. Built in 1978, Jean was originally supposed to be located much closer to Las Vegas in order to accommodate a work furlough program where prisoners would work in town by day and report to prison lockup at night. The taxpaying, law-abiding citizens of Las Vegas vehemently opposed the plan, and Jean was finally built in its more isolated present location.

The walk to Peters's office is uneventful. No riot, no guards beating prisoners, no "free" staff taken hostage. A few well-tended petunias are enclosed by the twin paths leading from one of the housing units. In the center of the yard, sparse and sporadic trees flout Jean's "garden" sobriquet. To my eyes, there is more menace in the unseasonably hot April sun than in the men strolling in denim-clad twosomes around the prison yard. They resemble anything but my idea of convicted criminals.

"These are dangerous men," Peters tells me later in his office, as if reading my thoughts and giving me warning. He is showing interest in my project. "Every one of them will be out of prison one day, so we better make sure they're rehabilitated before we let them out and they end up living next door to us." He offers this as his "selfish" reason for creating the job fair and for supporting projects like mine.

Before I leave, Peters introduces me to his staff and tells me that the inmate coordinator will contact me to arrange scheduling. In the meantime, he suggests that I meet with the warden as a formality. Although the Department of Parole and Probation is under separate jurisdiction and conducts programs within the prison as it sees fit, the support and cooperation of the prison administration and staff can only benefit my project.

Nevada's penal system consists of three separate departments operating more or less independently. The Department of Prisons is responsible for incarceration of adult offenders and is overseen by the director, who reports to the Board of Prison Commissioners. The Department of Parole and Probation maintains an office in each prison to oversee the release of inmates, ensuring that men eligible for probation or parole have met the necessary requirements. To qualify for probation, for example, an inmate must find a job (hence the November job fair) as well as a place to live. Juvenile offenders are under the jurisdiction of Youth Correctional Services, a division of the Department of Human Resources.

At the end of the interview, Peters escorts me back across the yard, following a gravel path defining its inner perimeter. For the first time, I take a good look around. The roughly rectangular yard runs about 150 yards north to south and is surrounded by low, two-tiered housing units of fifty cells each. A glass-enclosed guard station separates the A and B wing of each unit. Peters's office is in Unit 6 at the southeastern corner of the yard. At the southern tip lies the gymnasium. A small area in front of the building is sectioned off as the weight pile. We see a few bare-chested men hefting weights, sweating in the sun.

Just north of Unit 6 are the laundry, barber shop, and law library—all three housed in a single small building. Just beyond is the culinary facility. Its glass front and cooking odors as we pass recall the most ordinary of school cafeterias. Next is the infirmary, then the "psych ward," Unit 7. Inaccessible from the yard, its narrow, high windows are covered in bars and wire. The absence of bars throughout most of the rest of the prison is conspicuous in contrast. The guard tower and administration building lie at the northern tip of the rectangle. Farther along the path are the education building, the glass and wood shop, and the chapel. Two additional towers, one to the south, the other to the north, lie outside the perimeter of the prison yard.

Jean is part of a six-prison system. Forty miles northwest of Las Vegas is Indian Springs, a medium-security facility, officially the Southern Desert Correctional Center.

Northern Nevada, with a smaller population, has more than its share of prisons. Nevada State Prison (NSP) in Carson City was the old "max," but a new one was built in Ely this year [1990]. NSP has been redesignated a medium-security facility. It stands in shouting distance of the only women's institution in the state, the Nevada Women's Correctional Center. The Northern Nevada Correctional Center, also medium-security, is located in Stewart, Nevada, near Carson City. The system also supports eight work camps for nonviolent offenders nearing release or serving short-term sentences.

Walking beside Peters, it is easy to imagine the prison yard as the whole world—as though nothing else existed. The effect of the fence and barbed wire is to discourage the eye from looking beyond. I make a conscious effort to look through the fence at the twin casinos outside: the Gold Strike, a few hundred yards below, and Nevada Landing, just across the interstate.

"What an odd place to put a prison," I think. And then, "What an odd place to put a casino!" I imagine them as a trio of cautionary symbols: the casinos, garishly painted ladies of the night promising pleasure and profit, and Jean, the sober sister standing in the shadows to scold those who take those promises seriously.

PUBLIC ENEMY APRIL 12, 1990

Sami Martinez is the inmate coordinator at Jean Prison. His weathered eyes and hard-set, chiseled features make it difficult to guess his age. Businesslike, although shy, he seems to hide behind his thick Mexican accent. I was to meet with the warden on my visit two days ago. Because of a conflict, we reschedule for Thursday next week. In place of the meeting, I took the opportunity to spend time with Sami, who will be working closely with me over the course of the research project. Sami's regular day job is scheduling guest speakers for the Street Readiness Program, designed to prepare inmates for life outside the prison. According to Sami, the program is a novelty, the brainchild of a Nevada State Prison System graduate, a lawyer who once served time. Nationwide, very few programs address the practical problems an ex-convict will encounter in his day-to-day life: opening a bank account, paying bills, developing successful relationships, dealing with employers. The Street Readiness program is intended to reorient prisoners to life on the outside—a goal less lofty than rehabilitation.

"The program might actually do some good," Sami tells me, "if it was done the way it was designed. We bring the guys into class for fifty hours and then give them a certificate saying they've completed the course. What can you learn in fifty hours? But it's something to show the parole board and everyone pretends that it actually does some good."

Tuesday's meeting with Sami quickly developed into an informal gathering of the entire five-man staff of the Parole and Probation Office at Jean Prison. Over the next few hours, they give me a quick lesson about prison life. The first thing I learn is that "inmate" in Sami's job title refers to what he is, not who he serves.

"It's a common mistake," he tells me. "Because we work in an office, no one guesses that we live here on a permanent basis." Officially, I'm supposed to call him Inmate Martinez. That gives me the uncomfortable feeling, though, that I'm participating in his shame, like being asked to sew Hester Prynne's garments or to carry stones for the crowd gathering around the biblical adulteress. I notice that Don Peters calls him by his first name, so I decide to follow suit.

J. B. is the resident law clerk. He files briefs and researches legal matters for other inmates. In an aside, Sami tells me that J. B. is a bit of a rabble rouser.

"Just two months ago he refused to submit to a piss test."

"For drugs," J. B. adds.

"They threw him in the hole for a week," Sami continues. "But he challenged them and won."

J. B.'s accent is as thick as Sami's, although purely American. He speaks in a sing-song of grammatical errors, evoking wind-blown hills and dying scrub grass. He mentions a small town near Carson City as his birthplace. J. B. tells me he wants to be a lawyer; he's currently completing courses for his Academic Associates degree through the Community College. In response, the rest of the office staff shout with derisive laughter: "They ain't going to let you be a lawyer. First off, you're never getting out."

I haven't ventured to ask the men in the group what their crimes were (how do I introduce the subject politely into the conversation? "Whadda'ya in for?" sounds far too blunt), but I already know that all of them are serving life sentences. "They prefer to hire lifers for the office jobs," Rick explains. "Once they train you, they like to know you're going to be around awhile." Rick grew up in Las Vegas. His family is one of the city's oldest and most respected. He appears to be in his forties and well-educated and wants to cultivate the image that Jean is an in-teresting—although exceedingly annoying—interlude in his life.

Angus—Canadian-born, of Scottish descent—is J. B.'s cellmate, so is afforded the special privilege of hanging out in the Parole and Probation Office although he doesn't actually work there. Angus is nearly half as wide as the narrow office. He spends a good deal of time at the weight pile, he tells me. He is also the most "criminal" looking of the group, if one puts faith in TV images of a criminal type: the jutting brow, deep, dark circles under his eyes, and a slight forward hunch to his massive shoulders suggest the ability to intimidate by presence alone. But he is as articulate as Rick, if given to more frequent use of expletives.

Little Ricky, also known as Rick Two, or The Kid, is barely eighteen but appears to be many years younger. He spends little time with the group and leaves soon after being introduced. Ricky works under the direct supervision of Sami, who tells me later, "The Kid is a bit *loco* at times." I ask him what he means.

"Every conversation he has eventually ends up being about suicide."

"Does anyone take him seriously?" I ask.

"No one talks seriously about suicide," Sami tells me. "You're serious? You do it."

"What is he doing here?" I ask. I figure Sami's given me the lead.

"When he was about thirteen he stole a neighbor's shotgun and opened fire on a bunch of people."

"Why?"

"He says his girlfriend was cheating on him."

"Is that true?"

"It's true that he shot all those people. Who knows why? I think he's just trying to impress the cons."

Earlier the guys explain the difference between inmates and convicts. Inmates cooperate with the prison cops. They do what they're told and try to stay out of trouble. Convicts never cooperate with cops. Think James Cagney.

"Inmate" is a derogatory term. Convicts are looked up to. Sami's reputation as a convict was earned a long time ago. He no longer has to live up to the demands of the role. Convicts don't hold responsible prison jobs, for example. The other men respect Sami all the same.

Rick (the elder) is a self-confessed inmate. "It's much safer that way," he explains. "No sense in putting on airs you can't live up to."

Part of being a convict, the men tell me, is defending the role, sometimes with your life. Little Ricky aspires to be a convict but, according to Sami, doesn't quite know how. "The problem with these kids coming into prison today is they don't know how to act. You don't just come up and start talking to a guy who is sending out signals that he doesn't want to be talked to. They don't understand any of the signals. These kids don't pay attention to the Code. They don't show any respect."

THE TEST APRIL 19, 1990

I arrive for my meeting with the warden on time, but the appointment, set at 2:00 P.M., begins at 2:35. The warden is on the phone when his secretary leads me into his office and invites me to take a seat. I gather he is talking to his daughter. He makes no sign of ending the conversation until the door opens again and the assistant warden walks in, trailed by an officer. The latter is the only one to acknowledge my presence. As they talk, I politely stare at a cactus outside the warden's window. Over time, the yard crew have adorned the spiny leaf points of a five-foot yucca with multicolored gum wads. Nearly every leaf tip sports a hardened ball of gum, giving the cactus a cartoonish appeal.

The conversation begins to sound interesting.

"We've been over at Unit 5," the assistant warden says.

Warden: "Is everything moved out of the cell?"

Assistant Warden: "Most of it. Some of it still has to be checked."

Warden: "When do we transfer?"

Officer: "Tomorrow, sir. I need the signatures from Unit 7."

Unit 7 is the psych ward, where they teach you the Thorazine Shuffle, the Zombie Dance, the Catatonia Two-Step. J. B. has his own colorful description of inmates on psychotropic drugs. "You can always pick them out on the yard by the way they walk. They're so full of dope, they don't probably remember they're in prison."

I notice the warden is watching me. "Is he locked down in psych?" he asks.

The officer responds, "He's put away for now."

The warden finally addresses me directly. "One of our boys in Unit 5. He took a clothes hanger and straightened it out, then pushed it through his cellie's head from ear to ear. Right through the middle. Now why do you suppose he did that?"

"Who gave him the hanger?" is all I can think to ask.

The warden addresses his assistant, "This can wait till I'm finished here."

"It happened before you came. About two weeks before," Sami tells me later. "They're still tying things up. This guy is 'way out there.' He had a kiester stash, you know? He hid some dope up his ass. Later he sold it on the yard. During re-call he went back to his house—his cell—for a nap. When he woke up he forgot that he'd sold it. Thought he still had it hidden. When he couldn't find it, he accused his cellie of stealing it while he was napping. Told him he better return it, or else."

VERSIONS I AND II APRIL 27, 1990

Over the past two days I've been conducting interviews with inmates. I'm interested in hearing how they explain why they committed the crime that brought them to prison. I haven't seen their jackets, so Sami fills in the details.

Joseph is from a small, central Nevada township.

"Tell me about why you're here at Jean." I have already asked five previous interviewees this. Most of the men address me as "Ma'am," but Joseph is the first to whom it comes naturally. He hesitates before answering. I wait, hoping that I haven't betrayed scientific neutrality in edging my chair away from his pervasive, greasy body odor. His very large frame nearly obscures his chair.

"I was transferred here from Ely," he tells me at last. "They say I molested my daughters. Uh, my stepdaughters."

"Tell me what your thoughts were just prior to committing the crime."

Joseph hesitates again. Finally, "I'm not sure I can."

"Why is that?"

"Well, see. At the time I didn't know I was committing a crime."

"What do you mean?"

Joseph thinks for a moment. "Well, I admit I did like when the girls would sit in my lap. I always gave them a squeeze or a kiss. I never had no kids of my own and I sure loved those little girls. When I threw their mama out for getting drunk all the time, she took those girls with her. I missed them a lot, but they weren't my kids. I would've taken Evelyn back if she could've stayed from being drunk. About six months later they came to me and told me what I done was wrong. Holding them girls, sitting 'em on my lap, giving them hugs. That was abuse that I done. I didn't know I was doing anything wrong so I'm not sure how to answer your question. But it's true. I did do those things."

Later in the day, I interview Doug. Doug is from a well-to-do family of doctors. "This is really hard on my family," he tells me. "My family is pretty well known here. I come from a good family. I didn't need to pull this crime."

"Tell me about why you're here at Jean."

"Drugs," Doug says simply, then explains. "I got greedy. I was working for this company that sells stereo equipment, except that was just a front for what they were really doing."

Doug is about twenty-five. He has sandy-brown hair that curls around his ears. A full beard and mustache cover most of his face. His eyes—a clear, bright blue—are his most striking feature.

"My friend, who was working at this place too, had a plane," Doug continues. "One day the boss asks us if we would like to do some extra work and earn really big money. So, we started smuggling drugs. Trips down to Mexico. Then we would bring them up here and drive them someplace, sometimes to Vegas, sometimes north to some little desert town. It was always the same guys we met. They'd pick up what we had and a couple days later we'd get paid. Then, one night it's these different guys. We were suspicious, but what the heck? My partner starts walking towards them with the delivery. The guy in the other car starts driving towards us. Runs my friend down. I ran to my friend and grabbed his gun. I just started shooting when the car came back for me. I never killed a guy before. I still have nightmares."

Sami tells a different story. "Yeah, he comes from a rich family, but his jacket says he's here for raping his girlfriend. Beat her up pretty bad too."

SOME KIND OF JUSTICE MAY 6, 1990

The routine of the prison has come to occupy my days. At 8:00 each morning I arrive at Jean through the side entrance to the Admin Building avoiding the obligatory exchange of pleasantries with the warden's secretary. The walkway to the side entrance also gives me a view of the yard and the men hanging out near the gate, as if anticipating their eventual release.

At the guard station, my satchels are examined for contraband—drugs, money, or weapons that might be hidden among the books and materials. Under the scrutiny of the guards, I feel the same hypersensitivity as when I notice a police car behind me on the road—a misplaced sense of guilt, as though the very presence of armed authority implied wrongdoing.

The routine search takes longer some mornings than others, depending on the thoroughness of the prison cops. Sami and Rocky always wait for me at the end of the walkway outside the guard station, on the other side of the gate. Whatever time is left before class begins at 8:30 is spent in the Parole and Probation Office talking with the staff. The time spent with the men in the morning, or between sessions, is invaluably informative. They tell me about prison life, and I talk about books and philosophy. Sometimes I talk about my life outside the prison, although I have recently discovered that the administration greatly frowns upon my doing so, if not expressly forbidding it.

Last week, when Sergeant Gunderson searched my belongings at the guard station, she noticed the wedding photo mounted under plastic on the inside lid of my briefcase. It shows Edward and me flanking the children; he holds my youngest in his arms, while the elder beams proudly at his new father. The photo was taken on Bridger Street in downtown Las Vegas, not far from the Justice of the Peace. Edward's sense of dignity would not allow us to consider any local wedding chapel as an option. He is wearing a dark sweater in the photo and looks a bit like Robert Young. I'm wearing a pink and navy suit; my eyes squint tight from the sun. The photo is recent enough to qualify me as a new bride.

My other wedding photo was taken next to the Lady Luck Casino and Hotel on Third Street, just before we treated the boys to a trolley ride, then lunch at the Golden Nugget. Edward keeps that photo on his desk back in Los Angeles.

"Have the inmates seen this?" Sergeant Gunderson asks me the day she discovers the photo. She points and repeats the question to my puzzled silence.

"For security reasons," she explains, "You shouldn't be bringing any personal items, like photos, into the prison."

"Security?" I repeat, inflecting the word into a question. "Do you think one of the men might steal it?"

"They can use it against you. You better take it out of there," she adds as she clears me through the gate.

I'm inclined to ignore the sergeant's warning. Most of the students have already seen the photo because of my habit of sometimes leaving the briefcase open during lectures. Like students anywhere, they are curious to know about my life apart from teaching. They also feel free to comment on my decision to stay in Las Vegas for my degree, rather than return to Los Angeles with Edward; incredulous, too, that he would allow it. Decision making is the primary subject of the classes at

Jean. The students want to know how I apply the principles in my own life. I ask Sami and Rick what the sergeant meant about violating security.

"You show photos to friends and co-workers," Rick explains, "not to convicts. You aren't supposed to be friendly with us."

Sami's explanation is more cynical. "Gunderson just wants to give you a hard time. You come here smiling and in a good mood in the morning and all of a sudden she's Robocop."

"Maybe she's jealous," Rick suggests. "It's unlikely *she'll* ever get married."

I press the men to return to the subject.

"The friendlier you are with us, the easier it would be to con you into bringing us things—to turn you into a mule. You know, get you to smuggle for us."

"Is that what you would do?" I ask.

"You shouldn't ever trust us," Sami says. But it is hard to reconcile the Sami and Rick who greet me each morning with the violence of their past crimes (I had finally found the opportunity to ask). Should I be forgiving? Will it matter once they've served their time?

Many years ago I knew a man who had been to prison for killing his infant child. He had shaken the girl in a fit of irritation when she wouldn't stop crying. I found this out after knowing him for several years.

"Is it true?" I asked. I knew him as a patient, kind, and generous man.

"*That* was a different person," he answered. I accepted his response. His good character seemed adequate proof.

In the present I wonder to Sami and Rick, "How are you ever supposed to get back to normal if I treat you like criminals instead of like men?"

"We're not normal," Rick counters.

"We're criminals," Sami adds.

In the hours I spend away from Jean, I wrestle with these thoughts. Las Vegas, I easily discover, is an unfortunate place to encounter one's conscience. Downtown, homeless men are rousted and beaten to keep streets clean and safe, and alleged pimps are shot in their beds as they sleep. A neighbor tells me about a scheme to steal her boyfriend's truck.

"He deserves it you know. That truck is his whole life."

Reading between the lines I realize that someone new has been occupying his passenger seat.

"It'd be more like a joke," the neighbor explains, "I'll drive it down to Lake Mead and leave it there. Then I'll mail the keys to his new girlfriend."

Another kind of justice, I wonder?

WHO AM I TO JUDGE? MAY 21, 1990

We spend a good deal of time exploring "eternal" concepts like "justice," "freedom," or how to define "crime." I am curious what these things mean to men serving time.

"Should we judge others?" I ask one day in class. One man raises his hand.

"What do *you* mean by the word 'judge'?" he asks. "The dictionary says, 'to decide or punish.' What do you mean by that word?"

I decide not to correct him. But it leads me to question my own understanding. What *do* I mean when I say "to judge"? It has a very specific meaning at Jean Prison. On the "outside," as my students refer to everything beyond the second fence, things are judged to be good or bad, right or wrong, and sometimes points in between. On the inside, "to judge" is always negative. "Judging" is synonymous with punishment. What does it mean to judge? A five-year minimum sentence.

Today marks the midpoint of the project. Some of the men have already dropped out. "They don't like having their brains picked," Rick tells me during our discussion after yesterday's class. Sami, Rick, and J. B. give me regular feedback on the students' reactions to the class.

"Too many questions," is J. B.'s response. "All that philosophy stuff is just a bunch of questions. Never any answers."

Those who stay seem to like the challenge. Compared to university undergraduates, the men at Jean are model students. They are hungry for something. They devour each concept with such intensity—as if the things we discuss in class really mattered in their lives. At the same time, there is an underlying disquiet that I'm not sure how to deal with.

"Just don't call anyone a cop," J. B. reminds me half-jokingly. The guys have told me that the surest way to "get cut" is to insult someone's mother or to call him a cop. The latter is tantamount to accusing him of being a snitch, a rat, a cheese-eater. I am beginning to appreciate the underlying humor of prison jargon.

When the outbreak comes, it is from an unexpected source. The class is on break, and Vic, an early dropout, has been talking to me. He wears an expression of exaggerated sincerity. Sami dislikes him intensely and over the past several days has been trying to discourage me from letting Vic hang around during breaks.

"He's showing off to his friends, talking to the pretty schoolteacher."

"He's not bothering me," I counter. "If he was still in the class it wouldn't be a problem."

"But only students are allowed in the classroom. He's not supposed to come in here," Sami says, falling back on the rules.

I dismiss his objections.

When Vic shows up today, Sami storms out of the room. A few moments later, he's back.

"You're not supposed to be here," Sami tells Vic.

"It's okay, Sami. I invited Vic here."

"Only students are allowed in the classroom," Sami insists.

"Look man, I'm just talking to her."

"You're not supposed to be here," Sami repeats.

"I didn't know you were wearing a badge, man."

"Fuck you! Fuck You! FUCK YOU!" Sami shouts at Vic, who backs out of the room.

I expect the guards to descend. The other inmates make way for the two men, but the fight I'm expecting doesn't materialize. At the door to the classroom, Sami turns back as Vic disappears.

"He called me a cop," Sami mutters.

"Well, you were going on a bit about the rules," I point out.

"Yeah, but he's not supposed to be here," Sami insists, much more subdued. This is obviously a territory issue and I stake my ground.

"Sami, we're in *my* classroom."

"Yeah, but he called me a cop."

PRISON BLUES JUNE 5, 1990

Convict stripes first appeared in the nineteenth century in New York at Auburn Prison, built in 1816, and were later adopted at Sing Sing, built in 1825. The characteristic uniform remained in general use throughout the United States until the 1950s. Uniforms, of course, make it possible to differentiate inmates from outsiders at a glance.

Appropriately, the inmates at Jean wear denim. Officially, the uniform consists of blue jeans and a blue work shirt. Rules are relaxed, however. Jeans are mandatory, but T-shirts, pullovers, cotton Henleys, and bare chests are equally displayed, depending only on weather, personal taste, and financial capacity. The Department of Prisons issues the standard uniform when the inmate first enters prison and thereafter, as needed, when the old one wears out (the worn uniform must be presented as evidence before a new one is issued). Additional clothing may be purchased at the inmate's expense or donated by family. Visitors and staff are prohibited from wearing denim and discouraged from wearing any blue clothing.

The "uniform" at Jean may make identification of inmates easier for the guards, but it carries no stigma for anyone who has spent time on a university campus. In attire, inmates differ little from students, and blue jeans appear far less intimidating than the quasi-military khaki of the prison guards. Convicts are distinguished more by an abundance of tattoos—for some, covering every available inch of skin.

Sami compares life at Jean to the "joints" in Texas. There, the inmates wear white, resembling, I imagine, so many milkmen behind bars. He says the prisons there are completely self-supporting. Inmates grow the cotton for the uniforms, harvest it, and mill it. Women prisoners sew the uniforms. Everything the prison needs, from soap, to brooms, to dairy products, is produced by inmates, so all inmates must work if they are physically able. Sami picked cotton in Texas alongside other prisoners, watched by rifle-toting guards or "bosses" on horseback. The bosses spur the men on to increased productivity with liberal use of racial slurs, pitting "niggers" against "greasers." The men work faster in order to gain privileges.

"You want to be in 'one hoe.' That's what we called the first squad, the first to bring in ten acres. You get better treatment, better privileges. You get to be the first to eat."

Sami, a model employee in the Parole and Probation Office, prefers prisons in the West where they don't make you work. "The cops don't harass you. If you want to stay in your house all day, that's up to you. Those that *do* work get good-behavior time—a reduction in their sentence."

When Sami left Texas in 1982, many of the bosses he knew were leaving. "An order came down from some federal judge that they couldn't use racial slurs anymore talking to us. A lot of the guards just plain quit rather than obey the rule." Upon release, Sami moved to Nevada, and within a year, he was doing time here—back in prison. But Sami is not the only well-traveled one among my students.

"It's all gangs in California," says J. B. "It's a whole different way of doing time."

Angus agrees. "I won't ever do time in California again. The gangs have infiltrated and control everything. It's like the guards aren't the ones in charge."

"It's worse for the blacks and Mexicans," J. B. says. "Right up front they put you in a segregated housing unit 'cause they figure you're in a gang. And if the gang sends you on a hit, you go. Otherwise you go into PC—protective custody. That ain't no cakewalk either."

Protective custody is an option for inmates who feel in danger of harm from other prisoners. Requesting PC, though, calls attention to yourself, often resulting in heightened scrutiny from the guards. In practice, it is much like serving time in "the hole," or solitary confinement. And even that doesn't last forever. Most of the men agree: if you have to do time, Jean isn't a bad place to do it.

I have no point of comparison. Jean is the only prison I know, and it ain't no cakewalk as far as I'm concerned. Jean is a dangerous place, all the more because I'm never sure where the danger lies. Beneath the prison's outward serenity hums a pervasive anxiety. I am drawn to my students as a teacher to her pupils and as a person to other human beings, but at the same time I recoil from my knowledge of their crimes. Still, I find room for compassion. Signs above the drinking fountains at Jean warn about lead; microbes multiply inside the air ducts. I hear rumors of abuse by the guards and amorous trysts between inmates and free staff. Many of these things seem to happen behind the scenes, but I am convinced they do occur. The occasional military helicopters making practice runs over the desert only add to my image of Jean as a war zone, a no-man's-land, a point of no return. Exiting through the gate at the end of the day, I hear the voice from the tower call: ATTENTION ON THE YARD! RE-CALL! RE-CALL!

Then the sirens begin. Like mice caught in a torrent of rain, men rush to their cells. Others dare the guards with practiced nonchalance, hurrying only after the second warning.

I have come to regard Jean as a city of the condemned, set within the wider illusion of the impassive desert and a distant neon mirage.

LITTLE PIGEONS FEBRUARY 3, 1992

Los Angeles is a world apart from Las Vegas. Las Vegas is Jean Prison, the searing desert, and the neighborhood casinos, where a ten dollar bill buys me a roll of quarters, two free drinks, and the chance to win enough coins to cover my laundry for the week.

Los Angeles is Edward, the damp air that no one notices but me, the bumper-to-bumper slow dance on Highway 101, and the feeling that I've left a part of myself behind.

Edward says my work at the prison has left me morose. I say it's made me wiser and more aware, but I agree that I find conversations with his parents much less interesting. ("Really, Bernice, I can't think *where* you should plant the perennials.")

Jean closed in January, the same day the governor announced state-wide budget cuts, including the prison. When I arrived for classes that day, the yard was on lock-down in anticipation of protest riots by the inmates, and a small cluster of reporters and cameramen stood outside the fence. Everyone was denied entrance. I drove home wondering about the fate of my project.

Only the previous week, Sami and I had passed time between classes reading horoscopes from the newspaper. "Get out while you can," mine read.

"Yeah, well, mine says, 'Someone is thinking of you.' Wanna trade?"

The last time we spoke, Sami told me, "We're all little pigeons. You just have a bigger cage to roam in."

"Doesn't that make a difference?" I asked.

"You tell me."

I saw Sami and Rick once more, after the prison closed and before I left for Los Angeles. I went to collect my papers and books, which now sit, unused, in the corner of my office. Edward says they stink of cigarette smoke. But I know it's not smoke. It's prison smell. *Everything* seems to look and smell like prison to me.

"It's all you talk about," Edward complains. "The prison, your students. Your prize *pupils!*" His explosive sarcasm seems to surprise even him. In better moments, he remains supportive. "I just worry about your safety."

Jean closed just three months ago, but already some of the inmates have returned. The prison should reopen at full capacity later this year. Some people say that Jean was included in the budget cuts to deflect attention from health violations discovered as a result of inmate lawsuits. According to the story, repairs were quietly made during the time the prison was closed. Already the Parole and Probation Office has contacted me about restarting the program. I'm not sure how to tell Edward.

EDWARD JULY 11, 1992

Part of me remained sane the night that Edward was killed, although the sane, rational part stood off at a distance, observing my reaction, taking note of what people said and did, keeping myself upright and responding to questions, while the other part of me wanted to scream, tear my clothes and hair, or run away and hide in the same dark place where Edward had secreted himself to play his cruel and silly joke. Later, I thought about the way people in movies scream when they happen upon a scene of death. The scream of anguish, of fear, of realization that the person lying prone on the ground is—in fact—dead, indicates a level of understanding I was incapable of.

Edward was a big man, six foot five, 210 pounds; strong enough to bend the bars on our bedroom window the day we locked ourselves out. But everything stopped making sense the moment I found him lying cold and still on our bedroom floor. I must have slipped through some tear in reality. Sounds echoed strangely in my head and I moved laboriously through thick fog shrouding my eyes and my brain.

"What are you doing, Edward?" I heard myself ask—the thick, icy red liquid under his body offering no obvious clue, although the suspicion that something was horribly wrong struggled its way into my consciousness. I ran for the phone.

"Something's wrong with my husband," I told the 911 operator. "There's blood everywhere, you have to come right now."

"Is he breathing?" the woman at the other end asked.

"Breathing?" What a silly question, I thought, answering. "I don't know."

"Check to see if he's breathing. If he's not, hold his head back . . ." She gave me brief instructions for artificial resuscitation. I hurried to the bedroom and, kneeling by Edward, gently tilted back his head, exposing a slow trickle of yellow matter collecting on the wooden floor.

"No, no. She needs to come now," I heard myself saying. I gently lowered his head and ran back to the phone.

"You have to come now," I insisted.

"Stay there. We're sending someone."

It never occurred to me that someone was responsible for Edward's death until the detectives pieced it together for me later. A burglar, surprised in the act, shot him five times—in both legs, his stomach, his chest, and his head. Edward is dead, but the scene in my bedroom still fails to make sense.

The night Edward was killed, I spent more than an eternity in a police holding tank while the detectives verified that I was not responsible for his murder.

"You realize," they explained later, "most of the time, the person who finds the body is the one who committed the crime. We needed to be sure." Practical, of course, but it only compounded my shock. Mercifully, the children never wakened until the police came. They were whisked away to be questioned themselves. Sometime later the detectives drove us home. They left me with a cigarette and a piece of advice.

"Don't hold on to this incident. Remember that your children need you."

Returning to Jean was my way of finding answers. Ben's words, of course, came back to me. If I had wondered what it was like to be one of "them," my question—in part—is answered. The fact that someone else was responsible for Edward's murder does not mitigate the fear and shock I felt while the detectives arrived at the same conclusion.

The answers are not as simple as understanding why someone killed my husband. In some ineffable way, however, I have a clearer notion of what prison is about. While friends and family are sympathetic, I believe my students at Jean understand far better than anyone else how I feel, what I have lost. I see my pain reflected in their sympathetic gestures and eyes. There is no dividing line.

LUX ETERNA SEPTEMBER 5, 1992

Leaving Jean Prison at night is a very different experience from the day. The yard looks otherworldly, like the lights of a spaceship illuminating an isolated tract of land. There are no patches of darkness along the paths or under the sparsely leafed trees. Watching over us all are the men in the towers, whom I have never seen, even in the daytime. The guys on the yard tell me that they sit up there behind darkened glass, rifles trained on us as we make our way from Unit 6 to the main gate. It is a strange sensation, knowing you are always being watched. I'm not sure I trust these invisible men.

At other times the yard takes on the surreal tension of a gulag; lights scanning the perimeter in search of possible escapees.

Once through the second gate, the world resumes its normal shape, although "normal" is a relative term in Las Vegas. I stand in the parking lot with the tower still in view. The stucco Admin Building is silent and dark. The glare of the Gold Strike Casino shouts out to the sky.

The Gold Strike is invisible from inside Jean Prison at night. The inquisition of lights trained on the yard causes everything "outside" to recede into black. Standing outside, looking in, I realize that I am part of the blackness that surrounds the barbed wire gate.

As I drive away from the row of buildings hugging the hills, Jean's dome of lights and her neon companion triumph easily against the nighttime sky. I think about Edward and wonder, at the same moment, about the men inside. "Do *they* ever see stars?" I am ten miles closer to Baker when, at last, they fully conquer the sky.

AMIE WILLIAMS

Looking into a Dry Lake: Uncovering the Women's View of Las Vegas
A Film Journal

AUGUST 1994

I'm standing at the edge of what I think must be a dry lake. The air is perfectly still and brutally hot. The lake is waterless, but full to the brim with light. I'm ninety miles from Las Vegas, and I don't want to go any further. I think, this is it. This must be the place.

I've been making excursions to Las Vegas to interview women for a documentary film. I ask each of them—where's the woman's space in Las Vegas? There had to be something else, something other than the absurdly oversized MGM lion, the world's longest laser, and the Stratosphere tower (its unfinished erection stands at 850 feet and growing). Most of the women look at me, bewildered. They wonder what I'm after. I'd been wondering this myself on these long, hot drives from Los Angeles through the endless Mojave.

"Las Vegas means the Meadows, doesn't it?" one woman offers. She's a former nude dancer at the Palomino turned real estate broker. She sold the entire city block on which the "gentlemen's" club stood to its gentleman owner, earning a $14,000 commission, the exact same amount of money she earned in one year of taking her clothes off. The woman's space. It's what you make it. So much opportunity here. I stand on the edge of the lake that once was and wonder what The Meadows looked like before the Mormon men came.

291

Glitter Gulch sign.

SEPTEMBER

She's in her seventies, they suppose, although no one really knows. She's been cocktailing for over forty years at the Golden Nugget. Her father helped build the downtown hotel, but no, she won't be interviewed, because "I'm just too busy, honey—what are you looking for, anyway?" I shrug and look down at my own legs, and wonder what they would look like after forty years of eight-hour shifts in heels. The cracks in the dry lake seem to break wide open and laugh at me. What are you looking for? I realize I've been standing on the edge, peering in. It's time to take the plunge. I stalk back to my truck and let blast Sheryl Crow's "Leaving Las Vegas." Maybe it's time to move to Las Vegas. Become a Vegas woman myself.

OCTOBER

I'm thirty-three today, and the weather is finally bearable to sleep in, so that's all I do. Double digits should be significant in a town where numbers take you to the next level, the bingo palace, the bright promise. I'm still finding ways to survive in Las Vegas, with this terror of being crushed by pyramids instead of history or hand-me-down culture in give-away plastic cups that catch your change, your change of mood, your desire to flee.

THANKSGIVING

"It's that wild, wild West thing. Think about it, who built the West?" a change girl at the Riviera tells me. She turned tricks until she started taking women's studies courses at UNLV. She's third-generation Neva-dan. Her grandfather worked the mines. When the men were mining for silver, the women were mining the men for gold. So much opportunity. Like so many bulbs that burn out on the Strip, there's something missing. The broken signs spell it out: "Loosest Slots in Town," "Most Progressive Poker." Bodies on billboards. Boobs on the backs of taxicabs. "It's what influences your image of womanhood in this town, from a very early age," she tells me. "It's all a form of female labor, however you look at it. Whether you're making beds for 'em or in the bed with 'em. This town has been built on the backs of women."

EARLY DECEMBER

It's getting colder now, a desert dry cold. The nights are clear and black at my little apartment on a ranch in Calico Basin, seventeen miles from town. The green laser that shoots out and up from atop the Hilton parks its beam against the great red granite of Red Rock Canyon here. Canyon residents are protesting. The casinos now own the sky. Now that I live here, I'm starting to embrace the contradictions. The slapstick housing developments surrounded by faux stucco and transplanted palm trees. The unsung beauty of the desert at dusk. The excess of the Strip and the minimalism of the worker communities. I drive by dust-poor downtown residence motels with names like "Par-A-Dice Motel," "Desert Moon," and, my personal favorite, "The Blue Angel." I met the Blue Angel herself one day, maneuvering a shopping cart across the expanse where the pool once was. "Don't you take my picture, bitch." Above her a plastercast Marlene Dietrich in a blue gown waved a wand over the whole scene, revealing that one of her wings was chipped. My blue angel glowered and spat. I pretended to take a picture of the pool. Another dry lake. They're all over Las Vegas.

DECEMBER

To be a woman in Las Vegas is to be swinging madly on the madonna versus whore pendulum. On the one hand you have the showgirl, go-girl ethos. Glitz, glamour, a female mayor even, with big hair and nails. But to get that you have to look that, or have married into it. If you don't, your other options are a confusing contest between sexuality and anonymity. Unless, of course, you choose to ignore the whole scene and go about your business, which at some point—follow the yellow brick road to the yellow-brick walled community to the yellow-brick ceiling— " 'cause there ain't no glass ceiling here, it's cement, sugar"—will lead to the Strip.

It's the "mother of all strips," according to Robert Venturi, who's been learning a lot from Las Vegas ever since.[1] You can run but you can't hide, mother will haunt you. She literally and figuratively cuts the town in two. Not to mention what she does to women's bodies. All those maids bending, those waitresses serving, those clusters of women standing on street corners. Rosalyn, who runs the Friendship Corner, as a shelter for the homeless, wonders out loud: "If all the women stopped doing the work in this town, what would happen?" Rosalyn used to make beds at the Lady Luck Hotel. She broke her back (stepped on a crack in the dry lake) and was out of work. Out of luck. In the streets, where no one wants the tourists to see you, so you hide. So many opportunities, so you survive. Motherhood in Vegas is the Madonna thing. I film one mother at her place of work, a women's bathroom. She's the full-time attendant at the Barbary Coast, whose main job during graveyard is to keep the other women who work that shift from coming in and catching a wink. Wink, wink. We've got you. All you single mothers who see this town as a place to be a "full-time mother." Work swing shift and be home in time to get your kids off to school. Then off to work with you until dawn.

Winged angel.

One beat Mom tells me after ten hours of bussing tables: "There are two types of women here. The hard-working, usually two or three kids, who are happy to have a chance, and those who have had some bad knocks, lost their dreams." I try out titles for my film: *Lost in Las Vegas, Beyond the Neon, Stripped and Teased.*

JANUARY 1995

It's a New Year, and I've been hanging with the Corner Block Girls, a local gang of girls who have dropped out of high school. They're the young ladies of The Meadows, and they stride tall through the dead grass. The lionesses of another Oz. When they waited for the school bus, they were leered at from limos or offered drugs to be in "adult entertainment" videos. They laugh at the thought; they have loftier goals. They won't end up like their mothers, working three jobs and cashing their paychecks at Palace Station to play slots.

"This town is about greed, it's so stupid. All that money, and look where it goes." The Corner Block Girls check out guys on the corners in North Las Vegas. They have guns and know what they want. All that money, and their parents don't care what they do—they're always working. In a neighborhood called Naked City (popular myth has it showgirls once lived here and sunbathed nude), taggers tell the real story of "real" estate in Las Vegas. In the shadow of the Stratosphere tower, the Rapunzels attend an alternative high school here. They dropped out of their own accord, because "high school was stupid." The school is called Horizons. In Naked City, it's no telling how far that can be.

Maybe as far as across town in one of the "master-planned communities," where I interview the mistress of the mansion. The decor is all white leather and simulated marble countertops. She can't complain, the neighborhood is safe, the schools are well stocked, the streets are lined with precision palm trees and little man-made lagoons (no dry lakes here). With names like Paradise Cove, Green Valley, Desert Shores, The Lakes, these redundant developments beckon with the illusion of green grass, bodies of water. The desert, it seems, is not welcome behind their locked gates.

I love telling my filmmaker friends from Los Angeles that the real art scene is in Las Vegas. The maddening mirror, the self-referential amid exploding signifiers. But mostly, the second chance. The postquake, postriot, postmortem on the America that was and still is.

FEBRUARY

I find myself staring at an elderly woman dressed in pink, clutching a pink purse full of quarters, as one by one, they disappear into the video poker machine at Smiths Food. I've seen her here before—I ask her how often she plays. She tells me she's been here every day since her husband died. It was the only thing that could get her over it. I sit down beside her, and for the first time since I've been here, I do it. I pay a paltry sum for the possibility of pleasure. She's right. It fills the void.

Tonight, we (my producer and I) go to Crazy Horse II, one of the posher of the "gentlemen's clubs." We meet Corky and Cassandra (their stage names), two erotic dancers. Corky is retiring after twenty years, and Cassandra has been here only a few days. Corky reads Jung and talks about her shadow self. She sees what she's doing as a gift. "The service we are performing is not sexual, it's psychological, and that service is to make men feel OK about themselves." She is the self-prescribed avatar of the "self-empowered" woman. I love her perfect breasts (only $2,000, honey) and platinum red hair. I decide I could probably do this. Funds for the documentary are fast disappearing, and at $800 a night, it starts to look appealing.

Then I watch her lapdance, a strange, contorted ritual between unclothed female and unflinching male . . . the men are not allowed to touch. Corky says it's about power, getting off on that. I watch her lift her leg over a guy's shoulder, whisper in his ear. I wonder what she's saying, something about archetypes? I watch young men in dockers drinking rum and coke. An older, Mexican man in a big hat slinks up to me and whispers that he just put in the new carpet, how do I like it? I look down and see small renditions of Will Rogers riding multicolored broncos. I look up and watch another lapdance. I contemplate just who the horse is and who the rider.

On a break in the dressing room, Corky unleashes lore of her many years of doing this. "We were raised as women thinking that every man, all they wanted was us sexually. Think about it, what did your mother say, they only want one thing. Well, we don't think of them as human beings. And they don't care about us as human beings . . . in the club, we have a chance to change all that." I look at the array of women— all shapes and sizes in G-strings, slinky red slips, a metallic silver bikini. I have to admit, there's something incredibly human about all this exposed flesh. A kind of homespun erotica. They all seem so resigned to their bodies, so comfortable with their thighs. One girl is screaming at her boyfriend over the payphone in the corner, another is wondering if, at four months pregnant, she's showing.

Cassandra's different, doelike, shy. She sits alone in the corner of the dressing room, and it takes a while to get her to talk. She confesses she thinks she's the only virgin in the place. When she dances on stage, she closes her eyes. Covers her breasts with her hands when she walks off. She says she hasn't made much money because she just can't get the hang of it. Walking up to them, asking them to dance . . . you gotta be able to take rejection. "I hate the lying part. Some of these girls they tell the guys what they want to hear, that they look just like their boyfriend,

Billboard.

that they'll meet them after work, but it's all just lies to get them to pay more. You have to act sexual when you're not. Some girls say it's like acting, but it's not, it's lying."

I ask her why she's doing it, and like most of the younger ones, it's the money they never had. "I was broke, my car needed fixing, me and my boyfriend could never go out or anything . . . it was a way to get my life going." Cassandra also owns a show horse, something she's wanted all her life. Dancing helps her pay the steep boarding fees. She never won any shows " 'cause I never could afford the good-looking horse." I visit her at the stables one afternoon, and she's right, the horse is a beauty. So is the rider.

That night I can't sleep. I keep seeing Cassandra on her horse, then at the club. Like some pop incarnation of the prophetess Cassandra at the Gate of Lions. Corky in the lap of some guy, toying with his humanity. I get out of bed and stare at my body in the mirror. Even against all that I've read and coaxed myself into believing, I am fundamentally disgusted with what I see. Camille Paglia beware, these not-so-gentlewomen at gentlemen's clubs may have something, and it's not in some Demi Moore movie, some tiresome debate over pornography and victimization. It's basic: they work hard in a world where no one hides.

Hollywood wants me to believe that inside every woman, there's a stripper waiting to escape. I'm making this film to confront that myth, but my quest for the woman in Vegas has become a search for myself. I am fast learning how not to get sideswiped by illusions. Strip away the Strip, and you have profit, pure and simple. Inside every gambler is a yearning for escape. Another life. The kind that widows dressed in pink pull from their purses and place daintily into the slit that is the slot, the 7–11 collection plate, pass it on. The secret to Las Vegas is not "lost wages" but what you gain. It's all here for you in ways you never knew until you looked at yourself naked. And liked what you saw.

MARCH

Inside the Culinary Workers' hall, I'm taping a strategy meeting, led by Hattie Canty, president of one of the largest union locals in America. She's giving maids who have been fired for wearing union buttons a pep talk. She worked as a maid herself for fifteen years, raising ten children when her husband died of cancer. Vegas is the last union town in America. At 40,000 members strong, it sustained a six-and-a-half-year strike, one of the longest strikes in U.S. history. The Culinary Workers are today's equivalent of the mine workers of yesterday. The Frontier is one of the last family-run hotels, and the matriarch, Margaret Elardi wasn't budging. But the Culinary Union is nothing to mess with.

I film Hattie in the park on a sunny Sunday afternoon with her grandbabies. Being black in Las Vegas was never easy, and what was referred to as "Mississippi of the West" included a segregated Strip up until the late 1960s. Eartha Kitt and other black performers had to sleep in black family homes after they performed. They drained the swimming pool at the Sahara Hotel after Josephine Baker swam in it. Hattie still lives in the city-approved development she's been living in for thirty years. Its foundation is sinking. She's been promised a new house, but it's taken years to plan.

The *New Yorker* sent Annie Leibovitz out to photograph Hattie for an article. They took a picture of her ten kids and thirteen grandkids. Hattie was nonplussed. She casually told Annie, "I would've had eleven kids, but I lost one eight months pregnant, reaching up, trying to clean curtains. But I never missed a day of work, and I was never late."[2] You're a woman. You reach up in Las Vegas, and you pull down on that long-armed bandit. And sometimes you end up the president of a union. Sometimes you stare at two sevens and a cherry.

JULY

The Sahara tower reads one hundred degrees at midnight. That can't be right. There's something wrong about a city that never sleeps and never cools down, even after the sun is long gone. But the film is starting to heat up. Seems the working title, *Stripped and Teased,* is causing problems among some of the women. They don't want to be associated with anything "controversial" or degrading. "We're not about that . . ." I try to explain the title is ironic, a play on words, but it dawns on me that Las Vegas is a place with no irony. I stare stupidly at the Stratosphere tower, its absurd phallus still growing. Everything here is what it is. There is no subtext.

After six months here, I'm feeling this withering away of resistance. I no longer cringe at the sound of slot machines when I walk through a casino. I'm not as outraged at the incongruities between showgirl billboards and chain-smoking divorcees suffering from PMS (poker machine syndrome). I've arrived. I am a Las Vegas woman. I've learned to live in between the clanging contradictions and hold my head up. Hell, I just get through the heat of the day and I'm proud to say I drove without air-conditioning. Without irony. We can live this way when we have to.

OCTOBER

I meet a showgirl from Holland who moved here from Paris and married an American. She reclines on billboards all over town, proclaiming that she's the "Showgirl for the 21st Century." This no doubt means her nudity is of the postmodern kind. The Stardust Hotel, where she dances in "Enter the Night," has entered into a whole new arena of using woman-as-object. Her image is also splashed across an entire wing of a Western Airlines airbus. Fly the friendly showgirl.

We screen the movie *Showgirl* for a group of real showgirls, and film their reactions. For a film that so obviously misses the mark for all the obvious reasons, it still cut deep for these women. They laughed at the film, but couldn't laugh afterwards. Their lives are so badly, so bawdily misrepresented. They are all trained dancers, many of them from ballet companies. Here they are in Las Vegas because it's steady work. One of them, on pregnancy leave, points to her swelling belly. "This is real life, right here. We make fifty dollars extra if we dance topless. It's what you do, but not who you are." What was once all show is now technique, tough choreography. Fewer dancers, more lasers. In the twenty-first century, showgirls might, in fact, become extinct.

NOVEMBER

Then there's Anna, a Mexican-American mother from Texas, who moved here after her kids had grown, in search of her own adventure. Actually, she went to Reno first, but when her son was incarcerated in Jean Prison, thirty miles outside of Vegas, she moved down here so she could visit more often. Jean is an interesting study of an unlikely town. A friend once remarked that the town of Jean represented America's economic future: prisons and casinos. Except for a 76 mini-mart, that's all there is there.

Anna gets up at dawn to collect bread from a charitable outlet and distributes it around her neighborhood, to single moms, shut-in seniors, and disabled folk. She also ran a youth camp out of her home because "the kids had nothin' to do here." She gets no government help, no grants, no salary for what she does. She herself lives on food stamps. The Mother Teresa of the Other Las Vegas takes in bundles of clothes from all kinds of sources and redistributes them to those who need them. She even fixes VCRs and coffee machines that others have discarded. . . . In a city of pawn shops, Anna stands apart. She knows her customers, and they all know her. She's so busy, she laments, that her garden, a burst of brilliant color, isn't thriving as she'd like. "You can grow anything you want in this place, you'd be surprised—it just takes time."

Statue of Jesus and Mary in front of Our Lady of Las Vegas Catholic Church.

DECEMBER

The woman's space? I'm at that dry lake again, shooting the final scene of my film. The sun is setting, streaks of ochre and baby pink across an impossibly huge sky. I take off my shoes and feel the cracks of the earth between my toes. I see the faces and hear the voices of all the women I've interviewed, a chorus of laughter, bitter stories, some tears. Dancer bodies of precision, disciplined calves, lines across foreheads, varicose veins. I want to capture their defiance, their fatigue. I want to bring them all together for a drink, put it all on a number and forget that the wheel is spinning. It's been over a year since I started this project—I've come full circle, and as the light finally fades, I see their shadows, disappearing across the desert.

This is the women's Las Vegas, right here in the middle of nowhere, in the realm of the possible . . . and these, like so many fleeting shapes, are the women without whom the city of lights would just be a dry lake.

POSTSCRIPT: Amie Williams is not only still a Las Vegas woman, she married a Las Vegas man, and they now have a three-year-old baby. She completed her documentary *Stripped and Teased: Tales from Las Vegas Women* in 1999.

NOTES

1. Robert Venturi, Denise Scott Brown, and Steven Izenour, *Learning from Las Vegas: The Forgotten Symbolism of Architectural Form* (Cambridge, Mass.: MIT Press, 1972, 1977).

2. Hattie Canty quoted by Annie Leibovitz, *New Yorker,* February 26–March 4, 1996, 148–56.

PART V FROM PARIAH TO PARADIGM

Colony, Capital, and *Casino*
Money in the Real Las Vegas

Martin Scorsese's 1994 film *Casino* opens with a ball of flame. Sam "Ace" Rothstein, the character created from the life of the former Stardust casino headman Frank "Lefty" Rosenthal, played by Robert De Niro, strides authoritatively out of Tony Roma's restaurant on Sahara Avenue near the Strip and across the parking lot to his Cadillac. He enters the car, turns the ignition, and KABOOM! A human in flames hurtles out of the driver's seat, preceded by a blown-off door.

As Rothstein writhes on the ground and the camera pulls away, Joe Pesci, who plays Nicki Santoro, closely modeled on the mobster Anthony "Tony the Ant" Spilotro, offers a denouement. "This was the last time two little guys like us ever got this kinda chance and we fucked it up," he tells the audience, and indeed the story that follows as a narrated flashback offers a mythologized version of the last days of the mob in 1970s Las Vegas. Derived from Nicholas Pileggi's book of the same name, itself largely based on Rosenthal's reminiscences, *Casino* purports to tell the "truth" about the demise of organized crime's control of gaming in Las Vegas.[1] In this formulation, two vain and greedy hoods bring down a vast and powerful sub rosa empire. The individual failings of Santoro-Spilotro and Rothstein-Rosenthal are responsible for the demise of lucrative skimming operations at a number of casinos. The end of organized crime's purported control of the town is a casualty of the arrogance and stupidity of the two main characters. Their inability to keep their heads down and their pants zipped ruins the perfect setup:

unearned, unaccounted for, and untraceable money, forever. With its emphasis on individual failings, *Casino* is more fairy tale than social commentary or hard-bitten true crime drama.

This simple construction, with its characteristically Hollywood focus on the relationship between the two protagonists, patently misleads anyone who seeks to understand the workings of Las Vegas and Nevada. It ignores a crucial question: since when do people who have real power anywhere in the United States, no matter who they are, blow each other up in public? In this specific situation, there is an even more salient question: why would a sub rosa organization such as organized crime reveal the limits of its power in a public display of violence that would clear up any remaining doubts about the ownership of various casinos? The list of questions that stems from this portrayal is endless, and all lead to one conclusion. *Casino* is fiction. In the movie, the behavior portrayed in the film makes sense. In life, such explanations fall remarkably short.

Both the book and movie versions of *Casino* misunderstand the fundamental realities of Las Vegas and Nevada. Entranced by the power of narrative and the drama of larger-than-life figures, Pileggi and Scorsese assume that violence is power and mistake flamboyance for control. In the process, they fail to grasp the essence of the Silver State. Money is all-important in Nevada, but not only the money that flows like a river into the counting rooms of the casinos. Of even greater importance are the sources of capital that finance the construction of the Las Vegas Strip.

LIFE IN A COLONY

The most basic reality of Nevada is that the state is a colony, a point driven home by a trip to Hoover Dam, where vehicles inscribed with the insignia of the Los Angeles Municipal Utility District sport Nevada license plates. The fundamental relationship between Nevada and California is as clear as the insignia on the side of these cars: California runs Nevada, so completely and brazenly that the most needed resource in the desert state, water, is stored there for consumption in the great economic engine to the west. The control is so complete that the relationship seems natural: California entities wear Nevada license plates and no one notices, proof positive of the vast power of the Golden State in the adjacent Silver State. Nevadans need look no farther to see where their bread is buttered.

In Nevada, there is nothing unusual about this scenario; it is a capsule of the state's history. Founded as a result of the Comstock Lode and the need for another state in the Union to assure Abraham Lincoln's reelection in 1864, desolate Nevada has survived by catering to the needs of outsiders, in particular, Californians. From the mining industry, called "extractive" for a reason, to the development of divorce and gaming as the basis of the state economy, Nevada has always derived its sustenance from trading raw materials—gold, silver, and the possibility of quick freedom in personal or economic terms—for the finished products of American society. Nevadans have fashioned a world apart, one that cannot afford to rest too hard on any one image, in an effort to attract the interest of their neighbors. There is a malleability to Nevada, and especially to Las Vegas, that is unparalleled elsewhere in the nation and possibly the world.

In Nevada, as in other colonies, the relationship between core areas and their peripheries dominates life. The economic structure of a colony is different from that of a core area; a colony is dependent on a core for much, and often all, of its sustenance. In industrial economies, core areas produced products that were marketed in both cores and peripheries, and colonies were on the receiving end of the delivery system that brought them expensive finished goods in exchange for much less expensive raw materials.[2] Colonies ship out their raw materials until the source is exhausted, but the appetite for finished products remains insatiable. After the demise of traditional extractive commodities, successful colonies find a way to market other amenities or they decline. One of the clearest ways to survive is to provide services that the core culture eschews, scorns, or does not permit, but that are very popular with its people. In Las Vegas, the lure of fun, excitement, and a little bit of danger created an economy that allowed the distribution of the finished goods that signify the veneer of modernity and civilization in an outpost. Nearly everything that sustains the institutions of dominant cultures on a colonial periphery comes from outside. Nevada's power, water, food, economy, and raison d'être as an independent entity come from beyond its boundaries. Nevada imports almost everything.

Most important among the myriad commodities that Nevada has always imported has been capital. The Silver State, fountain of so much wealth for others, has always lacked indigenous capital. Since gaming became legal again in 1931, and especially since the end of World War II, capital formation outside the state has driven not only the growth of the gaming industry, but the growth of the entire state. In Nevada, the old journalistic adage to follow the money leads directly to where the power resides. The history of the rise and fall of the sources of capital that have supported the growth of Nevada's gaming industry illustrates the basic irrelevance of Spilotro and Rosenthal to the evolution of the industry by the 1970s, precisely the moment when they became closely linked to gaming in the public imagination. In effect, the film *Casino* obscures a far more significant story. The town was "lost," in Pileggi's and Scorsese's terms, before Rosenthal took over the Stardust and Spilotro arrived on the Las Vegas scene.

In Las Vegas, especially, capital regimes have been definitive. Since the return of gaming in 1931, southern Nevada has experienced a sequence of capital regimes. A federal regime came first, defined by spending for the Boulder (later Hoover) Dam and then by the development of heavy industry to support World War II. In 1946, the arrival of Benjamin "Bugsy" Siegel inaugurated a second capital regime, the mob era. From 1946 to 1969, mob financing held sway, first from the pockets of mobsters, who had no access to outside financing to build their casinos, and later through the mob-controlled Teamsters Central States Pension Fund.[3] In 1969, with the passage of the revised Corporate Gaming Act, which made it possible for large publicly held corporations to own casinos, the corporate regime began. Like the mobsters before them, the first financiers, such as Howard Hughes and Kirk Kerkorian, financed their operations out of their own pockets, but soon corporations such as Hilton, Holiday Inn, Ramada, and Sheraton bought existing resorts. In the 1980s, the impresario Steve Wynn raised the ante with junk bond funding, broadening the reach of the gaming industry and taking it mainstream. Each regime provided the dominant source of capital in its time period, shaping the forms of the community and inventing a different Las Vegas that suited the needs of its capital brokers. Each incarnation created a neonative population tied to that particular formulation; members of each of these groups thought of their Las Vegas as the only real one. Tied to time, place, and framework, each group of these people felt dramatically displaced in the aftermath of the transition to new capital regimes.

FEDERAL MONEY

As in most western states, the tale of where the money comes from begins with the federal government. In 1931, the economy of southern Nevada was precarious at best. The turn-of-the-century mining booms in places such as Rhyolite, Goldfield, Tonopah, and Bullfrog had ended after World War I, and the sale of the San Pedro, Los Angeles, and Salt Lake Railroad to the Union Pacific created another in the seemingly endless series of colonial relationships that dominated this periphery. The sale hurt Las Vegas, because in 1927, in response to the national railroad strike of 1922, the Union Pacific moved much of its shop from Las Vegas to Caliente. Early efforts to develop tourism also met with mixed success, and Las Vegas remained a dusty little town with no distinct purpose and little claim on the attention of the nation. After the railroad departed, Las Vegas came as close to becoming a ghost town as it ever would.[4]

Federal spending prompted a rebirth of colonial Las Vegas, as two events, the construction of the Boulder Dam, now Hoover Dam, which began in 1929, and the New Deal, which offered development programs across the nation, led the way. In southern Nevada alone, the federal government invested $70 million between 1929 and 1939—$19 million in the dam alone. Although the construction workers at the dam were eventually based in Boulder City, a few miles from the Colorado River canyons where the dam was constructed, Las Vegas benefited greatly from its presence. Boulder City developed its own retail district, which catered to the daily needs of dam workers, depriving Las Vegas businesses of that source of revenue, but Las Vegans recognized that the flow of visitors that began to pass through southern Nevada to view the construction of this magnificent edifice would continue after completion of the dam. Federal support for the many who came to Las Vegas in search of work at the dam but failed to find jobs, and, later, World War II military spending, replaced mining and the railroad in southern Nevada's economy.[5]

This first capital regime resembled that in many western locales. During the 1930s, federal projects were a dominant source of income throughout the nation, and especially in the West, and many towns were in the same position. This dependence on federal spending began earlier in southern Nevada, because work on the dam preceded the New Deal, but in many ways southern Nevada's experience in the 1930s was typical.[6]

One thing made 1930s Las Vegas atypical. In February 1931, the Nevada state legislature relegalized gambling. This was not an innovation but a return to the norm—although illegal from statehood in 1864 until 1869, gambling had been legal from then until 1913, when Progressive-era efforts to legislate morality put Nevada in compliance with the rest of the nation. Yet the revival of gaming took the state further down the colonial path than its liberal laws concerning prostitution, marriage, and divorce and its characteristic ignoring of Prohibition had done. The reinstatement of gambling gave Nevada an industry that could augment and ultimately redirect the federal capital so essential to the state. Especially after the dollars from the dam began to dry up, after its completion in 1936, this source of revenue proved increasingly important.[7]

This first modern capital regime illustrates the perils of colonial existence. Lacking industry or infrastructure, Las Vegas depended first and foremost on money from the federal government. Almost as an afterthought, in its effort to create a viable economy, the state of Nevada permitted activities that were seen as scandalous at best. Southern Nevadans, especially, recognized the perils of dependence. A change in federal policy could eliminate not only individual livelihoods but also the economic viability of the region. Before air-conditioning, attracting newcomers to a town where summer temperatures routinely topped 110 degrees Fahrenheit was a difficult task without the lure of easy prosperity.

As a result, Las Vegas shaped itself to the needs of the outside. In the 1930s and 1940s, this was not unusual in the West. It was as true of Los Alamos, New Mexico, and Richmond, California, as it was of Las Vegas. The difference was that Las Vegans recognized that their opportunity to capitalize was time-bound, and that other strategies would be necessary for long-term sustenance. Perhaps the much-trumpeted Nevada individualism promoted an attitude that developed industries to augment federal largesse; perhaps federal dollars seemed one more panacea in the long line that had come and gone. In any event, southern Nevada especially welcomed the federal money and engaged in strategies to encourage those dollars to stay in the area, while its people looked for new ways to diversify their income base.

After the completion of Boulder Dam, Nevadans cast about for a new strategy. Tourism and divorce filled a gap in the 1930s, but the prosperity of the dam years did not return. Only after Pearl Harbor, when the federal government again located important projects in southern Nevada, did Las Vegas recover from its post-dam doldrums. An air base northeast of town was commandeered by the federal government, which ultimately spent more than $25 million on the construction of facilities there. The Las Vegas Gunnery School, as the installation became known, supplied the Pacific theater with gunners, graduating 4,000 every six weeks by 1942. Another wartime project was the Basic Magnesium, Inc.

(BMI) factory, supported by federal dollars, in Henderson, a newly founded town on Boulder Highway, leading to the dam, between Las Vegas and Boulder City.[8] By the end of the war, federal dollars drove the local Las Vegas economy, while catering to gamblers and people seeking quick divorces provided backup. Federal dollars were the dominant capital regime of the era, driving local decision making. Access to the federal money, in the form of construction contracts, service work, or the opportunity to liberate dollars from the pockets of workers, was a clear charter for economic success. Federal dollars were so important that the community gave in to decidedly non-Nevadan demands: in 1942, Las Vegas closed its red-light district to accommodate the military, and after November 1942, bars and casinos were closed from 2:00 A.M. to 10:00 A.M., an unlikely prospect in southern Nevada. But closure was worthwhile if the consequence of failing to comply was being off-limits to military personnel.[9] In this manner, the colonial nature of southern Nevada was once again illustrated. As it had once catered to the mining industry and the railroad, it had come to cater to the demands of the federal government.

THE MOB ARRIVES

Meyer Lansky's mob henchman Bugsy Siegel launched the second capital regime in Las Vegas in 1946. Lansky and his associates had had an eye on Las Vegas as early as 1941, but in most accounts, Siegel is credited with envisioning the complicated relationship between gaming and status that would make the Flamingo Hotel and Casino a world-class destination resort. Siegel transformed Las Vegas from a western, institution-free center of vice into a world-renowned spectacle of gambling, entertainment, and fun by melding the themes of Monte Carlo, Miami Beach, and Havana with the resortlike character of the clubs that preceded the Flamingo on Highway 91 south of town on the road to Los Angeles. In the process, he inaugurated an era in which the capital to fund gaming resorts, which became the dominant industry in Las Vegas, came first from the pockets of organized crime and later from legitimate money the mob could control.[10]

Locals did not object to this seemingly nefarious involvement in what was becoming the primary local industry. In southern Nevada, the need for capital was so great that almost everyone looked the other way; even straitlaced southern Nevada Church of Jesus Christ of Latter Day Saints (Mormon) culture welcomed these newcomers. The mob had cash, and lots of it, a necessity in a colonial periphery such as southern Nevada, and Siegel benefited from his association with Hollywood. His arrival opened a new pipeline to the capital for which Las Vegans thirsted. Even his association with Murder, Inc. was not sufficient to deter locals, who embraced anyone who had money to invest.[11]

Initial investment by organized crime was masked by local involvement. At the end of 1945, when Siegel purchased the El Cortez, his investors included a number of locals as well as Meyer Lansky, Gus Greenbaum, an Arizona bookmaker, David and Chickie Berman and Israel "Icepick Willie" Alderman, who ran typical 1930s gaming road houses called "carpet joints" in Minneapolis, and Moe Sedway, a Siegel associate from Los Angeles. The purchase of the El Cortez initiated a pattern; in every subsequent purchase or development of a resort on the Strip, participation by "connected" illegal gamblers, who had become legal in Nevada, was evident. There was a visible relationship between locals and newcomers in nearly every new casino that effectively linked outside capital with some form of local respectability. Locals who could easily be licensed or individuals with ties to organized crime but no significant criminal record held visible and often sizable percentages of new casinos. Most of these "owners" appeared to have recently come into money and possessed expertise useful in the casino business. Who truly owned their percentages was not a good question to ask.

The funding of the Flamingo Hotel and Siegel's death illustrate the point. The construction of the Flamingo went well over budget; the initial estimate of $1.5 million ballooned to almost $6 million, aggravated by expenses such as the $1 million that providing a private sewer line to each room added to the cost. In 1946, when Siegel tried to extort $2 million from the Chicago mob to complete construction, he had $1 million of his own money in the project and $3 million that his connected friends had invested in $50,000-sized blocks of stock. Siegel was murdered in Hollywood as a result of the cost overruns. Not a dime of legitimate money financed the Flamingo after Siegel took it over from Billy Wilkerson, the founder of the *Hollywood Reporter*.[12]

This pattern of financing was typical of Las Vegas casinos and hotels throughout the late 1940s and 1950s. Even resorts with legitimate origins, such as Wilbur Clark's Desert Inn, became part of a vast organized crime network. Clark, his brother, and two investors had begun to build the Desert Inn in 1947 with $250,000. They soon ran out of money, and for nearly two years, the framed structure sat in the hot desert sun, looking more like an ancient relic than a nascent casino, as they searched for capital. Clark even tried to get funding from the nearly defunct New Deal-era Reconstruction Finance Corporation. In 1949, however, he met Morris B. "Moe" Dalitz, and within a few months, Dalitz and his partners in the notorious Cleveland Mayfield Road gang contributed $1.3 million in capital and owned 75 percent of the project. When Wilbur Clark's Desert Inn opened in April 1950, local residents called it "the most brilliant social event in the history of the Strip." Clark became a glorified front man at the resort that bore his name. The Desert Inn opened a pipeline of money from similar points of origin, and hotels such as the Sands, completed in 1952, the Tropicana, which opened in 1957, and the Stardust, following in 1958, soon had similar financing histories.[13]

These were the roots of the world that Scorsese and Pileggi recreated in the film version of *Casino*, set twenty years out of date. It was a world of individual investment, sometimes hidden, and, as a result, untaxed, with deliveries of paper bags and briefcases full of money to Italian-surnamed individuals in distant cities. These individuals held "points" in Las Vegas, percentage investments that were concealed, but returned monthly profits skimmed off the top of the casino's profits and never recorded in its ledgers. Insidious and nefarious to be sure, most of these were also small-time interests, amounting to as little as a few thousand dollars a month in profit. Jack Entratter, the ostensible head of the Sands in the early 1960s, held twelve points in the operation. Entratter, a former headwaiter at the Copacabana in Miami Beach, had become a player and philanthropist in Las Vegas (the social hall in the oldest synagogue in town, Temple Beth Sholom, was constructed with his donation and is named for him). He owned two of those points himself. The other ten he held for various people, including the real power at the Sands, an old associate of Meyer Lansky's named Vincent "Jimmy Blue Eyes" Alo.[14] The mythic Las Vegas was a personal world where everyone knew everyone else, and all knew who buttered their figurative bread.

There was much to celebrate in this world for the people who had come to Las Vegas after the war in an effort to legitimize their lifestyles. After the construction of the Flamingo, the town became a magnet for every gambler, hood, and small-time shady entrepreneur in the country. In every other state in the union, doing things that were commonplace in Las Vegas could land you a jail term. It was a relief to be in a place where their activities were legal. Such people came by the thousands, swelling the population of the city and creating what amounted to a company town. Even the political culture of the city was transformed, because the casinos were the only major source of campaign contributions. In effect, Las Vegas became one big carpet joint, a place where the mores of illegal gaming culture became the norm and where the only casinos that lost money—after Siegel's famous initial fiasco at the Flamingo—were ones run by people who did not understand the rules of this imported culture.[15]

Las Vegas became the center of gaming in the Western Hemisphere. The social cost was masked: although many casino employees gambled away their paychecks, most of the casino's winnings came from visitors, not locals. This obviated the problems associated with the redistribution of money that accompanied gambling by residents and gave the industry a positive impact on the state economy's bottom line. Nevada's preeminence in gaming was assured by political change elsewhere. With the rise of Fidel Castro in Cuba and the closing of the Havana casinos, there was only one location in North America where big-time gambling was legal and its operators were legitimate. After infrastructural improvements such as the expansion of McCarran Airport in 1963, Las Vegas was poised to take advantage of the growing wealth and changing cultural mores of American society.[16]

This new importance led to a much greater demand for capital than had existed during the 1950s, as well as to obvious changes in operations. Until 1963, when the Fremont Casino skimming scandal was derailed by illegal FBI wiretaps, Las Vegas was a small-time operator's paradise.[17] Accustomed to seeing their occupation as risky, the individuals who ran casinos continued to operate as fly-by-nights. They looked at the short-term profit that could be put in their pockets as the best profit, almost instinctively feeling that although they were entirely legal in Nevada, this idyllic environment could not last. They believed that like any gambler's lucky streak, their run of success would soon end.[18] But in a world of growing interest in recreation, in which gambling was increasingly seen less as a moral violation than as a legitimate pastime, such operators had to cater to a more general audience. To do so required different values in management as well as a lot more money.

The limitations of the individual capital phase of mob rule were evident in the layout of the city. After a spate of hotel construction during the 1950s—beginning with the Sands in 1952, and including the Tropicana, the gaming take for which was found on a piece of paper in the mob boss Frank Costello's pocket after a 1957 attempt on his life—that ended with the completion of the Stardust in 1958, no new Strip hotels were constructed until 1966. A New York stockbroker, Edwin Lowe, built a resort eschewing a casino, the Tally-Ho, but it soon ended in bankruptcy. The limitations of small-time mob rule and the capital to which it had access were evident. Siegel, Dalitz, and the other early mob entrepreneurs dug into their own pockets and went to their friends for capital, but as the market expanded and the amount of capital necessary to build a competitive resort grew, the pockets that had previously funded the growth of the industry were not sufficiently deep. Nor would the financial markets support the development of gaming resorts; the only source of such capital in southern Nevada was a local bank, the Bank of Las Vegas, founded in 1954 and reorganized as the Valley Bank in 1964. Although most of the bank's capital came from outside Nevada, its willingness to serve as a conduit for outside money helped legitimize the financing of the gaming industry. Among the first projects the Bank of Las Vegas funded were the development or expansion of the Fremont, the Sands, the Desert Inn, the Dunes, the Stardust, the Riviera, and the Thunderbird.[19] Despite the great importance of this local source of capital and its leading banker, E. Parry Thomas, who was instrumental in financing and handling transactions, the growth of the resort corridor had outstripped local funding. The capital to support the large-scale development necessary to turn Las Vegas from a huge carpet joint into a resort had to come from somewhere else.

The money was relatively easy to obtain. The Teamsters' Central States, Southeast and Southwest Areas Pension Fund, run by Allan Dorfman, the stepson of a mobster and an associate of the Chicago mob, provided the source. The initial conduit was Morris Shenker, an attorney who served as counsel to a small Texas insurance company, American National Insurance Corporation. Shenker was a confidant of the Teamsters' president, Jimmy Hoffa. Through the Bank of Las Vegas, American National became an early source of capital for casino funding. Shenker soon held a stake in a number of casinos. Thomas received a $5 million loan from American National, which helped open the door for the Pension Fund and facilitated the building of an economic empire. By 1963, the fund had more than $167 million in assets and was administered by a sixteen-person board. Hoffa clearly influenced the board's investments; in 1963, more than 60 percent of its funds were invested in real estate, compared to the 2.3 percent typical of similar investing consortiums.[20]

The beginning of Teamsters' Pension Fund investment in real estate financing dated to 1956, long before Hoffa and Dorfman turned their attention to Las Vegas. A $1 million, ten-year mortgage granted to

Cleveland Raceways at 6 percent interest was the Pension Fund's first loan. Bill Presser, a Hoffa ally and the Teamsters boss in Ohio encouraged the loan, which was quickly paid back after the passage of the Landrum-Griffin Act of 1958, which spurred an investigation by Robert Kennedy. Further loans were made in 1957 on similar terms. One financed the construction of the Castaways Motel in Miami, Florida; another went to Benjamin Dranow, an old friend of Hoffa's, who owned a department store that was currently in the middle of a difficult labor negotiation with another union. As did many such loans, the one to Dranow had to be written off. By 1961, the Pension Fund was out $766,000 of the $1 million original loan.[21] Under Dorfman, the Pension Fund consistently made atypical loans, which frequently turned out to be losers.

Early Teamsters' Pension Fund forays into Las Vegas had little to do with the gaming industry. In 1958, the *Las Vegas Sun*'s publisher, Herman "Hank" Greenspun, who was one of a very few American newspaper publishers to challenge Senator Joseph McCarthy's reign of terror and had been loudly and publicly critical of the mob, received $250,000 to finance the development of a golf course; if the loan was offered to quiet Greenspun, it failed. He continued to expose organized crime and corruption in southern Nevada. Teamsters' money funded other developments as well. On April 14, 1959, the 100-bed Sunrise Hospital opened, built by the Paradise Development Company, whose officers included Moe Dalitz, Allard Roen, a casino executive who had been indicted in the United Dye and Chemical stock fraud case, and two young Las Vegas businessmen, Irwin Molasky and Mervin Adelson. The Paradise Development Company needed capital and the Pension Fund provided it, with Hoffa assuring its profitability by delivering the Teamsters' health care plan to the new hospital. Although the arrangement looked like a front for organized crime, the hospital was a benefit to the community, and the people of Las Vegas welcomed it.[22]

Subsequent construction, especially the 1967 Boulevard Mall, also drew accolades from the community. With its unique local access to capital for development other than casinos and resorts, the Paradise Development Company effectively planned the future of non-resort Las Vegas by turning Maryland Parkway, a two-lane road that paralleled the Strip about two miles to the east, into the main commercial thoroughfare for the growing city of Las Vegas. The denizens of the city, from workers to executives, came to live in the area that grew up to the east of this new commercial center.[23] The enclosed Boulevard Mall, the first modern shopping center in Las Vegas, was the capstone to this set of accomplishments. With its completion, Las Vegans could believe that their city had the amenities to match their resort.

This was the most complicated dimension of mob rule in southern Nevada. In a colony that lacked sources of internal capital, was in the middle of substantive growth, and was dominated by an industry that, for cultural reasons, mainstream financing would not support, fresh capital was essential, and people embraced it, no matter what its origins. That the Teamsters' Pension Fund invested in social projects such as the hospital and mall, albeit profitable ones, made that infusion of capital even more important. To most of greater Las Vegas, which had grown from roughly 8,000 in 1940 to 269,000 in 1967, and which was increasingly populated by casino service workers, who thought of legalized gaming as the solution to the economic doldrums and their legal woes elsewhere in the country, the hospital and mall were community assets, and the source of their financing and the profit that derived from them were expected consequences. The hospital, the mall, and other similar developments began to normalize Las Vegas, giving the people of the town a sense of typicality that had been hard to sustain in the 1940s and 1950s. For that, Las Vegans were grateful, and they were usually willing to overlook any machinations in the sources of their normalcy.

The new source of money and the flamboyant, visionary style traceable to Bugsy Siegel and the Flamingo led to the development of distinctive new hotels. Most important of these was Caesars Palace, funded by a loan from the Central State Pension Fund, and run by Jay Sarno, an eccentric but brilliant entrepreneur. Sarno had begun to borrow from the Pension Fund in the late 1950s to finance hotel projects in Atlanta and Dallas for his national Cabana chain; by the time he conceived of Caesars Palace, he had the combination of vision and access that allowed him to dream of even more grandiose projects. Sarno envisioned a new level of distinction in the casino industry. Caesars Palace would be the quintessential "high-class joint," and its $19 million price tag was the most ever spent to develop a Las Vegas resort. Reflecting Sarno's idiosyncratic belief that egg-shaped structures relaxed people, the casino was elliptical. A frieze depicting the battle of the Etruscan Hills graced the wall next to the Noshorium Coffee Shop, a name that merged the Yiddish term "nosh," snack, with the "-orium" that in American popular culture spells Roman origin. Roman-style fountains and statues decorated the property, with eighteen huge fountains bordering the 135-foot driveway. The 800-seat Circus Maximus Theatre, patterned after the Colosseum in Rome, hosted only the top acts of the day; Frank Sinatra and Barbra Streisand headed the bill.[24]

During this era, Pension Fund money also financed other, less distinctive new resorts. During the early 1960s, the fund granted loans that supported the construction of the Landmark Hotel, the Four Queens, the Aladdin, and Sarno's Circus Circus. The Landmark had begun as the project of a wealthy Kansas City, Missouri, developer, John Carroll, who began construction with $3.3 million in funding from the Appliance Buyers Credit Corporation, a subsidiary of Whirlpool. Lacking the additional $10 million the plans for the resort demanded, Carroll built apartments and a small shopping center while searching for additional funding. In a typical partnership between an unknowing legitimate front man and mob-controlled money, the Central States Pension Fund came up with a $6 million loan in August 1966, offering Carroll the opportunity to build his resort.[25]

By the time Carroll received the loan for the Landmark in 1966, the Pension Fund had become the dominant source of capital in southern Nevada, which was dependent on any sources of capital that could support its growth. The internal funding that had supported early development was insufficient to meet the growing costs of resort development, particularly after Caesars Palace was built. Valley Bank was the sole source of local funds, and the growing industry required upward of $100 million in development capital between 1960 and 1965 alone. Although the Golden Nugget made a public stock offering in the late 1940s, traditional sources of capital such as stock and bond offerings were by and large blocked. Wall Street was not ready to take a chance on gaming. This left its potentially lucrative rewards to the Pension Fund and the organized crime bosses who ran it. By the 1960s, Las Vegas was thus beholden, not to industrial America, but to parasitic forces that preyed upon it, and the people who were attracted to the gaming industry were not bothered by this. The veneer of typicality was quite thin in the Las Vegas of the 1960s. Las Vegans argued that, behind the glitz, they lived in a "normal" town, but their definition of normal was quite at odds with the rest of the nation's.

Nevada's gaming laws contributed to its unique form of well-paid colonial status. In an effort to counter what state authorities perceived as the organized crime menace, state-level regulation of gaming began during the mid 1940s; prior to that time, counties and their sheriffs licensed and administered the industry. The 1947 murder of Siegel contributed to new statutes, which also gave the Nevada Tax Commission the power to investigate, license, and monitor gaming. This remedy hardly succeeded—Clark County Commissioner Harley Harmon complained during 1952 hearings concerning the license of the Sands entertainment director, Jack Entratter, that the tax commission had "let every syndicate in the country into Las Vegas"—and subsequently, the Nevada Gaming Control Board and the state gaming control commission were created to administer the gaming industry. Even the establishment in 1960 of a mechanism to bar undesirable people from casinos, the so-called "Black Book," formally known as the List of Excluded Persons after 1976, amounted to little more than a public relations ploy.[26]

Beginning in 1955, one cardinal state regulation had determined the pattern of the gaming industry: every stockholder of a gaming establishment had to be licensed. Although the legalization act in 1931 permitted corporate ownership of casinos, the 1955 regulation effectively eliminated that prospect. This effectively barred large publicly held corporations from owning stock in the gaming industry.[27] Qualifying the seemingly infinite number of stockholders in any major publicly traded corporation was a daunting if not impossible task. In an era when Wall Street shied away from Las Vegas, this did not pose a problem, but as American culture liberalized during the 1960s and some of the stigma associated with gaming began to diminish, Nevada law effectively blocked the most important source of capital for the expansion of gaming.

In the process, there was a dramatic unintended consequence. Instead of freeing the gaming industry from the influence of organized crime, Nevada law enshrined it. The law made the Teamsters' Pension Fund the only source of capital upon which Las Vegas could rely, achieving exactly the opposite of its framers' intentions. As long as the only source of capital in town stemmed from organized crime and southern Nevada needed that capital for growth, the vaunted "cowboy" county commission and other civic leaders recognized that they needed the mob as much as the mob needed them. Rather than a place under control of local cowboys, as depicted by popular lore and films such as *Casino,* 1960s Las Vegas was a partnership between local interests that needed capital and mobsters who were the only source of it locals could reach. The combination of the stigma of gaming and the Nevada statute denied legitimate capital to the gaming industry when it needed it the most.

MOVING TO THE MAINSTREAM

Two events changed this equation, leading to the transformation of Las Vegas from a mob-dominated gambling town into a corporate-owned modern resort; neither of these had anything to with the actions of Frank Rosenthal or Anthony Spilotro. The first was the return of the reclusive billionaire Howard R. Hughes to a suite atop the Desert Inn in Las Vegas in a typically bizarre fashion on Thanksgiving Eve, 1966. After a few weeks, the management of the Desert Inn sought to persuade Hughes to leave so that they could return the suite to the use of the high rollers on whom the casino depended. Instead of leaving, Hughes thereupon paid approximately $13 million for the resort, where he remained cloistered in the penthouse for four years. His choice to locate in Las Vegas initiated a buying spree for Hughes. He bought the Frontier for approximately $14 million, the Sands for $14.6 million, and Castaways for $3 million, as well as the Silver Slipper, a television station, airlines, and small airport facilities. Hughes also made overtures to purchase Caesars Palace, the Riviera, and the Dunes in Las Vegas as well as Harrah's in both Reno and Lake Tahoe, but an antitrust suit halted negotiations. Even before the Nixon administration overruled Justice Department objections to the purchase of the famous Harold's Club in Reno and Landmark Hotel, just off the Strip, in a maneuver that was later exposed as resulting from a bribe, Hughes controlled about one-seventh of the state's gaming revenue, one-quarter of that in Las Vegas, and more than one-third of the revenue generated on the Strip.[28] Hughes's entrance changed the face of the gaming industry.

Hughes was a public-relations dream for the besieged state of Nevada and its most important industry. In 1966, another in the seemingly endless series of skimming scandals had broken wide open, pitting the state against the FBI and the federal government. The FBI had been engaged in a series of illegal wiretaps of casino offices, and the information from those wiretaps had been leaked to newspapers such as the *Chicago Sun-Times*. When the state initiated its own investigation, the information gathered through the wiretaps was not made available to state officials. This impugned the integrity of the state's oversight of gaming and enraged Nevada, where the doctrine of the individual's preeminence over any germ of community sanction was firmly ensconced well ahead of the rest of the nation. Hughes's reputation as a brilliant entrepreneur who would not invest in anything that was not a genuine money-maker served to remove some of the tarnish that was spreading across Nevada gaming.[29]

Howard Hughes's entrance into the gaming industry was pivotal. He was part of the old and a harbinger of the new, the first wealthy entrepreneur with the resources and the desire to compete with organized crime, the first set of truly deep pockets to seek to make Las Vegas his own. He arrived at the perfect moment for a new entrepreneur, exactly as his predecessors in the industry began to give way. As the first generation of mob impresarios, men such as Meyer Lansky and Jimmy Alo, aged, some tired of the constant federal surveillance that they experienced. From this perspective, selling out to Hughes, whom they likely regarded as the quintessential "sucker," seemed a good idea. They took their profits and largely left the field.[30]

In some ways, Howard Hughes was more like the gangsters he replaced than the corporate America that revered him. Gaming was a natural for Hughes; he was the sole stockholder of Hughes Tool Company, meaning that only he had to pass gaming commission investigations; a man of his stature and wealth had little problem stalling state regulatory bodies. Hughes also had immense assets and cash that he could use to finance any deal he wanted. Just like Bugsy Siegel, Hughes relied on capital that was personal and private. The reclusive billionaire was different because his vast empire had no public taint of organized crime associated with it. He was a forerunner of the new Las Vegas, whose interest helped legitimize investment in the gaming industry.

The second change made the mobsters who sold out look like geniuses. In 1967, at the behest of William F. Harrah and Baron and Conrad Hilton and with the support of Nevada's governor, Paul Laxalt, the state passed the Corporate Gaming Act, which eliminated the requirement that each stockholder had to pass a Gaming Control Board background check.[31] The door opened for an infusion of corporate capital.

The first purchases by major multinational hotel chains followed quickly on the heels of the new law. In 1970, the Hilton chain bought the Flamingo and the International from Kirk Kerkorian, a self-made multimillionaire who also sought to make Las Vegas his own. Kerkorian had made his money in crop-dusting and expanded into entertainment. The two Las Vegas hotels that he sold were a prelude to his dream of a new, world-class resort, the MGM Grand Hotel. The sale moved him closer to his goal at the same time as it fully inaugurated the new capital regime. With the arrival of the Hilton corporation and its enormous success in Las Vegas—by 1976, 43 percent of the gross revenues of the 163-hotel chain came from its Las Vegas operations—new and legitimate capital became available in ways it had never before been.[32] Holiday Inn and Ramada followed closely behind Hilton, and a new form of financing supported the development of Las Vegas.

In this climate, organized crime suddenly became financially obsolete. Wall Street could invest a great deal more money than organized crime ever could; the $269 million the Teamsters' Pension Fund had invested in Las Vegas in the late 1960s may have remained the largest single pool of capital in southern Nevada, but it had ceased to represent the growth sector of gaming capital. In an instant, the passage of the revised Corporate Gaming Act redistributed power in Las Vegas away from Teamsters' capital and toward Wall Street.

This was the context in which the story told in *Casino* took place. In 1974, Allen R. Glick, a largely unknown San Diego businessman, received a $62.7 million loan from the Teamsters' Pension Fund to purchase Recrion Corporation, which owned the Stardust, the Fremont, and the Marina. Glick was a Vietnam veteran and a hard-nosed enterprising businessman who worked in real estate. A partner directed him toward Las Vegas, where Glick bought the bankrupt Hacienda Hotel and Casino at the southern end of the Strip. Glick's takeover of another bankrupt casino, at Lake Tahoe, brought him into the orbit of the Teamsters' Pension Fund; soon afterward, he sought to pounce on an opportunity to purchase Recrion and needed money fast. After efforts to raise it elsewhere, he came to the Teamsters at almost the same time they sought out his clean-cut image. What followed was predictable. At the Stardust, a 1950s-style mob skimming operation was installed, under the watchful eyes of the chairman of Glick's Argent Corporation executive committee, Frank "Lefty" Rosenthal, utilizing the skills of the famed slot cheat–turned–counting room boss Jay Vandermark and supported by the enforcement power of Tony Spilotro.[33]

There was a difference in the result. In the mid 1970s, there were other sources of capital to support the tourism industry, and Nevada authorities neither needed nor chose to look the other way. In addition, the Stardust was beset by problems almost from the beginning; the 1975 murder of a San Diego woman tied to Allan Glick's real estate endeavors there opened some eyes, as did the earlier murder of a Caesars Palace employee with known mob ties who had had an altercation with Glick one week before his execution-style murder in the parking lot. In another suspicious move, Rosenthal received a ten-year, $250,000 per year contract from Glick the week before his licensing hearing. The contract stipulated that Rosenthal would be paid regardless of whether he received a gaming license. In January 1976, the Gaming Control Board informed Glick that Rosenthal, a gambler since his youth, could not be licensed to run casinos. Despite Vandermark's expertise, a May 1976 Gaming Control Board raid on the Stardust counting room uncovered a skim in process that was later thought to total more than $7 million from slot machines alone in the space of one year.[34]

Even more pivotal was a 1979 Gaming Control Board hearing in which Frank Rosenthal's license was permanently denied. After his ouster from the CEO position at the Stardust, Rosenthal continued to receive his $250,000 annual salary from Argent for serving as entertainment director of the Stardust. Rosenthal hosted a local television show and played the role of man about town while trying to clear his name. He took his case to the Nevada Supreme Court, challenging the state's right to regulate his ability to work in the gaming industry and, thereby, the state's right to regulate the industry at all. Rosenthal's defense was the old argument that legalized gambling had evolved from illegal gambling, and that everyone else in the industry had had "run-ins with the law" too. On the steps of the state supreme court, after the decision went against him, Rosenthal argued that the issue was constitutional in character and informed the press that he intended to pursue it. Perhaps naive, perhaps megalomaniacal, Rosenthal fully expected to have his license restored at the 1979 hearing.[35]

In the film *Casino,* De Niro-Rothstein-Rosenthal is shocked to find his license denied and responds with a tirade against the commission. It is a largely sympathetic portrayal. De Niro seems the embodiment of honesty and integrity, a businessman trying to leave his illegal past behind who is persecuted by the law and manipulated by the cowboy county commissioner, whose brother-in-law he recently fired. De Niro is livid in the film, but it is the righteous anger of one wronged by a venal and vindictive system.[36] Once again, *Casino* romanticizes a two-bit hustler operating within the confines of a worn-out system that had become anachronistic; once again, it elevates the individual above the institutional, belying the realities of corporate America.

Actual footage of the hearing reveals an entirely different picture. Replete in a yellow porkpie hat placed at jaunty angle, yellow suit, off-yellow necktie, and ascot, Rosenthal attacked the Gaming Commission's chairman, Harry Reid, who later became U.S. senator from Nevada. Rosenthal accused Reid of a range of duplicity, smirking for the camera, swearing, and belligerently threatening, not only the commission, but a county commissioner, members of the governor's staff, and members of the press. Rosenthal regarded the action as evidence of the "hypocrisy" of a state that permitted gaming but did not want a professional gambler to run a casino. When a reporter began to query the defensive and clearly uncomfortable Reid about the allegations, Rosenthal cut off the questions with one of his own that was designed not to incriminate Reid, as had the reporter's question, but to have Reid withdraw his characterization of Rosenthal as a liar. Vain, arrogant, and clearly wounded by the decision, Rosenthal cared only about vindication, not about exposing any manifestations of the corruption he alleged. "You're all so self-righteous," he sneered at the press just before he departed, transferring a characteristic he evinced in quantity to those seeking to report the events of the day to the society Rosenthal disdained.[37]

The drama of the situation and the inaccuracies of its portrayal in the film are significant, but the main thing was that the Gaming Commission rendered such a decision at all. Its new posture revealed the flexibility of standards of suitability for licensing at the same time as the beginning of a pattern of normalizing the casino industry, and, with it, the state of Nevada, became evident. The burden of proof of suitability fell on the applicant for a gaming license; it was the acknowledgment of suitability that in effect demonstrated community standards. By the 1970s, those standards had changed. Throughout the 1950s and 1960s, gaming regulators routinely licensed a range of thugs to run casinos. During the 1950s, the Sands was run by Joseph "Doc" Stacher, who had a record of arrests that dated from the 1920s and included New York and Nevada convictions during the 1950s and a grand jury appearance in Los Angeles in 1962. Stacher's preeminence in gaming testified to the ineffectiveness of regulation. L. B. "Benny" Binion, who arrived in Las Vegas in 1946 with an arrest record in his home town of Dallas, Texas, that dated back to 1923, was granted a gaming license in 1951. Listed hotel owners in 1963 included Moe Dalitz, Ruby Kolod, Morris Kleinman, and Sam Tucker at the Desert Inn, Edward Levinson, Stacher's known front man, at the Fremont and the Horseshoe Club, Ben Goffstein and the Gus Greenbaum estate at the Riviera, and Jack Entratter at the Sands. These legal listings were the tip of an iceberg. Even in the 1960s, all kinds of people were licensed to own and work in casinos.[38]

Clearly, the world of Las Vegas had changed. The most important source of capital in the 1960s, the Teamsters' Pension Fund, still had

immense sums of money invested in the town, but it no longer dominated local politics and the state gaming board. The suitability standards
applied to Rosenthal, whose worst crime was to be unethical as an illegal
gambler, held the gaming profession to a new corporate standard. No
one from the first generation of Las Vegas gaming executives could have
passed without the application of considerable political influence, dem-
onstrating the shift to corporate capital and power. The cowboys of the
county commission did not get even, as the film *Casino* suggests; they
had no such pretension. They simply behaved as colonials around the
globe do and moved on from that source of capital and power to the
next, more powerful source. In the process, they used the tools of political power to reshape the nature of gaming in Nevada, moving it away
from career gamers and tainted Teamsters' capital and toward more
conventional sources.[39]

There were still problems with access to conventional capital for casino development in Las Vegas. Throughout the 1970s, large national
banks continued to shy away from Las Vegas, even after the Hilton
Corporation purchased the Flamingo and Kerkorian built the MGM
Grand, after taking over MGM Studios in California. Only the legalization of casino gambling in Atlantic City and the large profits that
investors raked in persuaded East Coast and California banks that Las
Vegas might be a legitimate place in which to invest. Through the aus-
pices of the Del Webb Company, the Sahara received $135 million from
New York banks for improvements to the resort. It was $10 million
more than requested. At about the same time, Aetna Insurance Company
loaned Caesars World, the parent corporation of Caesars Palace, $60
million. Soon afterward, First Interstate Bank began to develop a sizable
casino and gaming loan portfolio. By 1980, the five dominant gaming
organizations in Nevada, Harrah's, the MGM, Del Webb, the Hilton,
and Caesars World, were all publicly held corporations.[40]

Given the nearly unlimited capital that public financing could potentially generate, Las Vegas was again transformed. Two visionary entrepreneurs, Kirk Kerkorian, who sold his interests and departed Las Vegas
in the mid 1980s, but returned even more grandiosely a few years later,
and Steve Wynn, who raised the ante of casino financing, laid the basis
for the reinvention of a new and presumably competition-proof Las Vegas. Their genius lay in seeing the possibilities that the broadening of
access to capital provided. Large-scale funding meant that Las Vegas
could become more than a mecca of glitz and excess; as its capital came
from the mainstream, its attractions could be shaped to the tastes of the

mainstream audience. The gradual easing of the stigma on gaming and the willingness to meld gaming with conventional postwar attractions on the scale of Disneyland meant broader reach for Las Vegas. Not only did people who wanted to gamble come to the transformed desert town, so did people who wanted to see the spectacle and enjoy a vacation. Sin City became more palatable and maybe marginally even less sinful.

The two catalysts were typical of the breed of entrepreneurs that built Las Vegas. As the apocryphal story goes, Wynn was a protégé of E. Parry Thomas, who had parlayed a small share of a casino and a liquor distributorship into the purchase of the only piece of land that Howard Hughes ever sold, a parking lot next to Caesars Palace. Wynn sold the property, netting a $766,000 profit, enough to let him buy a sufficient stake in the downtown Golden Nugget to develop a controlling interest. By June 1973, he was running the Golden Nugget as vice president. In 1978, Wynn bought into Atlantic City, securing the backing of the financier (and later convicted felon) Michael Milken and the Wall Street firm of Drexel Burnham Lambert. Before the end of the decade, Wynn had made his casino the most profitable in Atlantic City and secured his ties to a major source of development capital. He had also built a tower on the Golden Nugget in Las Vegas and begun to plan to take it upscale.[41]

By the early 1980s, Wynn had larger plans. Milken, who had had dealings with Wynn since the latter's entry into the Atlantic City market in the late 1970s, was the obvious source of capital. In 1989, Wynn opened the $630 million Mirage resort, adding the dimension of fantasy embodied in its title in a new and spectacular way at a cost of $500 million more than any previous casino resort. Through Milken and Drexel Burnham Lambert, Golden Nugget, Inc., the parent company of Wynn's enterprises, borrowed $535.1 million to finance the Mirage, in what observers of the financial markets called "a work of art." The money came from junk bonds sold through Milken. Wynn's equity came from the sale of the Nugget in Atlantic City. With "fantasy become reality" as a theme, and a volcano kept cool by water in a desert locale, the Mirage embodied the essence of what Las Vegas could offer a tourist: it invented a reality that only rarely required the suspension of disbelief. Siegfried and Roy and their famed white tigers were part of this ambience, as were dolphins, and, later, the Cirque du Soleil. In the process, Drexel Burnham Lambert became the dominant financial force in Nevada gaming. By 1989, the $2.57 billion invested through the firm in the Silver State represented as many as 100,000 new Nevada jobs during the 1980s. No less a financial luminary than E. Parry Thomas recognized the impact; in 1989, he told a reporter that "Milken has been the primary mover [in Nevada] for the last several years." In a nod to the difficulties of acquiring capital before corporate gaming, Wynn referred to Milken's influence as being on a par with that of Thomas during the 1960s and 1970s.[42]

Kerkorian continued to set new standards with his plans for the second MGM Grand hotel and theme park, complete with an Emerald City and Wizard of Oz motif, which was first announced in the late 1980s. After selling out to Bally's in 1986, Kerkorian began to contemplate a return to Nevada gaming. His $594 million arrangement with Bally's forbade him to use the MGM name in Nevada for three years. In 1987, Kerkorian had bought the Sands and Desert Inn hotels from Hughes's Summa Corporation, and in early 1988, the Sands became the MGM Sands. Within a year, however, Kerkorian had sold the hotel to the casino impresario Henri Lewin. By 1989, he planned a full-fledged return and began to put the financing together for a new resort of unparalleled proportions. After selling MGM-UA to Turner Communications, run by Ted Turner, for $1.5 billion, Kerkorian had the capital to finance his newest endeavor. A sale of $140 million of stock in his parent MGM Grand, Inc., reduced his holding in the company from 98 to 72 percent and allowed the financing of what became the MGM Grand. By the time it was completed, the cost approached $1 billion.[43]

As gaming spread, Wynn, Kerkorian, William Bennett of Circus Circus, and others in Las Vegas recast the town as a family entertainment resort. The exotic themes of earlier resorts—the Dunes and its Sahara Sultan motif, the Tropicana's Cuban decor, Caesars Palace and its Greco-Roman theme, the Rio and its "Carnival" theme, and others— were replaced by an iconography derived from popular culture and directed at younger people. The opening of the Grand Slam Canyon at Circus Circus, the Luxor, Wynn's Treasure Island resort, and the MGM Grand in 1993 signaled a new Las Vegas, designed to appeal to adults and young people alike and eager to continue the adaptable traditions of its past. "This is part of a major metamorphosis in Las Vegas," Mayor Jan Laverty Jones said when the MGM plan debuted. "Las Vegas is changing from just adult entertainment to a resort destination.[44] Sin City was hardly sinful any more; as it had so often done before, Las Vegas had obliterated its past in its ongoing search to fulfill the desires of the

American and international public. Its unparalleled malleability made it once again timeless, always chameleonlike and supple, always prepared to reinvent itself as it catered to a broadened and different audience.

In a 1994 cover story, *Time* magazine declared that Las Vegas had become an All-American city, the new typical American home town. The rest of the nation had become more like its capital of sin, *Time* averred, arguing that there had been a convergence between Las Vegas and the rest of the nation and assigning Las Vegas a leading role in the service economy that has become, for better and worse, the future of the nation.[45] What the magazine failed to note was that at the same time that the rest of the nation had become more like Las Vegas, Las Vegas had become more like the rest of the nation. As the nation moved toward a service economy, the advantages of Las Vegas seemed more and more apparent. In this mecca of gaming, unskilled individuals with high school education levels could still earn a middle-class income. The Culinary Union helped keep wages high, and some hotels, most notably the second MGM, were willing to pay higher than union wages and provide better than contract benefits in order to discourage unionization by employees. Las Vegas had become like the Detroit of the 1950s in the way it provided solid pay for unspecialized work; for anyone with a modicum of skill and grace, it was an easy place to do well in service positions.

The transformation was completed by the way in which the Las Vegas experience became ordinary. By the 1990s, ITT-Sheraton, Hilton, and other major hotel chains owned big casino-hotels. Graduates of the Wharton Business School made decisions. The new hierarchy of the gaming industry resembled that of the army. Special training was essential for leaders. There was even a glass ceiling in gaming. No longer could dealers work their way off the floor to management positions. In the large resorts, the upward mobility that being "connected" had assured during the reign of organized crime disappeared. Pit boss was now as high as a dealer or floor worker could expect to go. The management positions were filled by MBAs, professional businesspeople, who although they did not repeat Howard Hughes's mistakes, also did not truly understand the gaming industry. The personal side of gaming, the floor manager who recognized and took care of patrons, had become scarce. Gaming had become an industry just like any other.

Although still a colony, Las Vegas had begun to have more in common with the rest of the nation. It depended on the same sources of capital that other communities did and had become subject to many of the same rules and regulations. It was not only that the rest of the nation had normalized the Las Vegas lifestyle, had become more like the center of gaming, cheap sex, and easy living; in the locations of its power, in its hierarchy and distribution of wealth and status, in the stratification of its labor force, Las Vegas had become more like the rest of the nation as well. The transformation of gaming and tourism had truly become a two-way street.

NOTES

1. Nicholas Pileggi, *Casino: Love and Honor in Las Vegas* (New York: Simon & Schuster, 1995), 11–12, 322–25, tells the story of the car bombing. Pileggi attributes the line "This was the last time . . . and we fucked it up," spoken by Santoro-Spilotro in the film, to Spilotro's henchman Frank Cullotta (ibid., 348).

2. Immanuel M. Wallerstein defines colonialism in *The Modern World-System: Capitalist Agriculture and the Origins of the European World-Economy in the Sixteenth Century* (New York: Academic Press, 1974); *The Capitalist World-Economy: Essays* (New York: Cambridge University Press, 1979); *The Modern World-System II: Mercantilism and the Consolidation of the European World-Economy, 1600–1750* (New York: Academic Press, 1980); and *Geopolitics and Geoculture: Essays on the Changing World-System* (New York: Cambridge University Press, 1991).

3. Stephen Brill, *The Teamsters* (New York: Simon & Schuster, 1978), 22–24.

4. Eugene P. Moehring, *Resort City in the Sunbelt: Las Vegas, 1930–1970* (Reno: University of Nevada Press, 1989), 6–12.

5. Ibid., 13–20.

6. Richard Lowitt, *The New Deal in the West* (Bloomington: Indiana University Press, 1984).

7. Russell R. Elliott with William D. Rowley, *History of Nevada,* 2d ed. (Lincoln: University of Nebraska Press, 1987), 248, 275–85; Joseph Stevens, *Hoover Dam* (Norman: University of Oklahoma Press, 1988).

8. Elliott with Rowley, *History of Nevada,* 310; Richard W. Mingus, "Breakdown in the Broker State: The CIO in Southern Nevada during World War II" (M.A. thesis, University of Nevada, Las Vegas, 1995).

9. Moehring, *Resort City,* 31–40; Elliott with Rowley, *History of Nevada,* 313.

10. Ed Reid and Ovid Demaris, *The Green Felt Jungle* (New York: Trident Press, 1963), 14–34; Ralph Pearl, *Las Vegas Is My Beat* (Seacaucus, N.J.: Lyle Stuart, 1973), 23–33; Moehring, *Resort City,* 13–23; John Findlay, *People of Chance* (New York: Oxford University Press, 1986), 136–45; Hal Rothman, "Selling the Meaning of Place: Tourism, Entrepreneurship, and Community

Transformation in the Twentieth-Century American West," *Pacific Historical Review*, 525–58; Robert Lacey, *Little Man: Meyer Lansky and the Gangster Life* (Boston: Little, Brown, 1991), 150–51.

11. Jerome H. Skolnick, *House of Cards: The Legalization and Control of Casino Gambling* (Boston: Little, Brown, 1978), 111–12; Burton B. Turkus and Sid Feder, *Murder, Inc.: The Story of "The Syndicate"* (New York: Farrar, Straus and Young, 1951).

12. Reid and Demaris, *Green Felt Jungle*, 24–26.

13. Ibid., 61–70; Moehring, *Resort City*, 74–77, 83–85; Peter Wiley and Robert Gottlieb, *Empires in the Sun: The Rise of the New American West* (New York: Putnam, 1982), 194–96. Skolnick, *House of Cards*, 124–33, details the federal and state response to the skimming that characterized these resorts.

14. Wiley and Gottlieb, *Empires in the Sun*, 197; Lacey, *Little Man*, 298; Skolnick, *House of Cards*, 127–31. Reid and Demaris, *Green Felt Jungle*, 233–42, provides a list of registered Las Vegas casino owners in 1963. A glance shows significant representation by members of organized crime and their associates.

15. Wiley and Gottlieb, *Empires in the Sun*, 195; Pearl, *Las Vegas Is My Beat*.

16. Skolnick, *House of Cards*, 115–16, 127–31; Lacey, *Little Man*, 299–300; Moehring, *Resort City*, 132–35, 238.

17. Lacey, *Little Man*, 294–301; Reid and DeMaris, *Green Felt Jungle*, 31–35.

18. Wiley and Gottlieb, *Empires in the Sun*, 198.

19. Moehring, *Resort City*, 115–16, 244–45.

20. Steven Brill, *The Teamsters* (New York: Simon & Schuster, 1978), 22–24; Wiley and Gottlieb, *Empires in the Sun*, 197–200; Reid and Demaris, *Green Felt Jungle*, 98–101.

21. Brill, *Teamsters*, 208.

22. Reid and Demaris, *Green Felt Jungle*, 62–63, 100–04; Moehring, *Resort City*, 242–43; Brill, *Teamsters*, 208.

23. Moehring, *Resort City*, 238–41.

24. Ibid., 116–18; Brill, *Teamsters*, 210.

25. Moehring, *Resort City*, 119.

26. Skolnick, *House of Cards*, 113–18, 122; Moehring, *Resort City*, 55; Ronald A. Farrell and Carole Case, *The Black Book and the Mob: The Untold Story of the Control of Nevada's Casinos* (Madison: University of Wisconsin Press, 1995).

27. Skolnick, *House of Cards*, 140–41; Moehring, *Resort City*, 55.

28. Moehring, *Resort City*, 118–19; Skolnick, *House of Cards*, 134–37; Wiley and Gottlieb, *Empires in the Sun*, 201–3; Donald Bartlett and James Steele, *Empire: The Life, Legend, and Madness of Howard Hughes* (New York: Norton, 1976).

29. *Nevada Report* 1, 1 (July 15, 1969): 2; Skolnick, *House of Cards*, 134.

30. Lacey, *Little Man*, 299–301; Skolnick, *House of Cards*, 139–40.

31. David Spanier, *Welcome to the Pleasuredome: Inside Las Vegas* (Reno: University of Nevada Press, 1992), 35–38, 95–96, 135–66; Elliott, *History of Nevada*, 333–36; Moehring, *Resort City*, 86–87, 243–44; Howard Stutz and

David Finnigan, "New Resort to Open Door for Union," *Las Vegas Review-Journal,* May 12, 1989, A1: 5.

32. Vern Willis, "Kerkorian Has Played Major Role in LV Success," *Las Vegas Review-Journal,* January 23, 1983, J3–5; Skolnick, *House of Cards,* 142–45; Moehring, *Resort City,* 120–22.

33. Pileggi, *Casino,* 120–33, gives Glick's ex post facto account; Brill, *Teamsters,* 232–37; *Mob on the Run* documentary, Channel 3 News, Las Vegas, 1987.

34. Skolnick, *House of Cards,* 206–21, offers the most analytical account; see also Pileggi, *Casino,* 175–215; Brill, *Teamsters,* 232–37; *Mob on the Run.*

35. Pileggi, *Casino,* 224–36; *Mob on the Run.*

36. *Casino.*

37. *Mob on the Run.*

38. Skolnick, *House of Cards,* 172–75; Reid and Demaris, *Green Felt Jungle,* 172–85.

39. Wiley and Gottlieb, *Empires in the Sun,* 204–6, is the best description of efforts to use regulatory powers to divest mobsters of their position in Las Vegas; see also Skolnick, *House of Cards,* 135–45.

40. Robert Macy, "Kirk Kerkorian Still Very Bullish on Vegas," *Las Vegas Review-Journal,* April 24, 1986, D1–2; Wiley and Gottlieb, *Empires in the Sun,* 206–9.

41. Jack E. Sheehan, "Milken Gives Wynn Key to Atlantic City," *Las Vegas Sun,* March 13, 1989, 1A-2A; Howard Stutz, "Drexel Paved Path of Gaming in 1980s," *Las Vegas Review-Journal,* February 12, 1989, 1B–2B; Fen Montaigne, "What Makes Steve Wynn a Winner?" ibid., November 13, 1983, 4L–5L, 14L–15L; Sergio Lalli, "Wynn Plans Big Hotel on the Strip," ibid., October 30, 1986, A1: 1–4; Sergio Lalli, "Wynn Envisions New Magic on the Strip," ibid., March 1, 1987, B1: 3; Sergio Lalli, "Wynn Unveils Plans for Strip Resort," ibid., May 28, 1987, B1: 1; "Planning Board to Review Wynn Resort," ibid., June 16, 1987, B2: 4; Ed Vogel, "Wynn Applauds Las Vegas as Worldwide Vacation Spot," ibid., November 20, 1987, B1: 5; Howard Stutz, "Steve Wynn's New Mirage Resort No Optical Illusion," ibid., December 10, 1988, B1: 2; Howard Stutz, "Mirage License Clears Hurdle," ibid., October 12, 1989, B1: 6; Ed Vogel, "Gaming Commission Grants License to Wynn to Operate the Mirage," ibid., October 27, 1989, B5: 1; Robert Macy, "Here's a Peek Inside the Mirage," ibid., October 29, 1989, A1: 2; Howard Stutz, "The Mirage to Become Reality," ibid., November 20, 1989, B1: 2; Howard Stutz, "The Mirage Opens Doors to Public, Special Guests Today," ibid., November 22, 1989, 3B; Howard Stutz, "Thousands Welcome the Mirage," ibid., November 23, 1989, A1: 2; Spanier, *Welcome to the Pleasuredome,* 36–38.

42. Jeff Burbank, "Four White Tigers Resort's First Guests," *Las Vegas Sun,* November 23, 1989, 1A, 5A; Stutz, "Drexel Paved Path of Gaming in 1980s," 1B; Spanier, *Welcome to the Pleasuredome,* 36–38.

43. Spanier, *Welcome to the Pleasuredome,* 17–59; Dial Torgerson, *Kerkorian: An American Success Story* (New York: Dial Press, 1974); Susan Gould, "Kirk Kerkorian," *Signature* 4, no. 9 (September 1969): 1–5; "Kerkorian Ventures Range from Air Charter Service to Movie Theme Park," *Las Vegas Review-*

Journal, October 1, 1989, 8B; Vern Willis, "Kerkorian Has Played a Major Role in LV Success," ibid., January 23, 1983, J3; "MGM Grand Inc. Earns $6.2 Million Profit in '88," ibid., March 22, 1989, C7; Howard Stutz, "Kerkorian Poised for Vegas Return," ibid., October 1, 1989, B1: 2; Ed Vogel, "Panel OKs Kerkorian's Plan to Sell Stock to Finance Park," ibid., October 27, 1989, 5B; Howard Stutz, "MGM Cleared for Marina Takeover," ibid., December 7, 1989, B1: 2; Howard Stutz, "Gamers Approve Kerkorian Deal," ibid., December 22, 1989, B1; Jay Greene, "Kerkorian: Mysterious and Rich," *Las Vegas Sun,* April 8, 1991, B4; Lynn Waddell, "Again, Kerkorian Operates on a Grand Scale," ibid., October 7, 1991, A1; Lynn Waddell, "MGM Gets Big Boost," ibid., May 16, 1991, A1; Lynn Waddell, "MGM Financing Nearly Complete," ibid., April 7, 1992, A1.

44. Lynn Waddell, "Shot in the Arm: MGM Viewed as Possible Recession-Buster," *Las Vegas Sun,* October 8, 1991, A1; Dan Njegomir, "New Resort Proposed for Southern End of the Strip," *Las Vegas Review-Journal,* September 23, 1988, B1: 2; Howard Stutz, "Success under the Big Top," ibid., November 11, 1989, 1B, 4B, 5B; Vern Willis, "Circus Circus, with Profitable History, Looks Good for Future," ibid., December 22, 1991; R. E. Tammariello, "Grand Slam Canyon Plans Unveiled," ibid., August 27, 1992, 1A, 3A; Lynn Waddell, "It's a Wonder: Circus Circus to Build Grand Slam Canyon, *Las Vegas Sun,* August 27, 1992, 1A, 7A; Cy Ryan, "LV Key to Nevada Economy," ibid., January 31, 1993, D1; Mike Weatherford, "The Adventure Begins: New Grand Slam Canyon Offers Thrills and Chills," ibid., August 22, 1993, 1J–8J; Jeff Rubio, "Las Vegas: A Sure Bet for the Entire Family," *Hemisphere,* August 1993, 119–21; Spanier, *Welcome to the Pleasuredome,* 83–85, 99–101; analysis of the major hotels and their themes courtesy of Gene Moehring.

45. Kurt Andersen, "Las Vegas, U.S.A.," *Time,* January 10, 1994, 42–51.

Who Puts the "Sin" in "Sin City" Stories?
Girls of Grit and Glitter in the City of Women

Those who fail to reread are doomed to read the same story everywhere.

Roland Barthes, *S/Z*

The Universe isn't made of atoms, it's made of stories.

Café bathroom graffiti

INTRODUCTION: THE PARADOX

Las Vegas is a city of stories. Stories of a lush green valley in the desert with little more than a ranch and a railroad stop that was turned into the world's most notorious twentieth-century city; celebrity stories about Bugsy Siegel, Frank Sinatra, and Elvis; origin stories about the birth of a neon resort dreamland from the vice-ridden loins of the mob; stories of decadence, delirious riches, and debt; fantasy stories of love, lust, and loss; old stories about money, sex, power, and artifice, all are intimately interconnected with new stories of families, suburban growth, Little League sports, churches, and tradition building. All of these and countless other tales are woven together to form the delicate fabric of a community. Las Vegas is a culture full of exuberant and exhausted tourists, visionary creators building fame from the gritty sandbox of the Mojave Desert, and immigrants, who settle here at the astounding rate of 6,000 per month in search of a new script for the story of their lives.

Las Vegas is the classic tourist town with a twist: namely, there is little that is classic about it. Neither city nor country, it is all simulation along the Strip and all suburbs around it. It is an urban landscape whose history is cinematic and entertaining: we know Las Vegas because of its legends, and its lore is its lure. The two words—Las Vegas—traditionally connote images of big-time gangsters, the Rat Pack, the "ching-ching" of slot machines loosening up for lucky players, swank cabarets and shows, and the favorite local pet: lounge lizards. The surface of this city space is smooth and alluring in its unique decadence. It is the new land of promise and possibility, where taking a gamble is more normative than deviant.

In this simulated world, the childishly innocuous term "gaming" has replaced "gambling," with its connotations of vice. Sex is entertainment, another commodity to be bought. Everyone is beautiful under the neon lights. The desert landscape is watered and dotted with imported flowers; palm trees are transplanted from Central America. Anything appears possible. No street in the world imports more delicacies than Las Vegas Boulevard, the Strip. From every corner of the earth, exotic vegetables, meats, cheeses, drinks, spices, and fruits travel to the heart of Las Vegas. The four corners of Tropicana and Las Vegas Boulevards are said to have more hotel rooms than the entire city of San Francisco. In this version of Las Vegas, everything is bigger than life: the buildings, the extravagance, the characters, and the stories.

Coexisting with this is a social environment characterized by the largest tourist-based service economy, the most highly organized and unionized service workers, and the fastest-growing residential community in the country. As the title of this anthology suggests, there is grit beneath the glitter, and an unassuming urban and suburban culture amid the grit. This is the invisible Las Vegas: the city that sleeps, the community that votes and builds and educates and grows and does all the mundane things that individuals, families, and communities do all across the country. There is a twist: this quotidian experience is enacted daily in the shadow of the Las Vegas neon, and billboards, slot machines even in grocery stores, and well over a hundred pages of listings for private entertainers and strippers in the city's yellow pages swamp the residential landscape with the values and images of the tourist culture of Las Vegas.

Las Vegas sits at a crossroad between these two worlds. The city nestles uncomfortably between at least these two different realities: on the one hand, it is a typical southwestern Sunbelt city, with its familiar pastel architecture, strip malls, suburban sprawl, and influx of opportunity seekers; on the other, it is a mold-breaking carnivalesque hub of gambling, sex, and entertainment. This tourist side of Las Vegas is itself multifaceted. There is the glimmering vacation getaway and conference destination of tourist brochures and convention bureau ads, and there is the harsh and gritty reality of vice and addiction that comes with this 24/7 town. From *The Green Felt Jungle, Fear and Loathing in Las Vegas,* and countless other literary excursions into the heart of Las Vegas darkness, to *Ocean's Eleven,* the Beavis and Butthead movie, and a tantalizing array of films made in and about Las Vegas, the stories of this city are replete with as much glamour, glitz, and glitter as grit, gore, and guts. It is a sparkling wonderland at the surface, but the enigmatic magic of Las Vegas works because of persistent hints of a dark and dangerous underbelly that lures the lascivious and titillates the dreamer and the voyeur.

In its persistent contradiction, Las Vegas is a playground of paradox, a collection of stories that merit reading and rereading if one hopes to generate a new understanding of the complexity of this city. One such rereading is a closer inspection of the production and consumption of "sin" in "Sin City": legalized and extravagant gaming, legal brothel prostitution in rural counties outside of Las Vegas, and plentiful illegal prostitution within the city, all meld together to construct the Sin City façade. While gaming receives exorbitant amounts of attention and analysis, the sexual economy of "sin" in Las Vegas has garnered less serious consideration. This is the story I want to tell about Vegas.

This Las Vegas is a city clothed in its lights, its architecture, and its vibrant and miraculous sanctuary-like splendor; beneath these sheaths is the fleshy seduction of the body of the city. The curves of its underbelly fattened by the coffers of gambling, its moist breath warmed by the heat of desire and fanned by a burgeoning sex industry, and the adrenaline heartbeat pulsing to the rhythm of showgirl revues and high-tech production shows. This is the postcard Las Vegas, where the suburban sprawl of communities is little more than glimmering lights around the glowing Strip in a standard nighttime photograph, the brightest spot on Earth from outer space, a visual icon of both human ingenuity and vice. In the stories, in the community, in the collective imagination of the world, there are few absolutes about Las Vegas; that it is an enigmatic city whose public persona barely masks a permanent tension between the paradoxes that saturate it may be its only secret truth.

For this reason I liken this touristic, lore-laden Las Vegas to a woman. Despite a long history of being debated, controlled, and examined by science, medicine, psychology, psychoanalysis, the law, and the state, the concept "woman" is unknowable, uncontainable, irreducible, and excessive. One need only travel a short metaphorical distance to move from the notion of the "dark continent of women's sexuality" to the seductive allure of Las Vegas: that which is contradictory, elusive, multifaceted, sensual, and mysterious. At this gendered interface is the lore of Sin City waiting to be reread and retold.

With the phallic grandeur of Bob Stupak's wet-dream casino fantasy, the Stratosphere Tower, situated midway between the heart of Las Vegas Boulevard casino development to the south, and the newly renovated Fremont Street Experience at its northern base, the Strip opens up like a woman's legs straddling the spectacle. All along it, posters, placards, handbills, statues, billboards, and actual bodies of working, walking, and consuming women dot the landscape like holographic reminders of the larger character of the city. And yet the suburbs grow, the number of families and retirees making their homes and building community here expand. A woman as mayor, a woman president of the university, women-owned building and development companies, a woman as state attorney general: mothers, grandmothers, professional women, these models of women flourish here, too, beneath the showgirl billboards, down the road from the adult bookstores and strip clubs. And, of course, the showgirls are mothers, suburban wives are strippers, and unionized culinary workers, cocktail waitresses and maids are grandmothers: this is a world of women, and the lines and categories between sex and suburbs, bad girls and good girls, are endlessly blurred.

It is in this fantasy space between the contradictions of real women's lives and the images of showgirls and strippers that soak up the sunlight of the bright desert and turn it into a dimly lit eroticized zone, that the new script of my life, the Vegas chapter, unfolds. I was just another girl amid the grit and glitter, trying to build a career and make a life like all the other immigrants to this enigmatic metropolis. My story is twofold: it is the tale of my personal transformation within this ironic funhouse of a city and of my professional emergence as a sex industry researcher and theorist. In the process of writing and rereading these personal vignettes, I want to tell a slightly different story that is bigger than my own: a story of Vegas as a city of women, replete with "girls" doing the gritty work and wearing the glitter that makes this playground possible.

THE GRIT: ONE "GIRL"'S STORY

As a new bottle-blonde by choice, I was beginning a critical feminist ethnography of my body as a cultural site in the late summer of 1995 as I moved between the East and West coasts to start an academic career in a town scarcely known for its avant garde intellectual culture. I was moving to the state with the lowest percentage of high school students going on to college; to a community where collegiate basketball trophies are the holy grail; where castles and pyramids sit side by side down the gold-paved road from an erupting volcano and a live action buccaneer battle that ends with a barrage of cannon fire, plumes of smoke, and fully costumed sailors tumbling into the water as the perfectly simulated British ship sinks into the abyss in front of the hotel-casino complex. This is a pirate's town; everyone is searching for a treasure, and none of them are hidden in Umberto Eco's books or on the shelves of wonderful old libraries. Nonetheless, here I was embarking on a new life adventure as an academic in this deliciously lowbrow city.

With these and a thousand other thoughts racing through my mind, my little red car lurched along the curves of the road, through the dark night, into the Vegas valley, a jet-black canvas splashed with Jackson Pollock–like neon designs. Sin City engulfed me like a tsunami. Around a treacherous bend on the side of a desert mountain, the valley below was suddenly awash in a hazy glow. My pulse quickened, like Poe's telltale heart on speed. The normal tick-tock of my pulse vibrating in my veins, rumbling through my body, suddenly felt like a tribal drum pounding an unfamiliar rhythm: "I live here? I live here."

The city looked as though it was built within rigid boundaries: the pulsing fluorescent and neon lights were packed in, and then it simply ended. The edge wasn't soft; there was no gradual fading of lights indicating breathing space between built environs. It was simply an explosion of light and life, and then it stopped, like an invisible wall encircling the city, with the harsh, dark oblivion of the desert mountains on all sides. I had the distinct feeling that I was landing in a brave new world. It was an epiphanic moment; I could feel my life changing inside me, as if the process of adapting to this space had somehow already begun. It was as if I was at the top of the first great peak on a roller coaster about to plunge down the tracks—too fast and too steep to let the scream escape from the constricted chamber of my throat. My red car dipped with the shoulderless mountain road, and the bounce jolted me to my senses. I was on the edge of possibility staring into the impossible: 1.2 million residents and a world of tourists in the middle of the Mojave Desert.

My only prior visit to the city had been five months before, when I flew in for my job interview at the university. The plane was struck by lightning about half an hour outside of the city, but we landed smoothly, with a rainbow stretching across the sky: a plane full of tourists cheering about the pot of gold at the end of the rainbow. Mine came in the form of a set of prescription medication bottles after getting so sick that I passed out during my job interview. It was not an auspicious beginning. At 2:30 A.M. on my second night in town, sitting in a hotel room whose walls, carpet, bedding, and curtains were thoroughly saturated with stale cigarette smoke from the thousands of gamblers who had rested if not taken solace here before, I realized that my fever was soaring. I needed aspirin or Ibuprofen, and for the first time I appreciated the fact that I was sitting in the belly of the 24-hour beast: surely I could find a gift shop open in the hotel casino. Wearing shorts and a tank top that I had packed for sleepwear, my blonde hair swept into a messy ponytail, and with a fever-flushed face and flu-weary eyes, I descended upon the lobby with my room key in one hand and a five dollar bill in the other. It was closed. "So much for the city that never sleeps," I thought. I was directed to walk through the parking lot, diagonally across the first busy street I hit, and into one of the countless 7–11 convenience stores dotting most every intersection in the city.

It was dark; I was sick, dizzy, and exhausted. The parking lot was mostly empty, and a patch of scraggly desert littered with garbage stretched out next to it. Despite the neon mega-resorts just a block away, I felt alone and vulnerable. I crossed the street without the benefit of a stoplight, because the nearest one was a long block away; this required darting cautiously around cars careening at seemingly outrageous speeds. I heard honks; and a loud deep voice yell something; and a "whoooooeeeeee" catcall from a car going in the other direction.

It felt as though I had stumbled into a foreign world when I opened the door to the brightly lit store. It was crowded, especially for the middle of the night. Everyone looked like a character out of a pulp fiction detective novel, and I giggled about my first real Vegas moment. It wasn't until a minute or two later that I realized just how "Vegas" an experience this was: the tall, paunchy, chalky-faced man behind the counter stared blankly at me when I asked for aspirin or Tylenol. He shook his head woefully as he reached behind him to grab the bottle, then held it in front of me so that I had to reach up and out to get it from him. I thought it odd when I caught a glimpse of the young man behind me in line in a stainless steel reflection behind the counter. He was staring at me, looking me up and down, and chuckling. I turned, startled. He looked away laughing, and the clerk said in a slow, low voice, "Do you want me to call somebody for you? Are you okay?" "Yeah, I just have the flu. I'm here on a job interview at the university and this sucks. How much for the aspirin?" The man behind me laughed out loud, and the clerk told me to be really careful. "Are you sure you don't want me to call the cops or something? You're in bad shape."

It hit me so hard I gasped, blushed, and raged inside my head in the same instant: they all thought I was a prostitute. As I walked out of the store, an old man with a big bottle of beer asked leeringly and jokingly, "How much tonight, baby?" The catcalls from cars made sense, the looks from the clerk and other customer made sense, the city suddenly made sense, everything made sense in a burning instant except one thing: I didn't make sense to myself. How had I, a young but serious grad student, whose biggest concern was presenting herself as a legitimate academic at the job interview, come here and ended up with a flu that transformed me in the eyes of the streets and the city into an entirely different kind of working girl?

It took two and a half weeks after moving to Vegas, for reasons wholly unrelated to the tourist economy or sex industry, for me to be propositioned once again. Sitting in my red car at an intersection, I felt the burn of eyes on the side of my face and glanced at the car next to me. A clean-cut middle-aged man was cranking his fist in a circle in a signal for me to roll down my window. I did, noting the arid early September heat and the politeness of this fellow citizen, who, I speculated, would be asking for directions or informing me of a need for air in one of my tires. Instead, he yelled, "How much?" I felt my head cock sideways just a bit as I wondered why he cared how much my car cost. "Huh?" He repeated his question with a lascivious grin and a chuckle. I recognized the laugh from the man outside the 7–11. Blond hair. Youngish woman. Red car. A mile from Las Vegas Boulevard. At a red light half a block from the "Palomino All Nude Dance Club" billboard. The equation was as simple as 1–2–3: I must be for sale. It began to make sense, and I began to make sense of myself in this city.

Two months later, there was a major electronics convention. The city was swamped with conventioneers, and even the nightly news did a piece on the crowds at restaurants and strip clubs. I was at a red light at the intersection next to campus when it happened again. This time the line was, "Hey, do you work?" from a man with a plastic-covered badge still stuck to his plaid shirt, driving a rental car. I had only rolled my window down because I assumed he was lost and in need of directions. Wrong again. This time, though, the response in my head was different.

I decided, for certain, then and there, to start studying the sex industry. I didn't choose it; the industry and Sin City chose me.

It chooses all women, really. In my new role, trying to make sense of the contradictions of femininity and sexuality in Las Vegas, I frequented strip clubs, adult stores, S&M shops, and even a swingers' club. With my colleague Barb Brents, another feminist faculty member, who had been living and thinking about these Vegas issues for eight years, I visited legal brothels and spoke to local officials and insiders about illegal prostitution. What became evident was that the culture of sex that sells the lore of Sin City inevitably sexualizes its inhabitants, especially women. From the revered and legendary showgirls, many of whom perform topless, to the strip club dancers, Internet porn stars, and prostitutes of every ilk, the "sin" of Sin City takes the shape of a woman's body with a price tag.

These same women leave their work and stand in line unobtrusively at the grocery store, the bank, along the first base line at the Little League game, or waiting to get into church. They are mothers, students, activists, wives, voters, moviegoers. And women who don't work the gritty jobs that fuel the Sin City coffers, from professors to waitresses, from business women to cleaning ladies, from poor women to suburban wives, are always subject to the undressing assumption that they might be, or must have been, an entirely different kind of working woman. Some signs of femininity and sexuality—red cars, lipstick, and dresses; blonde hair; high heels; even just simply jeans and a T-shirt on a woman's body—become nearly universal symbols of sex for sale. The evanescent and evolving realities of Las Vegas lend themselves to this kind of Möbius loop femininity: every woman may be a sex worker, and sex workers are every woman. In the paradox playground of Sin City, the vice isn't the reality; it is the seductive illusion that anything is possible. And, where anything is possible, every woman may be a "working girl."

THE GLITTER: "SIN CITY" SEX?

Girls wear the glitter in Las Vegas. Actually, maybe the glitter wears the girls. From thirty pounds of sparkling costuming adorning the bodies of showgirls to the glitzy uniforms of cocktail waitresses, the sexy and sparkling clothes worn briefly between sets by strippers, and the women of Caesars Palace who are literally sown into their costumes at the start of each shift, it is the shimmering fantasy space of women's bodies that secures the image of Las Vegas as opulent and high-energy. Sure, the neon, the glimmering chandeliers, the intricately designed carpets, and detailed decor that swallows visitors upon entry into the clockless, white-noise-laden space of casinos helps to make the city glamorous. But it is the moving, floating, all-pervasive presence of sexy and glamorous women that transforms intense interior decorating into a more visceral and immediate reality. And yet even the glitter-clad women are mere surfaces, costumed and playing a part in the scripted stories of Las Vegas.

Behind the sequined scenes is a different reality. Las Vegas's glitter barely covers the grit, not unlike the miles of hidden tunnels full of costume shops, heavy machinery, and exhausted workers that make Disney Land/World into the family fantasy space that it is. Pawnshops, trailer parks, urban ghettos, suburban slums, homelessness, and bail bondsmen all give peeks into other sides of the Las Vegas experience. For example, an accountant who is being sexually harassed by her boss and does not earn as much as her colleagues tells me about "reading" men to gauge who will give her the most tips tonight in the strip club, where her business suit is replaced by a shiny gown, which she will slink out of for the next guy who gives her $25.

Other glances behind the glitter would reveal complex lives as well. A curious voyeur may peek behind the scenes at the young mother who wears a simple white underwear set ("It doesn't matter, it's coming off anyway," she says plainly) with lots of sparkly makeup on her eyes and cheeks. She is a dancer and strips nude on a stage at a peek show on Las Vegas Boulevard; between sets, she types feverishly on a computer terminal hooked up to a video camera working an online paid Internet site where she writes provocative notes to interested netters, e-mails them a photo of herself to preview, and then secures their credit card number before stripping nude and writhing in a little cushioned cubicle for them through the computer. This young woman goes home after ten hours of this double-work life to a husband she believes is her soul mate, and to a daughter she dreams will go to college to avoid the hard work of this, her mother's, life. There is the mature phone sex worker who met her current husband "at work" and who bakes cookies for her grandchildren while she tantalizes her clients with hushed whispers and moans through the telephone line. Or, the single mother who spends a month of her summer allegedly camping and traveling through the Southwest while her child visits her dad, when she is really working as a prostitute in a licensed brothel in Nevada to make money to finish cosmetology school. A cocktail waitress at a gentleman's club goes to law school during the day; a sociology undergraduate starts her own Internet sex business on the side; and a welfare mother works the streets at the end of every month to support her family.

Despite these scenes of high-gloss glitz and hard-edged grit, Las Vegas is not really best described as Sin City, if by sin we mean access to sex. While this city is the symbolic center of the American sex industry and famous for the array of illicit delights it offers tourists, conventioneers, and locals, it is neither particularly sexually libertine in its culture nor expansive in the number of adult businesses it contains, relative to the size of the tourist and residential population. Sin City is an alluring façade, where sexy images and sexualized women are plentiful, but where actual sex and businesses that sell it are rather well hidden and under nearly constant siege by police, local government officials, and licensing agencies.

The shimmer of Las Vegas's aura covers these realities: prostitution exists but is illegal in Las Vegas itself; there are fewer strip clubs here than in several other large American cities (San Francisco, Atlanta, and Houston, to name a few); a local dominatrix had her "dungeon" business closed down on prostitution charges despite the fact that she only sold "discipline," never consummating with sexual contact; and the outcall stripper services are nearly constantly in a court battle over the ability to advertise and exercise their First Amendment rights as legal businesses. If this is a city of sin, real sexually oriented businesses and activities are excluded from a truly bawdy celebration of vice. Without passing normative judgment on whether this is good or bad, it is once again an interesting paradox that the glitter sells the town, the appearance of sin characterizes the city, but the actual sex industry remains on the (no doubt profitable, but still marginalized) periphery of this paradoxical paradise.

CONCLUSION: "GIRLS" IN A CITY OF WOMEN

In a city that depends on the labor of working women for the smooth functioning of its hotel and casino culture and expansive service industry, and that commodifies and glorifies at least one prevailing notion of women's sexuality, it is paradoxical that negative stereotypes of sex workers persist, and the airbrushed fantasy space of typical "Vegas girls" lends itself to a devaluing of all women through their objectification. And yet there are other realities here as well. Like Las Vegas—

diverse, enigmatic, contradictory—the images and roles available to women in this community are plentiful. The multiple realities of gender and of "woman" that are identifiable in Las Vegas open a playful space for envisioning and articulating gender roles and identities that resist the traditional good girl versus bad girl dichotomy. Just as the city continues to grow, implode old casinos and erect new ones, and evolve in its character, the competing histories and identities of this schizophrenic city and the women in it make rereading Sin City, and rewriting the script of gender in the service industry, in the suburban world of strip malls, in the strip clubs and adult industry, and in the urban spaces of fantasy cities, not only possible but inevitable.

Through my own lived experience of Las Vegas, and in incident after enlightening incident doing sex industry research, I began to reexamine the story of Sin City and narrate it differently. I don't do sex work, but I research it: does that make me a type of sex worker? I am just another woman moving about Las Vegas, but I have repeatedly been solicited by total strangers. The lines that blur the "reality" of Las Vegas are even more obscured when it comes to being a woman and enacting femininity and sexuality amid the multiple messages in this city. Sin City is not a town rife with sex, but it is a city that systematically uses women's bodies to sell *everything other than sex*. The hint of sin coded in the very presence of the female form is sufficient to connote vice, intrigue, glamour, and sex: not necessarily in the service of a massive and visible sex industry, but in the service of cultivating a unique tourist experience that sells *potential*.

The ability to consume the image of sexy women, to experience a safe proximity to the "seedy" world of sex, or to purchase a sexual encounter is sufficient; the actual deed is less important than its apparent availability. This is the bottom line: potential, a belief in the possible, is the most valued commodity in a city that defies reality. Dreams fill casinos and hotel rooms and draw exuberant optimists and weary desperados alike. This is the role of the sex industry in Las Vegas: to cultivate a sexualized climate that makes visitors comfortably and seductively aware of their power to purchase these unusual delights, without actually growing into a massive, visible, seedy, highly accessible industry. A contained amount of smut and grit is essential to Vegas culture and lore, especially as it is evidenced through the display of women's bodies and sexuality, but too much defeats the purpose of cultivating an atmosphere of clean, safe, glimmering potential.

Las Vegas is the new exotic: where women sell the city, and "girls" of all ages juggle the complexity of their lived gender experiences within the conflicted context of this gritty and glittering town. If the universe is made of stories, and Las Vegas is made of its lore, it is time to peek behind the veneer and reimagine the scripts of women and sex. I did, and it has permanently changed the plot line of my life. I became a tenure-track professor in Las Vegas, and a woman who takes sex workers seriously. I'm still learning how to live and make sense of the paradoxes here, and of the paradoxes in me that this town emphasizes. Fortunately, Las Vegas has almost as many storytellers and commentators as it does stories, and I continue to learn from them. On one occasion, after I gave a talk on the sex industry in Las Vegas at a conference, a man told me that he loved and hated my new hometown. He went on to explain that it reminds him of his days in Saigon when he was on leave from the army during the Vietnam War. "It was crowded, noisy, full of shops and signs and excitement. You never knew what was going to happen, but you could get anything at all you wanted. Nothing was impossible if you had some money in your pocket. You could buy absolutely anything or anyone."

This is the secret "sin" of Sin City, the invisible magnet of the tourists' playground that is Las Vegas: gluttony, excess, rabid commodification, and, most important, a belief that you can be anyone and can have anything if money is in your pocket or Lady Luck is on your side. Who puts the "sin" in "Sin City"? Girls, women, our bodies, our sexuality: but it is all in the service of selling the image of endless potential, the seductive myth that everyone can be beautiful, glamorous, and have their deepest desires fulfilled, more than it is about actual sex. Even I find myself wanting to believe that this can be the land of opportunity. In this town, Lady Luck herself is the emblem and mascot, and she wears glittery costumes and keeps things sexy. But the real fantasy is bigger than sex: it is success, or at least the temporary fantasy that the world really is your oyster. Here is my Vegas dream, which feels very possible (but I might be seduced just like everyone else by a well-packaged faith in making the impossible probable!): that with a little rereading, the fantasy world of gritty and glitter-clad girls that is Sin City can and will give way to a more deft analysis of Las Vegas as a city of women, full of potential and the possibility of a more diverse, equal, and enlightened model of gender and female sexuality. I'm still working on it, but I'll send a postcard with a pirate's treasure and a showgirl on it when I get there.

WILLIAM N. THOMPSON

Nevada Goes Global

The Foreign Gaming Rule
and the Spread of Casinos

In 1993, I got a call from Jack Binion's secretary asking if I could come to the Horseshoe Casino and meet with him. I said, "Of course," and we set up an appointment. When I met Jack, the son of the legendary Benny Binion and CEO of the Horseshoe, famous for its "World Series of Poker," he told me: "I saw you on that Culinary Union video and I didn't like the way you appeared to be speaking for the union." I said, "If you listened to my words, it was clear I was being neutral on labor issues." He conceded that he could tell that, "but it was obvious they were using you. I didn't like it. You shouldn't have done that." Then he said, "Well, forget about that. I want you to do a job for me. I want to get a casino in Louisiana, and I want you to tell the Louisiana Gaming Board why I should have it." I accepted the assignment, and we discussed the spread of gambling around the country. He suggested that "they" (meaning the Nevada casino industry) had probably screwed up. "We should have gone into Iowa and Colorado and put our money down against the spread of gambling. We would have all been better off just staying in Nevada. It wouldn't have taken much of an effort to stop all of this, but now we got it."

"Now we got it." The Las Vegas casino industry now has competition from casinos in half the states in the United States plus half the provinces of Canada. And now Jack Binion is very happy that casino gambling has spread. He is the proprietor of a leading revenue-producing casino in Louisiana, and also the number one casino in Mississippi. He continues to pursue casino licenses in other jurisdictions. So do Philip Satre, the CEO of Harrah's Casinos, Mirage Casinos' Steve Wynn, and the managements of the Hilton, the MGM-Mirage, Circus Circus, Lady Luck, Stations Casinos, the Boyd Group, and every other large Nevada gaming interest. Now we got it. We didn't want it, but we got it.

This essay looks at two considerations: first, how the Nevada gaming industry became a major participant in the forces spreading casino gambling throughout the United States, and, second, how the spread of gaming into other jurisdictions has affected Nevada.

In 1956, shortly after the Nevada Gaming Control Board was created (in 1955) as a specialized agency within the state Tax Commission, the subject of "foreign gaming" was placed on the decision-making agenda in Nevada. It was first thought that the board should use its discretion in deciding whether a Nevada casino operator could have an outside gaming interest. Gaming Control Board Rule 3.060 of 1956 provided that licensees could not engage in illegal gaming, but that the board would examine requests to be involved in legal gaming elsewhere. After casino control was reorganized and the Control Board was made the enforcement arm of a new Nevada Gaming Commission in 1959, new ideas prevailed. An amended Nevada Gaming Regulation 3.060—referred to as the Foreign Gaming Rule, "foreign" meaning "outside of Nevada"—was adopted. It clearly prohibited Nevada casino licensees from being involved in gaming activities outside of the state. The rule was in appearance absolute, but the commission could allow for exceptions, as in the case of a licensee who already had outside interests and was operating in an acceptable manner.

Regulation 3.060 was adopted in part in response to federal pressure. Indeed, the entire Nevada regulatory structure was set up in the 1950s to assure the federal government that gambling in Nevada could operate without unsavory criminal elements. A U.S. Senate organized crime investigatory committee, under the chairmanship of Tennessee's Senator Estes Kefauver, met in 1950 and 1951 and held televised hearings throughout the United States.

The committee concluded that gambling was the most important economic activity of organized crime in America. Voices in Washington, D.C., actually suggested that all casino gaming be terminated. (As an aside, it is interesting to note that our federal government at the same time was helping Hilton establish a casino in Puerto Rico as part of President Truman's Operation Bootstrap. Congress also permitted U.S. taxpayers' funds to be dispensed to Travemunde, West Germany, to open a casino—as part of the Marshall Plan strategy for getting western Europe "back on its economic feet." These cases are evidence of an ambivalent public attitude toward casino gambling—an ambivalence that continues today.)

While the creation of a specialized Gaming Control Board and independent Nevada Gaming Commission was reassuring to the federal authorities, their probes into Nevada gaming did not end. Arkansas Senator John McClellan chaired another committee investigating organized crime and casting its scornful eye on Nevada. Part of the state's response was the creation of the "Black Book" listing notorious individuals that would be banned from entering any casino in the state. Another response was the Foreign Gaming Rule.

The Foreign Gaming Rule was thought to be necessary to give the federal government an assurance that Nevada operators would not be joining hands with bad people who were outside of the reach of state regulators. There were also concerns that casino operators might commingle funds from Nevada casinos with those from other casinos and somehow become vulnerable to skimming schemes, whereby funds are subtracted from the flows of gaming money without the knowledge of government regulators. Skimming is done to avoid taxes and to give profits to unauthorized (hidden) owners. Additionally, Nevada wanted to guarantee the federal government that our gamers would not be part of the flimflam-type gaming houses proliferating in many parts of the world—stimulated in part by the rush of marginally honest casino operators out of Cuba when Fidel Castro took over that island.

The Foreign Gaming Rule wasn't adopted just for the federal government. Nevada interests also saw advantages in the regulation. As a commission chairman said, "I don't want Nevada operations to be dragged into a bankruptcy because of a licensee's activity somewhere else."

The Foreign Gaming Rule gave comfort to both federal and state authorities, who feared that Nevada casinos might promote campaigns for casino legalization in other jurisdictions. Officials were relieved that Nevada casino owners would not be spreading the "evil effects" of what one sociologist labeled a pariah industry. Nevada officials were also relieved that state casinos would be spared competition with gaming in other parts of the country.

One small break in the rigid application of the Foreign Gaming Rule came in 1973. Steve Wynn owned legal bingo halls outside of Nevada. After purchasing a volume of stock in the Golden Nugget, he gained an appointment to the board of the casino company. The move required licensing. The state examined his bingo interests, which in comparison to his Golden Nugget position were quite minor, and granted him licensing, permitting him to keep the bingo interests. Caesars Palace was also given a waiver so that a facility it owned in Pennsylvania could sell Pennsylvania lottery tickets.

A federal position that casino gaming should be confined to remote regions separated from urban centers was expressed in 1976 by the Commission on the Review of the National Policy toward Gambling. Ironically, in the same year, the voters of New Jersey authorized casinos for Atlantic City. It was not a Nevada gaming operator, but rather Resorts International, a casino interest operating in the Bahamas, that pushed the legalization campaign.

The New Jersey situation changed Nevada's thinking about the Foreign Gaming Rule. Atlantic City promised to be a gold mine for gambling companies, and Nevada wanted to share in the new bonanza. In 1969, Nevada had altered its licensing laws so that publicly traded corporations could have casinos. Several nationally based companies entered the casino field. Most of these, especially Hilton Corporation, were not Nevadan. Like Nevada resorts, they wanted to go into New Jersey. The casinos turned to the Nevada legislature for a remedy. They were not disappointed.

The Nevada General Assembly took cognizance of the fact that New Jersey was adopting a very strict regulatory framework, and on May 16, 1977, it passed Assembly Bill 375, abolishing Regulation 3.060. In its place, it provided that the Nevada Gaming Commission could give prior approval for a Nevada licensee to be involved in outside gaming under certain conditions. The outside gaming had to be legal, and it had to be judged not to pose a threat to the interests of gaming control in Nevada. Nevada regulators had to receive full access to information regarding the outside activity and any persons associated with the Nevada interests in the outside ventures. The act was later amended to allow the commission to use its discretion to waive these provisions under certain circumstances for specific companies.

The Nevada Gaming Control Board made a study of New Jersey regulations, and the go-ahead was given. In rapid fashion, the Golden Nugget, Sands, Harrah's, and Elsinore entered Atlantic City. Caesars Palace, the Tropicana, and the Showboat followed. But that was New Jersey. From the beginning, New Jersey was so suspicious about gaming that regulators assumed that without constant surveillance, operators deemed to have a clean bill of health would lose control of their casinos to organized crime.

The New Jersey official position resulted from the lack of a general consensus about the desirability of casino gaming. Only 56 percent of voters favored casinos, in a campaign in which proponents outspent opponents nearly 100 to 1. That was New Jersey. In Nevada, there is a consensus that casino gambling is not only legitimate but desirable. There is a lot of second-guessing in New Jersey. There has been no second-guessing of the legislative decision of 1931 that legalized casinos in Nevada. The concern in Nevada has always been the legitimacy of the casino industry in the eyes of outsiders.

The Foreign Gaming Rule lay dormant as a policy consideration throughout most of the 1980s. The industry was reconciled to the notion that it would get prior approval for ventures in New Jersey. It also had a tacit understanding with the gaming authorities that it would not actively lobby or otherwise influence efforts to legalize gambling in new jurisdictions. Indeed, what lobbying it did was to stop the spread of gambling—specifically gambling on Native American lands. U.S. Senator Harry Reid, himself a former chairman of the Nevada Gaming Commission, was instrumental in drafting federal legislation that was "supposed to" block expansion of Native American gaming. The Indian Gaming Regulatory Act of 1988 was passed after the U.S. Supreme Court ruled that states could not regulate Native American gaming without congressional authorization. Tribal gaming interests were able to block a federal rule that would have delegated regulatory authority to the states, and Reid crafted a provision for Native Americans to enter into compact negotiations with states. The compacts would provide for mechanisms for regulation of the gaming.

The Nevada interests thought they were stopping Native American gaming, perhaps because a tribe in Nevada had voluntarily negotiated a casino compact that provided for full state regulation of its casinos. Tribes in other states, however, were not so cooperative. Where the states did not allow Native American groups to operate casino facilities, they sued in federal courts and frequently won judgments forcing the states to allow them to have casinos. In 1996, the U.S. Supreme Court ruled that provisions of the 1988 law authorizing tribes to sue states in the federal courts violated the 11th Amendment of the U.S. Constitution. However, by then, it was mostly a moot issue, because Native American gaming had spread across the land. Native American casinos existed in more than twenty states.

Nevada state officials and congressional delegates and the Nevada Resorts Association, a key lobbying group for the largest casinos, vigorously protested that the federal judiciary and the executive branch were misreading the 1988 act, but other casino operators in Nevada wanted to operate some of the Native American casinos.

Toward the end of the 1980s, other external developments also affected the Nevada casino industry. In 1988, the voters of South Dakota authorized limited stakes (maximum $5 bets) for casinos in the town of Deadwood. In 1989, the Iowa legislature passed a law permitting limited betting on riverboats. Casinos opened in Deadwood in November 1989, only eight days before the Berlin Wall fell, followed by a general rapprochement between eastern and western Europe. Former Eastern Bloc nations wanted casino gambling too. Canada also opened its first permanent casino—the Crystal Casino in Winnipeg—in 1989. As the 1990s began, the Nevada casino industry looked out upon a very different world. Casino gambling was being legalized in a majority of U.S. states, and casino companies were financing attempts at legalization. Canadian and European casinos were being established at a rapid rate, and these foreign jurisdictions sought experienced companies to run their new operations.

Nevada casinos had a tremendous opportunity. They also faced their own wall—the Foreign Gaming Rule. Nevada's big companies reached out to win licenses for gaming boats and for contracts to build and run Native American gaming facilities in some places. They began looking around the world for new jurisdictions where it might be possible to reap the benefits of a temporary monopoly. But they were at a disadvantage. They could not be trailmakers because they needed Nevada board approval, and that delayed processes to the point where non-Nevada competitors were in the door while they were still checking out addresses.

A case study from 1990 is illustrative. A Nevada licensee had the correct entrepreneurial spirit. He wanted to find opportunities, exploit them by rendering good service, and cash in. He was a good, clean operator. The Nevada gaming authorities had raked him over the coals, as they do everyone applying for a license. He had passed muster. He was competent, fiscally sound, of good moral character, and without any disqualifying baggage in his background. He was licensed in Nevada, and he ran a casino honorably. He wanted to pursue his American dream in a country that used to be behind the Iron Curtain. He had an opportunity to become a partner in a casino. His partner was to be the government of that country.

The Nevada licensee traveled to the country. There he found a commercial disaster of sorts—he found people that needed a lot of commercial advice. The bookkeepers had no understanding of profit-and-loss statements. The workforce had no work skills, and, on top of this, they had bad work habits. They needed equipment and supplies. Worse, no bank or financial house would loan money for such a venture. All costs would have to be met up front. The country had no public laws on casino gambling. And as if that wasn't enough, it was going to be difficult getting money out of the country if profits were realized.

The Nevada licensee concluded that he could participate in a casino in the country only if it was small, at least at the beginning. If it was successful, he could reinvest all profits in expansion. He wanted to start with twenty-five slot machines. His investment in the machines—100 percent of their cost—would be totally at risk. But the key to the formula was to start small. Also, starting small, the Nevada operator could be influential in developing local standards that would assure that future larger casinos in the country would operate with high standards of integrity.

The foreign government agreed to allow the Nevada operator to come in and start the small casino. However, as soon as the Nevada licensee had put his plan on paper and identified all the resources he would need to make the project work, he realized that he could never make it fly. The stopper was the Nevada foreign gaming law. He calculated that in order to install twenty-five machines, he would have to pay to have Nevada gaming agents travel to eastern Europe, he would have to pay for translation services, and he would face impossible delays, because the foreign government itself would have to be persuaded to open up its books to Nevada regulators. When they opened the books, moreover, they would not meet Nevada accounting standards, and the gaming commission would see no gaming regulatory structure based upon written laws. The prospects of getting Nevada approval for such a foreign gaming venture were remote. Even if the Nevada Board gave its permission, the cost of a positive ruling would not be justified for a small casino.

This was a real-life case where a Nevada operator—fully qualified, certified as clean by virtue of his Nevada license, knowledgeable about gaming, and commercially wise—was denied the opportunity to export his expertise to a gaming establishment in another jurisdiction. Nevada was thus denied an opportunity to display its gaming technology and skill in a foreign country. A chance for Nevada to built a positive image abroad was lost.

This licensee could have been reassured that neither the board nor the Nevada Gaming Commission had turned down any applications for foreign gaming permission. That is, they never turned down requests from applicants who were informally told to take their cases for a foreign gaming approval all the way to the board and commission for approval. Others, no doubt, had been dissuaded from going through the process. On the other hand, the costs and delays incurred by having to go through the process amounted to a constructive denial of permission.

There are other situations where prospects of foreign gaming regulation by Nevada authorities had a similar chilling effect of stopping potential ventures. I asked this licensee who he thought would jump into the void and undertake the venture in the eastern European country. He thought that perhaps the Germans, Austrians, or Italians, who had more experience dealing with eastern Europeans, might be interested.

A few weeks later, I picked up a copy of the *Las Vegas Review-Journal* and found out that the "who" jumping into the void was not a European but an American, a Las Vegan at that. A businessman who has been involved in casinos all over the world negotiated to work with the country in question. He made an agreement to start small casinos in partnership with the government. He didn't have to worry about the Nevada Gaming Board. He didn't have a Nevada casino license. Actually, at one point in his career he had been denied a Nevada license. His career was replete with episodes of questionable casino practices in many places. He was the subject of one of the stories in Ed Reid and Ovid Demaris's *Green Felt Jungle*, a 1963 exposé of the seamy side of Las Vegas.

Nevada regulators had not certified his managerial and financial capabilities, as they had done with the Nevada operator who gave up on the foreign venture. Instead of one of Nevada's licensees overseeing the casino in the eastern European country, this man was given the opportunity.

Some Nevada regulators might say that this was all to the good. We would not want Nevada's reputation to be put at risk in a country where rigorous regulations are not in place. Perhaps so, but the conclusion does not necessarily follow. The gentleman who won the opportunity to go into the country named his casino "Las Vegas."

The case study suggests why the Foreign Gaming Rule was simply untenable as public policy for Nevada in the 1990s. Casino gaming was spreading to new jurisdictions within the United States and around the world, and the best operators, with proven records of integrity, were being placed at a competitive disadvantage. Unqualified, incompetent, and unscrupulous operators were put in a position of competitive advantage.

The policy was also untenable as a matter of constitutionality. The Foreign Gaming Rule was constitutionally suspect, because it represented an unreasonable state burden upon interstate commerce. Certainly, the rule restricted interstate commercial activity. Such a restriction would be permissible only if there were an overriding state interest in protecting the health, safety, and social welfare of Nevadans. In 1990, two state interests—the integrity of the industry and the economic health of Nevada—were no longer served by the application of the act. The legitimacy of the industry was no longer under challenge, and it was economically healthy. The state no longer had to carry the unique burden of protecting the reputation of casino gambling. Indeed, in the 1988 Indian Gaming Regulatory Act, the federal government had proclaimed that gambling was "good" as a tool for economic development. The casino industry no longer belonged solely to Nevada. Forces that might compromise the integrity of the industry might lurk "out there," but if they did, the Foreign Gaming Rule was counterproductive. It kept good operators out of other jurisdictions, heightening the possibilities of all kinds of hanky-panky on the Mississippi or Missouri rivers or in South Dakota.

In the case reviewed above, we see the absurdity of having the Nevada Gaming Control Board and Commission directly regulating officials of a foreign government that proposed to act as partner to a Nevada licensee in running a casino wholly within its own national boundary.

There was no easy opportunity for challenging the constitutionality of the Foreign Gaming Rule. In the court system, a party needs standing—an individual interest in the outcome—to make a challenge. A Nevada licensee is constantly under the scrutiny of the Nevada Gaming Board and Commission. It was difficult politically for a licensee to make a judicial challenge. The only practical way of challenging the rule was to appeal to the commission, and then to the state assembly to make changes. In 1991, that process began.

The board and the commission were somewhat responsive to the need for changes. They allowed for some selective adjustments in the rule. They invited gaming licensees to apply for special prior permissions to make arrangements for gambling operations outside the state. To get such prior permissions, the license holders had to come before the board and commission and justify their need for prior approval. A few larger companies did so, including Caesars Palace and Harrah's. They could make any outside arrangements to run gambling operations they thought appropriate for a one-year period of time. After they made the arrangements, they had to come back to the board and commission and report on the activity. Prior approvals were called "shelf approvals." A similar process has been used by agencies such as the Securities and Exchange Commission in giving certain companies the right to make IPOs (initial public offerings) and report the fact later.

The Nevada gaming authorities turned down several requests for shelf approvals, based on the rationale that outside gaming operations might hurt Nevada. They feared that a small company's outside casino might fail, and that companies might shift revenues from their stronger Nevada operations to the other places—hence hurting the state economy. The 1991 attempts at reforming the Foreign Gaming Rule with shelf approvals thus proved inconclusive.

The following year, the atmosphere surrounding the rule changed. While licensees had a tacit agreement with the board and commission that they would not encourage or influence the spread of gambling into new jurisdictions, several large companies simply ignored it. In 1992, Circus Circus, Hilton, and Caesars Palace approached the city of Chicago and the state of Illinois with a plan for resort casinos within the city. The companies risked the ire of the Nevada authorities, because the stakes were very high—the proposed Chicago projects had potential revenues well in excess of $1 billion a year. The companies might have rationalized their "disobedience" with the thought that the state of Illinois already permitted riverboat casinos outside of Chicago. Nonetheless, the Nevada Gaming Board was being presented with a frontal challenge to its informal if not its formal authority. Yet these were three of the biggest and best companies in Nevada gaming.

The board is charged by the Nevada gaming act to meet the policy goals that recognize that "the gaming industry is vitally important to the economy of the state and the general welfare of the inhabitants. [That the] continued growth and success of gaming is dependent upon public confidence and trust that licensed gaming is conducted honestly and competitively. . . ."

The decision regarding what to do about foreign gaming was, however, taken away from the board and commission in 1993. The essence of the Foreign Gaming Rule was repealed with the passage of Assembly

Bill 470. The new law did require that licensees notify the board of their outside gambling ventures after the fact, and that the board be allowed to review the involvements to assure itself that they were proper.

Assembly Bill 470 meant that all Nevada companies—big and small—could immediately go out and seek to win licenses elsewhere. The Horseshoe jumped at the chance, so did Station Casinos, the Boyd Group, the Lady Luck, Fitzgerald's, and Harvey's. The big companies also sought new ventures with renewed enthusiasm. There was a rush of activity, infusing the national gaming scene with a flow of new capital for expanded projects everywhere gaming was legal.

The legislative decision of 1993 coincided with eagerness on the part of Wall Street to embrace casino gaming. Many IPOs were issued in 1993 and 1994 for casino ventures. Established Nevada companies with commercial track records gave Wall Street the confidence to back the issues. An inflation in the value of casino stocks naturally occurred, and as a result, IPO activity was reduced in 1994 and 1995, when stock prices took an inevitable fall. The Nevada companies were also able to command far greater loans from traditional lending sources than casinos had ever done before. New sources of capital has been funneled into casino projects throughout the country.

For the first time, Nevada companies were freed to openly and vigorously campaign for proposals to legalize gambling in new jurisdictions. The Nevada industry became heavily involved in the Florida casino campaign of 1994, which spent $17 million, the largest amount spent on any referendum campaign in the United States up to that time. In 1996, casino supporters spent $8 million in Ohio. While these two campaigns were unsuccessful, the industry won several bids to legalize riverboat gaming, and it also won a contest in Michigan that resulted in the authorization of three major land-based casinos in Detroit. Everywhere gambling has been legalized, Nevada companies are ready to move in and operate new casino facilities. The spread of gambling across the United States in the years since the 1993 legislative decision on foreign gaming has been greatly influenced by that decision.

The 1993 decision to abandon the restrictive Foreign Gaming Rule has had positive benefits for the Nevada gaming industry. By participating in gaming in other locations, Nevada concerns can enhance their abilities to develop and train personnel. Casinos in other jurisdictions, especially ones that may be restricted to lower gambling limits or to smaller gaming areas, can be great places for training dealers and managers. These personnel can then aspire to move to their company's home casino in Nevada. For years, Casinos Austria has used cruise ships and foreign casinos as training centers for dealers and managers. Once trained, they return to a "home" casino in Austria.

By the same token, a home casino in Nevada can improve the morale of its staff by offering career ladders that have geographic diversity. Americans are people on the move. Certainly, all of us in the American West have the relocation bug. With branch casinos, operators can satisfy employees' desire for mobility.

Additionally, Nevada casinos operating casinos elsewhere can market their Nevada operations through them. New jurisdictions generate new customers for established casino jurisdictions—for both Nevada and New Jersey. Nevada can best exploit new market possibilities if Nevada operators are out in the field. A few examples are illustrative. Land's End, a catalog merchandiser of clothing, found that many people were reluctant to buy clothing from a catalog. To overcome that barrier, the company opened small stores to sell its products. The stores are not designed to turn a profit. Rather, they give potential catalog customers a chance to examine the quality of Land's End products. Once customers have bought Land's End products over the counter, they are more willing to order from a catalog.

In the gaming field, Aspinall's of London reached into the Asian market in a similar manner in the 1980s. The exclusive London casino was prohibited under British Gaming Law from advertising in England. Aspinall's opened a casino in Darwin, Australia, without advertising restrictions. Asian players were brought to Darwin and exposed to Aspinall operations and Aspinall hospitality. When these players went to London, as Asian business people frequently do, they made Aspinall's of Curzon Street their preferred London casino.

With satellite casinos in other jurisdictions, Nevada operators will also be able to identify valuable junket players more accurately and provide them with complimentary services and credit play.

Nevada needs new investors. A wealthy investor wishing to enter the casino gaming industry as an equity participant can choose among New Jersey, Nevada, riverboats, reservations, South Dakota, and other locations. Once successfully involved in gaming, the investor may decide to expand and start more casinos, maybe in several jurisdictions. An investor starting up in Nevada must, of course, be licensed by the Nevada Gaming Board and Commission. But then, under the Foreign Gaming Rule, the investor would have had to go through the Nevada gaming regulatory bureaucracy every time he or she moved into another jurisdiction, in addition to having to go through the other jurisdiction's licensing process. If the investor had any concern about government bureaucracy and overregulation, he or she would have invested outside of Nevada first and saved Nevada for last. By abolishing the Foreign Gaming Rule, Nevada has become much more attractive to outside investors.

Should Nevada be concerned that its licensees may take their profits out of Nevada and invest them in casinos elsewhere? Why? Isn't this what all owners do? There is no rule saying that casino stockholders can spend dividend checks only in Nevada. If there are better opportunities to make money from investments outside their state, Nevadans would be foolish to confine all their investments to it. But, on the other hand, if opportunities are better in Nevada, those investment dollars will stay in the state, whether there is a Foreign Gaming Rule or not. If the Nevada operator has facilities elsewhere, it is quite likely that earnings in other jurisdictions will go to facility expansion in Nevada.

Perhaps the Foreign Gaming Rule was part of the Nevada gaming scene because officials in the Silver State feared that if there were a lot of casinos elsewhere, if Nevada did not have a monopoly on casino gaming, the state's basic industry would be hurt. In other words, they thought Nevada could not stand the competition. Is this the case?

Nevada should not fear losing markets to casinos in other states. Nevada still has a comparative advantage. Nevada is a casino specialty store—a vacation resort with a vast array of gaming possibilities offered in a free enterprise atmosphere. Nevada can offer a multitude of recreation opportunities, outside and inside its resorts. Las Vegas is "the Entertainment Capital of the World." The gambling product of Nevada is a specialty product. People make conscious planned decisions to go to specialty stores. People are willing to travel distances to go to specialty stores. People spend time shopping when they reach specialty stores.

Casino gaming is offered across the United States and Canada in the form of convenience products in convenience stores. People gamble on a riverboat, or in a Native American casino, or in Gary, Indiana, or Winnipeg, Manitoba, because that is the most convenient place. Large numbers of people do not travel great distances to gamble in Deadwood, South Dakota. Even Atlantic City, which attracts a large number of tourists, still has to base its economy on convenience gamers from the New York, Baltimore, and Philadelphia metropolitan areas. Nevada is a supermarket of gambling, not a 7–11.

The spread of "7–11" casinos can stimulate latent demand by people who otherwise would never have thought of buying gambling prod-

TABLE I

CASINOS IN NEVADA AND ELSEWHERE
IN THE UNITED STATES

Year	Non-Nevada Casinos				Nevada Casinos
	Casino States		No. Casinos	Revenue (billions)	Revenue (billions)
	Total States	(Commercial States)			
1989	7	2	53	$2.778	$4.996
1990	7	2	115	3.563	5.481
1991	11	5	144	4.186	5.569
1992	13	6	196	5.777	5.862
1993	15	7	237	8.914	6.218
1994	16	8	281	9.203	6.990
1995	17	9	300	14.688	7.366

SOURCES: *Nevada Gaming Abstracts* (several years); *International Gaming and Wagering Business Magazine* (several years of August–September issue on gambling revenues in the United States); William N. Thompson, *Legalized Gambling: A Reference Handbook* (Santa Barbara: ABC-CLIO, 1994).

ucts. And once they buy, they will start thinking about shopping at a store with a little more ambience—after all, Americans do enjoy shopping, and 7–11s do not satisfy all their shopping desires. So much for the arguments, but do the facts back them up? Has the spread of gambling been good for Nevada?

Table 1 shows the growth in the number of casinos in the United States outside of Nevada from 1989 to 1995, the growth of their revenues, and the growth in gaming revenues in Nevada itself. Table 2 shows the number of visitors to Las Vegas in those years and their economic impact. Table 3 shows the distribution of visitors to Nevada from different regions of the United States.

It is clear that the expansion of gambling across the United States has not cut into Nevada markets. Indeed, as gambling expands to new jurisdictions, the proportion of visitors from those regions to Las Vegas has remained roughly constant, and the numbers have actually increased.

From 1989 through 1995, the number of casinos outside Nevada increased from 53 to 300. Nevada revenues increased by $2.370 billion over the same period of time. With the addition of each new casino, Nevada revenues went up an average of $9.6 million a year. Gambling revenues outside Nevada increased by $11.910 billion during this pe-

TABLE 2

VISITOR VOLUME TO LAS VEGAS AND ECONOMIC IMPACT

Year	Number of Visitors	Economic Impact (billions)	per Visitor (dollars)
1989	18,129,684	$11.91	$656
1990	20,954,420	14.32	$683
1991	21,315,116	14.33	$672
1992	21,886,863	14.69	$671
1993	23,552,593	15.13	$643
1994	28,214,362	19.17	$679
1995	29,800,000 est.		

SOURCE: Las Vegas Convention and Visitors Authority, *Visitor Profile* (1989–1994).

TABLE 3

PERCENTAGE DISTRIBUTION OF LAS VEGAS CUSTOMERS
BY U.S. REGION

Year	Midwest	East	West	South
1989	18% − (4)	10% − (1)	57% − (2)	15% − (0)
1990	19% − (4)	10% − (1)	57% − (2)	14% − (0)
1991	18% − (6)	10% − (1)	56% − (4)	16% − (0)
1992	20% − (6)	12% − (2)	53% − (4)	16% − (1)
1993	20% − (6)	9% − (3)	58% − (4)	13% − (2)
1994	17% − (6)	10% − (3)	58% − (4)	15% − (3)
1995	17% − (6)	10% − (3)	58% − (4)	15% − (4)

SOURCES: Las Vegas Convention and Visitors Authority, *Visitor Profile* (several years); William N. Thompson, *Legalized Gambling: A Reference Handbook* (Santa Barbara: ABC-CLIO, 1994). Figures in parentheses represent the number of casino states, excluding Nevada, in the region.

riod, while they increased by $2.370 billion in Nevada. For every new $5.02 of outside casinos' revenue, Nevada casinos brought in an extra dollar. Also, for each extra $1 million wagered outside of Nevada, Las Vegas gained 900 new visitors.

"There is not a shred of evidence to support the hypothesis that riverboat gambling will take gambling away from Nevada or New Jersey," Michael Evans, a professor of economics at Northwestern University, told the 1996 International Gaming Exposition in Las Vegas. He is right. It hasn't happened. It won't happen.

Not with riverboat gaming, small stakes gaming in Deadwood, or even high stakes in Native American casinos. The competition only makes Nevada gaming stronger.

A few years ago, I got a call from Steve Wynn. "Why do you say casinos that have local gamblers just suck money out of local economies?" he asked angrily. "What's your proof? Come on. Come on, you said that in the newspaper, now what's your proof? What makes you think you can get away with saying these things?" He was yelling at me. This was the "God" of casino heaven berating me. It was good practice for a future encounter with St. Peter. I tried to explain that, before speaking to the press on the subject, I had interviewed 785 players on Illinois riverboats and 697 in Wisconsin Native American casinos. "Yeah, is that proof?" he demanded. "Well, it's evidence, anyway," I replied.

"What about Mississippi?" he asked. "Mississippi is doing a fair job of drawing in tourists," I said. Wynn was planning on having a major casino property on the Gulf Coast. But he was still irritated that I could think that riverboat casinos in Illinois that draw money out of the pockets of poor local residents might be a bad thing. We ended the conversation with a fundamental difference of opinion over the value of non-tourist casinos.

I continue to wonder why Wynn, who has run very successful commercial casinos, aimed almost exclusively at tourists, got angry over someone advancing the idea that other casinos might be bad for local economies. Maybe there is a very good reason. Perhaps he, too, sees a linkage between all the casino gaming in America and the interests of Nevada.

He knows that the spread of gaming in America—whether to the beaches of the Mississippi Gulf Coast, the semi-sleazy riverboats of Galena, Illinois, or Keokuk, Iowa, or the spartan gaming halls of Red Lake or Leech Lake, Minnesota—is a good thing for Nevada, and he wants to see casinos perpetuated—even in their worst form. The spread of gaming has given the state of Nevada a renewed legitimacy in the eyes of all America and won Nevada new customers, who can satisfy their demand for casino gaming by visiting Steve Wynn's "must see" properties. Moreover, the abolition of a very unwise policy—the policy enunciated in the Foreign Gaming Rule—contributed to the making of a gambling America that can only help Nevada.

POSTSCRIPT: In 2000, Kirk Kerkorian's MGM Corporation purchased the Mirage Corporation and all of Steve Wynn's interests in casinos. Wynn subsequently purchased the Desert Inn and announced plans for yet another mega-resort.

Canto: Las Vegas

Cadillac and sphinx, Las Vegas, 1995.

Artificial lake, Las Vegas, 1992.

Suburb, Las Vegas, 1995.

Putting green, artificial lake, and night lights, Las Vegas, 1992.

Pine tree and lawn, new housing development, Las Vegas, 1992.

Boating on Lake Mead, Nevada, 1990.

Lake Mead, Nevada, 1986.

Signs warning of radioactivity, Yucca Mountain, Nevada, 1994.

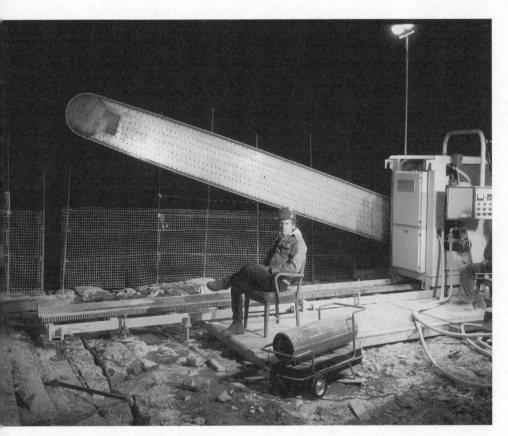

Nineteen-foot diamond-studded chainsaw for drilling bedrock, Yucca Mountain, Nevada, 1994.

Princesses against Plutonium, an anti-nuclear protest, Nevada Nuclear Test Site, 1988.

Cloudburst, Nuclear Test Site, Nevada, 1987.

Dying saguaro cactus, Las Vegas, 1992.

Caesars Palace, Las Vegas, 1992.

Contributors

COURTNEY ALEXANDER is research director for the Culinary Workers Union Local 226.

JAY BRIGHAM is a staff historian with Morgan Angel Associates in Washington, D.C.

JON CHRISTENSEN is a freelance investigative reporter and writer based in Carson City, Nevada.

MIKE DAVIS is professor of history at the State University of New York, Stony Brook, and the author of *Ecology of Fear: Los Angeles and the Imagination of Disaster.*

CONSTANCE DEVEREAUX is a freelance writer and artist in Las Vegas.

BRIAN FREHNER is completing his doctoral degree at the University of Oklahoma.

PETER GOIN is professor of art at the University of Nevada, Reno.

JOANNE L. GOODWIN is associate professor of history at the University of Nevada, Las Vegas.

KATHRYN HAUSBECK is associate professor of sociology at the University of Nevada, Las Vegas.

NORMAN M. KLEIN teaches at the California Institute of the Arts, Los Angeles.

SHANNON MCMACKIN is a native of Las Vegas.

FRANCISCO MENENDEZ is associate professor of film and the director of film studies at the University of Nevada, Las Vegas.

KIT MILLER is a freelance writer and photographer in Carson City, Nevada.

RICHARD MISRACH is a professional photographer in Emeryville, California.

EUGENE MOEHRING is professor of history at the University of Nevada, Las Vegas.

ROBERT E. PARKER is professor of sociology at the University of Nevada, Las Vegas.

HAL ROTHMAN is professor of history at the University of Nevada, Las Vegas, and the author of *Devil's Bargains: Tourism in the Twentieth-Century American West* and *Neon Metropolis: How Las Vegas Started the Twenty-First Century*.

WILLIAM N. THOMPSON is professor of public administration at the University of Nevada, Las Vegas.

AMIE WILLIAMS is a filmmaker and the principal of Balmaiden Films.

Index

Compositor:	Binghamton Valley Composition
Text:	10/13 Sabon
Display:	Sabon, Radiant Display, Akzidenz Grotesk
Printer and Binder:	Thomson-Shore